NEW ORLEANS:
A PICTORIAL HISTORY

28 may 1830.

Vue prise... sur le bayou St Jean

NEW ORLEANS:
A PICTORIAL HISTORY

by LEONARD V. HUBER

with a foreword by CHARLES L. DUFOUR

AMERICAN LEGACY PRESS
New York

For Audrey

This edition is published by American Legacy Press,
distributed by Crown Publishers, Inc.
1981 EDITION

Manufactured in the United States of America

Library of Congress Cataloging in Publication Data

Huber, Leonard Victor, 1903–
   New Orleans : a pictorial history.

   Bibliography: p.
   Includes index.
   1. New Orleans (La.)—History—Pictorial
works.   2. New Orleans (La.)—Description—
Views.   I. Title.
F379.N543H8   1981   976.3′35   81-12679
ISBN 0-517-318954   AACR2

h g f e d c

CONTENTS

FOREWORD BY CHARLES L. DUFOUR   ix
PREFACE   xi
INTRODUCTION   1

1. DISCOVERY AND DEVELOPMENT   16

The French Regime   16
The Spanish Regime   32
The Louisiana Purchase   37
Immigration from Saint-Domingue   42
Battle of New Orleans   44
Texas and the Republic   51
Three Municipalities: Creoles vs.
    Americans   51
The Melting Pot   54
Civil War   58
Reconstruction   66
Spanish-American War   71
World War I   72
World War II   75
Present   76

2. ARCHITECTURE   78

St. Louis Hotel: Creole Elegance   79
St. Charles Hotel: Pride of Town   83
Gallier Hall: American Style   86
Lafayette Square   88
United States Mint   90
Canal Street   90
Jackson Square: Heart of the French
    Quarter   102
Custom House   107
Churches   110
Cities of the Dead   118
Indigenous Architecture   125
Suburban Architecture   136

3. CULTURE   142

Theatre   142
French Opera   153
Concerts   158

Jazz   161
Education   167
Literature   173
Newspapers   176
Fine Art   180
Cuisine and Restaurants   182

4. PERSONALITIES AND CUSTOMS   188

Famous Visitors   188
Notable Residents   190
Characters   195
Saloons   205
Voodoo   207
Storyville and Prostitution   208
Victorian Home Life   212

5. DIVERSIONS   214

Biggest Free Show on Earth   214
Parades   226
Movies   228
Resorts   230
Parks and Amusements   236
Cotton Centennial Exposition   240

6. SPORTS   242

Crossed Swords Under the Oaks   242
Fights Between Animals   243
A Gambling Town   244
Sport of Kings   248
Sailing   251
Boxing   253
Baseball   255
Football   257

7. NATURAL DISASTERS   261

Epidemics   261
Floods and Hurricanes   264

8. MUNICIPAL SERVICES   269

Early Mail   269
Waterworks   271
Fire Department   273
Police Department   278
Hospitals   285

9. TRANSPORTATION   288

Street Transportation   288
Vanishing Ferries   292

Railroads   294
Beginnings of Aviation   300

10. BUSINESS   303

When Cotton Was King   303
Sugar   306
Coffee and Bananas   310
Early Merchants and Merchandising   312
Telephones for the Businessman   319
Banks Come into Their Own   321

11. RIVER AND PORT   325

Golden Age of Steamboating   325
Captain Eads's Jetties Save the Port   333
A Second and Last Breath for
    Steamboats   336
Steamships and Steamship Lines   345
The Port Today   347

12. THE SPACE AGE   354

BIBLIOGRAPHY   357
INDEX   362

FOREWORD

NEARLY A CENTURY AGO—in 1873—Edwin L. Jewell produced *Jewell's Crescent City Illustrated,* a book that has long been a collector's item for the specialist in the history of New Orleans. In sketch and text, Jewell presented a graphic account of the city and its people still in the grip of Reconstruction. For subsequent generations, Jewell's book has been both an effective link with the past and an ideal view of New Orleans as it was in the first decade after the close of the Civil War.

Since Jewell, there have been no serious efforts to portray New Orleans in words and pictures on a comprehensive scale. Its colorful story, from the canebrakes along the "beautiful crescent of the river" to the towering International Trade Mart, which casts its shadow across the old city, needs retelling in modern dress.

Now comes New Orleans historian and collector Leonard V. Huber's fascinating pictorial narrative of the city, with authoritative accompanying text. Sometimes proceeding chronologically, sometimes topically, but within a chronological framework, his impressive book graphically traces the exciting stages by which New Orleans moved from a deserted riverbank to the second most important port in the United States.

Drawing on his remarkable private collection of photographs, prints, sketches, and maps of the New Orleans scene, and supplementing his own material from public and private libraries here and abroad, Leonard Huber has produced a lasting monument to the city he so passionately loves.

Few, if indeed any, could have brought to the task of compiling this work the peculiar assets of Leonard Huber—inexhaustible pictorial sources, a keen appreciation of New Orleans history, and years of research on various aspects of the city. To his material and talents, Mr. Huber added his usual painstaking zeal and infectious enthusiasm.

New Orleans: A Pictorial History is a book for all seasons and people, one that will win the respect of the trained historian, while delighting the general reader. Whether young, old, native, or visitor, all will derive pleasure and information.

Leonard V. Huber has contributed several very significant monographs to the history of New Orleans, some exclusively from his pen, some in collaboration with others. This book—as it would be for any other New Orleans writer—is his magnum opus.

CHARLES L. DUFOUR

PREFACE

FEW AMERICAN CITIES have had as colorful a background as New Orleans. Its people have seen good days and bad since its founding in 1718, somehow carrying on through plagues, war and its terrible aftermath, floods, and a hostile natural environment. The city has a history replete with stirring events and romantic incident.

New Orleans brings to the reader scenes of many of these events, including the actors in them. Unfortunately, too few contemporary pictures exist of a number of important happenings. Our forebears, with the exception of the early French engineers who sent home drawings of their buildings and a few historians who sketched, were too busy trying to build a city to take much interest in making pictures. It was not until about the beginning of the nineteenth century that talented and well-trained artists visited New Orleans and drew what they observed. And it was not until the middle of that century that eastern magazines sent quick-sketch artists to New Orleans to illustrate this "different" city for their readers. From these —and the photographs of Mugnier, Teunisson, Cormier, Genella, Franck, Richard Koch, Leyrer, Williams, DePaul, Methe, Cresson, Beach and Weber, and drawings of Waud, Pennell, Woodward, and Cruise— has been built a rich heritage, from which I have drawn.

In the last two decades, the pulse of New Orleans has quickened and the city has grown prodigiously. Change is in the air, and time has taken its toll. Customs, distinctive and often quaint, have disappeared, and a new generation is growing up knowing little of the city's fascinating history and background. It is the purpose of this book to cast nostalgic glances, and, in so doing, recapture in picture and text some of the memorable days that have made New Orleans loved.

The accompanying text, including the captions, has been carefully researched and checked by experts in their respective fields. Many persons helped, and I am grateful to all of them. I am especially indebted to René J. Le Gardeur, Jr., a scholar and historian of the first rank, for his patience and careful assistance in the writing of this book. To Charles L. ("Pie") Dufour, newspaper columnist, historian, lecturer, I am most thankful for his unselfish help and encouragement. To my colleague Samuel Wilson, Jr., I owe much for advice, for checking facts, and for the loan of rare pictures from his and Mrs. Wilson's collection. To David Kleck for his encouragement, many thanks. I am

greatly indebted to Henry W. Krotzer, Jr., who created the drawings of first colonial French buildings of New Orleans especially for this book from plans in the French National Archives. Thanks also goes to Professor Marcel Giraud of the Collège de France, Paris, and to Mademoiselle M. A. Ménier of the Archives Nationales, Paris, for help in the chapters on French colonization.

My thanks for their ever-ready assistance go to Mrs. Dorothy Whittemore, former Director of the Reference Department, and Mrs. Connie G. Griffith, Director of the Special Collections Division, Howard-Tilton Memorial Library, Tulane University, for the generous loan of pictures and help in research; to Miss Margaret Ruckert, former head of the Louisiana Section, and Collin B. Hammer, Jr., present head of this department, and to Mrs. Peggy Richards, Director of the Louisiana State Museum, and to W. Joseph Fulton, a former member, and Mrs. Nell Yates of the museum's staff for the loan of pictures; to Guy F. Bernard, photographer extraordinary, for the loan of pictures; to Hermann B. Deutsch for the use of his fine aviation pictures; to Richard Koch, Felix H. Kuntz, and Boyd Cruise for the loan of pictures; to Ray Samuel, Albert L. Lieutaud, Mrs. Ferdinand H. Latrobe, Henry Pitot, G. William Nott, Arthur Scully, Jr., Donald F. Schultz, Mrs. Raymond J. Boudreaux, Mrs. Henry Knaupp, Dr. Edmond Souchon, James Janssen and Erston Reisch, Mrs. Milton L. Reisch, Herbert C. Swan, Iris Fincke, Edward J. O'Brien and Chief Patrick Burke, Thomas A. Greene, Arthur O. Schott, Art Burke, Nat Fleischer; to Mary A. Waits, Elaine Baltz, Lena G. Held, Joseph Merrick Jones, Jr., Dr. John Dyer, Mrs. Kenneth McCleod, Major Henry M. Morris, the New Orleans Athletic Club and Irwin Poché, the Ursuline Convent and to Vernon R. Daste, Angelo J. Mariano, Ellis P. Laborde, Miss Rose Lambert, Eric W. Johnson, Jr., Robert M. Calder, Mrs. Charles Eichling, Eric Heyl, Dr. Willard R. Wirth, Mrs. W. H. Reisig, Joseph Wilhelm, Fred Knaps, John Wigginton Hyman, Waldemar S. Nelson, Mrs. William J. Lahare, Merlin ("Scoop") Kennedy, Augusto P. Miceli, Coryell McKinney, Louis O. Reuning, John E. Morrill, Mrs. David L. Chandler, Colonel Anthony E. Filiberto and Charles F. Weber; to New Orleans Public Service, Inc., Southeastern Bell Telephone Co., Southern Pacific Company, The Chamber of Commerce of the New Orleans Area, The City of New Orleans Public Relations Department, The Louisiana Stadium and Exposition District, The Boeing Company, Department of the Army, New Orleans District, Corps of Engineers, The Times-Picayune Publishing Corporation, Loyola University of the South, New Orleans Chapter, Louisiana Landmarks Society, The Vieux Carré Survey, and the New Orleans Jazz Museum; to Mrs. Cecile Franck Hoffman of Charles L. Franck Photography, Edwin Gebhardt, Ray Cresson, John Guidi, Jack Beech, and Dan S. Leyrer for their aid in photography.

I am very grateful to Herbert Michelman, editor-in-chief of Crown Publishers, who decided to publish this book, to Paul Nadan, Crown's editor, whose editorial skills are apparent on every page, and to Nancy Tousley, who "discovered" it for her firm on a trip to New Orleans.

And last, but not least, I am grateful to my wife, Audrey Wells Huber, for her aid in research and for her patience and understanding during the lonely hours she spent while this book was being written.

In compiling and writing such a voluminous work, some errors and omissions are unavoidable, and I assume full responsibility for them despite the able assistance graciously given me by so many people.

LEONARD V. HUBER

INTRODUCTION

The French Regime

TWO HUNDRED AND FIFTY-TWO YEARS have passed since founder Jean Baptiste le Moyne, Sieur de Bienville, and his men cleared away the thick canebrakes on the riverfront to lay out New Orleans's first streets. Many groups left their marks on this cosmopolitan city: the Frenchmen who built the original town, the Spanish who ruled it for a third of a century, the refugees driven from France and its colonies by revolution and war, the Americans who came before and after the Louisiana Purchase, the immigrants from Ireland, Germany, Italy, and other European countries who came in the nineteenth century, and the Negroes who have always made up a considerable part of its population.

New Orleans is a southern city, but not in the sense of Charleston, Memphis, or Montgomery. It is isolated from the rest of the South by distance and its watery environs. Also, the people who colonized it were largely of Latin origin, with entirely different temperaments from the Anglo-Saxons who colonized other parts of the South.

Traditionally, New Orleans has always been known for its tolerance of human frailty and its attitude of "live and let live." "The City that Care Forgot," as it has been known since World War I, remains beloved by tourists who enjoy its fine food and drink, its carnival season with its madcap climax on Mardi Gras, its living "museum" in the Vieux Carré (the French Quarter), and a dozen other attractions ranging from strip shows on Bourbon Street to beautifully preserved antebellum homes in the Garden District.

But there is another side to New Orleans: one of struggle. New Orleans was founded some twenty years after the first Frenchmen came to the Gulf Coast. They had come to occupy and colonize the southern end of the huge territory that had been taken possession of by La Salle when he descended the Mississippi River from Canada in 1682. For two decades, France tried without much success to establish secure settlements at Biloxi and Mobile. But it was not until 1717 that Scottish financier John Law, through his Company of the West (later the Company of the Indies), then the possessor of a monopoly of the colony, decided to build a city on the Mississippi River "thirty leagues up the river, a town that should be named New Orleans, which one could reach by the river or Lake Pontchartrain." The site was near an Indian portage that had been observed by Bienville's brother, Iberville, some years before. In May, 1718, Bienville,

then in command, went "to mark the spot where the capital is to be built on the banks of the St. Louis River [the Mississippi] . . . [which was to be] named New Orleans in honor of Monseigneur the Duc d'Orléans, then regent of the kingdom."

Bienville came with six vessels and a force of six carpenters, four Canadians, and thirty laborers, who were former convicts, to start the work of clearing the land and erecting the first buildings. Leaving Major Paillou de Barbezan in charge, Bienville returned to Mobile, and for the next three years, until the arrival of the engineer, Adrien de Pauger, in 1721, very little was done. Pauger had been sent by his chief, Le Blond de la Tour, who had made a good plan of the city to be, to lay out its streets. Pauger cleared a great deal more ground and built a substantial warehouse. The next year, Father Charlevoix, coming from Canada, visited the infant settlement. He later wrote:

> The town is the first that one of the world's greatest rivers has seen rise on its banks. . . . But there are only about a hundred huts placed without much order, a large warehouse built of wood and two or three houses that would not grace a French village. . . . This wilderness that canes and trees still cover almost entirely, will one day, and perhaps that is not far off, be an opulent city and the metropolis of a great and rich colony.

That same year the straggling town was struck by a fierce hurricane which knocked down most of the ramshackle buildings put up earlier. This was a blessing in disguise, for not a single building was aligned with the engineer's plans and all eventually would have had to be demolished.

In 1722, the capital of Louisiana was moved from Biloxi to New Orleans, there to remain until well into the American era.

New Orleans is, generally speaking, about one foot above mean Gulf level, and when the Mississippi rose in the spring, the little town would be flooded, sometimes with two feet of water in the houses. This necessitated the construction of the first levee, in 1723, and the next year, Pauger reported to Paris:

> At present everyone works, vying with one another. Workshops and buildings are seen to rise everywhere so that New Orleans is growing before your eyes and there is no longer any doubt that it is going to become a great city.

Le Blond de la Tour's earliest known plan of New Orleans, dated April 22, 1722, projected a simple

1

gridiron of streets with a public square in the center, four square blocks extending in each direction above and below and six blocks back of the river. The blocks flanking the public square were marked with a fleur-de-lis, indicating that they were to be reserved for royal use, and on the block facing the square, a site for the parish church was designated. The streets were given names such as Royal, Bourbon, Chartres, Conti, St. Peter, St. Ann, St. Philip, and St. Louis, probably to flatter the French court and the church. With slight change, the same streets serve modern New Orleans today and most retain their original names.

The early years of the French in Louisiana, and, of course, in New Orleans, its capital, were marked by continual quarrels among the leaders of the colony. Bienville, who had been able to keep peace with the surrounding Indians very well, seemed to have a marked capacity for making enemies among his superiors and subordinates alike. After an official investigation, the founder of New Orleans was recalled in 1725 from his post. He had served twenty-six years in Louisiana.

Bienville's successor, Étienne de Périer, a lieutenant in the king's navy, inherited a colony racked with dissension and by quarrels between Jesuits and Capuchins over religious jurisdiction. In 1729 a massacre of 250 colonists at Fort Rosalie (Natchez) by Indians threw the city into a panic, and Périer ordered a rampart and a moat constructed, and issued arms to the citizens. But the defeat of the Natchez tribe the next year ended the threat of invasion.

By 1731, the Company of the Indies, dismayed by Louisiana's problems and the lack of profits, petitioned Louis XV to take back the colony, and once more Louisiana became a royal colony. Périer was recalled, and in 1732 Bienville, then fifty-two years old, was summoned out of retirement by the king to be governor of Louisiana.

Bienville returned to New Orleans in 1733 to find the colony with a shortage of merchandise, provisions, and money. There had been a considerable decrease in colonists, and the disposition of the Indians toward the French had sharply deteriorated.

Internal problems, as well as those with the Indians, were many, and Bienville was getting old. Still, he managed to guide the destiny of the colony for ten years, but discouraged by his lack of complete success in routing the troublesome savages and by the trials and disappointments of office, in 1743 he reluctantly asked to be relieved of office and retired to Paris, this time for good.

The new governor of Louisiana was Pierre de Rigaud, Marquis de Vaudreuil-Cavagnial, forty-five years old, a Canadian by birth. With his wife, fifteen years his senior, he immediately captivated New Orleans with his good taste, elegant manners, and elaborate entertainments. He gained the nickname "The Grand Marquis." The ten years that Vaudreuil governed Louisiana were a period of peace and prosperity: contending religious orders left off their quarrels, peace with the Indians was restored,

and a modicum of growth in the colony ensued, including the establishment of high society in New Orleans and the plantations nearby. Although experiments with sugarcane planting had been made as early as 1742, the Jesuits, during Vaudreuil's tenure, in 1751, continued planting on a more ambitious scale. This marked the modest beginning of the great sugar industry in the state, which was to affect commerce in New Orleans in the years to come.

Vaudreuil was elevated to the governorship of Canada and left New Orleans in 1753. His successor, Louis Billouart de Kerlérec, a French naval officer with a distinguished twenty-five-year career, soon found himself with the same frustrations that had plagued Vaudreuil's predecessor, Bienville. In addition, the Seven Years' War had broken out, and Kerlérec was fearful of an attack by sea from the English.

Unfortunately for the governor, a conniving *commissaire-ordinateur* (intendant), Vincent-Pierre-Gaspard de Rochemore was sent over to report on the progress of the colony. Rochemore became Kerlérec's bitter enemy, and while sending back to Paris reports charging Kerlérec with mismanagement, he himself, with power almost equal to that of his superior, permitted merchants and officials in certain circles to accumulate fortunes through corruption and laxness in enforcing the laws of trade and by outright speculation. This laissez-faire policy in New Orleans sowed seeds of rebellion, which bore fruit in the next decade —the first rebellion in North America against a European power. Rochemore was eventually removed, and another intendant, Nicolas-Denis Foucault, was sent to report on Kerlérec's activities. Foucault was a master of duplicity; his charges resulted in Kerlérec's recall and eventual imprisonment in the Bastille.

While these intrigues were going on in Louisiana, Louis XV—urged by the Duc de Choiseul, his foreign minister, who had no love for the colony—consented to make a gift of Louisiana to his Spanish cousin, Charles III. France at the conclusion of the Seven Years' War had lost all of Canada and all of Louisiana east of the Mississippi except the "island" of New Orleans, and Choiseul was determined to rid France of a colony that had been nothing but a burden since its founding. Charles, reluctant at first, eventually agreed, and Louisiana was ceded to Spain by a secret treaty of November 3, 1762.

The Spanish Regime

The treaty of cession was kept a secret between the Bourbon cousins for a year and a half, and nearly two years were to pass before the reluctant Spanish government finally made efforts to take possession of the colony. Jean Jacques-Blaise Dabbadie, who had succeeded Kerlérec as acting governor of Louisiana in 1763, announced to the stunned Louisianians in October, 1764, that by the Treaty of Fontainebleau they were to pass under the rule of Spain. A mass meeting participated in by delegates from the surrounding country and by the leaders of the New Orleans community resulted in the sending of Jean Milhet, a wealthy citizen, to Paris with a petition to the king not to relinquish Louisiana. Milhet received no encouragement at the French court, and hope vanished when word reached New Orleans that Antonio de Ulloa had been named governor of Louisiana by Charles III.

Ulloa, a distinguished scientist and captain in the Spanish navy, disembarked in New Orleans on March 5, 1766. His entourage consisted of three civil officers and only ninety Spanish troops. The Spaniards had mistakenly held the idea that the French troops in Louisiana would join their forces; Ulloa himself was described as too punctilious and as a person who raised difficulties over trifles. The new governor's very presence irritated the Louisianians, and nearly everything he said and did increased their antipathy toward him.

This situation resulted in the formation of a plot to expel Ulloa. The leader of the conspirators was Nicolas Chauvin de Lafrénière, the attorney general, and he was joined by a number of wealthy merchants of New Orleans and a group of planters and military men. Most Louisiana historians have portrayed Lafrénière and his conspirators as patriots with a deep-rooted love of their native country, but recent studies bear out the idea that most of them had made fortunes under the lax rule of the French and feared economic repercussions to themselves under Spanish rule. A commercial edict forbidding trade with the French Caribbean Islands and limiting it to only a few Spanish ports brought matters to a head.

The conspirators succeeded in arousing the Acadians west of the city and the Germans upriver. The first Acadians had drifted into Louisiana about 1763, and within five years there were some fifteen hundred of these refugees from Nova Scotia. On October 28, 1768, the Acadians and Germans together with many excited New Orleanians "took" the city. A thousand armed men milled about, and Charles Philippe Aubry, the French commandant who succeeded Dabbadie, who had died, aided Ulloa and his wife to escape. They boarded a Spanish frigate which, fortunately, was anchored midstream before the city. There was much loud talk but no bloodshed; Lafrénière and his confreres harangued the members of the Superior Council with charges against Ulloa, and a new petition was framed to send to the French court.

Ulloa eventually returned to Havana and sent a report to the Spanish ministry detailing the names of the plotters and the events that forced his retirement.

For once, the Spanish were quick to react. Charles III sent one of his favorite generals, an Irishman, Count Alexander O'Reilly, with twenty-six hundred troops and fifty cannon to Louisiana. O'Reilly arrived on August 18, 1769, his troops deploying from twenty-six vessels and marching to the Place d'Armes where Aubry formally handed him the keys to the city's forts. Although O'Reilly had reports on the conspiracy, he made an independent investigation, and, acting on instructions from the king, tried the twelve ring-leaders (one in absentia since he was dead). He

sentenced six to death and six to imprisonment. After the sentences were carried out, O'Reilly granted amnesty or pardon to the others who had signed the petition to expel Ulloa.

The short-lived freedom that the colony had enjoyed thus came to an end; the first revolution in North America had ended in failure.

O'Reilly abolished the Superior Council of the French and substituted the Illustrious Cabildo, which was partly a legislative and partly a quasi-administrative council, similar to that in other provincial towns under Spanish rule. The main laws came directly from Spain, from the captain general in Havana or from the governor himself, since there was no real legislative body. O'Reilly ordered a census taken, which showed that the population of New Orleans was 3,190. After the execution of the conspirators, he did little to disturb the lives and customs of the Creoles, descendants of the early settlers who preserved their characteristic speech and customs, and, surprisingly, the population of New Orleans quickly became reconciled to Spanish rule. Luis de Unzaga, who had accompanied O'Reilly to Louisiana, was proclaimed governor by O'Reilly at the first meeting of the Cabildo on December 1, 1769. But because of his superior position as captain general, O'Reilly continued to exercise his influence until he sailed for Spain on October 29, 1770.

Unzaga was a man of considerable ability. He soon realized that the strict interpretation of Spanish commercial laws would strangle Louisiana and, therefore, winked at the contraband trade, largely British, which had supplied many of the necessities of the colony. He took the part of the French Capuchins, Franciscan monks who had emigrated under Père Dagobert when the latter's spiritual leadership was challenged by the Spanish branch of the order then under Padre Cirillo, and otherwise helped reconcile the community, still essentially French, to Spanish rule.

Unzaga left in 1777, and his successor was Bernardo de Gálvez, a dashing young soldier then only twenty-nine years old. Gálvez further relaxed trade restrictions and permitted American agents to establish bases in New Orleans through which they supplied the Atlantic colonies with supplies and munitions in their struggle with Great Britain. Oliver Pollock, a New Orleans merchant who had been granted freedom of trade in Louisiana in return for placing a shipload of badly needed flour at O'Reilly's disposal when he came in 1769, was most active in this work. He advanced credit and supplies totaling $300,000 to the revolting colonists, thereby playing an important part in the success of the American cause.

During Gálvez's tenure, in 1779, Spain, as an ally of France, found herself involved in a war with England in which Gálvez led successful expeditions against Manchac, Baton Rouge, Natchez, Mobile, and Pensacola. He found that the people of New Orleans supported his military undertakings with great enthusiasm.

Gálvez frequently was absent from New Orleans and, in 1782, he installed his military aide, Colonel Esteban Miró, as acting governor. Miró functioned as Gálvez's lieutenant for four years, and when Gálvez was named viceroy of Mexico, Miró succeeded him in 1785 as governor in his own right.

Miró has been called "an affable, good-hearted and honorable man, whose judgment was as good as his intentions." At first he enforced the burdensome provisions regulating trade, but as time went on he relaxed some of his restrictions over the commerce of the port. During his era, New Orleans came more and more to depend on American trade from the upriver states and territories. This in time would mark the extinction of the power of Spain in Louisiana and the inevitable acquisition by the United States of the control of the mouth of the Mississippi.

In Miró's administration the great fire of March 21, 1788, desolated New Orleans, destroying 856 buildings—most of the French colonial city. The population, then about five thousand, suffered from a scarcity of provisions, which taxed the resources of the governor to supply. It was also during his tenure of office that the great bulk of Acadians who had been languishing in exile in France were brought to Louisiana.

Like his predecessors, Miró married into a prominent Creole family, and under his benign administration the Creole population was finally reconciled to Spanish rule. Miró resigned in 1791 to return to Spain.

Louisiana's next Spanish governor was a Belgian in the service of Spain—Barón Francisco Luis Héctor de Carondelet, who took office January 1, 1792. Carondelet was an energetic and determined man who brought many improvements to New Orleans. Under him the city had its first streetlights—eighty oil lamps suspended on chains at street corners; its first newspaper, the *Moniteur de la Louisiane*, which he edited; its first theatre, which was opened on St. Peter Street by the brothers Henry in October, 1792; and its first night watchmen and police commissaries. He had the Carondelet Canal dug by slave labor and erected two forts, St. Charles and Bourgogne, since he was fearful of attacks by the British or by the Americans from upriver.

It was the time of the French Revolution, and its reverberations were audible in Louisiana. Carondelet was fearful of plots from within as well as possible invasion from the French and Americans. Writing to the Spanish ministry in 1794, he reported:

By the exertion of the utmost vigilance and at the cost of sleepless nights, by frightening some, punishing others, by driving several out of the colony, and particularly those Frenchmen who latterly came among us, and who had already contaminated the greater part of the province with their notions and maxims of equality, by intercepting letters and papers of a suspicious character, and by dissembling with all, I have obtained more than I hoped, considering that the whole colony is now in a state of internal tranquility.

During the years 1793–1794, the city was struck by three hurricanes, and on December 8, 1794, a second great fire destroyed practically all the remaining buildings left by the French. It was started by some boys playing in the yard of Don Francisco Mayronne on Royal Street and was spread by a brisk north wind. In less than three hours, two hundred houses and stores were consumed.

The first Catholic bishop of Louisiana, Luis Peñalver y Cárdenas, was appointed during Carondelet's administration; and Jean Étienne Boré planted a large crop of sugar, hired an expert sugar maker, and produced in 1796 the first commercially successful crop of that staple, which finally established the sugar industry in Louisiana.

Barón Carondelet was appointed president of the Royal Audience of Quito in 1797, ending a highly successful administration. A most important event that occurred during Carondelet's governorship was the signing of a treaty between the United States and Spain. Among other things, it granted Americans the use of the port of New Orleans as a "place of deposit." This allowed them the privilege of exporting their produce or merchandise without paying duty. Subsequently, it was not renewed, but Americans with the tacit consent of the Spanish government continued to use the port until October 16, 1802, when Juan Ventura Morales, the intendant, suddenly closed it. The action precipitated a crisis, since it effectively curtailed American trade down the Mississippi and eventually led to the Louisiana Purchase.

Carondelet's successor was Brigadier General Manuel Luis Gayoso de Lemos, the former governor of the Natchez district. An affable and kindly man, he was occupied during much of his short administration with disputes with the strong-willed intendant, Morales. A social highlight of his governorship was the visit in 1798 of three illustrious but penniless visitors: the Duc d'Orléans—the future king of France, Louis Philippe—and his two brothers, the Duc de Montpensier and the Comte de Beaujolais. They were the peregrinating sons of Philippe-Égalité, who had voted for the death of his royal cousin, Louis XVI, and the great-great grandsons of Philippe d'Orléans, the regent of France for whom New Orleans had been named. The visitors were on their way to join their mother and eventually left by ship for Havana after drawing a draft for expenses on a New Orleans firm. Louisiana historians say they were entertained royally by Pierre de Marigny, Governor Gayoso, and others in New Orleans, but there is a paucity of authenticated published information as to how they spent their time.

Gayoso died rather suddenly of a fever on July 18, 1799, at the age of forty-eight. He is the only Spanish governor to have been buried in New Orleans, his remains being entombed in St. Louis Cathedral.

Pending the arrival of a successor, both Francisco Bouligny and the Marqués de Casa-Calvo served as military governors, with Nicolás María Vidal serving as civil head until the arrival in 1801 of General Juan Manuel de Salcedo, the last Spanish governor. Salcedo was advanced in years and "somewhat infirm in mind as well as body." It fell to his lot to transfer the Louisiana Territory from Spain back to France on November 30, 1803, thus ending thirty-four years of Spanish rule.

By and large, Spanish rule had been quite satisfactory to the Creoles, and at least one historian even called it a wise government. Population in the territory had quadrupled—for New Orleans it almost doubled—and the commerce of the port had grown tremendously. But one fact stands out: the Louisianians resisted all efforts to convert them into Spaniards. They remained French to the end of the regime.

The Louisiana Purchase

Louisiana had retroceded to France by the Treaty of San Ildefonso in 1800, but the colony had not been formally notified of the transaction until Pierre Clément de Laussat, the colonial prefect sent by Napoleon to take charge, arrived four months before the actual transfer in 1803. Lausset had been welcomed with mixed emotions by the Creoles—some of them considered him a dangerous revolutionary, and a number of the Ursuline nuns were so frightened at the prospect of an anti-Catholic government that they left for Havana. Laussat's grandiose plans for a French colonial Louisiana had come to naught: in August, 1803, news of the sale of Louisiana to the United States, which had actually been concluded May 2, had been received in New Orleans. Chagrined, he had been able to contemplate only the taking of possession of Louisiana from Spain and its almost immediate cession to the United States. On November 30, the transfer from Spain to France took place. The principal actors were Laussat; the Spanish commissioner, the Marqués de Casa-Calvo; and Governor Salcedo.

On December 20, 1803, the transfer of the colony to the United States took place with Laussat conducting similar ceremonies with William C. C. Claiborne and General James Wilkinson, the American commissioners. American troops arrived at the Place d'Armes, and with the signing of the *procès verbal* in the Sala Capitular of the Cabildo, the French flag was lowered and the vast Louisiana Territory became a part of the United States.

New Orleanians were not completely happy with the transfer of the colony to the United States; they had been fairly content under Spanish rule. American customs, particularly the use of English as the official language, were not well received, and the new American governor, Claiborne, who could not speak French, irked them.

At this period in its history, New Orleans was still a comparatively small town extending about a mile along the bend of the river and over a third of a mile in breadth. Three suburbs skirted it: the Faubourg Tremé to the north, Faubourg Marigny on the lands below what is now Esplanade Avenue, and the Faubourg Ste. Marie upstream on land that was to become the American section. There were some thirteen hundred buildings in the town, and the population was approximately eight thousand, about half of which was black.

Thanks to the French, New Orleans had a fine public square, the Place d'Armes, which opened to the river. Facing the square were the twin-towered St. Louis Cathedral, plastered and painted in front "to give it the appearance of marble"; the Cabildo (City Hall), which was then only two stories high; and the half-completed Presbytère. Other public buildings included the Ursuline Convent, two hospitals, a barracks, the government house, a theatre, and a ballroom. Buildings along the principal commercial streets were constructed of brick with roofs of tile or slate. Dwellings in the rear of the city were of wood with shingle roofs, and many of the better-class houses were set up on pillars. It was impossible to dig cellars because of the high water table, and the pillars were also a precaution against flooding.

In the original city, the blocks were 320 feet long and the streets 37 feet wide. These unpaved thoroughfares were drained by open ditches; garbage and slop thrown into these gutters created a stench; and it was only after hard rains that these drains were flushed of their noisome contents. Banquettes, or sidewalks, were first made of cypress planks, but by 1803 a number of sidewalks were paved with brick.

Between 1803, when France turned over Louisiana to the United States, and 1812, when Louisiana became a state, mayors were appointed by Claiborne, the territorial governor, himself an appointee of the President of the United States.

Laussat, the French colonial prefect, had appointed the wealthy planter Jean Étienne Boré as mayor. Just twenty days after Laussat had turned over Louisiana to the United States, Claiborne, in his capacity as acting governor of Louisiana, confirmed Boré to the post of mayor, and on February 17, 1805, New Orleans was incorporated.

Boré served fewer than six months and resigned presumably for business reasons but probably because of the hostility he felt for Governor Claiborne. Claiborne then appointed James Pitot, a Frenchman who had emigrated from Saint-Domingue to New Orleans. First named to the municipal council, Pitot was elected by his fellow members to the office with Claiborne's approval, and on March 4, 1805, the first election to select aldermen was held. The municipal officers consisted of a mayor, recorder (assessor), treasurer, and fourteen aldermen.

Pitot resigned in July, 1805, and Dr. John Watkins succeeded him. In 1807 Watkins turned over the office to James Mather, an Englishman who was the last appointed mayor of New Orleans during the territorial period. When Mather resigned, because of age, ill health, and criticism of his administration, New Orleans was without a mayor for almost five months, and Charles Trudeau, the recorder, filled the functions of mayor during that interval. The first election for the city's chief executive was held in September, 1812.

Prior to 1812, election procedures were a little vague. There were no formal nominations, and one just wrote the name of his choice on the ballot, but in 1812 a large group of citizens met to discuss possible candidates, and they eventually nominated Nicholas Girod (who neither spoke, read, nor understood English) and James Pitot (who, because of his presidency of the New Orleans Navigation Company, some felt would have a conflict of interest).

Girod won the election with 859 votes; only 461 were cast for Pitot. Girod ran again in 1814 and was reelected with August Macarty a close second. When his predecessor resigned in 1815, Macarty was elected unopposed and reelected in 1816 and 1818.

A Period of Growth

During this period there were many changes. In 1805 the first Protestant church was founded and a library society incorporated. In 1807 an important fire ordinance—the famous "Bucket Ordinance," which ordered each householder to keep two buckets in readiness—was passed. The same ordinance provided that four pumps be kept under the arches of the Cabildo; a watchman was to be stationed on the roof of that building and was to ring a bell at the cry of fire.

The police force was poorly run; several times during the early part of the century it was reorganized, and it was not until 1840 that a fairly workable department came into operation. The French traveler C. C. Robin, who visited New Orleans at the time of the Louisiana Purchase, found much indolence, dissipation, and a singular indifference to law and order there. The influence of the church was negligible insofar as the daily conduct of its parishioners was concerned. Gambling among men of all classes was a common vice; and there were also the notorious and disreputable quadroon balls, about which so much has been written. Respectable white women had few opportunities for social and mental development, their lives being passed in a monotonous round of domestic duties. Education was neglected and opportunities for self-improvement were few and not valued very highly. Smuggling was so general that it was almost regarded as a profession. This was the city in which the straitlaced Claiborne found himself.

Governor Claiborne was shocked by youths who had no accomplishments but "dancing with elegance and ease" to recommend them. He blamed parents for their inattention to their children's education. Most boys were sent to small elementary private schools or, if their parents could afford it, to schools in France. The Ursuline nuns offered instruction to seventy or

eighty paying pupils and taught girls of indigent families without charge. Claiborne urged that the territorial legislature establish a college, and after a great deal of effort the Collège d'Orléans came into being in 1811.

On April 30, 1812, Louisiana was admitted to the Union as the eighteenth state, with New Orleans as its capital. On June 18, the United States declared war on Great Britain, marking the War of 1812. However, Louisiana's participation began with the siege of New Orleans in December and January of 1814–1815. This siege was the most dramatic event that had yet occurred in a city that had witnessed considerable conflict with still more to come. Andrew Jackson's rout of the British army on the plains of Chalmette, accomplished by city and state militia, including also that of Tennessee and Kentucky and the aid as well of Baratarian pirates, did much to weld the polyglot population of Louisiana, particularly of New Orleans, into *Americans.*

In 1815, New Orleans's population had reached thirty-three thousand, and the city was growing rapidly. By 1820 there were forty-one thousand people, and a flood of city ordinances were passed to regulate everything from the price of bread to the conduct of theatre audiences. Improvements were many. A steam waterworks to supply unfiltered river water to subscribers, begun by Benjamin H. B. Latrobe before his untimely death in 1820, was completed in 1823. In 1821, a better system of streetlighting was inaugurated, although the custom of lighting one's own way at night continued as late as 1837. In 1822, streetpaving with cobble stones and a gravel topping was first attempted, but most of the city's mud streets were quagmires in rainy weather, and dusty on dry days.

River commerce, the lifeblood of the growing city, was greatly increased by the coming of the steamboat; the *New Orleans* was the first to successfully navigate the Mississippi. In 1817, there had been fifteen hundred flatboat and five hundred barge arrivals from the upper river, but hardly any steamboats. A strangling steamboat monopoly had held down their number, but once the courts had ruled the monopoly illegal, more and more were built and put into river commerce. In 1821, there were 287 steamboat arrivals against 441 flatboats and 174 barges. The value of both exported and imported commerce that year was $10,651,000, a figure that would be increased to more than $53 million fourteen years later.

In 1820, Louis Philippe de Roffignac won the mayoral election, and he was such a good mayor that he was kept in office for eight years, being repeatedly reelected with little or no opposition. Of him, John S. Kendall says in his *History of New Orleans:* "He seems to have been the first official in New Orleans to appreciate its dawning commercial importance and set himself earnestly and laboriously to prepare the city for its coming greatness." He took steps to pave some of the city's muddy streets and to light and police them better. Roffignac resigned in 1828 and returned to France, where he met an accidental death in 1846.

In April, 1825, the city was honored by a visit from the aging Marquis de Lafayette, who was making a tour of the United States. The city council appropriated $15,000 to redecorate the Cabildo as a residence for their distinguished visitor, and for five hectic days the hero of American revolutionary days was entertained by almost every segment of the population.

Railroad fever struck New Orleans in the late 1820s, and in 1831 the Pontchartrain Railroad was put into operation. The line ran from downtown New Orleans to the shore of Lake Pontchartrain. Though only 5.18 miles long, it filled a long-felt need; it became the last land link of the Mobile–New Orleans steamboat and mail route. Another railroad—the New Orleans and Carrollton—was started in 1835. This was more of a suburban line, since it served the towns of Lafayette (a two-mile run) and Carrollton (a four-and-a-half-mile run). Also in 1835 a much more ambitious project—the New Orleans–Nashville Railroad, a line from New Orleans to Nashville, 564 miles away—was started with a subscription of $500,000 from the city. The company ran into many difficulties and built only twenty miles of track out of New Orleans before the project was abandoned. Nearly twenty years would elapse before the emergence of the New Orleans–Jackson Railroad from New Orleans at a time when the rest of the country was greatly expanding its railroad trackage.

Roffignac's successor was Denis Prieur, who served until 1838. Next serving were Charles Genois (1838–1840), William Freret (1840–1842), Denis Prieur again (1842–1843), and again William Freret (1843–1844). Mayor Freret was described as "one of few equals and no superiors and one of the most useful mayors the city ever had." Freret was defeated in 1844 by Joseph Edgard Montégut, who served until 1846.

New Orleans was visited by frightful epidemics. In 1832, it was cholera, and between 1817 and 1860 there were twenty-three yellow-fever epidemics. In this forty-three-year period, 28,192 deaths were recorded from "Bronze John" (yellow fever) alone. During the fourth term of Abdiel Daily Crossman, who held office from 1846 to 1854 and for self-evident reasons called himself plain A. D. Crossman, the horrible yellow-fever epidemic of 1853 carried off about eight thousand victims.

New Orleans with its high water table became known as the city of the wet grave, "where the hopes of thousands are buried," since those who could not afford to buy a vault for the burial of their dead were compelled literally to deposit them in the water. An observer in 1819 had written that the water filled a grave to within eighteen inches of the top. The marshy character of the New Orleans soil and the city's annual rainfall were compelling reasons why aboveground burial vaults or individual tombs came into common use, a custom that still persists today, although improved drainage has long ago lowered the level of ground water. The first city Board of Health had been organized in 1817, but had operated only a few years. Attempts had subsequently been made to reorganize this important body, but the medical society kept the records until the 1850's, when a state body was organized. A city Board of Health came into being in 1898.

In the early 1830s, Chartres Street was the retail center of the city. In its shops could be found the latest Parisian fashions in clothing and millinery, imported glass and tableware, "fancy goods," and beautiful jewelry. By the end of the decade, however, more and more of the 721 merchants who were in business in 1834 were moving to Canal Street, which was fast becoming the center of retail trade.

Royal Street was noted for its banks, its cafés and exchanges, and its fine residences. Bourbon Street became an elegant residential section; many of these buildings on Bourbon and Royal still stand.

Above Canal Street, the Faubourg Ste. Marie grew rapidly in the 1820s and 1830s. This section was the commercial center of the city and contained the offices and warehouses of wholesalers, commission merchants, exporters and importers, cotton and sugar speculators. The Anglo-Saxon element was predominant here, and fortunes, often quickly amassed, soon found expression here in public buildings (St. Charles Hotel, Gallier Hall, Banks' Arcade), in blocks of substantial commercial buildings, and in the fine residences of the rapidly developing adjacent faubourgs.

On the political front, as in most states, there were differences between New Orleans and the rest of the state, between the Catholics of southern Louisiana and the Protestants of the north, between the large landowners and planters of south Louisiana and the hill farmers of the northern section.

New Orleans remained the state capital, but in 1830 the rural majority, convinced that the wickedness of "The City that Care Forgot" was corrupting the state government, had succeeded in moving the capital upriver to Donaldsonville. However, the legislators were soon bored with meeting in such a small town, and after a very short period voted to return to the old fleshpots. It would take until 1850, after persistent urging, for the capital to be finally removed to Baton Rouge.

Texas had not entered the Union until 1845, but events in Texas in the 1830s keenly interested people in New Orleans. The Texans were engaged in a struggle with Mexico and were being aided by a New Orleans committee which held mass meetings in their support. This group sent money, mail, supplies, and "emigrants" (volunteer fighters) to Texas, to the distress of the Mexican envoy to the United States. In 1836, Stephen F. Austin, an American colonizer, raised $300,000 in loans in the city and wrote of New Orleans: "The cause of liberty and Texas stands high in this city."

During the era, numerous filibustering expeditions were formed, at first to assist Latin Americans to win their independence, and later to try to overturn existing governments. A great many of these had their birthplace in New Orleans.

Politics, though, did not interfere with growth. In the mid-1830s, cotton plantations, served by the steamboats, were producing more than half a million bales a year, and New Orleans was becoming the world's largest cotton market. The city boasted half a dozen compresses where baled cotton was recompressed by large steam-operated machines to reduce it in size to lessen freight charges on exportation. However, in 1837, a rupture in the growing economy caused a nationwide panic which seriously disrupted business and finance in New Orleans. Fourteen banks suspended payment in specie. Faced with a shortage of small bills and in an attempt to improve financial conditions, the municipalities and businesses began to issue their own money, which often depreciated as rapidly as it was issued. It was not until 1839 that this depression was overcome and New Orleans again began to forge ahead.

By 1840, with a population of 102,192, New Orleans had grown to be the fourth largest city in the United States and second only to New York as a port. "In that year," wrote one historian, "there seemed every reason to expect that New Orleans would soon be the greatest, as it probably was proportionately already the wealthiest city in America." Its ideal location, near the mouth of the Mississippi, and the rapid expansion of steamboat traffic had combined to bring this about.

Unfortunately, while its prosperity in this period grew enormously, forces were operating beneath the glittering surface which, at the time, were imperfectly understood but which would seriously menace the city's continued importance. The Erie and Ohio canals, built in 1831 and 1832, later seriously affected the shipments of wheat and flour from Ohio, which traveled a new, rather circuitous, safer, route to New York instead of via the Mississippi to New Orleans. Additional railroad building, too, was neglected, but the city had all the business it could handle, so why build railroads except as feeders for the river traffic? In 1845, when Henry Clay presided over a great convention held in Memphis to demand such improvement as dredging and canalization in the Mississippi and its tributaries, two-thirds of the river tonnage was finding its way to New Orleans, and regular steamboat lines ran as far as Pittsburgh and St. Paul. By 1900, this once lucrative business would all but vanish; the vessels that carried the rich cargoes of the Mississippi and Ohio valleys would disappear, victims of the Civil War and later of the railroads.

The increase in the size of oceangoing vessels also contributed substantially to the decline of New Orleans as a world port. Northeast Pass at the mouth of the river shoaled in 1837, and Southwest Pass came into use. By 1850, this pass, which was about fifteen feet deep, became too shallow for vessels of more than one thousand tons, and in one week in 1852 forty vessels were aground at its mouth. There were other factors, such as high port charges, but apparently none was recognized early enough for constructive remedies to be proposed.

In 1854, General John L. Lewis became mayor; he was followed by Charles M. Waterman, who was impeached; and Gerard Stith defeated Major P. G. T. Beauregard in a troubled election in 1858.

In 1859–1860, the business of the port had never been better—2,214,296 bales of cotton had come down the river and exports and imports valued at $185 million had passed over the wharves of the Crescent City. New Orleans banks had nearly $20 million in deposits and over $12 million in specie in their vaults. The state ranked second in per capita wealth in the nation.

But the clouds of disunion were beginning to gather over the South, and the golden tide of commerce that had made the city great was suddenly to recede, not to return for a long, long time.

Civil War

Louisiana found itself on the eve of the Civil War in a peculiar position. Never a protagonist of states' rights, Louisiana—New Orleans in particular—was bound by strong economic and social ties to the nation. Half its agricultural and nearly all its commercial interests depended upon its connection with the Union, and Louisiana had little cause to withdraw from it.

The election of Abraham Lincoln in 1860, however, marked a turning point in the feelings of Louisiana's citizens; more and more of them felt that the day of compromise was past, and when, on January 26, 1861, the vocal group of secessionists won control of a convention to consider Louisiana's future relation with the Union, the Ordinance of Secession was passed by a large majority. The state existed as an independent republic for nine days before joining the newly formed Confederacy.

In New Orleans wild excitement broke out; the forts below the city were seized, as were the federal mint and the customhouse, and the city became abustle with preparation for war. The Mississippi had been blockaded by a Federal warship, and trade and commerce gradually came to a standstill. The South's General Mansfield Lovell reached New Orleans in October, and though he was shocked at the chaotic conditions he found, he set to work to improve the city's defenses.

It was soon apparent to Southern leaders that the Federals intended to get control of the lower Mississippi and cut the Confederacy in half. In December, Union troops landed on Ship Island off the Mississippi Gulf Coast in preparation for the campaign to capture New Orleans. Under the command of Captain David Glasgow Farragut, a fleet was assembled, and on April 18, a flotilla began the bombardment of Forts St. Philip and Jackson, then New Orleans's chief defenses. After five days of incessant mortar fire, the forts still held out, and Farragut decided to run his ships past them. A fierce battle ensued. Most of Farragut's ships got past the forts, and the next day he brushed past the Confederate batteries at Chalmette and dropped anchor before New Orleans.

Farragut tried to effect a peaceful surrender of the city, and a series of fruitless conferences with the mayor and Confederate leaders ensued. By April 29, the admiral's patience was exhausted, and on that day he sent an expedition ashore which, without bloodshed, hauled down the flag to take formal possession. Thenceforth, throughout the war and until 1877, New Orleans was an occupied city.

Three days later, General Benjamin F. Butler arrived in New Orleans with fifteen thousand troops and began a rule that caused him to be hated not only in the city but throughout the South.

Butler was succeeded by General Nathaniel P. Banks, under whose direction a Union government was formed. Comparative quiet characterized the first few weeks of his administration in New Orleans, but the old defiance soon reasserted itself, and in January, 1863, Banks deported three hundred Southern sympathizers to Confederate-held territory across Lake Pontchartrain.

John T. Monroe, the heroic Civil War mayor who had taken office in 1860, had been removed by Federal military authorities after the fall of the city in 1862. Between May 16, 1862, and May 11, 1866, New Orleans had a succession of mayors all appointed by the military occupying the city: George F. Shepley, Godfrey Weitzel, Jomas H. French, Henry C. Deming, James F. Miller, E. H. Durrell, Stephen Hoyt, Hugh Kennedy, Samuel Miller Quincy, Glendy Burke, J. Ad. Rozier, and George Clark.

Reconstruction

The seemingly interminable years of the Civil War dragged on. New Orleans, occupied by Federal forces, watched the fortunes of the Confederacy sink lower and lower in 1863 when Vicksburg and Port Hudson fell. Finally, in June, 1865, the war in Louisiana ended when General Kirby Smith surrendered, but for Louisianians the struggle was not yet over. After Lincoln's assassination, the powerful Radical Republicans in Congress wanted to punish the South. Instead of the "soft" peace that Lincoln planned, the Radicals determined to treat the Southern states as conquered territory. Reconstruction and military occupation would last twelve more years, and New Orleans, together with the rest of the state, would suffer what George W. Cable called "a hideous carnival of political profligacy."

In March, 1867, Congress passed its first Reconstruction Act, and General Philip Sheridan, who commanded the Federal troops in Louisiana, interpreted the terms of the act so harshly that only half the white citizens of the state could vote in the election of delegates to a convention to revise the state constitution, although all adult Negro males could vote. The results could be foreseen—the new constitution en-

franchised the Negro and provided for full equality in common carriers and in the public schools. The freed Negroes provided Louisiana with one of its greatest problems. Beguiled by their new social status, they interpreted freedom as freedom from work. With little or no education, the ex-slaves became the tools of unscrupulous white scalawags and carpetbaggers, who for a time controlled the political and economic destinies of Louisiana.

Henry Clay Warmoth was elected governor, with Oscar J. Dunn, a Negro, as lieutenant governor. The new constitution gave the governor almost unlimited power—he could appoint local police, registrars, and returning boards, which, at his direction, could throw out votes he did not want counted. Graft became rampant and taxes confiscatory.

The Warmoth-Dunn regime had hardly taken office when the Republicans split into two factions; the easy pickings attracted Republicans William Pitt Kellogg and United States Marshal Stephen B. Packard, who had backing in Congress. Kellogg replaced Warmoth in the 1872 "election," but C. C. Antoine, a Negro, became lieutenant governor. The Democratic candidate, John McEnery, thought he won the election, but a corrupt returning board counted him out. Kellogg was installed with the aid of Federal troops ordered by President Grant, and his Republican henchmen were in control of the legislature by the same means. By 1874, Louisiana was bankrupt with a debt of $53 million, on which it could not even pay the interest, let alone the principal. For nine years, the decent citizens of the state had endured one corrupt government after another; many had suffered disenfranchisement and were forced to pay exorbitant taxes that were squandered by inept Radical politicians, who kept themselves in power by using the Negro vote and by collusion with the Federal government, whose soldiers were ever present. It was not surprising that reaction would set in, and it did with the formation of White Leagues, which declared war on carpetbaggers, scalawags, and "noncooperating" whites. In New Orleans, General Frederick N. Ogden organized the Crescent City White League, which soon had twenty-eight hundred men enrolled under a quasi-military discipline.

Events came to a bloody climax on September 14, 1874, when there was a fifteen-minute battle between the governor's Metropolitan Police and the local White Leaguers, in which twenty-seven men were killed and more than a hundred injured. The White Leaguers routed the Metropolitans. Next morning the remnants of the police and the Negro militia in the State House surrendered, and all state and city officials were deposed and the McEnery officials formally inducted into office. But victory was short-lived. President Grant issued a proclamation ordering the White Leaguers to disperse and "submit to the laws and constituted authorities of the state," and backed it up by sending troops and three warships to New Orleans. McEnery, thereupon realizing that he couldn't fight the United States Army and Navy, surrendered.

The election of 1876 was quite similar to that of 1872—two sets of candidates each claiming victory. The Democrats, who had nominated Francis Tillou Nicholls, had a clear majority of votes, but after the returning board was finished, the Republicans were counted the winners by a majority of 3,437. On January 8, 1877, there were two inaugurations in New Orleans. Stephen B. Packard, the Republican, a Maine-born carpetbagger, was sworn in as the last of the Radical governors at the St. Louis Hotel, and at Lafayette Square ten thousand persons looked on while General Nicholls took the oath of office. The next day, the Continental Guards, formerly the White League, under General Frederick N. Ogden, assembled three thousand strong and marched to the Cabildo, where they took possession of the Supreme Court chambers, the arsenal, and the police station. The Republicans were holed up in the State House, while Packard tried futilely to get recognition from Grant.

In Washington, Republican Rutherford B. Hayes, thanks to an electoral commission, gained the necessary twenty disputed electoral votes to win the presidency in an extremely tight election. The fraudulent returns from Louisiana had been counted in his favor. But Packard did not benefit by it, and most historians feel that some kind of deal was made by Governor Nicholls's representatives in Washington; they had explained Louisiana's predicament to members of Congress close to Hayes, and the new president sent a commission to Louisiana to investigate. As a result, on April 27, 1877, President Hayes ordered all Federal troops out of New Orleans, Packard surrendered the State House, and the long period of Reconstruction in Louisiana came to an end.

On the mayoralty level, Mayor John T. Monroe had resumed office May 12, 1866, and served until March 28, 1867. Succeeding him were Edward Heath (1867–1868), John R. Conway (1868–1870), Benjamin Franklin Flanders (1870–1872), Louis A. Wiltz (1872–1874), Charles L. Leeds (1874–1876), Edward Pillsbury (1876–1878), and Isaac W. Patton (1878–1880).

Continued Expansion

The city's expansion in the meantime resumed. Even as early as 1852, the city of Lafayette, the section between Felicity and Toledano streets, was absorbed by New Orleans, and in 1870, Jefferson City, further up the river, and Algiers, across the river, were annexed. The suburbs of Hurstville, Greenville, and Burtheville, and finally the town of Carrollton itself were absorbed. New Orleans developed downstream and toward the lake also. However, as a great part of the land "back of town" was swampy and had to be cleared and drained, development here was much slower.

In 1874, Captain James B. Eads with his jetties began the work of opening the mouth of the Mississippi River. Artificial banks forced the current of the river to deepen its bed, while at the same time the silt-laden water was carried out into the Gulf of Mexico. By 1879, Eads's work was completed, and New Orleans was again able to accommodate deep-draft ships, which greatly increased the port's commerce. The 1870s also witnessed the expansion of the railroads, and by 1880, five large trunk lines entered New Orleans, serving a population of some 216,000, which included over 57,000 blacks and 3,000 immigrants. With the coming of the railroads, steamboat traffic began to decline; within a hundred years after the arrival of the first steamboat in New Orleans most of the boats had disappeared from the lower Mississippi.

The city boasted a good transit system composed of 140 miles of track, mostly serviced by 313 mule cars with 1,641 mules available to draw them. On three lines, the cars were drawn by steam "dummies."

However, an inadequate waterworks fell far below supplying the needs of the city, as did three large steam drainage machines and a system of canals that were supposed to drain the city in heavy rainfalls.

Manufacturing and mechanical plants were relatively few—915 employed a total of 9,500. The port was the city's principal business. Exports were valued at over $90 million, and nearly 1½ million bales of cotton were shipped that year. Imports totaled over $10 million, the principal commodities being coffee, iron, sugar, and molasses.

The city's largest parks had not yet been developed, although the unimproved land was municipally owned. Of 659 acres of public squares, the best kept was Jackson Square, which, "much frequented and with its wealth of orange trees and other subtropical vegetation is extremely attractive. It is closed at night, and has a day and night watchman, and a gardener."

Besides five theatres, now long gone, there were three large public halls and the resorts of West End and Spanish Fort, which were patronized nightly during the warm months by the thousands who enjoyed the ride to the lakeside, the band concerts, and other amusements.

When Mayor Joseph Shakspeare came into office in 1880, the city had a total of eighty-three "important" gambling establishments. Gambling, always a great evil in New Orleans, had reached a point at which it had to be repressed. The vice was forbidden by law and only existed commercially because it was countenanced by corrupt police. After a visiting young Frenchman was fleeced outrageously in a poker game, Mayor Shakspeare, who had come into office on a reform ticket, was determined to act. He could not license the gamblers, but he broached a plan by which certain chosen "honest" establishments would contribute to a fund to build and operate a much-needed almshouse in return for permitting their operation under the supervision of detectives. His plan was put into effect, and the gambling houses were reduced in number to sixteen. It was estimated that this "practical" system brought in about $30,000 from the remaining gambling houses, most of which were on Royal

Street. The "Shakspeare Plan" continued in operation with varying success under succeeding administrations until it was finally abandoned in 1887.

In 1882, the end of Shakspeare's first term, Canal Street was first illuminated by electric light, and by 1887, nearly all the city had electricity available. Mule-car transportation, started just at the outbreak of the Civil War, persisted for nearly thirty years, and it was not until 1892 that the first electric streetcars were placed in operation.

A world's fair, the Cotton Centennial Exposition held in 1884–1885, while not a financial success, restored to New Orleans a feeling that the city was at last recovering its former commercial importance. By drawing hundreds of thousands of visitors, it did much to bring about a better understanding between North and South.

After Shakspeare's first term, he was succeeded by William J. Behan (1882–1884). The term of office was then increased to four years, and J. Valsin Guillotte (1884–1888) was elected. Shakspeare again came into office in 1888 and served until 1892.

In 1890, the city was thrown into a furor over the murder of its able chief of police, David C. Hennessey. Nineteen suspects, members of a gang of immigrant Sicilian terrorists, were indicted, and in March, 1891, nine were brought to trial. When after two weeks in court, six of the defendants were acquitted, feeling ran high that there had been a real miscarriage of justice, probably through jury tampering or intimidation. A meeting of prominent citizens resulted in a call for action, and on March 14, 1891, a large party of armed men gathered at the Henry Clay Monument on Canal Street, marched to the Parish Prison, broke in, and shot or hanged eleven of those who were indicted, some of whom had not been brought to trial.

The Louisiana lottery also came to an end. Chartered during the corrupt times of the Reconstruction in 1868, it had flourished mightily in New Orleans for a quarter of a century, making fortunes for its operators and exerting a sinister influence in politics and on the life of the community. When the charter came up for renewal in 1892, it was renewed for three years, but the effects of a bitter struggle by reformers in New Orleans and restrictions on lottery mail by the federal government, the "Octopus," as it was called, was finally outlawed in 1895.

As in most large American cities, New Orleans experienced an almost continual struggle between entrenched "ring" politicians and reform elements. Since the end of the Civil War, the New Orleans political scene had been characterized first by the struggle of the "better" elements in the community to rid themselves of the radicals and carpetbaggers, who took advantage of the South's defeat during Reconstruction days. Then, in the seventies, eighties, and nineties, very often wholesale corruption was rampant, and reform administrations almost periodically came to power when conditions became intolerable, only to fade, invariably.

In one of these reform administrations, that of Mayor C. Flower, who succeeded John Fitzpatrick (1892–1896), an ordinance was introduced in 1897 by Alderman Sidney Story and passed by the city council. It set aside an area near the French Quarter where prostitution was to be permitted, but not actually legalized, so as to control and regulate what had become a real civic nuisance. The theory of containment as a method of controlling prostitution was then in vogue. The prostitutes were herded into the thirty-eight-block area designated in the ordinance, and thus began what soon became one of the most amazing spectacles of legalized vice that few visitors to New Orleans missed viewing. Much to Alderman Story's disgust, the red-light district was soon called Storyville, and it operated full blast for twenty years until the federal government closed it as a war measure in 1917. Mayor Flower served until 1900.

Spanish-American War

Soon after Flower took office, on February 15, 1898, the battleship *Maine* was blown up in Havana harbor with a loss of 266 men, with circumstances pointing to Spanish guilt. The *Maine* had visited New Orleans the previous Mardi Gras, and its officers and men counted many friends in the city. Like the rest of the nation, New Orleanians were horrified, and when negotiations by which Spain might have cleared itself of the crime broke down, war was declared on April 25. On the President's call for volunteers, Louisiana's response was immediate. Camp Foster was opened at the Fair Grounds and Jackson Barracks was expanded, a training camp was opened in Covington, and volunteers offered themselves in a steady stream. The battle song, "There'll Be a Hot Time in the Old Town Tonight" quickly became popular. In all, six Louisiana outfits were mustered, but none saw action before the war ended, just eight months after it had begun.

In the last year of Flower's term, the population of New Orleans had increased to slightly over 287,000 —some thirty-five times its size of a century before. But it was a city that had but few paved streets, no sewerage system whatever, and a community dependent largely on cistern water for drinking. Work on a new system of drainage, begun three years before, had just been completed. The improvement was apparent almost at once in the mortality statistics.

Paul Capdevielle, the last of the Creole mayors (1900–1904), followed Flower. During this period, in 1903, New Orleans observed the centennial of the Louisiana Purchase—a three-day celebration included the reenactment of the historic event by descendants of the original participants, a military review, a naval pageant, an operatic performance, and a grand pontifical mass at St. Louis Cathedral.

Capdevielle was succeeded by the versatile and energetic Martin Behrman. Behrman, who made his home in Algiers, where he was very popular, was an astute politician. After his first term, he was reelected by a huge majority, and during his first two administrations he built the "Old Regular" (ring) organization into such a powerful force that, despite the change from aldermanic to commission form of city government in 1912, he was reelected for a third term and again in 1916, serving a total of sixteen consecutive years.

During the Behrman administrations, the city had expanded in every direction. A badly needed municipally operated sewerage system was put into operation in 1908, and in a year piped, filtered water became available. When a spectacular $3 million fire occurred in 1905 destroying the Stuyvesant docks on the riverfront, expanding port business made a new and larger replacement necessary. In 1908, a new library on St. Charles Avenue was opened, thanks to the generous gift of Andrew Carnegie, and that same year a much needed annex to the City Hall was constructed and work was started on a new Civil Courts Building on Royal Street. In 1912, a bronze monument to Jefferson Davis, located on the boulevard that bears his name, was unveiled. In 1915 a palatial marble post office and federal court building on Camp Street was dedicated.

During Behrman's first year, in 1905, the last of the New Orleans yellow-fever epidemics took place, but prompt measures to combat the spread of the disease (screening of cisterns and oiling of open gutters, screening of houses) cut the number of cases to 3,286 and the deaths to 423. Improvements in the drainage system and other sanitary measures caused a dramatic drop in the death rate. Between 1880 and 1889, the death rate was twenty-eight per thousand as compared with eighteen per thousand in the average American city. Outdoor cisterns were outlawed in 1918, and three years later the rate slid to eighteen per thousand. By 1940, it was less than fifteen, including nonresidents desperately ill and brought to the city for treatment; excluding nonresidents, the death rate was about eleven. In 1969, the rate was 12.68 including nonresidents and 9.61 excluding them.

Greatly increased attendance in the public schools made it necessary to construct more buildings, and between 1904 and 1920, twenty-four schools, including two high schools for girls and one for boys, had been opened. In 1908, the Public Belt Railroad had been organized and put into operation to better serve the city's shippers and industrial plants through its switching and car transfer service. The board of port commissioners, active since 1901, had greatly expanded the business of the port during Behrman's time.

World War I

The desperate struggle going on in Europe in 1914 was reflected in New Orleans. Business, at first bad, gradually improved, since increased tonnage in war materials poured across New Orleans's wharves. Imports and exports were $283 million in 1914 and $524 million by 1918. There was a marked increase in the prices of consumer goods, and the "high cost of living" was a topic on everybody's lips. The sinking of the *Lusitania,* and Germany's unrestricted submarine war on shipping and general arrogance eventually resulted in American preparations for war. A series of preparedness parades was touched off throughout the United States, and the one in New Orleans, held June 3, 1916, brought out forty thousand marchers. When the United States declared war on Germany on April 6, 1917, immediate steps were taken to train the eighty thousand men from Louisiana who joined or were drafted into the armed services. Camps and cantonments rose at the Fair Grounds, at the City Park Race Track, at the lakefront near West End, and at Tulane University. The Algiers Naval Station became alive with activity. New Orleans oversubscribed by $11,940,000 the city's quotas in the campaigns for War Savings Stamps, Liberty Bonds, Red Cross, Knights of Columbus, Y.M.C.A., etc., raising a total of $103,-300,000.

Between 1914 and 1918 the port's public facilities were greatly increased by the construction of its public cotton warehouse with a capacity of 2 million bales; the public grain elevator that could store 4 million bushels; the gigantic army supply base consisting of three six-story steel and concrete buildings 600 by 140 feet and by starting the digging of the Industrial Canal. The Great War also saw the rebirth of river traffic—this time by barges instead of steam packets. The Mississippi had all but been forgotten—abandoned except for dwindling local service—when Congress, acting because the federally controlled railroads could not handle expeditiously the greatly increased tonnage generated by the war's needs, passed the Federal Control Act of March 21, 1918. This resulted in the formation of the Mississippi-Warrior services and eventually the Inland Waterways Corporation. This concern built forty two-thousand-ton barges and six towboats, and by 1923 nonperishable freight was moving almost as rapidly by barge as by railroad. Eventually, privately owned towing-barge services returned to the river, and the Mississippi now carries more freight to New Orleans than in the palmiest days of the packets.

On the opposite side of the river, the old Harvey Canal, which was a water link between the Mississippi River and the Gulf of Mexico via Bayou Barataria, Lake Salvador, and Bayou Lafourche, was bought in 1924 by the United States government. It was extended and enlarged to become part of the Intracoastal Canal, an important link in the waterways along which enormous amounts of cargo move by barge.

On November 11, 1918, the news that the war had ended caused New Orleanians to join the frenzy that shook the world that day. Reported the *Times-Picayune:*

From early morning until long into the night the city was ablaze with colors as thousands of overjoyed patriots made the air rock with their shouts and cheers. Scores of bands, fireworks, a thousand and one parades, most of them impromptu, in streets that were literally packed with people, and a citywide tooting of whistles and ringing of bells were some of the features that stood out.

Unfortunately, the nationwide influenza epidemic was then at its height, and on some days there were as many as a hundred deaths in New Orleans. Also, the French Opera House was destroyed by fire on December 4, 1919. Efforts to rebuild an opera house have continued until today with the beginning of construction of a new civic center for the performing arts.

The mad 1920s—an era of speculation in stocks and real estate—saw another increase in large buildings in New Orleans's business district. In this decade were erected the Hibernia Bank Building, the Whitney Bank Building Annex, The Cotton Exchange, the Roosevelt Hotel Annex, the Père Marquette Building, the Masonic Temple Building, and the striking American Bank Building.

One of the most important civic movements to take place in the 1920s and 1930s was the rejuvenation of the Vieux Carré. With the coming of the Civil War and the passing of the steamboat era, the commercial importance of New Orleans lay shattered. For many years the city remained proud though impoverished. The old Creole families who had lived in the Vieux Carré gradually moved to new parts of the city and little by little the quarter degenerated, whole areas becoming slums. A few artists and perceptive writers saw the charm of the place but their paintings and writings could not save it. An entire block of the finest buildings in the quarter was destroyed to build the Civil Courts Building, and the once magnificent St. Louis Hotel was allowed to fall into decay and eventual destruction. New Orleans began at long last to realize that, unless something was done to preserve what was left, soon the whole quarter would disappear. Through a Vieux Carré commission, hundreds of buildings were renovated, restored, and remodeled, and put to new uses to make them pay their own way. New Orleans, having triumphed over adversities that few cities in the United States had been called on to bear, was transformed.

In politics, however, it was business as usual. The reform element wanted to rid itself of the Old Regulars who had put up Behrman for a fifth term. They nominated Andrew J. McShane, who by a combination of circumstances barely beat Behrman. McShane's administration, like that of other reformers before him, did not live up to the expectations of its backers, and when McShane ran again in 1924, against Behrman, "Papa came home" for his fifth term. Before he had been in office a year, however, Behrman died of a heart ailment, leaving a record of nearly seventeen years of service, which no other mayor of New Orleans exceeded.

Behrman was followed by Arthur J. O'Keefe, Sr., who held office until 1929, being succeeded by T. Semmes Walmsley. Walmsley was mayor during Huey P. Long's tenure as governor and United States senator, when he was a virtual dictator in Louisiana poli-

tics. Many of the acts of the legislature, which Long controlled, were aimed at New Orleans and its politicians and newspapers that opposed him. This struggle for power was exemplified dramatically in 1934 when Long ordered the militia to prevent the seizure of the Orleans parish registration office by a rival faction headed by the mayor, who employed a hundred policemen to oppose Long's move. This opéra bouffe went on for weeks, but in the end Long was victorious. After eleven especially convened sessions of the legislature, which obediently passed every bill that Long wanted, he called a twelfth, which was to meet on the night of September 8, 1935. As he walked down a corridor of the Capitol surrounded by his bodyguards, he fell, mortally wounded, apparently by the gun of Dr. Carl A. Weiss, Jr., a young Baton Rouge physician. A year after his death, the state organization he had built was still so powerful that it forced the resignation of the recalcitrant Mayor Walmsley, whose term of office had two years to go.

The man who succeeded Walmsley was Robert S. Maestri, a Long intimate, who was endorsed by the Long Democratic Committee. As no other aspirant appeared, no election was held. Maestri served from 1936 to 1946, winning the 1942 election. Within two years of taking office, Maestri had put the city, then nearly bankrupt, on a cash basis, and by constant personal daily inspections of the city's properties, its sidewalks and streets, he was able, with the assistance of federal funds—for his administration spanned the days of the New Deal agencies—not only to greatly improve municipal facilities, but to keep hundreds of needy jobless working during Depression days.

The Depression of the 1930s hit New Orleans very hard. The failure of five New Orleans banks in 1933 and of many "homesteads," or building and loan associations, worked great hardships on its citizens. In 1934, 11 percent of the people of Louisiana were on federal relief. Federal spending in New Orleans under various relief agencies totaled more than $50 million by 1939, in addition to grants for self-liquidating projects of a public nature.

Perhaps the only bright spot during this period was the return of real beer and the end of Prohibition. On April 13, 1933, New Orleans's three breweries turned out half a million gallons of beer, and in addition there were the trainloads of suds that came from breweries in Milwaukee, St. Louis, and Cincinnati. That day quickly became a holiday, with tooting whistles, parades by the American Legion, crowds surging through the streets, and beer parties everywhere. For five cents, one could get an eight-ounce glass with a kick in it; for ten cents, a "schooner"; and for fifteen cents, a twelve-ounce bottle.

World War II

World War II broke out during Maestri's administration. New Orleans's shipyards were quickly expanded—the Delta Shipyards turned out the first 10,500-ton ship, the *Wm. C. C. Claiborne*, less than four months after Pearl Harbor—and by May, 1942,

Andrew Jackson Higgins had gathered a force of more than forty thousand workers to turn out PT boats and landing craft for the Navy. Meanwhile, the realities of the conflict were vividly brought home to New Orleanians: thirteen ships—some of them from New Orleans—were sunk in the Gulf of Mexico by the end of May, and German submarines lurked not far off the mouth of the Mississippi. Rationing of meat and other foods, rationing of gasoline, scrap drives, practice blackouts, recapped tires, air-raid-wardens' meetings, and women streetcar operators soon became the order of the day. Mardi Gras festivities were canceled for the duration, and New Orleanians set about the grim business of producing more, shipping more, and doing with less. A brand new streamlined *Panama Limited*, crack Chicago–New Orleans train of the Illinois Central Railroad, began operations during this time.

The surrender of Germany came on May 7, 1945, and New Orleanians celebrated, "though not as noisily as in 1918," remarked the *Times-Picayune*. Business came to a standstill, and streetcars were routed off Canal Street. Whistles and horns were blown, "people yelled, sang and cried in happiness," and some five thousand marchers carrying Japanese lanterns paraded that night. The casualties for this "quiet" celebration were reported by the police as about a hundred arrests for drunkenness, nine shot, thirteen stabbed, five fractured skulls, and one person dead.

The surrender of the Japanese on September 2, 1945, brought only a mild reaction from the people—except the members of the Bourbon Street Chinese colony, who celebrated noisily by setting off $500 worth of firecrackers by special permission of the police, and by burning an effigy of Tojo.

Further Expansion

In 1946, the reform element looked for a successor to run against Maestri. They selected J. O. Fernandez, a lame-duck congressman who tardily withdrew from the race just two days before the time for filing was to expire. By good luck, the reformers persuaded Colonel de Lesseps S. Morrison, who had just returned from duty overseas, to lead an almost forlorn cause. Campaigning vigorously, Morrison defeated the entrenched Maestri, to the great surprise of politicians and citizens alike.

"Chep" Morrison was elected mayor four successive times. During that period he built a fine record of constructive civic improvements which included the passage of bond issues to eliminate hazardous rail crossings by building overpasses and underpasses; the erection of a new $8 million city hall and civic center; a network of expressways and new boulevards; a new bridge across the Mississippi; and a new terminal building at the Moisant airport.

One of Morrison's most important accomplishments was to secure an amendment to the state constitution that enabled a citizens' committee to draft a badly needed home-rule charter. After exhaustive study, the committee submitted the new charter—the

ninth since 1805—which was approved by the city's voters, becoming effective May 1, 1954. For the first time in its history, the city had a charter that was framed and adopted locally. The 1950 population was 570,445.

Just before the 1951 carnival season was to begin —and the destruction by fire of the "den" of Rex's floats and costumes—a national emergency was declared by the president during the Korean conflict. There was no time for Mardi Gras. The former Higgins aircraft plant at Michoud was reactivated by Chrysler to make engines for tanks, and before the tank-engine assembly program was terminated in 1954, hundreds of tank engines had rolled off the Chrysler assembly line. Operations at this huge plant, which was capable of accommodating nearly four football fields, ceased until 1961, when the National Aeronautics and Space Agency took it over.

Another large plant was built in the New Orleans area during the years 1951–1953. This was the Chalmette Works of the Kaiser Aluminum and Chemical Corporation. Occupying an area of seventy square city blocks, this plant, employing twenty-seven hundred people, is the third largest aluminum reduction manufactory in the United States.

It was now the time of racial strife. On May 31, 1958, "screens" (small wooden signs that read "for colored patrons only") were quietly removed from all transit vehicles in New Orleans. But desegregation of the public schools was another matter. After fighting a rearguard action against the ruling of the Supreme Court—by passing no less than forty-seven acts of the legislature and seventeen resolutions to preserve segregation in Louisiana, the most significant of which were eventually held to be unconstitutional—the public schools of New Orleans were desegregated by court order. Four little Negro girls were admitted into the William Frantz and McDonogh No. 19 elementary schools on November 14, 1960. These schools were in a low-income section of the downtown Ninth Ward, and were boycotted by the parents of white children. Crowds gathered hurling abuse at the federal marshals, the Negro children, the judge concerned, the school board, and the federal government. But integration—if only token—had finally come to Louisiana.

The Catholic schools were integrated in March, 1962. In the decade since the Frantz School incident, all New Orleans public and parochial schools have become fully integrated without further public occurrences.

In 1961, Morrison, who ran for governor of the state three times unsuccessfully, resigned after fifteen years in office. He became ambassador to the Organization of American States. He was succeeded by Councilman Victor Hugo Schiro, who ran for office in 1962 and won reelection in 1966. The Louisiana Municipal Association elected him Mayor of the Year in 1966. He faced a problem that has since harassed most mayors of large American cities—inadequate funds to pay policemen, firemen, and city employees, and a rising crime rate. During the nine years of the

Schiro administration, the city was selected as a site for the construction of the Saturn rocket booster. The old forty-three-acre Higgins plant at Michoud was again reactivated, and by 1966, at the peak of production by Chrysler and Boeing, the total labor force reached 11,500.

In the early sixties, the seventy-six-mile-long Tidewater Ship Channel was opened. This canal, which is soon to be widened and deepened in order to be navigable by very large ships, cuts forty miles from the trip between New Orleans and the Gulf of Mexico via the winding Mississippi River. Its potential as a tidewater port is unlimited.

The 1960s witnessed a further building boom in the construction of large buildings, especially in the business section. Changing the skyline of New Orleans were the International Trade Mart, Rivergate Exhibition Hall, Plaza Towers, and the Bank of New Orleans Building; a number of high-rise apartment buildings and additional buildings at Tulane, Loyola, and Louisiana State universities were erected, to say nothing of hotels, such as the Royal Orleans, Bourbon Orleans, Downtowner, Royal Sonesta, the Monteleone addition, Holiday Inn, and the downtown Howard Johnson's. Other buildings, notably the Lykes, One Shell Square, and the Marriott Hotel, went into construction in the early 1970s.

In 1970, Moon Landrieu was elected mayor in a hotly contested election, defeating eleven other aspirants. At the onset of Mayor Landrieu's term, a revolutionary change in the operation of New Orleans's most important business took place. To meet the challenge of the times, a program of construction that will ultimately center most of the port activities away from the Mississippi River to the Mississippi-Gulf outlet—which links New Orleans directly to the Gulf of Mexico—has been inaugurated. Instead of rebuilding the more than ten miles of riverfront docks, near obsolescence with the advent of containerized shipping and the specially designed LASH and SEEBEE ships that carry them, a master plan has been developed by the board of port commissioners. This provides for an industrial complex, called Centroport, for port, manufacturing, and distribution facilities in the lower part of New Orleans—on former swampland. The first segment, costing $30 million, is under way and the ultimate cost of the project is estimated at $395 million. Other great projects are either planned or in the course of construction, notably the $129 million domed stadium and the proposed medical complex and urban renewal to be developed by the Health Education Authority of Louisiana (HEAL), which would cover an area of 288 acres in a deteriorating section.

New Orleans long ago conquered most of its early handicaps and now is a pleasant and healthful place in which to live. Its long, warm summer climate with accompanying high humidity has been largely ameliorated by air conditioning, almost universal in homes, offices, shops, and automobiles. Though it has lost its place as the South's largest city, it is still the nation's second port and a manufacturing, distributing, and shipbuilding center of no mean proportions. Where else can one find a "living" early nineteenth-century museum—its Vieux Carré? Few cities can boast of a like number of well-preserved southern antebellum homes such as exist in the Garden District. And then there is that greatest free show on earth—Mardi Gras —and the Spring Fiesta and the Sugar Bowl and the Saints football games and the opera, the symphony, horseracing, boating, and nearby fishing and hunting, and some of the most superlative restaurants in America. Best of all, the attitude of its people—"live and let live"—happily persists, which alone makes New Orleans a delightful city.

1. DISCOVERY AND DEVELOPMENT

The French Regime

1

1 René Robert Cavelier, Sieur de la Salle, after descending the Mississippi River from Canada, takes possession of the vast expanse of Louisiana and the Mississippi for Louis XIV, king of France, April 9, 1682. Lithograph by Lemercier, 1868. *Courtesy Bibliothèque Nationale, Paris*

2 Copper engraving of La Salle. Realizing the necessity of establishing a French settlement near the mouth of the Mississippi, he obtained the king's permission to colonize Louisiana. But La Salle's expedition of 1684 in search of the mouth of the river, from the sea, ended in failure. Because of faulty navigation, he missed the river and landed in Texas where shipwreck, disease, desertion, and hostile Indians led to his assassination by his own men.

3 *Louis XIV with His Family*, 1708, by Nicolas de Largillière. Louisiana was named for Louis XIV, the Sun King of France (1638–1715), during whose reign France reached the zenith of her power as a Continental nation. Louis, seated, is shown here with his son, the Grand Dauphin, and to the right, his eldest

grandson, the Duke of Burgundy, and with his eldest surviving great-grandson, the Duke of Brittany, elder brother of the future Louis XV with his governess, the Duchess de Ventadour. These heirs of three generations all predeceased Louis XIV. When Louisiana was settled during the last sixteen years of Louis's life, the decay that eventually destroyed the monarchy had set in. *Courtesy Trustees Wallace Collection, London*

4 The intrepid Henry de Tonty, "Iron Hand," was an Italian nobleman in the service of France. His right hand was blown off by a grenade and an iron one was put in its place. Arriving in Canada in 1678, Tonty came down the Mississippi with La Salle on his voyage of discovery and later made two trips in search of La Salle. He settled in Mobile where he died of yellow fever in 1704. *Courtesy Phoenix Museum, Mobile, Alabama*

5 Pierre le Moyne, Sieur d'Iberville, known as the Canadian "Cid," was born near Montreal in 1661. He was a skilled soldier-sailor, who had distinguished himself on the seas against the British. Twelve years

2

3

from the time of La Salle's death, the French determined to try again to make a settlement in Louisiana. Louis XIV chose him to head an expedition. With four ships and two hundred colonists, he arrived at Ship Island off the Mississippi Coast early in 1699. Exploring the region, he rediscovered the Mississippi River. The portrait by Charles Gill, at the Château de Ramezay, Montreal, was inspired by one belonging to Charles Comore, seventh baron of Longueuil, grandnephew of Iberville. *Courtesy Charles L. Dufour*

6 Jean Baptiste le Moyne, Sieur de Bienville, the founder of New Orleans. Born in Canada in 1680, he was eighteen when he accompanied his brother, Iberville, to Louisiana. For more than forty years he struggled to carve a successful colony out of the wilderness of Louisiana. Four times its governor or acting in that capacity, he fought Indians, endured the neglect of the French court, and the backbiting and jealousies of fellow officials. In 1743, he returned to France for good, dying in Paris in 1768 at the age of eighty-eight. *Courtesy M. Chadenat, Paris*

4

5

6

11

12

7 Pierre de Rigaud, Marquis de Vaudreuil-Cavagnial (1678–1760), came to Louisiana in 1743 to succeed the aging Bienville as governor. "The Grand Marquis" was governor for ten years, during which time there was peace with the Indians, a lessening of strife between contending religious orders, and general prosperity.

8 The Marquise de Vaudreuil.

9 Louis Billouart, Chevalier de Kerlérec (1704–1770), Governor Vaudreuil's successor. Troubles with the Indians, discord between the Capuchins and the Jesuits, quarrels with his commissary, Rochemore, duplicity from Foucault who succeeded Rochemore, and imprisonment were his lot. The Jesuits were expelled from the colony, and the first Acadian exiles began to trickle into Louisiana. *Courtesy Vicomte de Villiers due Terrage*

10 Madame de Kerlérec.

11 Iberville's vessels—*Marin, Badine, Renommée, Gironde*—were of this type. *From* History of the French Colonies *by Hanotaux and Martineau*

12 This fanciful eighteenth-century drawing shows Iberville in 1699 finding the arms of France set by La Salle at the mouth of the Mississippi in 1682. Actually, Iberville made no such discovery. The document reads:

DISCOVERY OF THE COURSE OF THE MISSISSIPPI
AND OF THE LOUISIANA, 1699.

Monsieur Cavelier ʹde la Salle, in spite of the obstacles placed by his enemies, discovered the Course of the Mississippi as far as the sea in 1683. Wishing, some years after, to explore the mouth of the river from the sea, he erred and in going to seek it overland, he was assassinated. Monsieur d'Iberville, Canadian Gentleman, was more fortunate in 1699 and found the Post with the arms of France that Monsieur de la Salle had set up in 1683. This

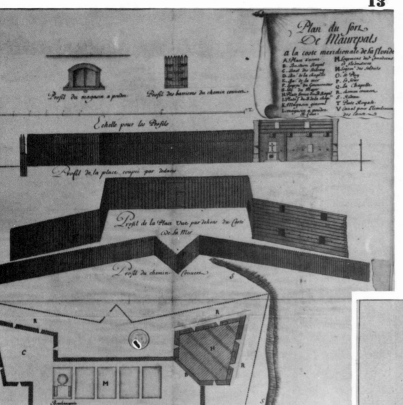

country was named Louisiana both to honor Louis the Great [the Sun King] and because the natives worshipped the Sun which was the symbol of the prince. *Bibliothèque Nationale, Paris. Courtesy Henry Pitot*

13 Plan of Fort Maurepas. This was the fort established by Iberville in 1699 on the shore of Biloxi Bay. The site of the fort is known today as Ocean Springs. Bastions H and I are indicated as being constructed of squared timbers laid horizontally. *Courtesy French National Archives, Paris*

14 This small marble tablet was found at the site of Fort Maurepas some years ago. *Courtesy Louisiana State Museum*

15 John Law, mathematical wizard, gambler in the grand manner, was one of the most fantastic pro-

moters that ever lived. After a flamboyant career, Law settled in France with a fortune of more than two million francs. Having gained the ear of the regent of France, Law was authorized to establish a bank. When Antoine Crozat, who had attempted to colonize Louisiana, returned his charter to the king, Law was ready with a scheme to take over the colonization of

Louisiana with a trade monopoly. Law spread promises of great and quick wealth, and his "Company of the West" stock was eagerly bought as speculation fever swept across France. The Company of the West in 1717 undertook to build New Orleans.

In 1719, the Company of the West merged with the Company of East India and the Company of China under the name of the Company of the Indies. The new group pushed immigration to Louisiana, which had been lagging. When not enough volunteers appeared, the company forcibly sent from Paris criminals of all ages and degrees. They made very poor colonists, and company agents were sent to Germany where they distributed glowing pamphlets about

Louisiana. About twenty-six hundred German peasants, attracted by promises of land, tools, and seed, left their homes for the colony. Many died of disease during the miserable voyage to the New World, but most of the survivors, unafraid of hard work, eventually settled about twenty-five miles above New Orleans. The fruits and vegetables from their gardens sent downriver to the infant city had much to do with keeping it alive. Engraving by Leon Schenk, Paris, 1720.

16 A cartload of undesirable colonists, the scum of France, being driven to ships (1719). *From* History of the French Colonies *by Hanotaux and Martineau*

16

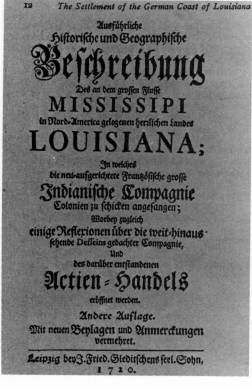

17

18

17 Title page of a pamphlet printed in 1720 in Leipzig, giving a glowing description of Louisiana to attract German emigrants to the settlements of the Company of the Indies. *From* The Settlement of the German Coast of Louisiana and the Creoles of German Descent *by J. Hanno Deiler*

18 In addition to the importation of convict labor, there was also traffic in slaves. The first shipment, numbering 147, arrived in Louisiana on July 7, 1720. This interesting engraving (ca. 1750), by Oursel from the Cabinet des Estampes, shows a slave ship with a dividing fence separating the sexes. After John Law's Company of the West took over, a considerable number had been sent to Louisiana, and the census of 1721 showed that there were 172 Negroes out of a total population of 470 in New Orleans. The *Code Noir*, or Black Code, was introduced by Bienville in Louisiana in 1724; this document was designed to regulate the conduct of the Negroes and to prevent cruelty and injustice to them by their masters. Negroes were used as troops during the French and Spanish regimes, and acquitted themselves well. Several companies of free men of color took part in the defense of New Orleans in 1814–1815. *Bibliothèque Nationale, Paris. Courtesy Henry Pitot*

19 Numerous tribes of Indians inhabited the regions near the site of the future city of New Orleans. In Iberville's voyage up the Mississippi (he was not quite sure that he was on the same river that La Salle had descended some seventeen years before), the first tribes that he met were Bayougoulas and Mongoulachas. The French quickly disarmed the Indians' fears by friendly actions and gifts. It was from the Bayougoulas that Iberville received a letter left a dozen years before by Tonty for La Salle when Tonty had set out from Canada to search for his friend. Dutch copperplate engraving (probably eighteenth century).

20 21 *Dance with Peace Pipe* and *General Dance*. The Indians were fond of dancing, and early writers observed that on occasion they danced all night, till daybreak, to singing accompanied by drums. There are many references by Du Pratz and Pénicaut to "singing the calumet"—a custom of offering the peace pipe, or calumet, to visitors, while the savages kept singing to show how happy they were to welcome them. *From* The History of Louisiana *by LePage Du Pratz, 1758*

19

20

21

Naturels en Eté

Femme et Fille

22 23

22 23 *Indian in Summer* and *Mother and Daughter*. The summer costumes of the Indians were extremely brief—a *braguette,* or breechclout, for the adult males, and a brief skirt for the females; children ran about nude: girls six to eight, boys to twelve. *From* The History of Louisiana *by LePage Du Pratz, 1758*

24 This Indian temple and the chief's hut were sketched in 1732 by Alexandre DeBatz, an architect who spent nearly thirty years in the Mississippi Valley. The building was in a small village of the Collapissas Indians on the shores of Lake Pontchartrain near New Orleans. DeBatz described the temple as a rectangular building twenty-two feet long and fourteen feet wide. It was constructed of posts, sheathed and roofed with cane mats, and having its rounded roof ornamented by three crudely sculptured and brightly painted figures of turkeys perched atop three pyramidal peaks equipped with sharp canes to discourage climbers from reaching the bird figures. DeBatz mentioned that this temple also served as a burial vault for the chiefs of the nation. Pénicaut describes the huts of one of the tribes that he visited when the French first came to Biloxi: "They are made of mud and are of a round shape almost like windmills. The roofs of the houses are made mainly from the bark of trees. There are others that are covered with leaves of a bush called locally *latanier* [palmetto]." *Smithsonian Miscellaneous Collection, LXXX #5 (1927)*

25 An elaborate commission, illuminated with the royal coats of arms above representations of an Indian and a Frenchman. It was presented to Okana Stolé, chief of the Cherokee nation, by Governor Kerlérec, February 27, 1761, to flatter the chief's vanity. The original is in the Library of Congress.

26 New Orleans was named for Philippe, Duc d'Orléans, regent of France, acting for his young cousin, Louis XV. This brilliant, dissolute, and utterly corrupt prince ruled France for eight years (1715–1723). Painting by Jean Baptiste Santerre. *Courtesy Versailles Museum*

27 Bienville founding New Orleans in 1718 by New Orleans painter Alexandre Alaux. Clearing of the site and the erection of the first buildings were started in May, 1718, by six carpenters, four Canadians, and thirty convicted salt smugglers who had been sent to Louisiana in lieu of jail. Bienville left Major Paillou de Barbezan in charge and returned to Mobile. *Courtesy Louisiana State Museum*

25

26

27

28 Adrien de Pauger, second engineer in the colony, brought order out of the haphazard scattering of huts that was New Orleans between 1718 and the time he came in March, 1721. He soon cleared enough ground with only a small force of labor to trace the principal streets running perpendicular to the river. Pauger had his troubles with those who had built houses before he arrived, and a document dated September 5, 1722, relates that he beat one Traverse on the head with a stick when the latter refused to move his house, which was apparently in the way of the new street layout. *From Maurice Thompson,* The Story of Louisiana. *Courtesy Library of Congress*

29 This interesting map dated January 10, 1723, less than two years after Pauger had come to New Orleans

V EÜE DE LA N OUVELLE O RLEANS

to lay out its streets, shows, in light color, the original clearing made prior to 1721 and, in the darker shade, the work done between 1721 and 1723. The streets have been laid out as far as Bourbon, but the forest was not far away. This plan of New Orleans is signed by Le Blond de la Tour, chief engineer. *Courtesy French National Archives, Paris*

30 New Orleans's first mill was a windmill erected on the banks of the river (*right*) to catch the breeze. Also shown on this small section of a crude but interesting

early map by Jean François Dumont, who came to Louisiana in 1716, are Bienville's house and garden (*center*), and the concession of the Jesuits (*far left*). The canal, crossed by a small bridge, was probably no more than a ditch. *Courtesy French National Archives, Paris*

31 View of New Orleans (1720), probably the earliest, which appears as an ornament on a larger map of that date. Louisiana historians have suggested that the houses are at the entrance of Bayou St. John. *Courtesy Bibliothèque Nationale, Paris*

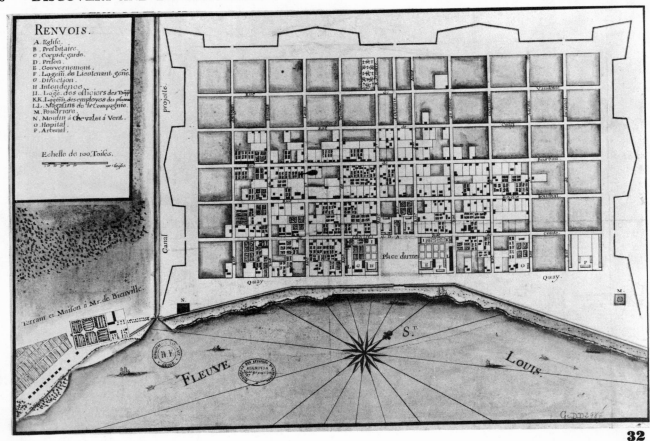

32

32 A plan of New Orleans dated May 30, 1725. This early plan, which is unsigned, probably was made either by Adrien de Pauger or his staff. Shown are "The lands and house of M. Bienville" (*lower left*), the projected canal (never built), the first cemetery on St. Peter Street near the edge of town (*top*), and the principal public buildings, most of which were then just projected. *Courtesy French National Archives, Paris*

33 *Veue et Perspective de la Nouvelle Orleans,* one of the first pictures of the infant city, drawn by Jean Pierre Lassus in 1726. He was a surveyor who did not remain long in the colony. Aside from its charm as an interesting watercolor, its great documentary value

becomes apparent when one studies it closely. In a site surrounded by tall trees with few clearings runs the Mississippi; on the right bank, men are cutting trees, while huge fires are burning, fed by large tree trunks. One man (*left*) is about to kill a snake, another (*center*) is forcing a pole down an alligator's mouth, and a strange-looking animal (*far left*), probably a deer, is nibbling leaves from a tree. Across the river, New Orleans raises its scattered houses, its windmill, its church spire; a crowd of tiny people walk in the square near the riverbank where several merchant ships are at anchor. Several canoes are on the river. One of them (*left*), filled with Indians, has a severed head on a pole for a masthead. Another boat (*center*) on an inspection tour, probably belonging to

33

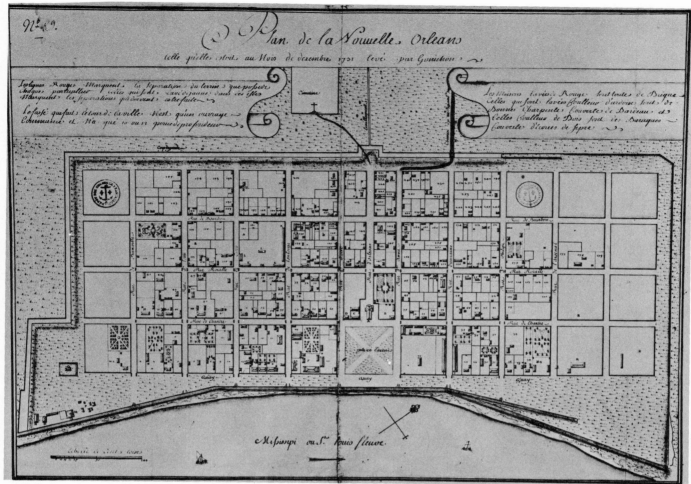

34

the governor, boasts a covered stern and flies a flag. A bayou (*left center*) pierces the forest, while a triangular flight of migratory birds indicates the presence of a lake. *Courtesy French National Archives, Section Outre-Mer, Paris*

34 New Orleans as it was in December, 1731. Ten years had elapsed since Adrien de Pauger's first streets were laid out, when this plan by Gonichon was made. On it he designated public buildings, houses made of brick, those made of wood, and "huts covered with cypress bark." At that time, the streets extended back only as far as Dauphine Street (four blocks from the river), and there was a shallow ditch "only 10 or 12 inches deep" around two sides of the little town. *Courtesy French National Archives, Paris*

35 The Directors' House, built in 1724, near the corner of Levee (Decatur) and Toulouse streets, facing the river. It was of frame construction with a wood shingle roof, and like most of the early buildings built directly on the ground. This caused its timbers to rot and the house to fall into decay. *Renderings by Henry W. Krotzer, Jr., from plans in the French National Archives, Paris*

36 In 1726, the house was modified by the addition of two wings and what was probably the first gallery to be built on a New Orleans house.

35

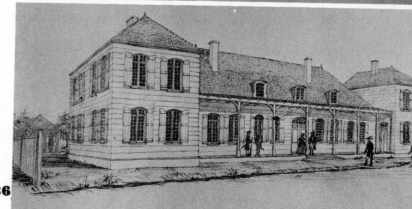

36

37

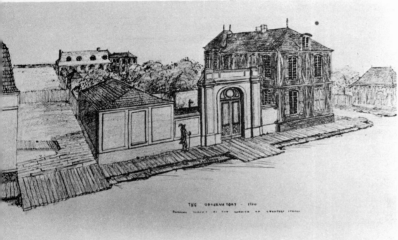

38

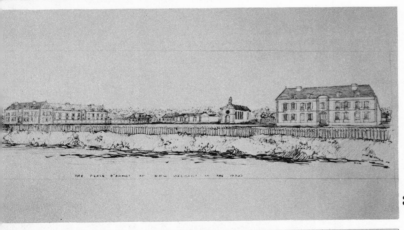

39

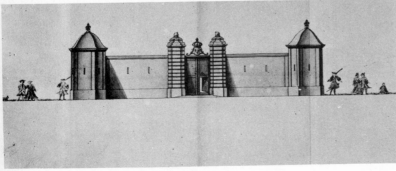

40

37 The Governor's House, on the corner of St. Ann and Chartres streets facing the Place d'Armes on the site now occupied by the library of the Louisiana State Museum in the Lower Pontalba Building. This house was built in 1726 and occupied by Governors Périer and Bienville. The Governor's House was on a large lot, 330 feet deep, which extended along Chartres Street to Dumaine. The house itself contained seven rooms with galleries at front and back; in addition, there were an adjoining two-storied building to one side, a large courtyard, a separate kitchen, bakery, two storerooms, woodshed, chicken and pigeon houses, and an extensive garden. From an excellent description in the Library of Congress, from drawings in the French National Archives, and from early city maps, it has been possible to make this accurate conjectural restoration. *Rendering by Henry W. Krotzer, Jr.*

38 The Observatory, on the same site as the Governor's House, but at the Dumaine Street end. It was a two-storied building of half-timbered construction, designed and built by the architect-scientist Pierre Baron in 1730. For a very brief period, the French constructed buildings with exposed woodwork, generally filled in with brick, but they soon found out that in the climate of New Orleans, the exposed woodwork quickly rotted, and they learned to cover the woodwork with wide boards or plaster stucco. The building was designed with two small triangular terraces on the second floor to enable Baron to make celestial observations with his telescope. A monumental gateway and a small service building adjoin the Observatory. *Rendering by Henry W. Krotzer, Jr.*

39 The Place d'Armes, as it was in the 1730s. This rendering was drawn as if the viewer were standing at a point just above the upper end of the present French Market. The large buildings on each side of the square were the military barracks erected 1734–1739 at a cost of 235,350 livres or about $47,000. The first barracks in the city were dilapidated and largely unusable, and it was through Bienville's urging that two imposing brick barrack buildings were erected on each side of the Place d'Armes. These buildings could house several hundred soldiers; with their completion, the square, after eighteen years, achieved a style in the best French baroque tradition, originally envisioned by La Tour and Pauger. Also shown in this rendering is the Parish Church of St. Louis, the Corps de Garde, and the Officers' Barracks. A wood fence runs along the levee at the riverbank. *Rendering by Henry W. Krotzer, Jr., from drawings in the French National Archives, Paris*

40 A powder magazine built in 1730 on the river edge of the city (present-day Iberville and Decatur streets). This interesting sketch is by Ignace Broutin, designer of the structure. *Courtesy French National Archives, Paris*

41 The Ursuline Convent, 1903, at the downtown riverside of Chartres. It was constructed between 1748 and 1752, designed by Ignace Broutin, the king's engineer, and completed by his successor Bernard de Verges. It is quite probable that some of the doors and windows, and for certain the stairway of the earlier building, were reused in this well-built structure. It is the oldest building in the Mississippi Valley. *Courtesy Library of Congress*

42 These Ursuline nuns were lodged in a house at Chartres and Bienville streets, while their convent was being built. The first Ursuline nuns reached New Orleans on August 6, 1727, having come to establish a school for girls and to attend the hospital. The Ursulines still conduct an excellent school for girls. *Courtesy Mother Mary Ann, O.S.U., Ursuline Convent and Academy*

43 The first Ursuline Convent was built between 1727 and 1734. Of half-timbered construction, the structure was so long in building that its timbers were in an advanced state of decay by 1745. This rendering shows the Convent (*extreme right*) and the wings containing the hospital (*left center*), kitchen (*extreme left*), and pharmacy (*right*). Architects were Alexandre DeBatz, Pierre Baron, and Ignace Broutin. *Rendering by Henry W. Krotzer, Jr., from plans in the French National Archives, Paris*

44 *The Embarkment of the Casket Girls,* a nineteenth-century engraving by Charles Edouard Delort. Shortly after the arrival of the Ursulines, a cargo of poor but marriageable girls of good character was sent to the colony. Each girl had been supplied with a *cassette,* or small chest, containing articles of clothing. These girls, known as *les filles à la cassette,* or "Casket Girls," were placed under the care of the nuns until they married, which was very soon, for there were many prospective husbands.

45 Monplaisir, one of the finest houses of the French period. Another Alexandre DeBatz design, it was built for Chevalier Jean de Pradel in 1750, across the river from the Place d'Armes. In later years, it was the home of John McDonogh, and survived until after 1860.

46 Government House, 1800, built in 1761, one of the last buildings constructed under the French regime. It occupied the site of the Directors' House, the first capitol of the colony, on Decatur and Toulouse streets. A large raised building, with shaded galleries, Government House was situated 200 feet from the river, and its gardens, stables, and outbuildings stretched 336 feet to the rear. It escaped the great fires of 1788 and 1794 and was in use by the Louisiana Legislature at the time of the Battle of New Orleans

46

47

EXTRAIT
DE LA LETTRE DU ROI,
A M. D'ABBADIE, DIRECTEUR GÉNÉRAL, COMMANDANT POUR
SA MAJESTÉ, A LA LOUISIANNE.

48

when General Jackson threatened to blow up the legislature meeting in it when he heard a rumor that this group wanted to capitulate to the British invaders. The Government House, then the Louisiana State Capitol, burned in 1828. *Conjectural sketch made from contemporary drawings by Henry W. Krotzer, Jr.*

47 Louis XV of France (1710–1774), by Louis Michel Van Loo. His gift of Louisiana to Spain in 1762 was the end of an era. *Courtesy Wallace Collection, London.*

48 The 1764 broadside that informed stunned Louisianians that Louis XV had ceded the colony to Spain.

49 New Orleans at the end of the French regime, part of a panoramic view, made by an unknown English artist (probably an intelligence officer), taken from the opposite side of the river in 1765. The original, preserved in England, was presented to the Louisiana State Museum in the 1940s.

49

50   **51**

DE PAR LE ROI,

DON ALEXANDRE Ô REILLY
Commandeur de Benfayan dans l'Ordre
de Alcantara, Lieutenant-Général & Inf-
pecteur-Général des Armées de Sa Ma-
jesté Catholique, Capitaine-Général &
Gouverneur de la Province de la Loui-
fianne.

EN vertu des Ordres & Pouvoirs, dont Nous fommes muni de Sa Majefté Catholique, dé-
clarons à tous les Habitans de la Province de la Louifianne, que quelque jufte fujet que les
Evénemens paffés ayent donnés à Sa Majefté de leur faire fentir fon indignation, Elle ne veut
écouter aujourd'hui que fa Clémence envers le Public; perfuadée qu'il n'a péché, que pour s'être
laiffé féduire par les intrigues de Gens Ambitieux, Fanatiques & mal intentionnés, qui ont té-
mérairement abufé de fon ignorance & trop de crédulité; ceux-ci feuls répondront de leurs cri-
mes & feront jugés felon les Loix.
Un Acte auffi généreux doit affurer Sa Majefté, que fes nouveaux Sujets s'efforceront chaque
jour de leur vie de mériter par leur fidélité, zéle, & obéïffance la Grace qu'elle leur fait, &
la Protection qu'elle leur accorde dès ce moment.

A la Nouvelle Orléans, le vingt-un Aouft mil fept cens foixante-neuf.

52

53

50 Antonio de Ulloa (1716–1795), the first Spanish governor. He lacked the iron will necessary to control the sullen Louisianians who resented being made Spanish subjects. After two futile years (1766–1768), his attempt to take over the colony for Spain ended in his being expelled by the Superior Council—the local governing body.

51 Count Alexander O'Reilly, sent to take over from Ulloa. He served from 1769 to 1770, in his capacity as captain general. On August 18, 1769, he came with twenty-six hundred Spanish troops, arrested the leaders who had expelled his predecessor, tried, convicted, and executed five of them, and sentenced six to prison.

52 O'Reilly posted this broadside, dated August 21, 1769, which granted amnesty and pardon to all Louisianians who had signed the petition to expel his predecessor, Ulloa. It read in part:

> [the king] is persuaded that the inhabitants of Louisiana, . . . would not have committed the offense of which they are guilty, if they had not been seduced by the intrigues of some ambitious, fanatic and evil-minded men who had the temerity to make criminal use of the ignorance and excessive credulity of their fellow citizens. . . .

53 Bernardo de Gálvez. After Luis de Unzaga's tenure of office (1769–1777), which had been marked by a conciliation between Spanish rule and the Louisianians, the brilliant young Gálvez, then in his early twenties, became governor. During his governorship and under his leadership, the Spanish captured Manchac, Baton Rouge, and Natchez from the British in 1779, Mobile in 1780, and Pensacola in 1781. Gálvez supplied arms and ammunition to aid the American colonies in the fight with England. Gálvez relaxed trade restrictions and encouraged commerce. *From* A History of Louisiana *by Alcée Fortier, 1904*

54

RELATION

DE l'Incendie qu'a éprouvé la ville de la Nouvelle-Orléans, le 21 mars 1788.

VERS une heure & demie après-midi, le feu s'est déclaré à peu près au centre de la Ville. Le vent du sud, qui souffloit pour lors avec une grande violence, l'a animé à un tel point, qu'aussitôt il s'est manifesté en plusieurs endroits à la fois. Toute la vigilance des Chefs, & les prompts secours qu'ils ont fait apporter, sont devenus inutiles, même les pompes, dont quelques-unes ont été brûlées par l'ardeur des flammes, qui se portoient à une distance incroyable. Dans un péril si imminent, chacun craignant pour soi, s'est retiré pour voir s'il étoit possible de sauver quelques effets; la frayeur des plus proches voisins du danger leur a fait perdre le peu d'instants qui leur restoient, & la confiance de ceux qui étoient plus éloignés & qui cherchoient à soulager les autres, les a jeté dans le même

55

57

54 Esteban Miró as a young officer. For nearly four years, Miró, as chief military aid to Gálvez, served as acting governor of Louisiana. In 1785, Miró was named governor; he served until 1791. Under his able leadership, the Creole population became largely reconciled to Spanish rule.

55 During Miró's tenure. First printed account of the great fire of March 21, 1788, printed at Cap Français, Saint-Domingue.

In the afternoon of the 21st of March, at 1:30, . . . the residence of the Army Treasurer Don Vincente José Nuñez caught fire, reducing to ashes 850 buildings, among which are all the business houses and the residences of the most aristocratic families. . . . The Parochial church and the Presbytery have been among those stricken by this misfortune, and the majority of their books have been destroyed by fire. The Capitol House, the watch house and the Arsenal with all the arms which are kept there have all suffered the same fate.

Courtesy Felix H. Kuntz

56 During Miró's tenure, the largest mass migration of Acadians, some sixteen hundred, took place in 1785 when the Spanish government brought to New Orleans nearly four hundred families who had been abandoned in France. They settled along the bayous of southern Louisiana. The view is of the exiles leaving Grand Pré.

56

57 The Golden Age of Spanish rule came with the administration of Barón Francisco Luis Héctor de Carondelet, a Belgian nobleman in the Spanish service. During this period (1792–1797), New Orleans saw its first theatre opened, read its first local newspaper, had its streets lighted by lamps, and enjoyed the protection of a small force of night watchmen called *serenos*. Carondelet also had the canal bearing his name dug in the rear of the city to facilitate drainage, and built fortifications around New Orleans. In fourteen months during 1793–1794, New Orleans was struck by three

58

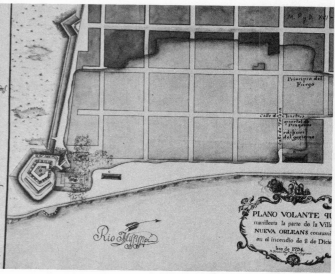

59

60

61

hurricanes, and a second devastating fire leveled almost all that was left of the original French town.

58 Juan Ventura Morales, Spanish intendant under Carondelet at New Orleans, who, on October 16, 1802, closed the port of New Orleans to upriver American traffic by canceling the American "right of deposit" that had existed since 1795. Morales's action led to the realization that increasing American trade down the Mississippi demanded a solution that would eliminate the bottleneck—America must either seize the city or negotiate for its acquisition.

59 The great fire of Carondelet's regime. Two weeks after the fire destroyed a great part of the upper portion of the Vieux Carré, on December 8, 1794, a draftsman named Juan M. Perchet made this plan showing the extent of the damage. The newly erected St. Louis Cathedral (more easterly on Chartres, but not seen here) and the Government House (B) survived, due to a change in the direction of the wind. Most of the section adjoining, with the excepion

of the Merieult house on Royal Street (north of Chartres, but unmarked) which still stands, was burned. *Courtesy Archivo General de Simancas, Spain*

60 Damaged in the fire of 1794, this building, photographed by Mugnier about 1890, is typical of the Spanish period. Begun in 1789, and completed in 1798 after the damage, it stood until 1962 when it was rebuilt for the Little Theatre, of which it is now a part. Located on the corner of St. Peter and Chartres streets, its occupants varied from the first bishop of New Orleans to restaurants and bars, before it became part of the theatre. The fine wrought-iron balcony railing was on the original building.

61 During Carondelet's administration, Bishop Luis Peñalver y Cárdenas came to the city in July, 1795, to find a very low state of religion and morality in his see. Upon his arrival, the Parish Church of St. Louis became St. Louis Cathedral. The bishop, a cultured, retiring, and pious man, instituted needed reforms, but was sent to other fields before they could be carried out.

62

63

64

65

62 Pastor of the St. Louis Cathedral for over forty years, Father Antonio de Sedella was affectionately known to New Orleanians in later years as Père Antoine. His real name was Francisco Antonio Ildefonso Moreno y Arze, and he was born in Sedella, in the province of Málaga, Spain. Having become a Capuchin priest, he arrived in New Orleans in January, 1781, as a commissary of the Inquisition. Contrary to the generally accepted belief, however, he made no attempt to establish the Inquisition in Louisiana, and it was because of his insubordination in an entirely unrelated matter that he was sent away from the colony. He returned in 1795 with Bishop Peñalver to become one of the most beloved though controversial figures in New Orleans church history. He died in 1829 at the age of eighty-one. *Courtesy Felix H. Kuntz*

63 The short term of Governor Manuel Luis Gayoso de Lemos (1797–1799) was marked by the visit of three illustrious visitors: the Duc d'Orléans—the future king of France, Louis Philippe—and his two brothers, the Duc de Montpensier and the Comte de Beaujolais, sons of Philippe-Égalité, cousin of the ill-fated Louis XVI. Gayoso died of a fever at the age of forty-eight and was buried in St. Louis Cathedral, the only Spanish governor to be buried on Louisiana soil. He was succeeded by General Juan Manuel de Salcedo, the last Spanish governor.

64 One of the most interesting figures of the Spanish regime, Don Andrés Almonester y Roxas was born in Spain in 1725, and came to New Orleans shortly after the arrival of General O'Reilly. Appointed royal notary, Almonester quickly became wealthy, largely through real-estate speculations. Marrying for a second time late in life, he became the father of Micaela, who eventually married Joseph Xavier Célestin Delfau de Pontalba. Almonester was ambitious for a "title of Castile," which he sought from the king of Spain. A very charitable man, he built a home for lepers, he built the Cathedral, rebuilt the Charity Hospital, and even loaned money and supervised the construction of the Cabildo (City Hall). Just prior to

his death in 1798, he was made Knight of the Royal and Distinguished Order of Charles III. Portrait by Salazar. *Courtesy Archdiocese of New Orleans*

65 Portrait, about 1798, of Pierre d'Aunoy and his son, during the tenure of Governor Gayoso. D'Aunoy was born in New Orleans about 1775. He began service in the Spanish Army and rose to the rank of lieutenant general after having distinguished himself against the

French in the Peninsular War (1808–1814). His descendants still live in New Orleans. *Courtesy Louisiana State Museum*

66 The portrait of the family of Dr. Joseph Montégut, painted about 1797 during the last years of the Spanish regime, gives us a glimpse of domestic life in the best circles of the city. Dr. Montégut was a much-respected physician. *Courtesy Louisiana State Museum*

67 The signing of the official documents transferring the colony from Spain to France took place at the Casa Capitular, meeting place of the Illustrious Cabildo, or Spanish municipal governing body, on November 30, 1803. It was built in 1796–1799 from the design of the architect Gilberto Guillemard. The Cabildo met in it for only three and a half years when Spain relinquished Louisiana. This view is from a sketch made many years later by Joseph Pennell.

66

67

68   **69**   **71**

70

PROCLAMATION.

AU NOM DE LA RÉPUBLIQUE FRANÇAISE.

LAUSSAT,

PRÉFET COLONIAL,

AUX LOUISIANAIS.

68 Portrait of Napoleon Bonaparte (1769–1821), first consul of France, by Baron François-Pascal-Simon Gérard, 1803. He had succeeded in getting Spain to retrocede Louisiana to France under the secret Treaty of San Ildefonso (1800). Expeditions to take possession of the colony were organized, but yellow fever and the Negro uprisings in Saint-Domingue, and a winter of great cold forced Napoleon to abandon his plans.

69 Portrait of Pierre Clément de Laussat, by Jean François Gille Colson. Laussat was sent by Napoleon to New Orleans as colonial prefect to prepare for the arrival of the French troops.

70 On March 26, 1803, Laussat published a "Proclamation in the name of the French Republic." To a large extent, the Creole population—though predominantly French in origin, language, and customs—faced the prospect of the change in regimes with little enthusiasm. *Courtesy Louisiana State Museum*

71 The first mayor of New Orleans was Jean Étienne Boré, the New Orleans planter. He was appointed by Laussat during the short interval that he governed after the end of the Spanish regime (November 30 to December 20, 1803). Boré's cane fields were in the vicinity of present-day Audubon Park. This portrait once hung in the New Orleans Sugar Exchange.

72 Following the Spanish transfer, President Thomas Jefferson (1743–1826) instructed United States Minister Robert R. Livingston in France to try to negotiate the purchase of New Orleans. Livingston worked tirelessly to get Napoleon's foreign minister, Talleyrand, to open negotiations. Portrait by Rembrandt Peale. *Courtesy Marcus Greve*

73 Bonaparte discussing the possibility of the sale treaty with his ministers Talleyrand and Barbé-Marbois, illustrated by André Castaigne. Napoleon was slow in making up his mind to sell Louisiana to the Americans. He felt he could not keep it if war broke out with England. *From* Century Magazine, *June, 1904*

72

73

74

74 James Monroe (1758–1831), a Jane Stuart copy of a portrait by Gilbert Stuart. Appointed by President Jefferson minister extraordinary to join Robert R. Livingston in Paris to purchase New Orleans and the Floridas, he participated in the final negotiations during the latter part of April, 1803. *Courtesy Felix H. Kuntz*

75

76

75 After several days of haggling over the price, Livingston and Monroe agreed to pay 60 million francs ($11,250,000) and to assume 20 million francs ($3,750,000) for American claims against France. Here artist André Castaigne portrays the signing of the Louisiana Purchase Treaty by Marbois, Livingston, and Monroe.

76 The beginning and end sections of the Louisiana Purchase Treaty, which, although dated April 30, 1803, was not signed until May 2. Several copies were made, of which this is the American original. *Courtesy National Archives, Washington, D.C.*

77

78

77 In the Place d'Armes before the Cabildo, December 20, 1803, the French flag was lowered and the American flag raised. It is reported that the American flag stuck while being raised, and that the spectators gave signs of cold hostility, while only a handful of Americans voiced a small cheer. Painting by Henry Hintermeister. *Courtesy Louisiana State Museum*

78 Moved perhaps by the sheer joy of knowing that New Orleans was soon to come under the democratic sway of the United States, the artist, J. L. Bouqueto de Woiseri, depicted a soaring eagle, carrying in his beak the inscription, "UNDER MY WINGS EVERY THING PROSPERS." Woiseri lived in New Orleans at the time of the Louisiana Purchase and called himself a "designer,

79

80

81

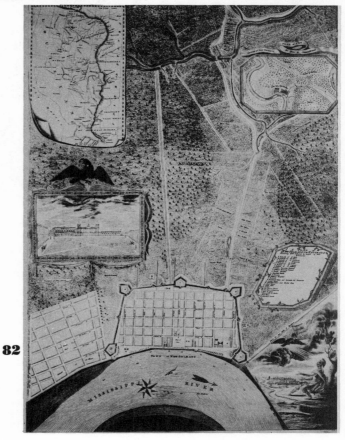

82

drawer, geographer, and engineer." This is a wonderfully graphic panoramic view of New Orleans. Its buildings, its church, the ships in the harbor, the road on the levee are all faithfully delineated. *Courtesy Chicago Historical Society*

79 Miniature of General James Wilkinson, who with William C. C. Claiborne, governor of the Mississippi Territory, acting as commissioners for the United States, signed with Prefect Laussat the *procès verbal*. *Courtesy Hugh M. Wilkinson*

80 Sketch by G. Birch, ca. 1805, of General Wilkinson's military headquarters, the original Delord-Sarpy plantation house then owned by Armand Duplantier, a compatriot and friend of General Lafayette who had served as his aide-de-camp in the Continental army. At the time of the purchase, the house was located on the outskirts of the town on a site now occupied by the old Lane Cotton Mills, at Annunciation and Poeyfarre streets. The house was demolished many years ago. *Courtesy Boyd Cruise*

81 Engraving of William C. C. Claiborne, by J. B. Longacre. On March 26, 1804, Congress established the Territory of Orleans (virtually what is now the state of Louisiana), and President Jefferson appointed twenty-eight-year-old Virginian Claiborne as governor. Claiborne was Anglo-Saxon, a Protestant, and a serious-minded official who found the indolent, careless ways of the Creoles of his territory hard to understand; by the same token, the Creoles complained that Claiborne could not speak the language of the country and did not understand them.

82 De Woiseri's plan of the city. Indicated are the five Spanish forts that were falling into decay when Claiborne arrived, and the first few streets of what was to become the uptown portion of the city. *Courtesy Louisiana State Museum*

83

83 84 The revolution in Saint-Domingue, and Napoleon's unsuccessful attempt to recapture the colony, were among the factors that influenced his decision to sell Louisiana to the United States. The revolt of the free people of color and the slaves, in the former French colony of Saint-Domingue (now Haiti), in the last decade of the eighteenth century, had brought the French Revolution close to the shores of the North American continent. Two of the major events of this uprising are pictured here. The first illustration, by an unknown German engraver, represents the artist's conception of the bloody revolt of August, 1791, in the northern plain. The scene from the hills, drawn from

life by Defontana and engraved by Berthault, is a view of the burning of the port city of Cap Français in June, 1793, in which thousands of colonists were massacred, and from which some ten thousand refugees escaped and fled to the Atlantic seaboard cities of the United States.

In early 1802, Napoleon, having taken advantage of the freedom of the seas accorded him by the recent Treaty of Amiens with Great Britain, sent an army to recapture the colony; but despite early successes, the ravages of yellow fever and the rupture of the treaty in the late spring of 1803 forced the French troops to withdraw and surrender to the British fleet that now

84

blockaded the island. The rebel forces then gained complete control of Saint-Domingue in the fall of 1803, and all the colonists who could do so fled for their lives, a number of them coming to Louisiana, just about the time that the United States took possession of the province.

These new immigrants, plus the few refugees that had drifted in during earlier years, gave a tremendous impetus to the intellectual, cultural, and commercial life of lower Louisiana. Many were men of ability and energy; they reestablished and revived the theatre in New Orleans, making it the first permanent operatic theatre in the United States; they published newspapers, a number of which had long and influential careers; they founded schools and colleges; and they became prominent in law, politics, and commerce.

In 1809, New Orleans was again flooded with new arrivals of refugees when some 9,000, of whom 2,137 were whites, who had previously fled from Saint-Domingue to Cuba, were expelled from the latter country by the Spaniards in retaliation for Napoleon's invasion of Spain in 1808. By 1810, New Orleans had tripled its 1803 population. *Courtesy Bibliothèque Nationale, Paris*

85 Toussaint L'Ouverture, the brilliant Negro leader, who, by keeping Saint-Domingue practically independent of France, made possible America's ultimate acquisition of Louisiana. *From* The French Revolution in San Domingo *by T. Lothrop Stoddard, 1914*

86 James Pitot, first mayor of the incorporated city, and one of the most successful and distinguished of the Saint-Domingue refugees to settle in New Orleans. Born in France in 1761, he went to the French colony of Saint-Domingue as a young man. After living there for eleven years, he was forced by the slave revolution in 1793 to seek refuge in the United States. Before coming to New Orleans, he lived for two years in Philadelphia where he became an American citizen. He arrived in New Orleans in 1796 and soon had a flourishing business. He took an active part in municipal affairs and was first a member of the municipal council before Governor Claiborne appointed him mayor of the city, and in 1805 mayor of the newly incorporated New Orleans. He soon resigned the mayorship because of the press of his business activities. Bank director and head of the New Orleans Navigation Company, he gave up all business connections in 1813 when Governor Claiborne appointed him judge of the city's Parish Court, a position he filled until his death in 1831. Pitot is the author of an unpublished memoir entitled *Observations sur la Colonie de la Louisiane de 1796 à 1802*, which he took with him to France just before the Louisiana Purchase to give French authorities and businessmen information about the colony of Louisiana. France was then about to take it back from Spain. *Courtesy René J. LeGardeur, Jr.*

87 The Pitot House about 1885. From 1800 to 1809,

85

86

87

the Pitot family lived in this once elegant three-story brick house at 630 Royal Street, a showplace in its time. Traces of its former grandeur are evident in this photograph. The house was destroyed in the closing years of the last century.

Battle of New Orleans:
January 8, 1815

88 The best-known picture of the Battle of New Orleans was made by a participant in the battle, Hyacinthe Laclotte, architect and assistant engineer in Jackson's army, and lithographed by Case and Green, Hartford, Connecticut. Clearly shown (*bottom left*) are the house and garden of the Edmund Macarty plantation, Jackson's headquarters. The Battle of New Orleans and the American victory had a profound effect upon our history. It not only saved New Orleans from conquest by the British, and made the Mississippi an American river, but it opened the way for westward expansion. It increased our nation's prestige in the world, gave the young United States confidence in its military powers, and increased the national feeling of unity. It made a popular hero of Andrew Jackson, and did much to stamp the effects of frontier democracy on the American social and political order. The Battle of New Orleans was the last major battle of the War of 1812. This war, which had been going on for nearly a year and a half without any decisive military action, suddenly became alive when the British, after defeating Napoleon in April, 1814, were able to turn their mighty war machine toward the United States. An expeditionary force under Admiral Alexander Cochrane raided Washington and burned the White House and attacked Fort McHenry at Baltimore. Joining a fleet of troopships from England in Jamaica in the West Indies, Cochrane and General John Keane sailed for the Louisiana coast and arrived with fifty ships carrying one thousand guns on December 9, 1814.

The British decided not to sail up the river past Fort St. Philip, but approached the city from the rear, through Lake Borgne, a shallow arm of the Gulf of Mexico. On December 14, after a sharp engagement, British barges captured five small American gunboats guarding the water approaches to the city, thus laying the way open for invasion. The British made their way in small boats to the mouth of Bayou Bienvenu, the entrance to an unguarded route to New Orleans on the Mississippi River. During the night of December 22–23, they had advanced to a point just nine miles below New Orleans. Pushing upriver during the day of December 23, they spread over the Villeré, Lacoste, and de La Ronde plantations and made camp for the night.

Meanwhile, General Andrew Jackson, then commander of the military district that included Louisiana, had arrived in New Orleans on December 2, bringing with him his regulars and elements from the Tennessee militia. Jackson had hardly time to organize his forces when the British were on American soil; when he received news of the British approach he decided upon a very bold move. He struck the enemy on the night of December 23, in their camp. Catching

them off guard, he gave the leaders the impression that they were being met by a very formidable force. Jackson withdrew his men to the Rodriguez Canal, a ditch about fifteen feet wide that separated the Chalmette and Macarty plantations. Along this ditch his men threw up a mile-long shoulder-high rampart, using mud, rails, fence posts, wooden kegs, and anything they could get their hands on. This rampart occupied a most fortunate position between the Mississippi River on one side and an almost impassable swamp on the other.

On Christmas Day, 1814, General Sir Edward M. Pakenham, brother-in-law of the Duke of Wellington, arrived to take command of the British forces. Pakenham ordered an attack on the Americans on December 28. His men began advancing in two columns, one near the river and the other near the swamp, through the stubble of the plantation cane fields.

The American sloop *Louisiana* came downriver and began firing into the nearest British column, and artillery fire from the American lines forced the column by the river to withdraw. The commander of the British column near the swamp, seeing that he had no support on his left, called off his attack.

On January 1, 1815, Pakenham ordered his artillery to try to silence the American guns and break through the rampart. The British had brought up heavy artillery from the fleet with incredible labor, and a battery was erected about seven hundred yards from the American line. Pakenham's forces began a terrific fire, accompanied by a shower of rockets that were designed to frighten the defenders. The American guns answered, and so great was their accuracy that by noon the British guns were completely silenced.

Fearing that further delay would demoralize his army, Pakenham made preparations for a head-on assault against the Americans, even though some of his junior officers thought that such an attack would fail.

In the half light of the early morning of January 8, Pakenham sent his forces in a frontal attack on the Americans. He had hoped to take advantage of the darkness to get his troops within a few yards of the American line without being seen, but a delay caused by one of his junior officers in forgetting to bring ladders and bundles of sticks to throw in the ditches to help scale the ramparts cost him the advantage. Pakenham, nevertheless, determined to proceed with the attack. General Samuel Gibbs attacked the American left and center with a brigade of three thousand men. As the British advanced across the open fields, the artillery fire from the American batteries quickly tore huge gaps in their ranks. The redcoated British troops quickly filled in where their comrades had

88

fallen and continued their advance in measured time until they came within musket range. Then the crack shots from Tennessee and Kentucky, who made up this part of the line, opened up on them with their long rifles. This checked their advance and killed many, including their commander, General Gibbs.

On the British left along the river, General Keene divided his brigade. One force under Colonel Robert Rennie was sent against the extreme right of the American line. Keene then took a regiment of Scottish Highlanders obliquely across the field to help General Gibbs. The regiment suffered frightful casualties from the galling fire of the batteries. Keene rallied the remainder of Gibbs's men, and again assaulted the American center. This time he was severely wounded, and as his attack on the right was failing, General Pakenham himself rode forward to rally his men for a third assault. In this action, Pakenham was shot and killed. Colonel Rennie's attack on the right was repulsed after fierce hand-to-hand combat. A British

force across the river, successful at first, had to be recalled, and because of the bitter defeat suffered by their main force, General John Lambert, now commander in chief, ordered an end to hostilities. The casualties in this dreadful battle were 2,057 British, 71 Americans. Rarely had professional veteran soldiers been defeated in so one-sided a battle.

Some days later, far down the river at Fort St. Philip, the British sent four ships of war in an attempt to silence the batteries of the fort, and although they fired more than a thousand rounds, the fort never failed to respond. After ten days the British left off. On the plains of Chalmette, the Americans discovered on January 19 that the enemy, leaving campfires burning, had stolen away, returned to their ships, and sailed off. Ironically, two weeks before the final Battle of New Orleans, on January 8, representatives of the United States and Great Britain had signed a treaty of peace at Ghent, Belgium, a fact not known by any of the participants in the battle.

BATTLE OF NEW ORLEANS.

89

90

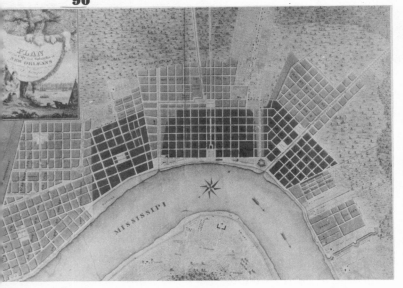

89 A view of the Battle of New Orleans from the American ramparts, by John Andrew. Jackson's ragtail army is shown mowing down the British. *From* Ballou's Pictorial, *Drawing Room Companion 1856*

90 Plan of the city and suburbs of New Orleans from an actual survey made in 1815 by Jacques Tanesse, city surveyor. Published later, the map revealed New Orleans's new faubourgs, or suburbs, that had sprung up around the little colonial city barely a dozen years after the Louisiana Purchase. The population at the time of the British invasion in 1814–1815 was about eighteen thousand. The fortification at the southeast end of town is Fort St. Charles. *Courtesy Richard Koch*

91 Drawing of Fort St. Charles made in 1817 by the United States Engineers Department, topographical bureau. General Jackson quickly found that New Orleans had no defenses worthy of the name, and he realized that the city had to be defended outside its limits. The last of four forts, which had been built at each corner of the town by the Spanish, remained standing on what is now the corner of Esplanade and North Peters. The others had decayed and were demolished after the Louisiana Purchase. In 1814, Fort St. Charles was fast going the same way—its parapets and glacis were decaying and its platforms rotting. When Jackson arrived, this fort was useless. Nevertheless, it was manned. On his third day in New Orleans, the general inspected two occupying detachments of the 7th and 44th regulars commanded by Major Peire and Colonel Ross.

92 Capture of the American flotilla on Lake Borgne, December 14, 1814, by T. L. Hornbrook. The first engagement of the siege of New Orleans was the unsuccessful effort of the Americans to prevent the British from landing on American soil. Under Lieuten-

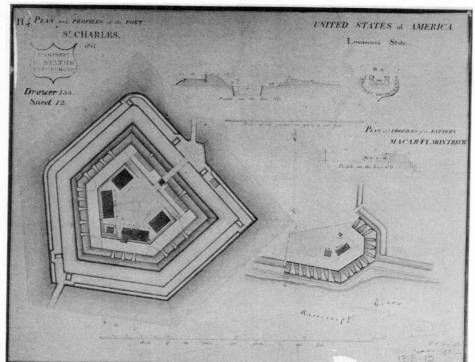

91

92

ant Thomas ap Catesby Jones, 5 American gunboats and 2 tenders with a total of 25 guns and 204 men fought about 1,000 armed sailors and marines on 42 British barges. Hopelessly outnumbered, Jones fought bravely, but was overwhelmed and had to surrender. *Courtesy Chicago Historical Society*

93 On the day the American flotilla capitulated, the steamboat *Enterprise,* the fourth to be built on the western rivers, arrived at New Orleans with a cargo of badly needed ordnance stores from Pittsburgh. Gen-

93

eral Jackson, desperate for supplies, ordered the small forty-five-ton boat, commanded by Captain H. M. Shreve, upriver to search for three keelboats carrying small arms. The *Enterprise* also was employed to remove women and children from the danger zone at New Orleans. Then Captain Shreve undertook to pass the British batteries on the bank of the river nine miles below to bear supplies for Fort St. Philip. He put the supplies aboard and ran the *Enterprise,* covered with cotton bales securely fastened to the vessel with iron hooks, past the British batteries at midnight. He reached the fort in safety, discharged his freight, and on the next night passed undiscovered, until beyond the range of the enemy's guns. This was undoubtedly the first time that a steamboat had taken part in a military operation. *From* Lloyd's Steamboat Directory and Disasters on the Western Waters, *1856*

94 On the night of January 7, 1815, the eve of the final Battle of New Orleans, nuns, relatives and friends of soldiers prayed at this old Ursuline chapel. The building, built for the nuns by Don Andrés Almonester y Roxas in 1787, was incorporated into a school on the grounds of the old Ursuline Convent, which still stands.

95 Lithograph of Our Lady of Prompt Succor, under whose statue the citizens prayed for victory. Just before the Mass ended, a courier from the battlefield burst in with the news of Jackson's victory. General Jackson himself came to the convent after the battle to thank the nuns for their solicitous prayers. A statue of Our Lady is still preserved in the Ursuline Convent, and each year on the anniversary of the battle a Te Deum is sung. *Courtesy Samuel Wilson, Jr.*

96 General Andrew Jackson (1767–1845), hero of the Battle of New Orleans, by John Vanderlyn, painting executed in 1819. Born of Irish parentage in South

95

Carolina, he was taken prisoner as a boy in the War of Independence by the British, and the treatment he received resulted in a lifelong dislike for Great Britain. *Courtesy City Hall, New York*

96

94

97 General Sir Edward Michael Pakenham, 1812. Pakenham was sent to America to replace General Alexander Ross, who had been killed at Baltimore. Admiral Sir Alexander Cochrane, in charge of the expedition, had resolved that New Orleans, with its rich trade, would be his prize, and Pakenham was directed to join him as commander in chief, which led to his death at the Battle of New Orleans. *Courtesy Duke of Wellington Collection*

98 General Pakenham being carried, fatally wounded, from the field, a detail from a print by West, published in 1817 by McCarthy and David, Philadelphia. His last words were "lost through want of courage."

99 Commander of the *Louisiana*, Master Commandant Daniel T. Patterson. His handful of light warships played a very important part in the defense of New Orleans. Commanding the *Carolina* first, Patterson harassed the British during Jackson's first attack upon them. After the loss of the *Carolina*, he continued operations in the river with the *Louisiana*, and built up land batteries on the opposite side of the river to continue to harass the British with cannon fire. General Jackson later credited him: "To your well-directed exertions . . . must be ascribed in a great degree that embarrassment of the enemy which led to his ignominious flight." *Courtesy United States Navy*

100 Jean Lafitte, the famous pirate. He spurned the British request for aid and, despite a raid on his stronghold at Grande Terre by United States naval forces, volunteered to help Jackson against the British invasion. Lafitte himself did not take part in the Battle of New Orleans, but served as a guide in outlying sections. One of his lieutenants, Dominique You, was in command of a battery in the battle of January 8, which performed very well. But aside from some of Lafitte's followers who joined Jackson's heterogeneous army, apparently the most valuable service Lafitte rendered was supplying some seven thousand flints from his lair.

97

98

99

100

101

101 In 1819 while the city was still a little intoxicated over Jackson's victory over the British, a Madame Plantou, a painter who had studied under David, came to New Orleans to exhibit her huge painting, which she called *The Peace of Ghent 1814 and Triumph of America.* Done in allegorical style with figures of Hercules, Minerva, Mercury, Britannia, and the United States, it was exhibited at the home of former Mayor Girod, with an admission charge of $1 per person. The architect, Benjamin Latrobe, then in New Orleans, saw the painting and commented that "it was an excellent painting in many points of view," but thought it a caricature, painted with poor judgment. The city council thought otherwise and appropriated $50 with which to buy, from the artist's husband who had accompanied her, an engraving of the painting to be placed in its Session Hall. The original engraving by Phelippeaux has disappeared. *This photograph is from a copy courtesy Bibliothèque Nationale, Paris*

102 The Chalmette Monument. In 1855, the state of Louisiana began the erection of a one-hundred-foot monument on a tract of ground that included the most important part of the battlefield of New Orleans. For many years it remained unfinished until in 1907 the state transferred the monument and grounds to the federal government. It was then completed, and the state donated thirty-six additional acres including the Rodriguez Canal to the park. Chalmette was established as a national historical park in August, 1939, and enlarged in 1966. *Photo by Manuel C. De Lerno*

102

Texas and the Republic

103 New Orleanians had not yet put the Battle of New Orleans out of mind when they looked at Latin Americans who were fighting for their independence. Filibustering expeditions were formed to try to overturn existing governments. There were expeditions to Texas, Mexico, and Cuba. Conspirators met in Maspero's Exchange on Chartres Street and later in Banks' Arcade on Magazine Street, and the newspapers of the time reflect the interest of New Orleanians, many of whom joined the plotters. Of all the filibusters, the best known in New Orleans was William Walker, the gray-eyed man of destiny. Walker possessed a brilliant mind. He was born in Tennessee in 1824, and after his graduation from the University of Nashville at the age of fourteen, he studied medicine at the University of Pennsylvania and went to Europe for further study. When he returned, an accomplished surgeon, he came to New Orleans where he studied law and opened a law office on Canal Street, later turning to journalism. Walker left New Orleans in 1849 and joined the march of the forty-niners to California. Out West he resumed his newspaper work, but again the old restlessness asserted itself, and before long he led a filibustering expedition into Mexico that made him the temporary master of an entire Mexican state. When this failed, he was sent to California where he was tried for violating neutrality laws, but he was soon freed by a sympathetic jury. In 1855, he went to Nicaragua at the request of a faction of the Nicaraguan government and soon seized power, becoming the president-dictator. A coalition of Central American states defeated his forces, and he surrendered himself to the United States Navy and was returned to New Orleans to stand trial. Acquitted, he twice made attempts to conquer Nicaragua, but both efforts failed. A third attempt got as far as Honduras where he was arrested by a British naval commander who turned him over to the government of Honduras where he was shot by a firing squad on September 12, 1860. Engraving by J. C. Buttre.

104 The Texas Republic war schooner, *San Antonio*, 1841, from a contemporary sketch made by midshipman Edward Johns, T.N. In 1842, the *San Antonio* with Lieutenant Charles F. Fuller of the Texas Navy aboard had just reached New Orleans after a nine-day trip from Yucatán, and her commander had ordered no shore leave for the crew. The sailors had been drinking, and when Lieutenant Fuller, senior officer on board, refused their repeated demands, they shot and battered him to death with their rifle butts. Two of Fuller's fellow officers were injured in this melee, and the mutineers locked them below deck and escaped in two boats. Several of the mutineers were caught and hanged. *Courtesy University of Texas*

103

104

Three Municipalities: Creoles vs. Americans

105 While New Orleanians could unify to help their Texas neighbor, at home the Creole element had resented the American element. The Creoles were "a warmhearted generation" and a "mild and amiable people with much less energy and irascibility than the emigrants from other states," noted observers who

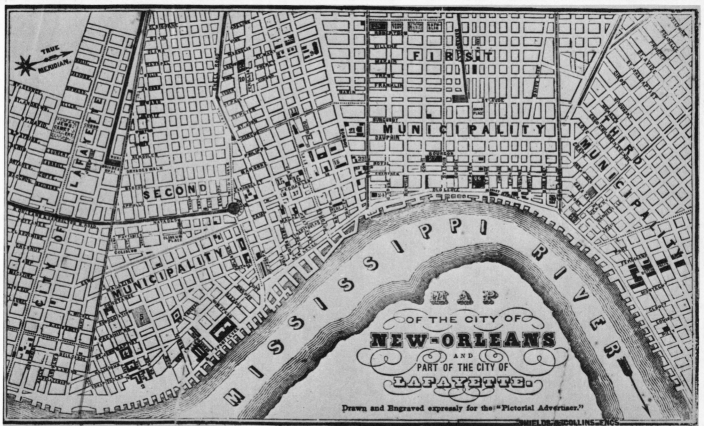

105

came to New Orleans. But the natives were being eclipsed by the invasion of wave upon wave of people from the United States and Europe. During the 1830s, a duel between a Creole and an American brought matters to a climax; the American lost his life, the Creole was tried and acquitted, and a mob of the dead man's friends attacked the judge at his home. Shortly thereafter, state authorities withdrew the city charter and provided another, which divided the city into three separate municipalities, each with its own separate council, recorder, police force, and taxing power, but with a single mayor. The curious division persisted for sixteen years until 1852 when a new charter abolished the system and returned the city's government to a single municipality. The first municipality was basically the Creole Vieux Carré, from

106

Canal to Esplanade streets and from the river to the lake. The second, which had been largely developed by the American groups after the Louisiana Purchase, extended from Canal to Felicity streets and from the river to the lake. The third municipality extended below the first municipality to the shores of Lake Borgne. It was during this strange municipal division that the American element erected the City Hall (now Gallier Hall) on St. Charles Street. Not to be outdone, the council of the first municipality, envisioning the great improvements that the Baroness Pontalba had announced that she would make to her properties facing Jackson Square, added mansard roofs to the Cabildo and the Presbytère. *From* Pictorial Advertiser, *ca. 1845*

106 The three municipalities were sketched in 1842 by P. Cavailler from the opposite side of the river. This first municipality view shows the Place d'Armes (with its flagpole), and the Cathedral directly behind (with

its three spires), flanked by the Cabildo on the left and the Presbytère on the right. Also shown are the St. Louis Hotel with its dome (*left center*), the French Market (*right center*), and a line of masted vessels along the levee and other shipping.

107 This second municipality is the American section of the city. Note the dome of the St. Charles Hotel and the tower of St. Patrick's Church visible above the cluster of buildings and steamboat shipping at the levee. In the foreground are a steam towboat pulling two sailing vessels and the steamboats *Giraffe, Brilliant*, and *Tallerand*.

108 This third municipality is viewed from a boatyard, and shows the lower part of the city. Smoke pours from several chimneys of the industries in that part of town. Also in view is a visiting French warship, the *Neptune*, approaching the towboat *Panther*. *Three views courtesy Howard-Tilton Library, Tulane University*

109

109 In 1852, this official seal symbolized the unification of the three municipalities. The seal was authorized June 18, 1852, and the design was approved June 26 of the same year. It contains thirty-one stars for the thirty-one states then in the Union. Twelve stars in an inner circle at the top and one at its center represent the original thirteen states. Twelve stars in an outer circle are for twelve states admitted into the Union from March 4, 1791, to June 15, 1836. Three stars at bottom left and bottom right represent six states admitted from January 26, 1837, to September 9, 1850. The center shows two Indians beside three wigwams, over which the sun's rays are slanting. An alligator at bottom center brings to mind the swamps of Louisiana. Reclining prominently at center is a white-bearded Neptune, mythical god of waters and the sea, representing Old Man River.

This official seal, that has embellished city documents for nearly a century, is noted but briefly in Book 130 of the minutes of the New Orleans city council: "Paid John Douglas, 17 St. Charles Street, for engraving die and printing of a seal, according to the ordinance of June 26, 1852—$16.00."

The Melting Pot

110 Immigration greatly swelled New Orleans's population and added considerable color. Waves of immigrants from Ireland and Germany landed at New Orleans, and although many of them journeyed upriver or to Texas, thousands remained. Of the 168,675 people in New Orleans in 1860, about 40 percent were foreign-born—the Irish leading with twenty-four thousand and the Germans next with about fourteen thousand. Fascinated by the heterogeneous types he met in New Orleans, Alfred R. Waud, an English illustrator who came to the city in 1871, sketched them for *Every Saturday*, a Boston magazine.

111 While "lace-curtain Irish" were prominent, the Irish who came after the 1840s—who were escaping the dreadful potato famine—were of another class. A contemporary describes them as "drawers of water and hewers of wood." Mostly they were penniless and had to work as laborers. Those who survived the recurring epidemics of yellow fever and saved their money became small businessmen, or entered local

110

politics, which often helped them to prosper and gain prestige. A great many crowded into the section near the riverfront, around the market, and in Rousseau Street, in what is still known as the "Irish Channel." This sketch by an unknown artist shows two sons of Erin mixing it up after an argument.

111

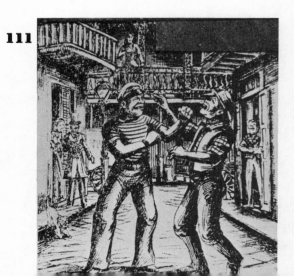

112

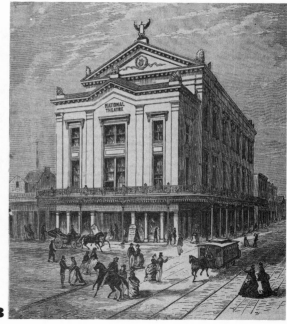

113

112 Intolerable living conditions and political and religious issues in the homeland caused many Germans to leave Europe to find a new life in America, typified by the family seen here. In three waves of immigration, thousands came to New Orleans. The first was from 1820 to 1850 when 53,900 German immigrants arrived at the levee. The second wave came prior to the Civil War, and a third began after the war and continued until the middle nineties. Most of the immigrants continued on to points in the interior, but by 1870 there were more than fifteen thousand persons of German origin living in the city. Sketch by J. Dallas, 1857.

113 The German theatre, the *National.* German plays had been given in New Orleans as early as 1839. In

the period 1870–1871, nearly two hundred German plays were presented in New Orleans at various theatres. The number gradually decreased as the Germans became Americanized, until by the end of the century the German theatre had almost disappeared. *From* Jewell's Crescent City Illustrated, *1873*

114 The Volksfest was a New Orleans institution that sprang into existence in the 1850s and continued until World War I. The illustration shows a Volksfest held in May, 1859, at the Union Race Course on Grand Route St. John. Hundreds of Germans, headed by Mayor Stith and other invited guests, marched with decorated floats to the racetrack where all sorts of amusements were provided for a day of fun. *From* Frank Leslie's Illustrated Newspaper, *May 28, 1859*

114

THE VOLKSFEST, OR GERMAN MAY FESTIVAL AT NEW ORLEANS. See page 408.

115

116

115 116 The last wave of immigrants to come to New Orleans were the Italians. By 1890, there were fifteen thousand in the city, with more arriving around the turn of the century. Like the Germans and Irish before them, they had to start at the bottom of the economic scale, competing for jobs as unskilled laborers, peddlers, and market people. There was a sprinkling of cultured Italians who emigrated before the Civil War, but most Italians came to New Orleans from impoverished Sicily during the latter part of the last century. Many of these immigrants settled around Pontchatoula and Independence, Louisiana, where they became small farmers. Those who came to New Orleans settled in the decaying Vieux Carré, which at the turn of the century had become a slum. In time, they turned the French Market into an Italian market. Like other ethnic groups, by dint of hard work, thrift, and the opportunities afforded all immigrants in America, the Italians improved their lot. These illustrations are of an Italian lemon vendor and Italian fruit stand in the French Market.

117 The French Market. Peddling was the first step above a laborer's job.

117

118 Few Italian immigrants were as successful as Joseph Vaccaro. Born in Contessa Entellina, Sicily, in 1882, he was taken to New Orleans by his family and started his business career by peddling fruit from a basket. With his brothers Luca and Felix, together with Salvador, Vincent, and Carmelo Dantoni, he imported bananas from Central America and then bought ships for the purpose. Thus was born the firm of Vaccaro Brothers, which later became the Standard Fruit and Steamship Company, owners of large banana plantations in Central America.

119 A famous son, Henry M. Stanley, at fifteen, discoverer of the long lost Livingston. In 1858, the question, "Do you want a boy, sir?" caused a cotton merchant, reading his morning paper in front of his establishment, to look up. He saw a youth of seventeen, John Rowlands, who, after a most unhappy childhood in England, had shipped to America where at New Orleans he jumped ship to search for a better life. The merchant, Henry Hope Stanley, gave young Rowlands a job, and the youth's earnest manner and hard work so won Stanley and his wife that they took him to live with them and adopted him. The house in which young Stanley lived, 904 Orange Street, still stands, and a pane of the window in his room still bears the name he scratched on it more than a hundred years ago.

120 Immigrants had come from other countries as well. Samuel Zemurray (1877–1961) came to America from Rumania as a youth. He worked hard and saved enough money to enter the banana business in Mobile, and, having prospered, moved his operations to New Orleans where he founded the Cuyamel Fruit Company, which merged with the United Fruit Company. Before Zemurray's death in 1961, he made many gifts to New Orleans institutions, notably to Tulane University and Touro Infirmary, and endowed the New Orleans Institute of Mental Hygiene. *Courtesy Coryell McKinney*

118

119

120

121 Immigrants, neatly tagged and accompanied by all their worldly goods, arriving at the New Orleans immigration station about 1900. Immigration by this time was but a trickle. *Courtesy Howard-Tilton Memorial Library, Tulane University*

121

122 The election of Abraham Lincoln and a fiery sermon (later published) by Dr. Benjamin Morgan Palmer, a Presbyterian minister, on Thanksgiving Day in 1860, seemed to have crystallized a major change in public thinking on the subject of secession. By February, 1861, Louisiana was part of the Southern Confederacy. Reverend Palmer was a native of South Carolina, pastor of the First Presbyterian Church of New Orleans, and a passionate believer in states' rights, defending slavery as something bestowed on the South by God as a trust. *From* Jewell's Crescent City Illustrated, *1873*

122

123

123 A slave pen in New Orleans—before the Auction. In New Orleans just before the Civil War, there were only 13,000 Negroes and free people of color out of a population of 168,000. Emancipation brought many Negroes from the plantations into the city, and since that time the percentage of Negroes in New Orleans has increased until today they make up about 40 percent of the total population. *From* Harper's Weekly, *January 24, 1863*

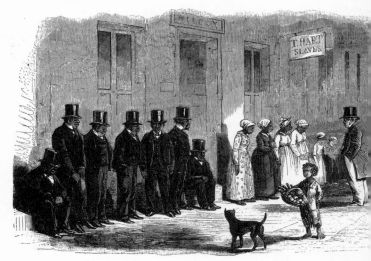

124 Camp Walker, Métairie Ridge, Louisiana, 1861, in the early days just after the formation of the Confederacy, lithograph by Adrien Persac. New Orleans was gripped with "war fever" with companies drilling, uniformed men marching, and all sorts of preparations being made for the impending struggle. Camp Walker was set up on the grounds of the Métairie Race Track, and soon two thousand men were training there. The campsite proved unsuitable, however, and a new camp, Camp Moore, was laid out in the piny woods near Tangipahoa, about eighty miles north of the city. *Courtesy Confederate Museum*

124

125

126

125 126 Local "stamp money" (June, 1861) and stamps (July, 1861), issued by New Orleans's postmaster John Leonard Riddell after the city was cut off from the federal postal system. In addition, New Orleans was cut off from all ocean trade by the blockading of the mouth of the Mississippi by the U.S.S. *Brooklyn* in May, 1861, and as summer wore on, food and commodities became scarce and prices in the city rose drastically. The stamp money facilitated making change as there was a dearth of small coins. The rare cover shown bears double the postage for the usual rate of ten cents.

127 Commissioned a brigadier general in the Confederate Army, Pierre Gustave Toutant Beauregard, called by an eminent Louisiana historian "Napoleon in Gray," was sent to Charleston, where at his command the first guns of the Civil War were fired on Fort Sumter. Then followed Bull Run, Shiloh, again Charleston, Dreury's Bluff, Petersburg, and surrender

at Greensboro, North Carolina. For many years his soldierly, white-haired figure was one of the sights of New Orleans. A Creole who loved life, he participated in the social affairs of those of his class—opera, balls, the Jockey Club. He was alert and active until his death at the age of seventy-five on February 20, 1893.

128 The Washington Artillery battalion, a colorful volunteer company that was the pride of New Orleans, at Camp Louisiana, July 25, 1861, after the Battle of Bull Run. The officers took along their own horses and servants and their own French cook, Edouard, from Victor's restaurant. The battalion served with Lee's Army of Northern Virginia; a reserve battalion known as the Fifth Company served with the Army of Tennessee. Together they participated in more than sixty great battles and achieved an incredible record, which made the Washington Artillery one of the best-known military units during the Civil War.

128

127

129
130

131

133

burned in 1862, and all that remained was its front wall, which was moved and reerected in Bienville Plaza opposite Jackson Square in 1939.

130 The battalion was originally organized in 1838 and saw service in the war with Mexico. Members were from the best families of New Orleans. The men shown here are in the uniforms of those days, the 1840s. This cover of a piece of sheet music was dedicated to the First Company of the Washington Artillery. *Courtesy Samuel Wilson, Jr.*

131 Adjutant William Miller Owen, a typical Washington artilleryman, 1861. Owen was selected to be the adjutant by Major James E. Walton, the battalion's commander. Owen produced *In Camp and Battle with the Washington Artillery,* a lively account of its most brilliant years.

132 In 1880, the Washington Artillery, reorganized after the Civil War, bought the huge building that had housed the 1872 Grand Industrial Exposition. This three-storied structure, which faced St. Charles Street and ran all the way through to Carondelet, was used as an arsenal, and its ballroom was the scene of many carnival balls. The battalion has been merged with the National Guard a number of times; it was mobilized in the Spanish-American War and marshaled in World War I as the 141st Field Artillery Regiment, but saw no active service; it fought gallantly in Africa, Italy, and France during World War II in two battalions (the 141st and 935th Field Artillery); and at present is known as the First Howitzer Battalion of the 141st Artillery of the Louisiana National Guard, with a complement of 583 men. *From* Scientific American, *May 4, 1872*

129 While the outfit was away fighting during the Civil War, their armory at 721 Girod Street was seized by the occupying Federal forces and sold. It was

133 The Washington Artillery's insignia, a snarling tiger, above the motto, "TRY US."

132

134

134 The bombardment of Forts Jackson and St. Philip by the United States Navy. Confederate leaders, not sure at first whether New Orleans would be invaded downriver or from the sea, moved with what seems to us today incredible slowness to defend their most important city. Not until the fall of 1861, when they sent General Mansfield Lovell to New Orleans, did real preparations begin. Nearby Forts Livingston, Macomb, and Pike were garrisoned and armed, and New Orleans's main defenses, Forts Jackson and St. Philip, were repaired and nearly a thousand men sent to man their 115 guns. The chain barrier across the Mississippi near the forts was strengthened. Ordered to take New Orleans, Captain David G. Farragut with a fleet of twenty mortar boats and seventeen ships of war entered the Mississippi, eventually cut the chain barrier, and, after failing to soften the defenders in the forts with mortar fire, on the night of April 23 and morning of April 24, boldly got fourteen of his warships past, despite terrific resistance. He steamed toward New Orleans, virtually undefended. *From* Le Monde Illustré, *Paris, ca. 1862*

135 David Glasgow Farragut was sixty-one years of age when he commanded the West Gulf Blockading Squadron, which passed the forts and captured New Orleans in April, 1862. Flag Officer (later Admiral) Farragut had been in the navy for fifty years before the expedition was planned, and was selected by the naval high command because of his great professional ability and long experience. The successful reduction of the forts was done "with a skill and caution" that won him the love of his followers, and with a dash and boldness that gained him the admiration of the public and the popular name of "Old Salamander"—in federal circles, that is.

135

136

136 Excited populace of New Orleans. After the Yankee ships had passed the forts below New Orleans, the news was telegraphed to the city, and the populace, awakened from their dreams of security by tolling bells, became almost frantic. Confederate officials abandoned their posts and mobs roamed in the streets. Shops and businesses were closed; transportation stopped, and cotton, corn, sugar, and rice were sent to the levee to be burned. *From* Harper's New Monthly Magazine, *August, 1866*

137 The Federal fleet at anchor in New Orleans harbor on April 25. Note the cotton and shipping burning along the levee. Farragut immediately demanded that the city surrender. General Lovell, with no means to combat so formidable a force, evacuated his troops and turned the city back to civil authorities. *From* Harper's Weekly, *1862*

138 Captain Theodorus Bailey and Lieutenant George H. Perkins on their way to demand the surrender of New Orleans, sketch by T. de Thulstrup. *From George W. Cable's* New Orleans Before the Capture

137

138

139

140

139 Scene at the City Hall—hauling down the state flag, which consisted of thirteen stripes: four blue, six white, and three red. A yellow star on a red field was in the upper left corner. After a period of prolonged correspondence between Farragut and Mayor Monroe, during which the mayor had refused to haul down the Louisiana state flag flying over City Hall, Farragut sent a detachment to remove it. On April 29, 1862, Captain Henry Bell went ashore with all the marines of the fleet, accompanied by two brass howitzers. He made his way through sullen, defiant crowds to the City Hall. The howitzers were placed in position to command St. Charles Street in both directions.

Captain Bell requested the mayor to lower the Louisiana flag. Upon Monroe's refusal, Bell sent some men to the roof. The mayor walked out of the hall into the crowded street and placed himself in front of one of the guns, folded his arms, and fixed his eyes on the gunner who stood ready to fire. Captain Bell and his men then safely returned to their ship with the flag. While city authorities had not actually surrendered, the city was, nevertheless, firmly in Federal hands. *From* Century Magazine, *July, 1889*

140 New Orleans's mayor, John T. Monroe, who defied Farragut. He was eventually sent to prison by General Butler, who took command of the city following Farragut's arrival.

141 General Benjamin Franklin Butler, chosen by the federal army to head the occupation of New Orleans. On May 1, he marched troops into the city and took up headquarters in the St. Charles Hotel. General Butler was forty-four years of age when he came to Louisiana. Born in comparative poverty, he had been a successful lawyer in Massachusetts where he was also a powerful Democratic political leader. Like many Northern generals, he had obtained his commission more by political influence than by military experience. He was a stout, ungainly man with eyes contemporaries called "cocked," and his squeaky, high-pitched voice was a source of amusement to his men. Although Butler was pompous, often tactless, and sometimes coarse, he, nevertheless, possessed a brilliant mind and kept his soldiers well-disciplined,

levied taxes to feed the poor, cleaned the long-neglected gutters of the city, and repaired the levee. But, from the beginning, New Orleanians loathed Butler, and rightly or wrongly, bestowed upon him the nickname "Spoons" before he left the Crescent City. During his seven and a half months in command, his associates, particularly his brother, Andrew Jackson Butler, were reputed to have made fortunes by illegal and extra-legal practices. Engraving by H. B. Hall from an original sketch by Thomas Nast, 1863.

142 Registered enemies taking the oath of allegiance, sketch by J. R. Hamilton. To those who refused to sign the oath of allegiance to the United States, Butler invoked the Federal Confiscation Act, subjecting their property to confiscation and themselves to deportation. Butler seemed obsessed with the idea that the people of New Orleans should be punished for having seceded from the Union. He hanged William Mumford, a North Carolinian, although a long resident of New Orleans, on June 7, for tearing the United States flag down from the mint; deposed Mayor Monroe and sent him and Pierre Soulé, the mayor's adviser, to prison; and exiled three Episcopalian ministers for refusing to pray for the President of the United States. *From* Harper's Weekly, *June 6, 1863*

143 As commander of the army occupying the Confederacy's largest city, General Butler found himself in a trying situation, surrounded by hostility, anger, and frustration. The inhabitants went out of their way to

141

142

145

General Order
No. 28.

HEADQUARTERS DEPARTMENT OF THE GULF.
New-Orleans, May 15, 1862.

As the officers and soldiers of the United States have been subject to repeated insults from the women [calling themselves ladies] of New Orleans, in return for the most scrupulous non-interference and courtesy on our part, it is ordered that hereafter when any female 'shall, by word, gesture, or movement, insult or show contempt for any officer or soldier of the United States, she shall be regarded and held liable to be treated as a woman of the town plying her avocation.

By command of   MAJOR-GENERAL BUTLER.
GEO. C. STRONG, A.A.Gen., Chief of Staff.

143

annoy, ridicule, and insult the Federal officers and men. The women of New Orleans, even those of the upper classes, directed their scorn toward the Yankees at every turn. Exasperated, Butler sought to solve his problem by issuing his infamous "General Order No. 28," which is reproduced here from an original broadside. The order stopped the insults, but brought down upon Butler denunciation from Jefferson Davis, Southern newspaper editors, Confederate generals in the field, who read it to their men, and even from the Northern press. It was read in the English Parliament where Lord Palmerston said, "an Englishman must blush to think such an act had been committed by a man belonging to the Anglo-Saxon race."

144 *Women of New Orleans Insulting Federal Officers. From* The Autobiography of Major General Benjamin F. Butler, *Boston, 1892*

144

146   **147**

145 *The Ladies of New Orleans before General Butler's Proclamation* and *After General Butler's Proclamation. Northern cartoon from* Harper's Weekly

146 General Banks's government was based on a small number of voters, and Michael Hahn, a German-born New Orleans lawyer, was elected governor of Louisiana by voters in the occupied portions of Louisiana, barely 30 percent of the state. He resigned in February, 1865, to become United States senator. *From* Harper's Weekly, *1864*

147 As lieutenant governor, J. Madison Wells, a scalawag from Rapides Parish, assumed the governor's chair. Unpredictable, a self-seeking politician, he turned from a fairly conservative position to that of radicalism, and it was under his regime that the riot of July 30, 1866, over the reconvening of the state's constitutional convention took place. He was removed by General Philip Sheridan, at which a local paper remarked, "All's well that ends Wells." *From* Harper's Weekly, *November 11, 1865*

148 Even though New Orleans's war experience was not as harsh as that of some other cities in the South, the city's ordeal under Reconstruction was traumatic. For a short time in 1865 ex-Confederates again were in control in Louisiana, and the Radical Republican element, dissatisfied, determined to reconvene a constitutional convention to oust them. A meeting was called on July 30, 1866, and a riot ensued in which 38 persons, mostly Negroes, were killed, and 147 wounded. These federal troops marching by the St. Charles Hotel were called out too late to quell the riot. Sketch by Alfred R. Waud. *From* Harper's Weekly, *August 15, 1866*

149 Henry Clay Warmoth (in old age), first governor under the new constitution. Warmoth was an Illinois-born lawyer and a Union officer who settled in New Orleans. In 1868, at the age of twenty-six, handsome and ambitious, with a grace of manner and skill as an orator, he plunged into politics and was elected governor of Louisiana. The elected House was almost half Negro, while one fifth of the Senate were ex-slaves.

149

148

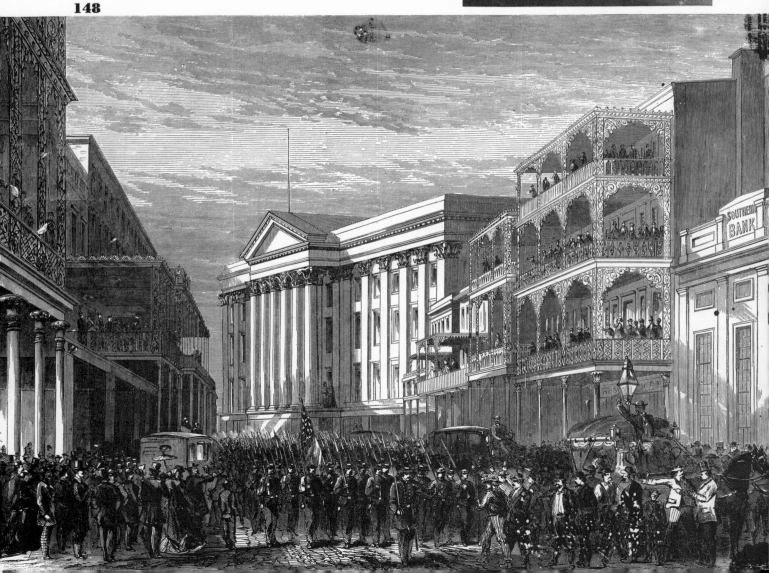

Both the House and Senate "belonged" to Warmoth, and with his inauguration began a period of scandalous bribery, official plundering, crushing taxation, racial strife, and official disregard for the rights of white citizens. The legislature appropriated huge sums of money, much of which was shamelessly squandered. The legislature in 1871 cost $958,956.50, whereas no prewar session cost more than $100,000. Thousands of dollars were wasted on an army of useless clerks, in publishing proceedings in fifteen obscure journals, in a bill for "stationery," which included ham and champagne, and so on. Warmoth amassed a fortune, although his salary as governor was only $8,000 a year. His career was marked with strife. A near riot occurred when he and his faction denied admission to certain members of the House of Representatives, who thereupon took up quarters above the Gem saloon on Royal Street. His career as governor terminated when the House impeached him, suspending him from office just before the end of his term. Warmoth lived to the ripe old age of ninety, dying in 1932. In his memoirs, he denied ever being a carpetbagger, but conceded he might be termed a scalawag.

150   **151**

150 P. B. S. Pinchback, Negro lieutenant governor of Louisiana (succeeding Dunn who died in office), became governor for about a month in 1872 when Henry Clay Warmoth was impeached. *From* Jewell's Crescent City Illustrated, *1873*

151 William Pitt Kellogg, the Vermont-born carpetbagger, who was declared "elected" in 1872 by a Radical returning board, despite election returns which showed that John McEnery, the Democratic-Liberal candidate, had won by more than seven thou-

sand votes. Kellogg's term was marked by civil disorders and bloody riots, and his regime depended on armed force to keep it in power.

152 The battle of September 14, 1874. After a riot in Coushatta, Governor Kellogg ordered the seizure of arms; and learning on Saturday, September 12, 1874, that a shipment of rifles and ammunition was to be unloaded from the steamer *Mississippi* on Monday, ordered the weapons seized. This precipitated the gathering of the White League on Canal Street on Monday, September 14, and after calling for the immediate abdication of Governor Kellogg, a call that went unanswered, the crowd determined to drive out the usurper. Returning armed at 2:30 P.M. and taking up positions behind barricades hastily constructed of any materials they could find, including streetcars and paving stones, the White Leaguers prepared to meet the assault of Kellogg's Metropolitan Police. Marching

152

up Chartres and Decatur to Canal Street, five hundred of the police with six pieces of artillery opened artillery fire on the White League positions. Returning their fire, the White Leaguers in about fifteen minutes forced the Metropolitans to flee in panic. The sketch shows the Metropolitan Police beating a hasty retreat down Canal Street after being badly mauled by the citizens of the White League. Note the unfinished Custom House in the background. *From* Frank Leslie's Illustrated Newspaper, *October 3, 1874*

153 A Metropolitan Police badge. *Courtesy Major Henry M. Morris, Chief of Detectives, New Orleans Police Department*

153

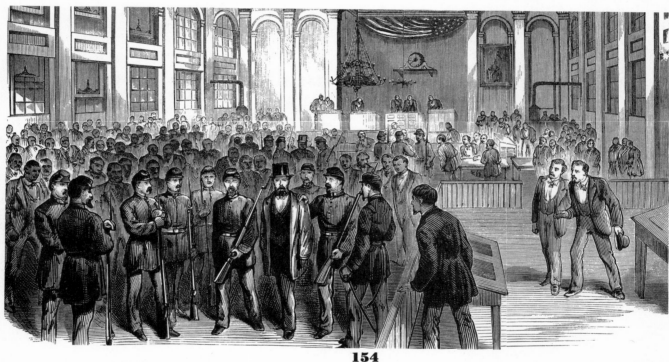

154

154 *The Conservative Members Leaving the Hall of the House of Representatives by the Intervention of Federal Troops,* sketch by Nathan W. Mills. This incident occurred on January 4, 1875, when five Democratic members of the newly organized session of the House of Representatives, controlled by Kellogg, but seated by the temporary chairman, L. A. Wiltz, were ejected by Republicans who returned with federal troops. *From* Frank Leslie's Illustrated Newspaper, *January 23, 1875*

155 Voters in the Nicholls-Packard presidential election to replace Kellogg. This sketch by S. W. Bennett, published in *Frank Leslie's Illustrated Newspaper,* December 2, 1876, shows a polling booth in Elephant Johnie's, a saloon on the levee. A Negro policeman and hangers-on are armed with clubs, and Federal soldiers in the background confront the prospective voters.

155

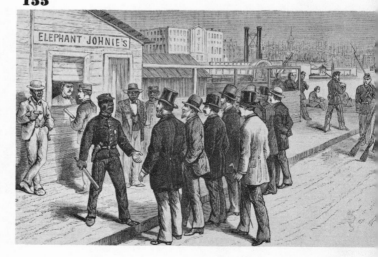

156 The inauguration of Governor Nicholls on the balcony of St. Patrick's Hall, January 8, 1877, sketched by S. W. Bennet. Francis T. Nicholls, a hero of the Confederate Army, had been nominated by the Liberal party in a final attempt to achieve home rule. In the meantime, the Radicals were swearing in their man, Stephen B. Packard, at the St. Louis Hotel, then being used as the State House. *From* Frank Leslie's Illustrated Newspaper, *February 3, 1877*

157 The day after Nicholls's inauguration, citizens and militia under the command of General Frederick N. Ogden organized in Lafayette Square. *From* Frank Leslie's Illustrated Newspaper, *January 27, 1877*

156

157

158

158 Ogden's forces in possession of the Supreme Court Building, which was in the Cabildo at that time. For four months, they patrolled the State House where Packard's government had holed up. *From* Frank Leslie's Illustrated Newspaper, *January 27, 1877*

159 Downfall of the Packard government in Louisiana—United States troops marching out of the Orleans Hotel, April 24, 1877. President Hayes then ordered all federal troops in Louisiana withdrawn, and Packard surrendered the State House. The era of Reconstruction was over! *From* The New York Daily Graphic, *May 2, 1877*

159

160

161

162

160 The sinking of the *Maine* in 1898 in Havana harbor turned New Orleanians' thoughts back to war. After declaring war against Spain on April 25, the President's calls for volunteers resulted in the opening of Camp Foster, a training camp at the Fair Grounds. About two thousand officers and men of the First and Second Louisiana regiments (militia) were mustered in here in May, 1898.

161 In the summer of 1898, this group of New Orleans young officers was in training at Mobile during the Spanish-American War. Of the 4,615 officers and men from Louisiana who answered the call to the colors, 152 died of disease and accidents, but none were killed in action as the war ended before they could be sent to the front.

162 Statue honoring the men who fought in the Spanish-American War. Members of the New Orleans Cuban colony placed a wreath in honor of these men in April, 1964, to observe the sixty-sixth anniversary of the date on which the United States Congress passed a resolution stating, "The Island of Cuba is, and, of right, ought to be free and independent." *Photo by H. J. Paterson. Courtesy Times-Picayune*

163

164

163 "Back the President—We are Prepared" read the banner carried by these World War I marchers in 1917. Once again, New Orleans mustered for war—this time following the sinking of the *Lusitania,* bound for New York, in 1915 by a German submarine. This parade is led by helmeted policemen, an army band furnished music, and many of the participants carried American flags. The scene is on Canal Street near Burgundy. *Photo by Charles L. Franck*

164 *The Sunday States,* August 2, 1914. *Courtesy Times-Picayune*

165 A day to remember, November 11, 1918. This group of truck-riding navy yeomen and yeomenettes was snapped on Canal Street in front of the Custom House, while riding around the city's streets in a de-

165

lirium of joy over the signing of the armistice ending World War I. *Photo by Gasquet. Courtesy Miss Lillian Roane*

166 That year New Orleans celebrated its two hundredth anniversary. A contest for the design of an official flag for the city was held. It drew 379 entries. The committee in charge had a hard time making up its mind, and the design adopted was the result of the combined ideas of Bernard Barry and Gus Couret, both of whom were awarded gold medals. The flag's field is white (for purity of government), with edgings of blue (for liberty) and red (for fraternity). The birth and infancy of New Orleans (under France) are represented by three fleurs-de-lis grouped in triangular arrangement on the white field. *Courtesy New Orleans Public Library*

167 Martin Behrman, 1904–1920, was mayor during the war years. He rose from obscurity to great personal popularity and political power. His sixteen years as mayor were unequaled in the office. After his fourth term, he was again elected, in 1924, but died in office January, 1926. Great civic improvements were initiated under his administrations—pure water supply, with much needed sewerage and drainage systems put into operation; an enlarged public-school system; improved fire and police departments; and the creation of the Public Belt Railroad and Parkway Commission.

168 Mayor Arthur J. O'Keefe, Sr., 1926–1929, succeeded Behrman.

166

167

168

169 Mayor T. Semmes Walmsley, 1929–1936. Walmsley became acting mayor in 1929, was elected in 1930, reelected in 1934, and served until political pressure from Governor Huey P. Long's stalwarts forced him to resign on August 17, 1936.

170 Toward the end of 1930, New Orleans had begun to feel the effects of the Depression. By 1933 when five New Orleans banks went into liquidation and 11 percent of the state's population was on relief, federal agencies such as the CWA and WPA were set up to aid the unemployed, who built roads, streets, bridges, public buildings, water mains, sewers, parks, and fields. They also engaged in compiling records; they acted, sewed, and contributed to art, to literary and historical research, and to scientific development. Maestri was mayor, and with federal money at his disposal, attacked problems of his day with great vigor. Maestri, a Long intimate, was endorsed for mayor by the Long-dominated Democratic Committee organization. No other aspirant for the office appeared, and no election was held. Here he is wielding a pickax to start a street resurfacing project near the Custom House, August 15, 1936. Maestri was reelected in 1942 and served during the crucial World War II days until 1946 when he was spectacularly beaten by De Lesseps S. Morrison.

171 Maestri, with his chief engineer, Hampton Reynolds, inspecting the work of clearing unsightly boathouses and shacks along the banks of Bayou St. John near City Park. This was part of the City Park extension for which the federal government spent nearly $5 million.

170

169

171

172 Mayor de Lesseps Story "Chep" Morrison, 1946–1961, during his army days before entering politics. Morrison began his career as mayor of New Orleans on his return from service in World War II, thereafter rising to major general in the reserves. As a last-minute entry in the mayoral campaign of 1946, Morrison defeated Maestri against overwhelming odds. For fifteen years under his dynamic leadership (he was reelected in 1950, 1954, and 1958), the Crescent City made great progress. Among many projects carried out during his administrations were the construction of the Civic Center complex, a new airport, the Pontchartrain expressway, railroad grade separations, and a union station. Morrison suppressed gambling and vice, created a highly successful recreational department (NORD), made street and housing improve-

ments, and saw the enactment of a badly needed home rule charter in 1954. During his terms as mayor, he made twenty-eight goodwill trips to Latin America, and when he resigned in 1961 he was appointed United States ambassador to the Organization of American States, an office he held until 1963. Morrison ran unsuccessfully three times for governor of Louisiana in 1950, 1960, and 1964. The city mourned his untimely death following a plane crash in Mexico on May 22, 1964.

173 This huge United States flag (seven stories high) hung in front of Godchaux's on Canal Street during World War II. The poster in the foreground urges support of the 7th War Loan; New Orleans's quota was $51,338,000. *Courtesy Times-Picayune*

172

173

174 On V-E Day (May 8, 1945), Hitler was hanged in effigy in New Orleans. *Courtesy Times-Picayune*

175 Scene on V-J Day. This picture was taken in the vicinity of St. Roch Avenue and North Galvez Street less than thirty minutes after the official announcement of the war's end was made by President Truman. Flags were waved, neighbors marched, huge victory bonfires were lighted, bells tolled, and people crowded the churches. *Photo by Oscar J. Valeton. Courtesy Times-Picayune*

Present

176 Mayor Morrison's new City Hall, west of the French Quarter, is one of the buildings making up the city's impressive Civic Center, which also includes the State Office Building, State Supreme Court Building, Civil Courts Building, and the main library surrounding beautifully landscaped Duncan Plaza. The Civic Center covers fourteen acres. *Courtesy Chamber of Commerce of the New Orleans Area*

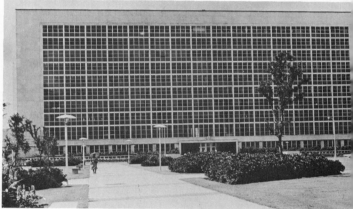

176

174
175

177

180

178

177 Mayor Victor Hugo Schiro, 1961–1970, was elected after Morrison resigned in 1961 and served until Maurice ("Moon") Landrieu won election from a field of eleven other aspirants.

178 Schiro inherited the problems of any major American city—racial strife, strikes, housing and employment needs, and a scarcity of money. Here mothers demonstrate in the front of the William Frantz Public School to protest the desegregation of the New Orleans public school system, 1960.

179 Youthful marchers protesting our presence in Vietnam, 1969.

180 Mayor Moon Landrieu, elected in 1970, fell heir to New Orleans's problems—the ever-increasing cost of government, demands of police and firemen, mounting relief costs, etc. *Photo by Tipery. Courtesy City of New Orleans*

181 Artists sketching visitors is a typical scene in the Vieux Carré today. Many of the artists hang their stock of pictures on the iron fence surrounding Jackson Square to tempt possible buyers. *Courtesy Chamber of Commerce of the New Orleans Area*

179

181

2. ARCHITECTURE

1

2

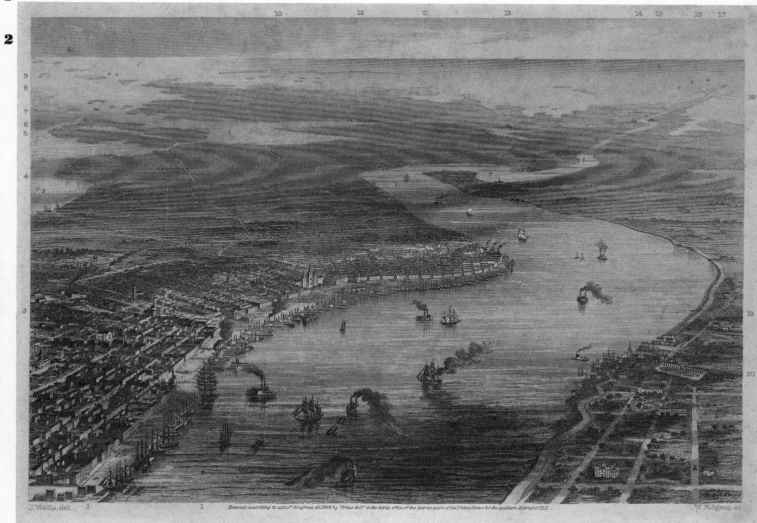

J. Wells. del.   Entered according to act of Congress A.D.1863 by Virtue & Co. in the clerk's office of the district court of the United States for the southern district of N.Y.   W. Ridgway. sc.

1. Mississippi River.	6. Rigolets.	11. Gulf of Mexico.	16. Balize.
2. Levee.	7. Lake Borgne.	12. Proctorsville.	17. South Pass.
3. St Charles Hotel.	8. Mississippi Sound.	13. Fort Dupré.	18. South West Pass.
4. Lake Pontchartrain.	9. Ship Island.	14. Fort St Philip.	19. McDonoughville.
5. Fort Pike.	10. Chandeleur Islands.	15. Fort Jackson.	20. Algiers.

1 Architecturally, the New Orleans of the early 1850s was a most attractive city. Contemporary visitors and many people who lived here have left glowing accounts of its buildings. The artists of this 1852 skyline view, B. F. Smith, Jr., and J. W. Hill, saw the city as it appeared from the tower of St. Patrick's Church (partly seen in the foreground). Starting at the extreme left-hand corner, we have the First Presbyterian Church; directly above it is the newly completed City Hall (Gallier Hall), located on St. Charles Avenue; and following along St. Charles Avenue is the St. Charles Hotel (*left center*). The dome of Odd Fellows' Hall is directly over St. Patrick's in the foreground, and the dome in the distance (on a straight line with Odd Fellows' Hall) belongs to the St. Louis Hotel. The spire of St. Louis Cathedral, slightly to the right and above the hotel, is barely visible. The busy levee is, of course, at the extreme right, at about the center of which (in this scene) is the Place d'Armes or Jackson Square. A traveler coming by steamer would first see the majestic white dome of the St. Charles Hotel rising high above the surrounding buildings. The St. Charles was undoubtedly New Orleans's most elegant building, and if the visitor would climb to the colonnade under its dome and look to the northeast across Canal Street (Canal is about dead center, horizontal, in this photograph), he would see the narrow streets and the closely built houses of the Vieux Carré. In addition to the St. Louis Hotel's dome and the newly rebuilt St. Louis Cathedral, he would see the recently erected Pontalba Buildings (at the Place d'Armes) with the dome of the Merchants' Exchange in the foreground (about dead center). He would also see the beautiful crescent of the Mississippi and the levee. Around the base of the hotel, the business blocks with their simple, well-proportioned facades might strike him as perhaps the finest examples of commercial architecture he had seen anywhere in America. Several church spires would be visible, especially the Gothic tower of St. Patrick's; to the south, of course, he would view City Hall's gleaming white marble Ionic portico. Further to the south he would see in the distance the columned residences and gardens in the suburb of Lafayette. To the west, toward Lake Pontchartrain (not seen here), was open country, with its wooded areas, canals, and suburban roads.

2 This 1863 bird's-eye view gives a broader picture of the relative location of the various sites. No. 3 is the St. Charles Hotel and between nos. 10 and 12 is Jackson Square, near the levee, with its impressive buildings as a focal point. It is an ambitious view of New Orleans and its vicinity, delineated by J. Wells and engraved by W. Ridgway. This view not only shows New Orleans, Algiers, and McDonoghville in considerable detail, but purports to give the viewer a glimpse of such far-off places as South Pass and South West Pass at the mouth of the Mississippi, and even includes the Chandeleur Islands and Ship Island on the Mississippi Sound!

St. Louis Hotel: Creole Elegance

3 The Exchange (St. Louis) Hotel, as it appeared in 1853 when it had been rebuilt after a disastrous fire that heavily damaged it in 1841. New Orleans in the fabulous years beginning with the 1830s had seen tremendous growth in population and wealth. Creole and American businessmen had realized that New Orleans needed something more than the comparatively small hotels and numerous boardinghouses that then operated for the influx of visitors from surrounding plantations and other cities. Accordingly, two hotels had been built—the City Exchange (St. Louis Hotel), by the Creoles, in 1836–1840, designed by the French architect J. N. B. de Pouilly; and the St. Charles Exchange Hotel, completed in 1842, by the

3

firm of Dakin and Gallier. Each hotel cost roughly about $1 million, and in building them New Orleans became the pioneer city to provide buildings for housing a large number of guests in comfort and luxury. *From* Gleason's Pictorial Drawing Room Companion

4 In 1842, the rates were $2.50 a day, and an early advertisement of the St. Louis Hotel advised visitors that the table for gentlemen would provide dinner from three to five o'clock, and the one for ladies at five o'clock. *From* Pitts & Clark New Orleans Directory, *1842*

5 The St. Louis Hotel in 1873. An elaborate cast-iron gallery on two stories was added later. *From* Jewell's Crescent City Illustrated

6 Exchange Passage (better known as Exchange Alley between Royal and Chartres streets) is a street cut through as an approach to the St. Louis Hotel. An early example of city planning, it was designed by the same architect who designed the hotel, and the lots were sold with the understanding that purchasers were to build in a uniform manner. Exchange Passage became known as the street of fencing masters since several had their ateliers in this thoroughfare. The photograph dates from 1901 before the block was demolished to build the former Civil District Courthouse in 1908–1909. Three blocks of the street from Canal to Conti still remain. *Courtesy Library of Congress*

7 A stone's throw from Exchange Alley was the courtyard of the home of Molly Moore Davis, 84 Royal Street, 1901. This house, together with all the others in

5

6

7

4

TO VISITORS,

ST. LOUIS

HOTEL,

ON ROYAL, ST. LOUIS, & CHARTRES-STREETS,

New-Orleans.

THIS splendid and elegantly furnished new Establishment opened under the charge of the Subscriber.

A LADIES' AND GENTLEMENS' TABLE IS PROVIDED.

☞ The Table for Gentlemen will be found very acceptable, as Dinner is kept warm from 3 to 5 o'clock.

☞ The Ladies' Table is at 5 o'clock.

EDWARD MILFORD,

Formerly of the American Hotel and Carlton House, New-York.

FEBRUARY 1, 1842.

the square bounded by Royal, St. Louis, Conti, and Chartres streets, was destroyed about 1908 as part of the site for the Civil Courts Building. Mrs. Davis, the wife of Thomas E. Davis, the editor of the *Daily Picayune*, wrote novels, poems, and plays. She was probably the most famous hostess of her day, who brought together in an informal and charming setting visiting celebrities and many local persons of note. *Courtesy Library of Congress*

8 The Girod House, popularly known as the Napoleon House, was opposite the St. Louis Hotel. Located on the corner of Chartres and St. Louis streets, it was built in 1814 by Nicholas Girod, mayor of New Orleans. This photograph was made about 1906. Part of the balcony of the old St. Louis Hotel shows to the left of center, and a typical ice wagon of the period is at the curb below. A well-proportioned three-storied building surmounted by a hipped tile roof and crowned by an octagonal cupola, the Girod House has long been associated with a tale that it was built as a

refuge for Napoleon Bonaparte who was to have been rescued from St. Helena and brought to New Orleans by some of his ardent admirers. Unfortunately, Napoleon died before the plot could be carried out, but the legend persists. *Courtesy Library of Congress*

9 Woodcut of the Louisiana Senate in session in the St. Louis Hotel, May 2, 1877. While during its early years the hotel was the scene of several elaborate balls, one reputed to cost $20,000, bad luck had dogged the management, and the Citizens' Bank, which owned the hotel, took it back several times, because of losses in operation. In 1874, it became the State House and headquarters for the Radical Kellogg carpetbag government. After the battle of September 14, 1874, between citizens aligned with the White League and Kellogg's Metropolitan Police, the citizens took possession of the building, but were ousted two days later by Federal troops. In 1875, when Democratic members of the legislature attempted to take their seats at an initial meeting on January 4 and organize for the session, the Republicans again had troops come into the building and eject their enemies. *From* The New York Daily Graphic

10 The block-long St. Louis Hotel's exterior was simple and dignified in design, but its interior boasted a large ballroom, a beautiful circular stairway, and a rotunda surmounted by a magnificent dome sixty-five feet in diameter, which rose to a height of eighty-eight feet above the floor. Under this rotunda, auctions of all sorts of property, including slaves, were held. The rotunda was eventually divided by a floor. The upper portion was used as a dining room, and eventually the senate chamber of the Radical state government met here. This fanciful engraving by W. H. Brooke is entitled *Sale of Estates, Pictures and Slaves in the Rotunda, New Orleans*

10

11

12

11 After the departure of the Radicals, the hotel was found to have been almost wrecked, and scarcely fit for use. It was repaired and reopened, but by 1903 again was in ramshackle condition. By 1912, it was a ruin with mules stabled in the rotunda and bats in the rooms. The great storm of September 30, 1915, did further damage, and its owners demolished it. Seen here is the dome of the rotunda after the hurricane. Visible are some of the hundreds of hollow clay pots that architect J. N. B. de Pouilly had cleverly used to lighten the weight of his huge dome.

12 The slave block, 1906. This platform in the lower section of the rotunda was pointed out to tourists as the block on which slaves were auctioned in the days before the Civil War. *Courtesy Library of Congress*

13 One of the reasons for the commercial failure of the St. Louis Hotel was its lack of rooms, for it could only accommodate two hundred persons. This photograph taken in 1917, when the hotel was being demolished, shows the outer walls of the rotunda and its dome, and the Tuscan columns, still standing, of its grand entrance. *Photo by Charles L. Franck*

13

14

14 St. Charles Exchange Hotel in its year of completion, 1842, lithograph by B. W. Thayer & Co. The St. Charles was the most admired building in the New Orleans of the 1840s. Named for the street on which it stood, this 350-room caravansary, with its huge barroom adorned with a range of Ionic columns and its stately ballroom above it, became the center of business and social life in the American section of the city. The first St. Charles was surmounted by a cupola and dome 46 feet in diameter, which, with its lantern, rose to a height of 185 feet above street level. The dome of the St. Charles was visible for miles, and guests of the hotel who cared to climb to the colonnade and porch, which supported the dome, could get a fine view of the city and the winding Mississippi.

15 Fire, which broke out on January 18, 1851, in the St. Charles's upper stories soon went out of control due to poor fire-fighting equipment and consumed the hotel, the Verandah Hotel across the street, and continued up St. Charles Street all the way to Lafayette Street, destroying fifteen buildings, including Dr. Clapp's Strangers' Church.

16 The Verandah Hotel, diagonally across the street from the St. Charles Hotel. It was erected in 1836–1838 by Dakin and Dakin, architects, at a cost of $300,000. This was a family-type hotel, and its name came from the cast-iron galleries that ornamented its facade. The hotel had an impressive eighty-five-foot-long dining room, and three elliptical domes were recessed into its ceiling to receive the chandeliers. *From Norman's New Orleans and Environs, 1845*

15

16

17

20

18

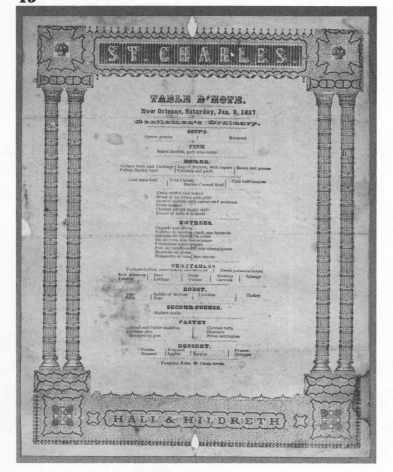

19

17 The second St. Charles Hotel rose from the ashes of the first within two years after the destruction of the original building. The hotel remained open during the final years of the Civil War, and after Appomattox (1865) it was returned to its operators who gave free accommodations to returning Confederate veterans, many of whom were penniless. Pictured here is a scene of great excitement at the second St. Charles Hotel in 1876; commissioners from Washington who had come to study the returns of the Hayes-Tilden election are seen leaving. In 1878 major repairs were made and the hotel enlarged so that it could accommodate as many as seven hundred guests. *From* Frank Leslie's Illustrated Newspaper, *December 9, 1876*

18 Some idea of the elegant lobby of the second St. Charles Hotel can be gained from this rare sketch by Nathan W. Mills. *From* Frank Leslie's Illustrated Newspaper, *January 23, 1875*

19 A menu of the St. Charles Hotel, Saturday, January 3, 1857. This fixed-price meal offered more than fifty items from soup to nuts.

20 The St. Charles's gold table service, used only on extraordinary occasions, was reputed to have cost $16,000. Part of it is seen here. *From* Gleason's Pictorial Drawing Room Companion, *March 19, 1853*

21 Like its ill-fated predecessor, the second St. Charles Hotel was also destroyed by fire. This occurred on April 29, 1894. The photograph shows how complete was its destruction. The present Sheraton-Charles was built on the same site not long thereafter.

22

Gallier Hall: American Style

22 Gallier Hall (Old City Hall). This fine Greek Revival structure is the best surviving New Orleans building designed by James Gallier. Built in 1845–1850 as the municipality hall of the second municipality, it became the city hall for the entire city when the city government was again reunited after the unsuccessful division of government into three separate districts was abandoned in 1852. Robert Seaton was the contractor; but after he had finished the basement the city ran out of funds and construction was halted, the roofed-over basement being used by the police department. The city even considered selling the unfinished building and site to the owners of the St. Charles Hotel, which had burned in 1851; but after much discussion the council, led by Samuel J. Peters, who personally guaranteed the money to finish the structure, gave Gallier the contract to resume building and the city hall was completed within two years. It was dedicated on May 10, 1853. Gallier Hall is 90 feet wide and 215 feet deep and three stories high. Its facade, which rests on a Quincy granite base,

is of Tuckahoe marble from New York. There are two rows of fluted Ionic columns—six in front and four in the rear. The entrance on St. Charles Street is reached by a flight of granite steps leading up between the columns. The pediment is adorned with the figures of Justice and Commerce, done in high relief by the sculptor Robert A. Launitz. The two upper floors have a twelve-foot-wide hallway, which runs the entire length of the building, and originally a large meeting hall, sixty-one by eighty-four feet with a high arched ceiling, occupied a great part of the third floor. This room, which contained extensive galleries on three sides, a stage, and an elaborately ornamented ceiling, was used for Lyceum lectures until the time of the Civil War. During reconstruction days, it was cut up into smaller chambers and used for offices. Gallier Hall, in the opinion of architectural critics, is hardly surpassed in dignity and proportion by any building of the Greek Revival period in the United States. *Photo by Dan S. Leyer*

23 James Gallier, Sr., born in Ravensdale, Ireland, 1798, son of a builder. By hard work and application he learned the building trade, studied architectural drawing at the School of Fine Arts, Dublin, and largely by self-education, mastered his profession, working with architects in Dublin and later in Liverpool, Manchester, London, and New York. Coming to New Orleans in 1834 with Charles B. Dakin, the architect, he soon became one of the busiest men of his profession. Failing eyesight caused him to retire in 1849, but his firm, headed by his son, James Gallier, Jr., continued to produce architecture that was a worthy ornament to the city. Unfortunately, most of Gallier's fine buildings have disappeared, lost through fire (St. Charles Hotel, Merchants' Exchange) and the inexorable march of time. Bust by J. C. King, ca. 1845. *Courtesy Mrs. Kenneth McLeod*

24 James Gallier the elder met death with his wife and many other New Orleanians, and the members of a French opera troupe who were coming to the city for an engagement, when the ship *Evening Star*, on which they were traveling from New York foundered in a terrible storm on October 3, 1866. *From* Frank Leslie's Illustrated Newspaper

25 The council chamber of Gallier's City Hall, December 6, 1889. The casket of Jefferson Davis, President of the Southern Confederacy, is lying in state. Before the Civil War, Governor Isaac Johnson's body lay in state there, to be followed as years elapsed by obsequies for Davis, General P. G. T. Beauregard,

Chief of Police David C. Hennessy (who had been killed by the Mafia), Bertie Sneed (the first casualty of the Spanish-American War), Mayors Martin Behrman and de Lesseps S. Morrison. During the stormy days of Reconstruction, the old city hall had also been the scene of many political demonstrations. In later years, President-elect Warren G. Harding addressed a vast gathering in front of the hall before he took office; and William McKinley, Theodore Roosevelt, and Herbert Hoover were received in the mayor's parlor. *Photo by C. H. Adams*

23

24

25

26

26 Leading from the front steps of Gallier Hall is Lafayette Square, seen here on a summer's evening in 1858. "The Square," wrote Kilburn, who sketched it, "is a great resort and on fine evenings presents the lively appearance shown in the engraving." In the background can be seen St. Patrick's Church and the First Presbyterian Church. Lafayette Square, bounded by St. Charles Avenue, Camp Street, North Street, and South Street, is the second oldest public square in New Orleans. It was laid out by Carlos Trudeau in 1796 as part of a plan for subdividing the Gravier plantation in the Faubourg Ste. Marie. When the sketch was made, there were no monuments in the square. In 1873, a monument to Benjamin Franklin was placed in the center of the park, but this was moved to a spot facing Camp Street when in 1901 the statue of Henry Clay was removed from the center of Canal at Royal–St. Charles and erected in its stead.

27

The John McDonogh monument, erected in 1898, faces St. Charles Avenue. Strangely, no statue to Lafayette, for whom it was named, was ever erected in it. *From* Ballou's Pictorial Drawing Room Companion

27 The center of Lafayette Square, featuring the marble statue of Benjamin Franklin, photographed about 1900. The statue has had a very curious history. It was ordered by a group of New Orleanians, headed by Richard Henry Wilde, from the American sculptor Hiram Powers. By 1844, Powers, then working in Florence, Italy, had received only $1,000 of his fee for the statue. Time passed, the Civil War intervened, Wilde died in 1867, and the purchasers forgot, until in 1869 someone discovered the contract and reminded Powers who apparently waived the balance due him. In 1871, he finished the statue. It arrived at New Orleans unclaimed and was advertised for sale by mistake; the granite for the base was ordered from Boston, but the ship carrying it sank. Another base arrived, the statue was set prominently in the Square, and was moved in 1901 to face Camp Street, making way for a statue of Henry Clay. The Italian marble, of which the Franklin statue was made, deteriorated so badly that in 1909 it was removed to the interior of the recently completed New Orleans Public Library. When that building was demolished, the figure was set up on the campus of the Benjamin Franklin Senior High School. Here more deterioration set in, and vandals sprayed the statue with paint in 1962. Cleaned

and repaired, it now stands, after nearly a century of its unveiling, in the corridor of the high school. *Photo courtesy Samuel Wilson, Jr.*

28 Odd Fellows' Hall at the corner of Camp and Lafayette streets, a site now occupied by the old New Orleans post office. Built in 1852, it was the scene of many brilliant gatherings, balls, and concerts by such artists as Gottschalk and Ole Bull. During the occupation of New Orleans after the Civil War, it had been used as a barracks, and it was returned to its owners in November, 1865, only to burn down the next year. Another structure, called St. Patrick's Hall, was built on the site, and this stood until 1905 when it was demolished to build the post office. *From* Jewell's Crescent City Illustrated, *1873*

29 One block beyond Camp Street was one of the largest and most important commercial structures in the second municipal district—Banks' Arcade. This block-long, three-storied building was situated on Magazine Street at a point between Gravier and Natchez streets. Built in 1833 after the plans of Charles F. Zimpel for Thomas Banks, it featured a glass-covered arcade, which divided the structure into two parts. In the lower stories in the 1840s were offices of businessmen, lawyers, notaries, and brokers, not to mention the famous restaurants of John Hewlett. The second floor contained the armory of the Washington Guards, more offices, and billiard rooms, while the third floor was a hotel for gentlemen. The newspaper office of the *Bulletin* occupied the corner of Magazine and Gravier streets. A grand "coffee room" on Magazine Street and on the arcade was adorned with pictures and engravings. This hall was for many years used for public gatherings, since five thousand persons "could be assembled without inconvenience." Banks' Arcade was the scene of many memorable meetings, particularly before the Mexican War. The building, then valued at $700,000, was the capital prize in an 1839 lottery, and it partially burned on March 4, 1851, but "everything valuable in the Arcade barroom was saved," reported one newspaper. Parts of Banks' Arcade are still standing. *From* New Orleans City Directory, *1842*

28

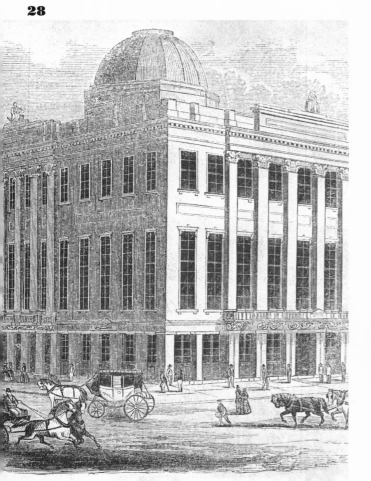

29

30

31

32

30 The old United States Branch Mint, 400 Esplanade Avenue. William Strickland designed this New Orleans landmark, which was erected in 1835. The site had been occupied by Fort St. Charles—one of several forts erected by the Spanish in 1792—and later by the first Jackson Square. In 1931, the mint was converted by the addition of cell blocks into a federal prison. This was later abandoned, and the Coast Guard used the building until a short time before it was turned over to the state of Louisiana for eventual restoration and use as a branch of the Louisiana State Museum. Two events are associated with the history of the old mint. One was the fancy dress ball given there by Joseph Kennedy, superintendent of the mint, for his daughters Rose and Josephine, in 1850. This was probably the only ball ever held in a United States mint, and one of those things that would probably happen only in New Orleans. The other event was the hanging on June 7, 1862, of William B. Mumford, forty-two years old, for hauling down the United States flag from the mint and tearing it into shreds shortly after the surrender of the city to the Union forces in the Civil War. Mumford was hanged from a gallows built in front of the main entrance to the building. *From* Ballou's Pictorial Drawing Room Companion, *1858*

31 The battery of stamping machines in the New Orleans Mint, 1890. *Photo by George F. Mugnier*

32 Gold coins from the New Orleans Mint. The mint coined double eagles, eagles, and half eagles in gold; dollars, halves, quarters, dimes, half dimes, and three-cent pieces in silver. From 1838, when it began coinage, to its seizure in 1861 by the state, the mint had turned out a grand total coinage of $69,913,093. After the Civil War, coinage was again resumed and continued until 1909. *Courtesy Mr. and Mrs. Ray Samuel*

Canal Street

33 Plan of the city commons, showing the location of the rope walk (shaded area) and the proposed navigation canal on the extreme left, which eventually became Canal Street, one of the widest main streets in the world. It has had a curious history. Originally a "commons," or unoccupied tract, adjacent to the old city boundaries, the city council claimed it for New Orleans, a claim that was recognized after the Louisiana Purchase by the federal government in 1807. The decision, however, contained a proviso that the city would "reserve for the purpose, and convey gratuitously for the public benefit, to the company authorized by the Legislature of the Territory of Louisiana, as much of the said commons as shall be necessary to continue the Canal of Carondelet from the present basin to the Mississippi, and shall not dispose of, for

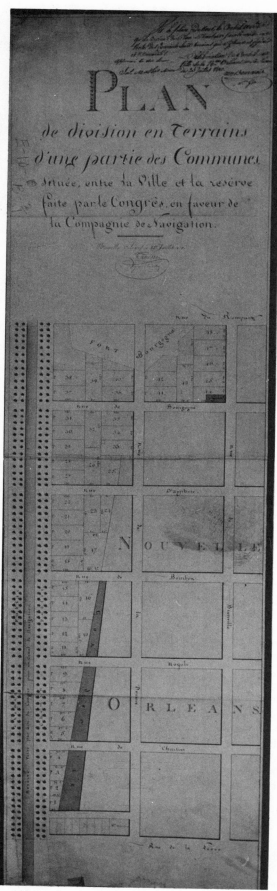

33

the purpose of building thereon, any lot within 60 feet of the space reserved for a canal which shall forever remain open as a public highway." The canal was to have been fifty feet wide, and the New Orleans Navigation Company was empowered by charter to dig it. This the company never did, and by 1852 it became insolvent and forfeited its charter. Long before this time, Canal Street, which ran crosstown from the river, had begun to develop as a thoroughfare. It separated the Creole section from the fast-developing American section. With legal hindrance to its growth gone, this 171-foot-wide street soon came into its own. Ink and watercolor drawing by Jacques Tanesse, 1810. *Courtesy City Engineer's Office, City of New Orleans*

34 Canal Street, from a map by T. G. Bradford dated 1838, showing "neutral ground" between the first and second municipalities.

34

35

35 In the early part of the nineteenth century, Chartres Street intersecting Canal was the principal street of retail merchants in New Orleans, but, as the city grew, a number of merchants established themselves in the upper part (the river end) of Canal Street, while in the lower part, toward Rampart, about halfway into the town, there were a number of private residences. Two of the largest structures on Canal Street were the State House, which had originally been built in 1815 as the Charity Hospital, and the first Christ Church on the river corner of Bourbon. The State House was located on Canal between Baronne and University Place, in the American section. In 1840, the block between Bourbon and Royal was sketched by J. Lion, who made this lithograph. At the left is the second Christ Church, erected in 1835 by the architects Gallier and Dakin to supplant the earlier church that had served the congregation since 1815. Next to it was the rectory, built in 1827, both being crowded by commercial structures.

36 State House, Canal Street, between Baronne and University Place, 1835. In 1834, Joseph Holt Ingraham, an extremely observant world traveler who visited New Orleans, described the street, including State House and Christ Church:

Canal Street with its triple row of young sycamores, extending throughout the whole length, is one of the most spacious, and destined at no distant period to be one of the first and handsomest streets in the city. Every building in the streets is of modern construction, and some blocks of its brick

edifices will vie in tasteful elegance with the boasted granite piles of Boston.

Ingraham continued:

The government house [State House], situated diagonally opposite to the church, and retired from the street . . . was formerly a hospital, but its lofty and spacious rooms are now converted into public offices. Its snow-white front, though plain, is very imposing; and the whole structure, with its handsome, detached wings, and large green, thickly covered with shrubbery in front, luxuriant with orange and lemon trees, presents, decidedly, one of the finest views to be met with in the city. These two buildings, with the exception of some elegant private residences, are all that are worth remarking in this street, which, less than a mile from the river, terminates in the swampy commons, every where surrounding New Orleans, except on the river side.

Courtesy Confederate Museum, New Orleans

37 In the 1830s, there were a number of hotels on Canal Street, nearby the river. This one, the Planters, came to an unfortunate end at two o'clock on the morning of May 15, 1835, "burying 50 persons, 40 of which escaped with their Lives." Repairs were being made on the ground floor of the hotel, which probably weakened the upper floors, and this very likely caused the crash. One lucky guest saw a big beam headed his way, but it struck his bedpost first and enabled him to escape. Lithograph by Nathaniel Currier.

38 Canal Street in the late 1850s, from a lithograph published by Louis Schwarz. The steeple in the right background is that of the third Christ Church, which was erected in 1847, on the site occupied by the present Maison Blanche building. The church with the dome to the left is the Jesuit Church on Baronne Street. The disorderly appearance on the neutral ground of the squares in the foreground contrasts with the tree-shaded strip further down the street. More than a dozen of the omnibuses, which were the principal means of transport before the advent of street railways, are shown in the picture.

36

37

38

93

39

39 Inauguration of the Clay statue at New Orleans. The statue of Henry Clay now in Lafayette Square originally stood here at Canal Street at the St. Charles –Royal intersection. Henry Clay, the great Kentucky statesman who "would rather be right than President," had been a popular visitor to New Orleans where he was greatly admired. After his death in 1852, the Clay Monument Association was formed, which eventually raised the money to employ the sculptor Joel Hart to create an heroic-size bronze of Clay. On April 12, 1860, amid great celebration and with a military parade and speeches, the fourteen-foot statue on its seven-tiered granite base was unveiled. Engraved as a woodcut, 1860. *Photo by J. D. Edwards*

40 Canal Street in the 1870s. This photograph made near the St. Charles–Royal intersection with the Clay monument in its center shows the open gutters and Belgian block pavement of the street. Loafers sit on the chains suspended between cast-iron posts, and grass grows in the roadway.

41 The Henry Clay statue as it appeared shortly after its dedication in 1860. Lithograph by Louis Schwarz, 1862.

42 The building occupying this corner site is one of the oldest landmarks on Canal Street still standing. It is the Musson Building at the riverside of Royal. It

40

41

was erected in 1833 by Germain Musson, and its front and sides are constructed entirely of granite from Quincy, Massachusetts. Musson, a cotton merchant, had the granite brought from the east as ballast in the ships that hauled away his cotton. The photograph dates from about 1890. *Photo courtesy Ray Samuel*

43 Twenty-four years after its erection, the statue of Henry Clay had become a traffic obstruction, as can be seen in this photograph taken of the St. Charles–Canal Street intersection in 1884. In 1901, the statue was taken down and reerected in the center of Lafayette Square.

42

43

44

45

44 Canal Street shortly after the removal of the Clay statue, which should have been at dead center. There are no automobiles, but the neutral ground is crowded with streetcars. *Courtesy New Orleans Public Library*

45 For forty years, the Clay monument stood at the busy intersection of Canal and St. Charles–Royal streets. On at least two occasions, it was the gathering place for citizens who felt outraged at the conduct of their government. The first of these was the meeting of the White League on the morning of September 14, 1874, when five thousand men met to try to end the usurpation of Governor William Pitt Kellogg, heard speeches, and then returned to their homes for arms and fought the Kellogg Metropolitan Police on the riverfront. On another occasion, depicted here, a mass meeting was called on March 14, 1891, at the base of the statue. The day before, a jury had acquitted six Italians and failed to convict the remainder of the nineteen, who had been arrested and charged with complicity in the Mafia murder of Chief of Police David C. Hennessy the year before. Infuriated at the action of the court, and after hearing speeches from several of their leaders, the mob marched to Parish Prison, broke in, and shot or hanged eleven of the nineteen accused. Sketch by T. de Thulstrup. *From Harper's Weekly, March 28, 1891*

46 This view of Canal Street, sketched by Theodore R. Davis, shows the block between Burgundy and Dauphine streets in 1866. The artist has drawn the four elegant private houses known as Union Terrace, which were erected in 1836–1837, "whose interior arrangements and architectural taste are in perfect keeping with their exterior chastity of design," to quote a contemporary who estimated their cost at $100,000. The illustration was made at the time of the riot over the Radical party's call for reconvening the state's constitutional convention in which 38 people were killed and 147 injured in this vicinity. *From Harper's Weekly, August 25, 1866*

47

47 Canal and Dauphine streets some thirty years later. The large department store at the corner, which dominates the area, is the predecessor of the present-day Maison Blanche building. The mule cars have been supplanted by electric cars, but no automobiles are visible. In 1898 when this picture was made there probably weren't any in New Orleans.

48 Canal Street in 1922. The new Maison Blanche building dominates the skyline. The curbs on both sides of the street are crowded with parked automobiles, and the neutral ground carries four sets of streetcar tracks. Aside from a few minor changes in facades, the buildings shown are essentially unchanged today. *Photo by Charles L. Franck*

48

49

49 The Touro block, the north side of Canal Street between Bourbon (a block up from Dauphine) and Royal streets, 1856. This group of stores was built by Judah Touro. The residence sandwiched in between the buildings was at one time the rectory of Christ Church, which once adjoined the church. After Touro's death, the executor of his estate approached the city council and offered to contribute a substantial sum to the beautification of Canal Street with the understanding that a monument to Touro would be erected and the street renamed Touro Boulevard. The offer was accepted, but, for some unknown reason, a short time afterward, the street was renamed Canal Street, and it has been called by that name since. *Courtesy Dr. Edmond Souchon*

50 The Touro block five years later. In 1861, just prior to the outbreak of the Civil War, the first horsecars were put into operation in New Orleans. This lithograph of Canal Street shows two of the new-style vehicles dashing along.

50

51

51 Bourbon Street, just off Canal. An artist from *Frank Leslie's Illustrated Newspaper* sketched this view of Bourbon Street in 1868. A small crowd is attracted by an organ grinder and his monkey. The large building in the left background is the Opera House, which a journalist described as "the largest and finest on this continent," and he found the street "the only one in New Orleans that has preserved the style and 'cachet' of the old French founders of the Gallic colony."

52 A composite view of typical Canal Street buildings standing in 1873 when *Jewell's Crescent City Illustrated* was published. These were clipped from advertisements and several are still standing.

52

53

53 A crowd of the curious are looking at the ruins left by a great fire on Canal Street, which destroyed most of the block on February 16, 1892. Visible is the burned-out Kreeger store to the left. The iron framework to the right was one of several 150-foot towers that had been originally erected, mostly in the business or American section, to carry electric wires. They were used for a few years to support ten thousand candlepower streetlamps. *Photo by C. Milo Williams*

54 A strange sight on Canal Street looking toward Carondelet Street in February 14, 1895. New Orleans's great snowstorm that day was an event that no one who experienced it ever forgot. Eight inches fell before midnight of the day before, all streetcar traffic was halted, and cars were abandoned on their tracks, while children threw snowballs, and improvised sleds made their appearance.

54

55

56

55 Just off Canal perpendicularly is Royal Street, looking toward Iberville, about 1905. The building to the right is the Merchants' Exchange, part of the lower floor of which was occupied by George Springer's New Royal Café. Adjoining it is the old Union Bank building, in which George Schroth sold shoes. Across Iberville Street is the Commercial Hotel, predecessor of the Monteleone Hotel. Solari's fancy grocery is across the street, and Fabacher's restaurant close by. Two boys are riding on the ice wagon, and one of them is undeniably sucking at a piece of ice. Today all the buildings on the right are gone, as is Solari's. *Courtesy Library of Congress*

56 At the opposite end of the French Quarter, moving away from Canal, is Esplanade Avenue, the historic residence portion of the city in later Creole days. Says a writer in the *Picayune's Guide to New Orleans* (1903 edition):

It is one of the most beautiful streets in New Orleans, and is to the Creoles what St. Charles Avenue is to the Americans—the aristocratic residence street. The avenue, through its entire length, from the river to Bayou St. John, is lined on either side of the car tracks with a continuous row of shade trees, which makes the street very pretty and attractive. The homes in the avenue are the center of Creole culture and refinement; fine old furnishings of the Louis Quatorze style adorn the interiors. Many romantic stories cluster about these homes and it is here, if you are so fortunate as to have a friend who can gain you admittance to the exclusive society of the old French Quarter, that you will see Creole beauty and society at its best.

The view is of Esplanade Avenue near Burgundy Street, 1900. *Courtesy Library of Congress*

57 Canal Street at night, about 1937. Rampart Street is at the corner of the Saenger Theatre, followed by Burgundy, Dauphine, and Bourbon streets. The Maison Blanche dominates the skyline. Canada Dry and Jax were competing for the attention of passersby, and the Saenger was playing *Gold Rush Masie* with Ann Sothern, and Lowe's featured Myrna Loy and William Powell in *I Love You Again. Photo by Charles Gennella*

58 Revamped Canal Street with four sets of streetcar tracks. This scene, made in 1947, was taken from a building overlooking Carondelet Street, in foreground. Canal had undergone a beautification program in 1930, costing $3½ million. From the river to Claiborne Avenue, for twenty blocks, the street was repaved, the sidewalks and neutral grounds being done in terrazzo, and new ornamental light standards—each with the French, Spanish, Confederate, and American insignia decorating their cast-iron bases—were installed. *Courtesy New Orleans Public Service, Inc.*

57

58

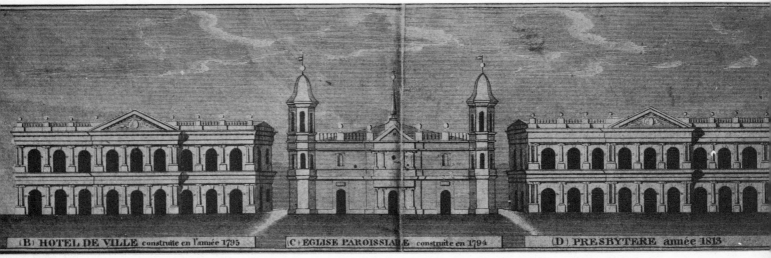

(B) HOTEL DE VILLE construite en l'année 1795   **(C) EGLISE PAROISSIALE** construite en 1794   **(D) PRESBYTERE** année 1813

59

59 New Orleans's proudest historical and architectural heritage is Jackson Square and the five buildings bordering it—the Cabildo, the St. Louis Cathedral, and the Presbytère, which face it, all above; and the faded red-brick structures, not shown here since they were begun in 1849–1850, known as the Pontalba Buildings, which flank it. Laid out by Adrien de Pauger in 1721 as the Place d'Armes, the square was used as a military parade ground for many years. During the two and a half centuries that have passed, the character of the buildings bordering it have changed several times, and the square itself has undergone several transformations. From a map by Jacques Tanesse, 1817. *Courtesy Richard Koch*

60 When G. W. Sully made this view of the Place d'Armes from the river in 1836, the three rows of maple trees that had been planted on each side of the Place d'Armes in 1806 had grown quite large. This sketch also shows a fountain in the center of the square. *Courtesy Howard-Tilton Memorial Library, Tulane University*

60

61

61 The Place d'Armes looked like this in 1845. Lithograph by Thomas Williams. The Cathedral is ornamented with a central steeple, with its bell-shaped roof. The fountain in the center of the square has disappeared, and the Place is a parade ground with soldiers drilling. The picture was evidently made in winter, as the rows of maples on each side of the square are bare.

62 Directly behind the Cabildo is the Arsenal, constructed as a state armory from plans of Dakin and Dakin in 1839. Its striking Greek Revival design makes it an interesting landmark. From 1846 until the Civil War, it was used by the Orleans Artillery. In 1858, it was seized by the vigilance committee; in 1860, it was used as headquarters for General P. G. T. Beauregard, adjutant general of Louisiana. In the early days of the Civil War, the Confederates used it to store military supplies, and after the occupation of New Orleans by the Federals it became a military prison. During Reconstruction times, the Metropolitan Police used it, and it was to its sheltering walls that they fled after their hasty retreat in a battle, September 14, 1874, on the riverfront. In later years it was used by the reorganized Orleans Artillery and as a state arsenal. On March 15, 1914, it was transferred to the Louisiana State Museum. *Photo by Richard Koch*

62

63

64

63 In 1849, Gaston de Pontalba, who had come to New Orleans from France, sketched the Place d'Armes to show the newly added mansard roofs on the Cabildo and the Presbytère. *Courtesy Louisiana State Museum*

64 The Cabildo. It was erected in 1796–1799 during the last years of the Spanish regime. On December 20, 1803, in its Sala Capitular on the second floor was signed the *procès verbal,* by which the formal transfer of Louisiana from France to the United States was effected. From 1803 to 1853, it served as the New Orleans city hall. At various times it has housed several libraries, a fire station, a police station, a police court, the city notary, and, from 1853 to 1911, the Supreme Court of the state of Louisiana. At its rear was a prison and later a police jail. In 1825, it was briefly converted into a fine residence for General Lafayette when he visited the city. Since 1911, it has become part of the Louisiana State Museum.

Note the addition of the mansard roof, in 1847. Through the years the Cabildo has been remodeled several times, but except for the roof the original character of the building remains largely unchanged. The American emblems on the pediment were added in 1821, the work of the Italian sculptor Pietro Cardelli. The wrought-iron-balcony rails, perhaps the finest of the Spanish period in New Orleans, were made locally by Marcellino Hernandez. The Cabildo had greatly deteriorated by the early 1960s, and $800,000 was appropriated by the state to repair it. Intensive restoration work was undertaken during 1966–1969, and the building was once again opened to the public in April, 1970.

65 In January, 1851, the city council changed the name of the Place d'Armes to Jackson Square in honor of the hero of the Battle of New Orleans, fulfilling a longtime desire of many citizens of the city. In fact, on General Jackson's visit to New Orleans in 1840, he had laid a cornerstone on January 13 for a monument to him to be erected in the square. Little had been done about setting up the Jackson memorial for a decade, but with the interest stimulated by the Baroness Pontalba's buildings the Jackson Monument Association renewed its efforts to raise funds. Eventually they got an appropriation of $10,000 from the legislature to aid the project. In 1856, Clark Mills's equestrian statue of Jackson was unveiled. This statue is one of three, the first cast for Lafayette Square in Washington and the third stands in Nashville, Tennessee. It is one of few equestrian statues in which the horse stands on his hind legs without the support of the tail or by the addition of a supporting rod. Strangely, the monument does not bear the name of General Jackson, but the inscription, "The union must and shall be preserved," a quotation from Jackson, was engraved on it at the order of General Butler when the city of New

Orleans was captured by federal forces in April, 1862. *Photo by Charles F. Weber*

66 After the equestrian statue of General Andrew Jackson was dedicated, the square was laid out as an attractive French formal garden, which we see in this lithograph by Louis Schwarz, which also shows the completed Pontalba Buildings—two block-long, three-storied row houses on each side of Jackson Square. These were erected by Micaela, Baroness de Pontalba, the daughter of Don Andrés Almonester y Roxas, from whom she had inherited the sites. Although she had lived in France since her marriage at sixteen, the baroness returned to New Orleans in 1848, and in 1849–1850 let contracts for the construction of the houses. They were designed by architect Henry Howard after the owner had had differences with James Gallier, whom she had at first consulted; but the baroness did most of the supervision herself while the buildings were being erected. The two structures, each of which contained sixteen houses, cost $302,000.

65

66

67

68

67 Close-up of the lower Pontalba Building. *Photo by Ray Cresson*

68 One of the most notable features of the Pontalba Buildings is the beautiful cast-iron railings of the galleries. The entwined "AP," which stands for Almonester and Pontalba, and the scrollwork were designed by the baroness herself, a fact documented by one of the builder's draftsmen who worked on the job. *Photo by Stuart Lynn*

69 Micaela, Baroness de Pontalba (1795–1874), as she appeared in later life. *Photo courtesy Baron Alfred de Pontalba*

69

70

71

70 One of the most interesting buildings in New Orleans, architecturally and historically, is the United States Custom House on Canal and Decatur streets, near the river. Designed by architect Alexander T. Wood, its massive granite facade features a harmonious combination of Greek Corinthian columns on Roman bases surmounted by lotus-type Egyptian capitals. Although construction started in 1848, the work stopped at the time of the Civil War and the building looked like this in 1873. *From* Jewell's Crescent City Illustrated

71 The original New Orleans Custom House, located in the upper section of the original city near the river, watercolor by Samuel Wilson, Jr. Built in 1807–1809—from the design of Benjamin H. B. Latrobe—by Robert Alexander at a cost of $19,000, this building was a small, simple edifice of red Philadelphia brick, with stone trim. It was one of the first American classical revival designs to be erected in New Orleans. A poor foundation and other factors caused its rapid decay, and when Jackson came to New Orleans, the building was falling apart. It was demolished about 1819. *Courtesy artist*

72

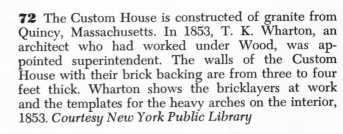

72 The Custom House is constructed of granite from Quincy, Massachusetts. In 1853, T. K. Wharton, an architect who had worked under Wood, was appointed superintendent. The walls of the Custom House with their brick backing are from three to four feet thick. Wharton shows the bricklayers at work and the templates for the heavy arches on the interior, 1853. *Courtesy New York Public Library*

73 The Marble Hall of the Custom House, 1901. This room, once termed "the finest business room in the world," is 95 by 125 feet and 54 feet high. Its ceiling is supported by fourteen lofty Corinthian columns forty-one feet high and four feet in diameter, which cost $15,000 each. *Courtesy Library of Congress*

74 Detail of the magnificently carved Corinthian capitals in the Marble Hall. These feature an image of Mercury, god of commerce (shown in the photograph) and Luna, goddess of the moon, always shown with a crescent on her brow, an allusion to the crescent bend of the Mississippi at New Orleans. *Photo by H. G. Richey*

75 At one end of the Marble Hall is a well-executed bas-relief carving of the great seal of Louisiana over an allegorical sculpture of a plow, for agriculture, a cog-wheel for industry, and a cask of sugar and bales of cotton for the state's principal crops. To the left is a life-size figure of Bienville, the city's founder and to the right is General Andrew Jackson, the city's defender in 1814–1815. *Photo by H. G. Richey*

73   **74**

75

76

76 Rebel prisoners in the New Orleans Custom House, sketch by J. R. Hamilton. The Custom House had several uses. It was the city's main post office from 1860 until 1906, and it served as a factory for the manufacture of shells and gun carriages during the early days of the Civil War. When Farragut landed in New Orleans, a mob broke into the building and looted the post office, and during the occupation of New Orleans it served as a Union prison, confining about two thousand Confederate prisoners of war. *From* Harper's Weekly, *August 29, 1863*

77 Like most New Orleans buildings built before piling came into use, the Custom House has settled, as careful measurements show, more than three feet. An apocryphal story, circulated by guides and still current, has the foundation resting on cotton bales. Actually, the building's foundation is built on a grillage of heavy timbers. Work was again started on the building after the Civil War and it was completed in 1881. At that time it had cost $4,179,854, but since then more than a million has been expended in alterations and improvements. This photograph was taken by Mugnier, ca. 1895.

77

78

79

78 The first St. Louis Church, the first permanent church in the newly founded town of New Orleans, as it appeared in the 1730s. It was designed by Adrien de Pauger, the French engineer who had come in 1721 to lay out the town's streets. Started in 1724, after many delays, the new church was dedicated three years later, at Christmastime, 1727. Unfortunately, Pauger did not live to see his creation complete; he had died the year before and was buried under the incomplete church. During the six decades that the church stood, there worshiped within its walls French Governors Périer, Bienville, Vaudreuil, and Kerlérec and Spanish Governors Unzaga, Gálvez, and Miró. In this first little church were baptized the children of the colonists and the children of the slaves. Here were married the lowly and the highborn, and through its doors were borne the mortal remains of the faithful for the burial rites of the Holy Mother Church on the journey to the cemetery on St. Peter Street. The church, with much of New Orleans, burned to the ground in the great fire of March 21, 1788. This restoration drawing by Boyd Denver was based on Adrien de Pauger's original plans in the French National Archives, Paris.

79 Old Cathedral of St. Louis, the second church of St. Louis, at the Place d'Armes, lithograph by Adrien Persac. It was the gift of the wealthy Don Andrés Almonester y Roxas, and was designed by Gilberto Guillemard, a Frenchman in the military service of Spain. Started in 1789, it was much larger than the first church and was a rather low, flat-roofed building flanked by bell-capped hexagonal towers, but without the central spire seen here (it was added in 1819–1820). The work dragged on, and it was not until five years had elapsed that the church was dedicated as a cathedral on Christmas Eve, 1794. By great good fortune, the new church was spared destruction for New Orleans had had a second great fire in early December when 212 buildings in the upper section of the Vieux Carré were destroyed. Almonester's cathedral served until 1849 when the church was found to be in such poor condition that it had to be rebuilt. The building to the left is the Cabildo and on the right is the Presbytère, the last completed. *Courtesy Howard-Tilton Memorial Library, Tulane University*

80 The rebuilt St. Louis Cathedral immediately after completion, flanked by the Cabildo and Presbytère in 1852. Lithograph by X. Magny. At first the architect, J. N. B. de Pouilly, and John Kirwin, an Irish builder, were to rebuild the original church. But structural faults were found in the walls of the old building and it was demolished; the architect redesigned the church making it wider and longer. During construction, the central tower of the new church fell, causing considerable damage, and the architect and builder were dismissed. The church was then finished by architect-builder Alexander H. Sampson. The Cathedral was

80

completed and blessed on December 7, 1851. De Pouilly's design here indicates the central spire with spidery tracery of wood and iron. This did not prove practical, and the steeple was enclosed in a weather-proof covering of slate in 1859.

81 With the influx of the American element after the Louisiana Purchase, Protestant churches began to appear—Baptists in 1816, Presbyterians in 1817, Metho-

dists in 1818. With the coming of the Germans, the first Lutheran churches were established, the earliest in 1829. Parson Clapp's church, seen here, was known as the Strangers' Church since nearly every Protestant visitor went to hear Mr. Clapp. It was situated on St. Charles Street between Gravier and Union. This lithograph shows the church as it was in the 1820s. Parson Clapp was originally a Presbyterian minister who ran into difficulties with his congregation, some of them leaving to form the First Presbyterian Church. He continued to preach as a Unitarian in this building. The building was eventually destroyed in the great fire, which burned down the St. Charles Hotel in 1851. The first synagogue for Jews was organized in 1828, although there had been Jews in New Orleans before the Louisiana Purchase, and the Christian Science denomination established its first church in 1895. Today practically all denominations are represented, and there are more than six hundred Protestant and non-Catholic churches, big and little, in the city, besides some one hundred Catholic churches. Lithograph by Félix-Achille Beaupoil de Saint-Aulaire. *Bibliothèque Nationale, Paris*

81

82

84

82 83 The Mortuary Chapel of St. Anthony, Rampart Street, in 1890 and before, the oldest church building in New Orleans, built in 1826 when funerals were forbidden to be held in the St. Louis Cathedral because of fear of yellow-fever contagion. Father Francis Turgis, Confederate army chaplain, served as pastor after the Civil War, and in 1875 it became a church for Italians. In 1918, it was renamed Our Lady of Guadeloupe, and since that time it has become the official chapel of New Orleans's police and fire departments.

83

84 85 St. Patrick's Church, Camp Street, 1873. The first building was a frame structure. St. Patrick's, established in 1833, is the second oldest Catholic congregation in the city and the first Catholic church established for English-speaking members of that faith. When the first pastor of the church died, he was succeeded by Father James Ignatius Mullen, whose driving enthusiasm led his Irish immigrant followers to build the present church, completed in 1841. The original design was by the architectural firm of Dakin and Dakin, but they withdrew during the construction of the church and it was finished by the celebrated James Gallier. St. Patrick's is an impressive edifice; its tower, 185 feet high (the equivalent of an eighteen-story building), was for years the highest structure in New Orleans, and its interior, patterned after the

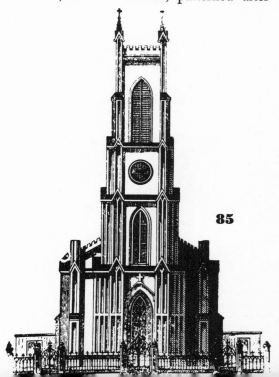

85

English Gothic churches of York Minster and Exeter Cathedral, was further ornamented by a beautiful altar and by three fine murals painted by Leon Pomarède, a talented artist of French birth who lived in the city at the time. Through the years, the character of St. Patrick's congregation has changed. The Irish, who lived in the neighborhood, long ago moved away as the section became more and more commercial. But St. Patrick's has many loyal members, and many Catholics from other parishes worship there since they love the old church. *From* Jewell's Crescent City Illustrated

86 St. Patrick's main altar, designed by James Gallier.

Pomarède's huge murals are in the background. *Photo by Guy F. Bernard*

87 This bird's-eye view of New Orleans was made about 1895 by George F. Mugnier, who probably photographed it from the steeple of St. John the Baptist Catholic Church. St. Patrick's Church spires (*left center*) at Camp Street, the Lee monument (*right center*), and the shot tower (*to the right and above*) are plainly visible. The shot tower, at the corner of Constance and St. Joseph streets, was at that time the highest building in New Orleans (214 feet); an anonymous writer in the *Historical Sketch Book*

and Guide to New Orleans in 1885 described a trip in a little elevator to the topmost room where molten lead was dropped to form shot. *Courtesy Samuel Wilson, Jr.*

88 The third Christ Church (1873), demolished in 1883, a New Orleans landmark for many years. The mother church of Protestantism in New Orleans, it had its beginnings in 1805 when a number of Protestants met and decided by vote to affiliate with the Episcopalian denomination. Their first church was erected at Canal and Bourbon streets, but was demolished in 1835, and another, designed by Gallier and Dakin, was built on the site. In 1847, that church was sold to Judah Touro, and this third church designed by T. K. Wharton was built on the corner of Canal and Dauphine streets. This church, of Gothic design, served the congregation until the site was sold and the present Christ Church Cathedral erected at St. Charles Avenue and Sixth Street. The original site is occupied by the Maison Blanche department store.

89 Old Church of the Immaculate Conception, Baronne Street, built between 1851 and 1857, photographed by Charles L. Franck about 1925. Designed by Father John Cambioso of the Jesuit Order, this unusual building is Moresque in style. Father Cambioso employed cast iron for the columns and pews and for the dome of the church. In 1928, it was closed because of structural weaknesses, and a new church of virtually the same design was constructed on the site, using much of the cast iron of the old church. The present church is noted for its impressive bronze Moresque altar, designed in 1870 by the architect James Freret, its stations of the cross in stained glass, and its bronze statue of St. Peter, whose foot has almost been kissed away by visitors through the years.

90 First Presbyterian Church, Lafayette Square, originally established in New Orleans in 1818. Built in 1854 at a cost of $87,000, this impressive building with its lofty spire was a New Orleans landmark until its demolition to build the present Federal Building. From the pulpit of the First Presbyterian, the celebrated Dr. B. M. Palmer preached during his long ministry beginning in 1856 until the close of the century. *Photo by L. E. Cormier*

91 First Presbyterian Church, 5401 S. Claiborne Avenue. This building incorporates parts of the second edifice on Lafayette Square, demolished to make way for the Federal Building. *Courtesy New Orleans Public Library*

92 Another example of the excellent brickwork in nineteenth-century New Orleans churches is that of the Jackson Avenue Evangelical Church on the corner of Jackson Avenue and Chippewa Street. Since the photograph was made in 1910, the church has lost its lofty spire. *Photo by L. E. Cormier*

88

89

90

91

92

93 Christ Church Cathedral, 2919 St. Charles Avenue, about 1910. The steeple was destroyed in the great storm of September, 1915, and never rebuilt. *Courtesy New Orleans Public Library*

93

94

94 New Orleans had an unusual grouping in one uptown section (the Irish Channel) of three Catholic churches: St. Alphonsus (1855), St. Mary's Assumption (1858), both still standing, and the Church of Notre Dame de Bon Secours (1858), since demolished. St. Alphonsus was the Irish church, St. Mary's the German, and Notre Dame the French, each serving the faithful of these nationalities who had settled

95

96

in the neighborhood during the era of heavy immigration. This view shows the clock tower of St. Mary's, an extremely fine example of New Orleans brickwork. *Photo by Richard Koch*

95 St. Mary's Roman Catholic Church, built by German immigrant Catholics in German Baroque style. Damaged heavily by hurricane Betsy a few years ago, it will now be repaired and restored. Note the tower of St. Mary's Assumption in the background. *Photo by G. E. Arnold*

96 View of St. Mary's Church showing the high altar. *Photo by G. E. Arnold*

116

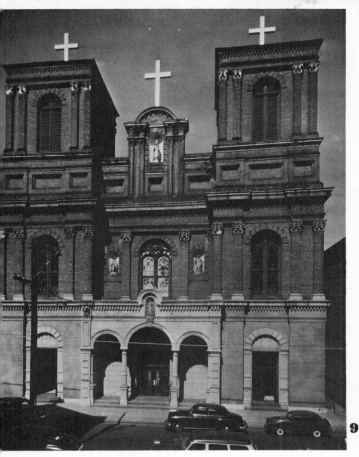

97 St. Alphonsus Church, ca. 1945. *Photo by Charles L. Franck*

98 St. Alphonsus's impressive interior was in the florid Renaissance style, ca. 1910. *Photo by E. Claudel*

99 Easter decoration of the altar in a German Protestant church (probably First Evangelical), about 1895. The words "Christ Is Risen" (in German) are spelled out in flowers. There is a floral cross in front of the altar, and palms are used in profusion.

100 The First Baptist Church, 4301 St. Charles Avenue, erected in 1952, is one of the leading congregations of this denomination. Its pastor is Dr. J. D. Grey, one of the most prominent Protestant ministers in New Orleans. *Courtesy Times-Picayune*

101

101 Holy Name of Jesus Church, with its soaring tower, erected in 1914. This handsome edifice, a memorial to the McDermott family, is adjacent to the Loyola University campus. *Courtesy Loyola University of the South*

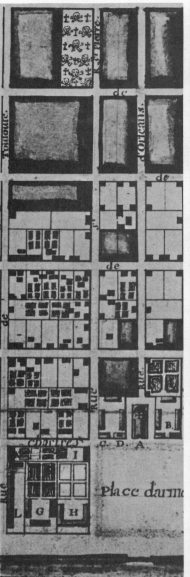

102

103

104

Cities of the Dead

102 103 When the French founded New Orleans in 1718, burials were made along the riverbank. In 1721, when Adrien de Pauger laid out the town, he designated a cemetery on its outskirts. An early plan of New Orleans dated May 20, 1725, shows the cemetery as extending along the upper side of St. Peter Street between the streets we now know as Burgundy and Rampart. Burial in this cemetery was entirely below ground, and because it was in a low and swampy site the area was surrounded by ditches and the earth from the ditches used to raise the level of the land. The cemetery was fenced with a wooden palisade and later by a brick wall. This cemetery served colonial New Orleans until St. Louis Cemetery No. 1 was

118

106

105

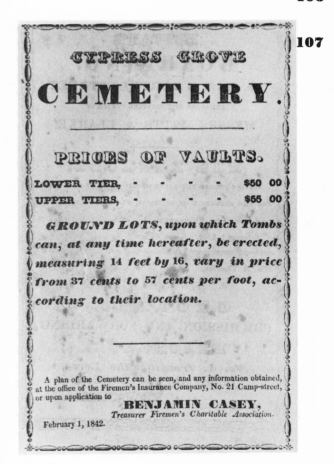

107

opened in 1788. This was eventually leveled and the land sold for building lots. Gonichon's plan of 1731 shows a path leading to the cemetery from Orleans Street. *Courtesy Samuel Wilson, Jr.*

104 105 Part of a row of vaults in St. Louis Cemetery No. 1 and plastered brick tombs in the same cemetery. It was in St. Louis Cemetery No. 1 that aboveground vaults and tombs first appeared. The Spaniards enclosed their colonial cemeteries in other parts of the world under their domination with walls containing vaults, and as New Orleans at that time was under the rule of Spain it was natural that this custom be adopted, especially since the marshy character of the soil and the heavy annual rainfall made ground interments less than desirable. The New Orleans tomb is but a series of several vaults (usually two with a receptacle below), one on top of the other. Built of brick and plastered to preserve the masonry, these tombs resembled miniature houses, and those families who could afford them had them erected.

106 107 Sketch of the type of wall vaults common in most old New Orleans cemeteries, and an advertisement. New Orleans's faubourgs, or suburbs, Ste. Marie, Lafayette, Bouligny, Hurstville, and Carrollton each had one or more cemeteries, inevitably platted on the outskirts of the living. Thus came into existence Lafayette Cemetery No. 1 in 1833, St. Joseph's in 1850, Lafayette No. 2 in 1853 (these three are on Washington Avenue), Carrollton in 1848, and St. Vincent's on Soniat in 1850. Below Canal Street, besides St. Louis No. 1 and No. 2, St. Louis No. 3 on Esplanade Avenue was chartered in 1856. St. Roch Cemetery was not laid out until 1868. *From* History of the Yellow Fever in New Orleans, *Summer, 1853. Courtesy Howard-Tilton Memorial Library, Tulane University*

108

109

110

108 St. Louis Cemetery No. 2, photograph taken about 1890 by Mugnier. Its wall vaults and its crowded tombs gave rise to the expression "Cities of the Dead." Cemetery No. 1 was filled by 1820, and the city authorities had decided that another cemetery was needed. Cemetery No. 2 was built at the edge of town on what is now Claiborne Avenue between Canal, St. Louis, and Robertson streets (four squares originally, later reduced to three). The new cemetery, consecrated by the church in August, 1823, like its predecessor, was surrounded with oven vaults (called "fours" by the Creoles). The city had grown in population and wealth, and in the succeeding thirty years the cemetery was filled with private family tombs, some strikingly handsome.

109 110 Avet and Lazzize tomb and Pilié tomb in St. Louis Cemetery No. 2 are among the most striking examples of wrought-iron work to be found in New Orleans. By the middle of the nineteenth century, iron craftsmanship in the city had developed to a high degree and much of it was lavished on the tombs. *Photo by Guy F. Bernard*

111 The Plauché tomb in St. Louis Cemetery No. 2, typical of the Greek Revival designs that J. N. B. de Pouilly designed. Many of the more elaborate tombs were designed by De Pouilly, who had come to New Orleans in the 1830s from France. De Pouilly, who had designed the St. Louis Exchange Hotel and the present St. Louis Cathedral, had brought with him a book of scale drawings of the best-known tombs in Père Lachaise Cemetery in Paris, which at that time was at the summit of Greek Revival design in the field of cemetery memorials. That book and a scrapbook containing De Pouilly's sketches still exist, and it is possible to trace the influence of the monuments in Père Lachaise on the work that De Pouilly did for his New Orleans clients. Other *marbriers*—marble cutters and tomb builders—soon imitated De Pouilly's designs, thus creating a style of mortuary architecture which, with improvements, has continued to this day. *Photo by Charles A. Lawhon*

111

112

112 Decorating the tombs in St. Louis Cemetery No. 2 on All Saints' Day, woodcut from a sketch by John Durkin. All Saints' Day, November 1, is New Orleans's Memorial Day. For several weeks prior, the older cemeteries would hum with activity. Weeds, which grew rank in some New Orleans cemeteries, were cut down, tombs patched and freshly whitewashed. The tap-tap of the marble cutter's mallet was heard, for the names of those who recently took up residence had to be carved. Vases of marble, cement, glass, and even bottles were brought. Then came the great day! Thousands and thousands of chrysanthemums were brought to the cemeteries and reverently placed at the tombs. From morning to late afternoon the cemeteries were thronged and by nightfall became huge bowers of flowers.

Customs have changed somewhat since those times. No longer are tombs draped in black and decorated with flags, and the nuns and orphans have vanished with the coming of the United Fund, but the custom of visitation and the bringing of flowers on All Saints' Day is still a distinctive New Orleans observance. *From* Harper's Weekly, *November 7, 1885*

113 The Girod Street, or Protestant, Cemetery, which had its beginning in 1822 at just about the same time as St. Louis No. 2. A rectangular piece of land in the

113

Faubourg Ste. Marie, fronting on what is now South Liberty Street between Perrilliat and Cypress streets, was bought from the city, a cemetery laid out in the 3½-acre tract, and remains removed from the Protestant section of St. Louis No. 1. This cemetery, which was owned by Christ Church, like its Creole predecessor was surrounded by walls and contained 2,319 vaults. During its 135 years' existence, about one thousand family tombs and more than a hundred tombs of benevolent societies were erected. Girod was the yellow fever and cholera cemetery; in it were buried thousands of victims of the epidemics that scourged New Orleans in the mid-nineteenth century. This view of the Girod Street Cemetery shows a man rowing a skiff with a coffin in it because the place was flooded. The cemetery was demolished in 1957. *From* History of the Yellow Fever in New Orleans, *Summer, 1853. Courtesy Howard-Tilton Memorial Library, Tulane University*

114 In the nineteenth century, it was customary for groups of friends or people of similar nationalities, or those who belonged to certain trade or religious or social organizations, to band together into mutual benevolent societies for the purpose of providing medical assistance (doctors and medicine), burial insurance, and, in many instances, entombment facilities. There were about fifty of these among the white inhabitants of New Orleans in the mid-nineteenth century, and one of the most prominent was the New

Lusitanos Benevolent Association, which erected a handsome tomb for the benefit of its six hundred members. This rare photograph shows the tomb decorated with black and silver draperies, probably at its dedication in 1859. Three of its officers in frock coats and top hats proudly pose before it. *Photo by J. D. Edwards Gallery of Photographic Art*

115 A whole colony of cemeteries (they were eventually to number fourteen) took root at the end of Canal Street. One of these was Cypress Grove. The entrance with its Egyptian-style pylons and sextons' offices is very much as it was a century ago. The Firemen's Charitable and Benevolent Association, volunteer fire fighters, started Cypress Grove in 1840 (and Greenwood in 1849). The Irish Congregation of St. Patrick's Church opened the St. Patrick Cemeteries in 1841; the Charity Hospital or Potter's Field for the indigent dead started in 1847 and The Odd Fellows' Rest opened in 1849. The Dispersed of Judah was founded in 1846, and St. John, then called the First German Evangelical Lutheran Cemetery, the second Protestant burial ground in New Orleans, came into existence in 1867. From a lithograph probably made about 1860. *Photo by Guy F. Bernard. Courtesy Howard-Tilton Memorial Library*

116 The Leeds family tomb (1844) in Cypress Grove Cemetery. Iron for the construction of buildings came into use about the middle of the nineteenth century,

114

and in New Orleans the material was employed in the construction of tombs. *Photo by Guy F. Bernard*

117 Métairie Cemetery. After the demise of the Métairie Jockey Club in 1872, a syndicate of New Orleans's businessmen formed the Métairie Cemetery Association and turned the erstwhile Métairie racecourse into New Orleans's largest and most elaborate burial ground. Memorials to the Army of Tennessee, the Army of Northern Virginia, and the Washington Artillery are features of Métairie, and many of the city's most prominent families own tombs there. Now nearing the century mark in age, Métairie's four thousand characteristic aboveground family vaults or tombs and an equal number of ground plots rank it among the most impressive cemeteries of the nation.

118

118 The Langlés cenotaph and its puzzling inscription at the base, "ANGELE MARIE LANGLES 105 La. 39," Métairie Cemetery. Angèle Langlés and her mother Pauline Costa Langlés were well-to-do residents of New Orleans. Planning a trip to France, they both made wills before sailing on the French steamer *La Bourgogne*. Two days out of New York on July 4, 1898, the steamer sank, with the loss of more than five hundred lives, the Langlés among them. Since the wills of both women involved different sets of heirs, the courts were called upon to decide which of them had died first. A lengthy legal dispute arose, and the case eventually went to the Louisiana Supreme Court. The court's decision was that the daughter, being younger, was presumed to have survived the mother. Since the daughter's will had called for the erection of a "tomb" for herself, the court, against the wishes of the heirs, ordered that the sum of $3,000 from her estate be used for the purpose of erecting a cenotaph in her memory. The executor of her estate caused her name and legal reference to the case to be engraved on this monument to suggest that all who pass might learn the circumstances under which the memorial was erected and read the opinion of the Supreme Court of Louisiana commanding its construction.

119

119 The descendants of the Creoles went into "deep mourning" when a member of the family died. This widow and her daughters, in full mourning, are carrying flowers and wreaths to adorn the graves of their relatives. Many of the burial sites in the older cemeteries were graced with funerary ornaments (floral emblems or immortelles) fashioned of wire, beads, and glass to form "everlasting" designs. They were used instead of fresh flowers and so impressed Mark Twain on a visit to the city in the 1880s that he wrote of them: "The immortelle requires no attention; you just hang it up, and there you are; just leave it alone, it will take care of your grief for you and keep it in mind better than you can; stands weather first rate, and lasts like boiler iron." *From* Frank Leslie's Illustrated Newspaper, *April 25, 1863*

120 A typical New Orleans street corner death notice, 1896.

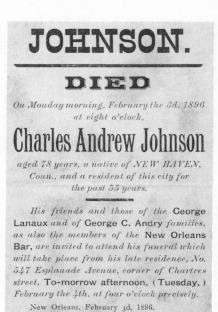

120

JOHNSON.

DIED

On Monday morning, February the 3d, 1896 at eight o'clock,

Charles Andrew Johnson

aged 78 years, a native of NEW HAVEN, Conn., and a resident of this city for the past 55 years.

His friends and those of the **George Lanaux** *and of* **George C. Andry** *families, as also the members of the* **New Orleans Bar,** *are invited to attend his funeral which will take place from his late residence, No. 547 Esplanade Avenue, corner of Chartres street,* **To-morrow afternoon,** (Tuesday,) *February the 4th, at four o'clock precisely.*

New Orleans, February 3d, 1896.

121

121 Reading a New Orleans death notice, 1890s. These black-bordered announcements, which were also invitations for the friends of the deceased to attend the last services, were generally tacked on buildings or lampposts.

Indigenous Architecture

122 The architecture of many of the oldest houses in New Orleans, particularly those in the Vieux Carré, is a blending of French, Spanish, and American styles, which have been adapted to the climate and soil conditions of the city. The French influence predominates, but one can discern Spanish touches and American adaptations in a great many structures. This is the Mérieult house, 527 Royal Street, built in 1792, which somehow survived the second great New Orleans fire in 1794. In the 1830s, the house was extensively remodeled and the Quincy granite pilasters, which are so characteristic of commercial buildings of the time in New Orleans, were substituted for earlier brick arches. *Photo by Dan S. Leyrer. Courtesy The Vieux Carré Survey*

123

123 Lafitte's Blacksmith Shop, 941 Bourbon Street. When this photograph was made in 1938, enough of the plaster from the wall had fallen away to show clearly the "brick-between-posts" construction, which was commonly used by French builders and continued by their successors. Unfortunately for a good story, no historical evidence links the pirate Jean Lafitte with this cottage. *Photo by Rudolf Hertzberg. Courtesy Howard-Tilton Memorial Library, Tulane University*

124 The Absinthe House, 327 Bourbon Street. This is a fine example of early nineteenth–century New Orleans combined commercial and residential building, with an intermediate floor, or *entresol*, and lighted by

122

124

126

125

the fanlight transoms of the doors on the ground floor. The structure was built about 1806 and is notable for its fine wrought-iron balcony railing and supporting brackets. For many years it housed a marble bar, which was deeply pitted in places by the thousands of absinthe drinks the bartenders frappéed on it. *Courtesy Library of Congress*

125 This quaint building served as a courthouse in which General Andrew Jackson was tried and fined $1,000 for contempt of court by Judge Dominick A. Hall. Jackson had resisted writs issued by Hall after the general had jailed Louis Louallier, a member of the Louisiana Legislature, who wrote in the *Louisiana Courier* against continuing martial law weeks after the Battle of New Orleans was over. This house was demolished in 1888. Sketch by Joseph Pennell, 1883.

126 A notable example of fine wrought-iron work adorns the gallery of the old building 337–343 Royal Street, which once housed the Branch Bank of the United States. This structure was erected about 1799 during the Spanish regime and is one of the few surviving from the period. *Photo by Rudolf Hertzberg. Courtesy Howard-Tilton Memorial Library, Tulane University*

127 New Orleans iron lace—cast-iron railing at 2103–2105 Baronne Street. *Photo by Guy F. Bernard*

127

126

128

128 Another well-known French Quarter building is the Lalaurie House, 1140 Royal Street. Called the "Haunted House" from the tale of slaves tortured by their mistress, the building was sacked by an infuriated mob in 1834 and reconstructed in its present form after that date. This photograph, made about 1906, shows that the corner downstairs was occupied at that time by a saloonkeeper by the name of F. Greco, who called it appropriately "Haunted Saloon." *Courtesy Library of Congress*

129 The stately Le Carpentier–Beauregard house, 1113 Chartres Street, erected in 1826. Confederate General P. G. T. Beauregard lived here a short time after the Civil War. The house and its adjacent garden were restored by the writer Frances Parkinson Keyes.

129

130

When this photograph was taken in 1903, Chartres Street was still surfaced with large Belgian granite blocks with which many New Orleans streets were paved during the nineteenth century. *Courtesy Library of Congress*

130 The Grima House, 820 St. Louis Street, now the Christian Woman's Exchange. It was built in 1831 by William Brand, an American architect-builder who had come to New Orleans a quarter of a century before. The house suggests the Georgian architecture found in the eastern part of the United States. *Photo by David Nelson*

131 As the city pushed out of its original boundaries, some of the wealthier inhabitants built fine houses on Esplanade. This one, with its pilastered facade, was built on Esplanade and Rampart, which was then called Rue d'Amour (Love Street). *Notarial Archives, City of New Orleans. Courtesy Samuel Wilson, Jr.*

131

132

133

132 The David House, now Le Petit Salon, a women's club, at St. Peter Street, built in 1838. This very fine Greek Revival city house is noted for the well-done detail of its entrance and its interesting ironwork. The bows-and-arrows design of the middle railing balcony is particularly fine. *Photo by Rudolf Hertzberg. Courtesy Howard-Tilton Memorial Library, Tulane University*

133 The iron lace balconies that are synonymous with old New Orleans are in full flower on the Labranche buildings, St. Peter and Royal streets. There are eleven of these buildings, erected in 1840 for the widow of Jean Baptiste Labranche. The cast-iron galleries were added when these became fashionable in the 1850s. *Photo by Rudolf Hertzberg. Courtesy Howard-Tilton Memorial Library, Tulane University*

134 A double parlor in the Vieux Carré. This was the home of the Labatut and Puig families. *Photo by Rudolf Hertzberg. Courtesy Howard-Tilton Memorial Library, Tulane University*

135 The residence of Simon Hernsheim, built in 1881 on St. Charles Avenue and Pine Street, a typical Greek Revival house of the post–Civil War period. Several houses of this type still stand today, although this one was demolished years ago to make way for the Fabacher residence. *Courtesy Library of Congress*

134

135

136

137

138

136 By the early part of the twentieth century, many of the once-proud town houses of the French Quarter had fallen into decay. This is the courtyard of a house on Royal Street, 1906. The two wooden cisterns to the right supplied drinking water. *Courtesy Library of Congress*

137 A typical example of servants' or slave quarters, as they are popularly known. These structures with their characteristic carpenter's chisel roofs generally adjoin or are in the rear of some of the more pretentious houses in the French Quarter.

138 Service quarters, sketch by Joseph Pennell, 1883.

139 For every great house in New Orleans there were of course hundreds of cottages. Even the most humble New Orleanians in the past preferred to live in little houses of their own rather than in quarters of large units, such as row, tenement, or apartment houses. These two small dwellings photographed about 1895 were located at 1926–1928 Bourbon Street and are typical of many cottages erected in the 1850s. The one on the left still retains the characteristics of the cottages in the Vieux Carré with its high-pitched roof, French doors, and batten shutters. The one on the right is a "shotgun" cottage, so called because if one opened the front door and fired a gun, the shot would go straight through the house to the back, since the doors to each room were in a continuous line from front to rear. The houses of this time were built flush on the property line, and the buttresses of the steps and the steps themselves were made of wood and called "box steps."

139

140

142

143

140 Old Spanish house on Orleans Street, sketch by Joseph Pennell, 1883. Most of the small houses of the early nineteenth century were built flush with the sidewalk and had a narrow alleyway at each side leading to the courtyard at the rear. Their plans were generally very simple—two rooms at the front of the house and two at the rear with a loggia or gallery at the back and separate kitchens or servants' quarters in the courtyard.

Generally the houses had steep pitched roofs with gable ends; they were constructed of bricks set between a heavy framework of wooden posts and then plastered. This was done to preserve the comparatively soft, locally-made bricks. Many had French doors and heavy solid shutters, which could be closed against the heat of a summer's day or for protection at night.

141 Typical small shop with adjacent residence, sketch by Joseph Pennell, 1883. The gallery was characteristic of many New Orleans dwellings of the time.

142 This house is typical of many erected in the last half of the nineteenth century. *Photo by C. Milo Williams*

143 A New Orleans "double" cottage (a two-family home) of the late 1890s. The facade of this little Cleveland Avenue house is completely covered with jigsaw ornament.

141

144

145

144 Gallery brackets on double cottages that in the 1870s, 1880s, and 1890s appeared on many New Orleans houses, including some of the least pretentious double cottages. These gingerbreadlike brackets could be purchased by builders from local millwork firms, turned out in dozens of standard designs.

145 This might be called the ultimate in jigsaw decoration. The capitals of the columns and the window cornices of this downtown residence are evidences of the trend in gingerbread ornamentation characteristic of the 1880s and 1890s.

146 The Victorian age spawned some odd architectural creations. This Canal Street baroque house, still standing although shorn of some of its more gorgeous trappings, was the ultimate in 1898 when it was the home of Charles A. Orleans, a successful cemetery-memorial builder.

146

147

148

147 The curious Doullut house, located on Egania Street and overlooking the Mississippi River, was given its name "Steamboat House" because of the resemblance of its cupola to the pilot house of a river steamboat. It was erected in 1905 by Captain Milton Doullut who operated riverboats at the turn of the century. *Photo by Rudolf Hertzberg. Courtesy Howard-Tilton Memorial Library, Tulane University*

148 The most unambitious of the city's folk lived rent and tax free in shacks that they put together of scrap lumber on the batture of the Mississippi. When this picturesque shanty was photographed in the 1890s, the river had risen and was about to enter the dwelling. *Courtesy Mrs. Samuel Wilson, Jr.*

149 While the Vieux Carré Commission, set up by law, jealously guards the buildings in the one-hundred-square area of the French Quarter, and the Garden District Property Owners' Association endeavors to protect buildings in the Garden District from mutilation or demolition, and the New Orleans chapter of

149

the Louisiana Landmarks Society is quick to oppose demolition or mutilation of important landmarks, there have been some notable exceptions when fine old structures have been razed in the name of progress. This handsome Greek Revival structure was erected in 1832–1833 for the Commercial Bank at a cost of $75,000. A writer in the 1842 city directory, describing it, said: "As it is chiefly of brick stuccoed, its durability cannot be counted on." He was entirely wrong as the building stood for a little more than a hundred years. In 1869, it was taken over by the Morgan's Louisiana & Texas Railroad and its successors, the Southern Pacific Company, who used it as headquarters until well into the twentieth century. It was demolished in 1938 to make way for a parking lot.

150 Work on the Moresque Building, which once covered the small square now occupied by the Pan-American and old Times-Picayune buildings on Camp, Poydras, and North streets, was begun in 1859. This unusual three-storied building was constructed with facings of cast iron in the Moorish style. Com-

150

pleted after the Civil War by John Gauche, who conducted a queensware (earthenware) business in it, the building was used until it burned in a spectacular $700,000 fire on April 15, 1897. *From* Jewell's Crescent City Illustrated, *1873*

151 The Story Building, also known as the Wells Fargo Express Building, during this period occupied a site at the corner of Camp and Common streets, now featuring a garage. *From* Jewell's Crescent City Illustrated *1873*

152 New Orleans's favorite grocery store, Solari's, an establishment at the corner of Royal and Iberville streets, founded in 1861. Solari's was in business for nearly a century and boasted a national clientele. Lovers of good food in New Orleans were saddened when the store was demolished in 1961. *Courtesy The Vieux Carré Survey*

153 The office of the New Orleans Gas Company was standing in 1873. This building with its mansard roof and dormer windows was later the home of New Orleans Public Service, Inc. The site at the corner of Baronne and Common streets is now occupied by the Sears department store. *Photo by Charles L. Franck*

151

152

153

154

154 The Abraham Building, erected in the 1880s with Charles Hillger as architect, was an ornate office building, located at the corner of Carondelet and Gravier streets. Its site is now occupied by part of the Richards Center complex. *Photo by Charles L. Franck*

155

155 Another nineteenth-century building, the Liverpool and London and Globe Insurance Company Building, at the corner of Carondelet and Common streets. It occupied the site of the present American Bank Building, for which it was demolished when the bank was erected in 1919. *Photo by Charles L. Franck*

Suburban Architecture

156 City of Lafayette, 1842. In the 1820s as the city continued to expand upstream, the nearby plantations were subdivided into lots and a cluster of faubourgs— Annunciation, Livaudais, and Lafayette—were developed. By 1833, these suburbs were combined by legislative act into the city of Lafayette and local govern-

156

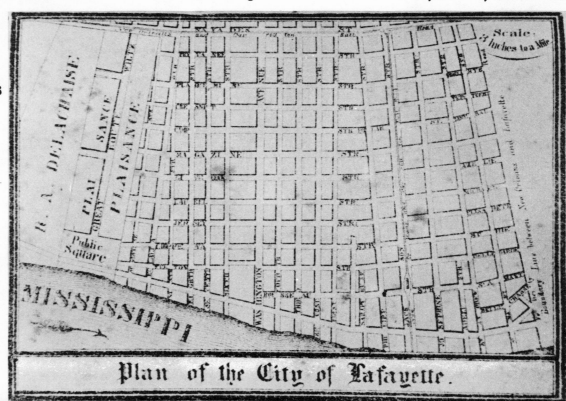

ment set up. The town presented curious contrasts. Along the riverfront there were flatboat and steamboat landings and cattle pens and slaughterhouses; in this neighborhood also settled German and Irish immigrants, who made up a goodly portion of the town's population. At the rear of the town around Chestnut, Prytania, and St. Charles were the charming suburban homes of well-to-do New Orleans merchants who built large houses surrounded by pleasant gardens; many of these great houses with their gardens exist today, collectively known as the Garden District. Lafayette had its own newspaper, the *Lafayette Spectator,* its street railway (on Jackson Avenue with connections to New Orleans), a fire department, and its own cemetery. Lafayette existed as a separate city for nineteen years. In 1852, this thriving community of fourteen thousand was consolidated into the city of New Orleans.

157 The elegant entrance to the Robb mansion. This structure, now demolished, was built about 1850 by James Robb, a banker. It occupied three acres of ground on Washington Avenue between Camp and

Chestnut streets. The house was large in scale, simple in design, but admirably proportioned, and it was at one time surrounded by a fine garden. In later years, the property was occupied by H. Sophie Newcomb College (1890–1918) and the Baptist Bible Institute. *Photo by Rudolf Hertzberg. Courtesy Howard-Tilton Memorial Library, Tulane University*

158 Garden District interiors were characterized by spacious, high-ceilinged rooms and well-detailed plaster and woodwork. This is the interior of the Payne-Strachan house at 1134 First Street, built about 1848–1850. *Photo by Rudolf Hertzberg. Courtesy Howard-Tilton Memorial Library, Tulane University*

157

158

159 The Robinson-Jordan house, 1415 Third Street, one of the largest in the Garden District, built in the late 1850s in Greek Revival style. Its elaborate interior features highly decorative painted ceilings. *Photo by Rudolf Hertzberg. Courtesy Howard-Tilton Memorial Library, Tulane University*

160 Madame Désirée Chaffraix's home, 2833 St. Charles Avenue, built in the late 1850s, was a particularly elegant New Orleans landmark for a century until it was demolished in 1958 to erect an apartment building. Through the years this house with its stately pillars and wide gallery was the scene of many social gatherings. Madame Chaffraix, a wealthy widow, divided her time between her New Orleans home and her French château. *Photo by Rudolf Hertzberg. Courtesy Howard-Tilton Memorial Library, Tulane University*

161 The Bradish-Johnson house, now the Louise S. McGehee School, 2343 Prytania Street, erected in 1872. Its rather florid design is attributed to James Freret, who studied in Paris at the École des Beaux-Arts. *Photo by H. S. Ragas*

162 The stairway of the Bradish-Johnson house is a masterpiece. *Photo by Rudolf Hertzberg. Courtesy Howard-Tilton Memorial Library, Tulane University*

163 One of two sets of cast-iron fences in the fascinating cornstalk design. One is in the Vieux Carré; this one ornaments the Short-Moran house, 1448 Fourth Street. A great many nineteenth-century cast-iron railings in New Orleans were erected by Wood & Miltenberger, the New Orleans branch of the noted Philadelphia foundry of Wood & Perot. *Photo by Rudolf Hertzberg. Courtesy Howard-Tilton Memorial Library, Tulane University*

159

160

161

162

163

139

164

164 Charbonnet house. This charming house, erected about 1810, faced the river in the lower part of the city. It was surrounded by a large garden and outbuildings. The Charbonnet house was typical of the large dwellings of its time. It was a raised house with large columns in a lower story and colonnettes in the upper story, with a French roof. *Courtesy Orleans Parish Notarial Archives*

165

166

167

165 *A street in the Faubourg Sainte-Marie*, one of New Orleans's first suburbs, is the title of this picture made about 1821 by Saint-Aulaire. *Courtesy Bibliothèque Nationale, Paris*

166 Bernard de Marigny's house, lithograph by Félix-Achille Beaupoil de Saint-Aulaire. This scene in the Faubourg Marigny was made about 1821. It shows the large house of Bernard de Marigny surrounded by a very nice garden, the whole enclosed by a picket fence. Note the Indian brave and his squaw crossing the street together with their children. *Courtesy Bibliothèque Nationale, Paris*

167 A number of houses built during the Spanish regime still survive. This one, known as the Spanish Custom House, although there is no record of such a function, is located at 1300 Moss Street on Bayou St. John. It was probably built about 1784, when the land on which it stands was the plantation of Don Santiago Lloreins. It is a charming example of French West Indian architecture.

168 In 1833, some 4½ miles upriver from New Orleans, land was laid out in lots, and the town thus created named for General William Carroll, who had encamped there in 1814 with a force of Tennesseans en route to the Battle of New Orleans. In 1835, the New Orleans and Carrollton Railroad began operations and soon Carrollton became a pleasant suburb. A racetrack, fine gardens, both beer and botanical,

and a hotel soon attracted visitors and home seekers from the city. Carrollton was incorporated as a town in 1843, and it became the county seat of Jefferson Parish after the Faubourg Lafayette had been absorbed by New Orleans in 1852. *From* Rand McNally's Family Atlas, *1889*

169 This ornate neo-Gothic carbarn was the terminus of the New Orleans and Carrollton Railway. *Photo by C. Milo Williams*

170 The Carrollton Hotel, like the carbarn, was falling into decay and was soon after demolished when the levee was moved back. *Photo by C. Milo Williams*

168

170

169

3. CULTURE

Theatre

1 The culture of Louisiana was French, and the Creoles inherited a fondness for "shows, the theatre, balls and assemblies," as well as opera. Theatre and opera performances, gambling, horse racing, and city social life made New Orleans a gay metropolis. By the 1840s, "the season" brought the rich planters and their families from upriver to New Orleans, and the city was one of the cultural centers of America.

The first theatre in New Orleans was built and operated by the Henry brothers, Louis Alexandre and Jean Marie, Parisians. It opened in 1792 in the closing years of the Spanish regime, and was located on St. Peter Street near Bourbon. Its early years were precarious ones, but despite poor acting and financial troubles, the St. Peter Street theatre somehow managed to survive until well into the American era. In 1808, a larger theatre on St. Philip Street, seen here, began operations. It was used both as a theatre and as a ballroom for quadroon balls. Drawing by Jacques Tanesse, 1815.

2 In 1813, the even more pretentious Théâtre d'Orléans opened its doors only to be destroyed by fire the following year. John Davis, an extraordinary impresario, rebuilt the Théâtre d'Orléans on the same site and it reopened on November 27, 1819. At the time of its opening, it was one of the most sumptuous in America, its spacious parquet was almost encircled by two tiers of boxes and a gallery; supper rooms were also provided. The theatre burned in the morning of December 7, 1866. The Théâtre d'Orléans was on Orleans Street near Bourbon, on a site since occupied until recently by the Convent of the Holy Family and now occupied by the Bourbon Orleans Hotel; a ballroom built by Davis adjoining his theatre still stands, now part of the hotel. Drawing by Jacques Tanesse, 1815.

3 Program of the Théâtre d'Orléans, February 28, 1828, featuring *The Vestal*, a grand opera in three acts, and *Monsieur Jovial*, or *the singing Constable*, a vaudeville skit. It was one of the first homes of grand opera in this country, and throughout its existence

1

(G) THEATRE St PHILIPPE annee 1810.

F) THEATRE · D'ORLÈANS annèe 1813.

2

3

French opera featuring troupes imported from France was performed there. However, occasional plays in English were produced, notably by William Duff in 1811, the pioneer of such productions. In 1817, a company headed by Noah Ludlow presented plays in English. *Albert L. Voss Collection. Courtesy Mrs. Raymond J. Boudreaux*

4 It was not until 1820 that a young Englishman, James H. Caldwell, then twenty-seven years old, came to New Orleans to establish a good English theatrical company at the St. Philip Street theatre. The *Honey Moon* ushered in the era of the English-spoken theatre in New Orleans. John S. Kendall in his *Golden Age of the New Orleans Theatre* states: "With them [the Caldwell players], the English language drama established itself in that city as a permanent intellectual institution. Thenceforth, for almost a hundred years, there was to be no interruption in the regular recurrence of the orthodox dramatic season."

James H. Caldwell, who died in 1863, was called "the architect of the fortunes of the second municipality." He engaged in many civic enterprises after his start in the theatre. Besides his theatrical ventures, he, together with Samuel J. Peters, another dynamic New Orleanian of the period, did much to develop the

4

Faubourg Ste. Marie above Canal Street. In addition to lighting the city with gas, he was an organizer of the New Basin Canal, the New Orleans and Nashville Railroad Company, the New Orleans Water Works, the Verandah and St. Charles hotels, and other projects. He served as a member of the city council, held the office of recorder (both for two terms), and served four years in the state legislature. Blessed with an engaging personality, Caldwell was not only a finished actor but a dynamic businessman, to whom New Orleans owed much in the years during which the city emerged from a small town to a southern metropolis. *Courtesy Donald F. Schultz*

5 This was Caldwell's tax bill on property and slaves that he owned in the Faubourg Ste. Marie assessed at $20,500. The rate was $2 per $1,000 assessed value.

6 Recognizing that inevitable changes were coming because of the influx of Americans, Caldwell cast his eyes on the yet undeveloped part of town above Canal Street as the site for a theatre. In 1822–1824, he erected the American Theatre on Camp Street near Poydras. From his English imported gas-making machine used to furnish illumination for his theatre came the formation of the gas company that provided street and household lighting for the city. The theatre, built by an architect-builder by the name of Gott, opened on January 1, 1824, with the play *Town and Country*, in which Caldwell played the leading part. The American Theatre soon was noted for its excellent entertainment, and almost every actor and actress of importance of the day appeared there. Drawing by H. Reinagle, 1830.

7 The first St. Charles Theatre, engraving by Lemaitre. Caldwell retired from the theatre for a short time to engage exclusively in his expanding gas enterprise, but in 1835 he returned to build his fabulous new theatre. He visited Europe to study the great continental theatres, and his ideas were embodied in the design of his new theatre by A. Mondelli, a talented scenic artist. On completion, the St. Charles was undoubtedly the finest theatre in America. This magnificent structure on St. Charles Street near Poydras cost $350,000 and contained 4,100 seats. Its

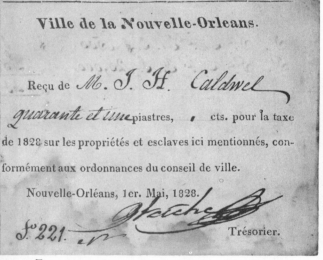

5

7

6

domed interior was lighted by a gas chandelier 36 feet in circumference and 12 feet high, with 250 gas jets and 23,300 crystal drops. Nothing like the St. Charles had ever been seen before in America. This magnificence was short-lived, for seven years after its opening, fire destroyed the building. *From* Histoire des Antilles, *Paris*

8 Cross-section plan of the first St. Charles Theatre. *Courtesy Labrot Collection, Tulane University*

9 A second St. Charles was erected on the site by Caldwell's rivals, Noah Ludlow and Sol Smith. Just as large as its predecessor, it was, however, not quite as ornate. Opening in 1843, this theatre operated until 1899 when it too was destroyed by fire. While quite opulent in its interior, it had a plain facade that in later years was changed by the addition of a gallery supported by cast-iron pillars. A third St. Charles Theatre, first known as the Orpheum, was built on this site, but after a varied career it was demolished in 1967 to create a parking lot. At the bottom is a view of the facade and the two owners. Lithograph by G. Tolti, printed by D. Theuret, ca. 1850.

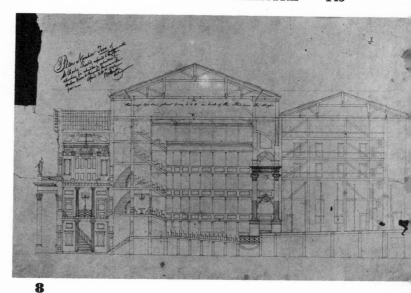

8

9

SAINT CHARLES THEATRE, NEW ORLEANS

LUDLOW & SMITH PROPRIETORS & MANAGERS

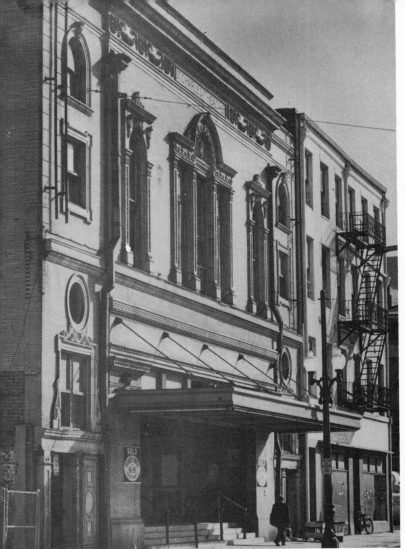

10 The third St. Charles Theatre, later known as the Orpheum, in its last days. *Photo by Frank Methe. Courtesy Clarion Herald*

11 Peeling paint, water-stained plaster—the boxes and upper galleries of the third St. Charles Theatre just before it was demolished. *Photo by Frank Methe. Courtesy Clarion Herald*

12 Among the many famous players who appeared at the three St. Charles theatres were Edwin and Junius Brutus Booth, Jenny Lind, Fanny Elssler, Joseph Jefferson, Lotta Crabtree, Charlotte Cushman, and Tyrone Power. But probably the best-known and certainly the most sensational actress to come from New Orleans was Adah Isaacs Menken. Born Adah Bertha Theodore in Milneburg in 1835, she made her one and only appearance in New Orleans on the stage of the Gaiety Theatre as a minor player. A beautiful woman, she taught herself to act, learned several languages, wrote poetry, and could ride, sing, and dance. Scantily clad, she was the first woman to play the part of Mazeppa, the Cossack chieftain who was lashed to the back of a wild horse and driven away as a punishment. This was at the start of a career that made her the toast of London, Paris, and New York. Menken was unconventional, completely uninhibited, wildly extravagant. She married four times and had a number of affairs. She died at the age of thirty-seven and is buried in Paris. *Courtesy Louisiana State Museum*

13 The Varieties Theatre, on Gravier between Baronne and Carondelet, was opened in 1848. Lola Montez, the sensational actress-dancer, who had been made Countess of Lansfeld by her friend King Ludwig I of Bavaria, played in this theatre in 1853. When the Varieties burned (for the second time) in 1879, the Variété Association, the club that owned it, sold the ground and built in 1871 a new Varieties shown here, on Canal Street where the Kress and Maison Blanche stores now stand. The new theatre, which cost $320,000, was one of the most elegant in the South and was famous for its magnificent staircase. The Varieties became the Grand Opera House in 1881, and the theatre continued in operation until 1906 when it was sold and the building demolished. Watercolor by Boyd Cruise. *Courtesy Joseph Merrick Jones, Jr.*

14 "Dixie's Land" was first heard in New Orleans in the Varieties Theatre, where it was wildly applauded at its first performance, and it has been popular in the South ever since. One of the first editions of the verse was printed in New Orleans by a fourth-district

13

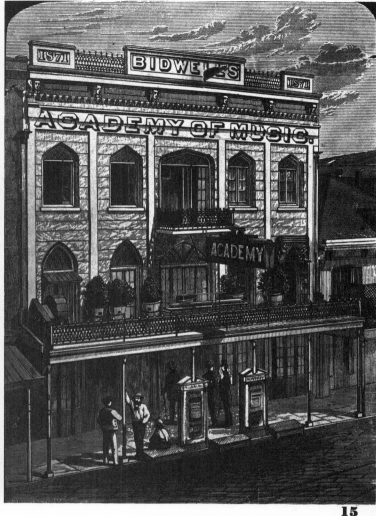

15

14

printer named John Hopkins at his shop at 823 Tchou-pitoula Street. The words had been composed in 1859 by Daniel Decatur Emmett, a minstrel actor, and the music by a German-born bandmaster named Herman F. Arnold. *Courtesy G. William Nott*

15 Another well-known New Orleans theatre was the Academy of Music, built on St. Charles opposite Perdido Street, very close to the St. Charles Theatre. Erected in 1853, it was originally called Dan Rice's Amphitheatre after Dan Rice, the famous circus showman. Succeeding Rice was the Spalding and Rogers's Circus, which played this theatre for several winters prior to the Civil War. With the coming of spring they loaded their actors, minstrels, animals, and curiosities aboard *The Floating Palace,* on which performances were given upstream during the summer. The theatre came under the ownership of David Bidwell, who remodeled it, and gave it the name Academy of Music. Bidwell elevated it to serious drama. It was he who inaugurated the matinee, so popular in New Orleans. The Academy of Music, then known as the Audubon Theatre, burned in 1903. *From* Jewell's Crescent City Illustrated, *1873*

16 David Bidwell (1821–1889), credited with inaugurating the matinee in New Orleans. For many years, he was one of the foremost theatrical producers in the Crescent City. On his tomb in Métairie Cemetery, his wife had engraved: "We part to meet again / Bid me not good night / But in some pleasant land / Bid me good morning."

17 The twin theatres Tulane and Crescent erected in 1898 by Klaw and Erlanger on land leased from Tulane University, as an artist envisioned them on the opening night's program of the Tulane (October 17, 1898). The play performed was *Nathan Hale* by Clyde Fitch, and the stars were Nat Goodwin and Maxine Elliott. The Crescent, which seated 1,800, was designed as a popular-price theatre to continue the sort of offerings that Klaw and Erlanger had been presenting at the St. Charles. The smaller Tulane catered to a clientele that had patronized the Academy of Music. The Tulane-Crescent with their glass-enclosed arcade were a familiar part of the New Orleans scene until their demolition in 1937. *Courtesy Felix H. Kuntz*

18 The glass arcade so familiar to thousands of New Orleans theatregoers had been added to the Tulane-

16

17

CHARLES
FROHMAN
PRESENTS

ETHEL BARRYMORE

18

19

20

21

Crescent theatres in 1906 when this photograph was made. The poster informed passersby that McIntyre and Heath soon would be playing in *The Ham Tree,* and that they might view "the most beautiful singing and dancing chorus in the world." *Courtesy Library of Congress*

19 20 Ethel Barrymore and Billie Burke appeared at the Tulane Theatre, as did New Orleans–born E. H. Sothern, who first saw the light of day in a boarding-house on Bienville Street while his parents were in the city on tour. The Tulane was accustomed to the cream

of the American stage, including Otis Skinner, James K. Hackett, Olga Nethersole, Richard Mansfield, Julia Marlowe, DeWolf Hopper, Maude Adams, Margaret Anglin, George Arliss, Joseph Jefferson, John Drew, Robert Edeson, William Faversham, Anna Held, Lillian Russell, Fritzi Scheff, David Warfield, Lou Tellegan, Walker Whiteside, Robert Mantell, and many others. *Photo of posters courtesy New York Public Library*

21 The interior of the Crescent Theatre. For many years it was a vaudeville house.

22

25

23

24

22 In 1903, Henry Greenwall, for a number of years the manager of the Grand Opera House, built the Greenwall Theatre on Dauphine and Iberville streets. Before its demolition in 1963, it ended its career as the Palace Theatre, a movie house. Shown here is the Palace Theatre, about 1935.

23 Henry Greenwall (1833–1913), the last of the great theatrical owner-managers on the New Orleans scene. He owned several theatres in southern cities simultaneously.

24 Greenwall also built the Baldwin Theatre in 1904, seen here in 1906, as the home for the Baldwin-Melville Stock Company. Eventually it became a burlesque theatre, known as the Dauphine, before it was entirely abandoned. It stood in 1967, forlorn and decrepit, a symbol of the decay of the professional theatre in New Orleans. Greenwall fought the Klaw and Erlanger syndicate for many years in securing bookings, but it was a losing fight and he died a comparatively poor man.

25 The Dauphine, just before it was torn down in 1970. *Photo by G. E. Arnold*

26 These glories of the old days were found when the Dauphine came tumbling down. *Photo by G. E. Arnold. Courtesy Times-Picayune Publishing Corp.*

26

27

28

27 *Timour the Tartar,* the "Great Spectacular Equestrian Drama," was the feature of another New Orleans theatrical character, Frederick Stempel, who changed his name to Faranta. Born in 1846, he came to New Orleans and was part of a minstrel show at the Academy of Music. After a disastrous trip to South and Central America, he returned to New Orleans almost penniless, but somehow managed to scrape up enough money to start a tent show at the corner of Bourbon and Orleans streets. Although Faranta charged only ten cents admission, he prospered sufficiently to erect the Iron Theatre, a sheet-iron-covered structure built over a wood frame; the barnlike theatre was large enough to hold 4,800 persons. Despite his low prices (he finally upped his best seats to thirty cents), Faranta presented artists of known ability and Faranta's show was very popular until it burned in 1889. The site is now occupied by the Bourbon Orleans Hotel.

28 "A Giant Show at Midget Prices" proclaimed this advertisement of the opening of another popular priced amusement center, the Dime Museum and Theatre. It was operated by Eugene Robinson in the 1880s. Located in a five-story building on Canal Street between Camp and St. Charles streets, this was the first dime museum New Orleans ever had. For ten cents, one could see fat ladies, living skeletons, bearded women, Siamese twins, gorillas, dwarfs and giants, and novel mechanical inventions. These occupied the top four floors. On the ground floor was a small theatre where continuous vaudeville was presented. Robinson eventually built a pair of gaudy showboats, Robinson's Floating Palaces Museum, Menagerie and Aquarium, and a floating Grand Opera House. This venture lasted only one season (1893–1894), when, owing to reverses, Robinson was forced to sell his properties at auction.

29 "Here I stand the Tallest Man on Earth, the $100 bill is yours if you can reach it." Advertisement of the Crescent City Dime Museum, Grunewald Hall, 1884.

30 Robinson's Floating Palaces Museum, Menagerie and Aquarium, and his attached Grand Opera House, as they looked at the beginning of the season 1893–1894.

31 In the early 1920s, a stock company headed by Leona Powers and Walter P. Richardson played for several years at the St. Charles Theatre. This versatile group, under the capable management of Lee Sterrett, presented a different show each week and put on such plays as *Three Faces East, The Green Goddess, Six Cylinder Love, The Cinderella Man,* and many others.

29

Saenger's St. Charles Theater Players First Birthday Souvenir

Presenting Ernest Truex's Broadway Stage Hit "Six Cylinder Love"

SAENGER'S ST. CHARLES THEATER PLAYERS WHO GAVE NEW ORLEANS ITS FIRST YEAR-ROUND "LEGITIMATE" THEATER.
Seated, left to right: Joseph Echazebel, Lora Rogers, Lee Sterrett, stage director; Leona Powers, Marion Grant, Kathryn Givney.
Standing, left to right: Vincent Dennis, Donald Gregory, stage manager, Grace Deming, Julian Noa, Lester Al. Smith, William Melville;
Robert Bentley, Val Winters, Emily McPherson, O. W. Wegner, scenic artist; and Orris Holland.

31

30

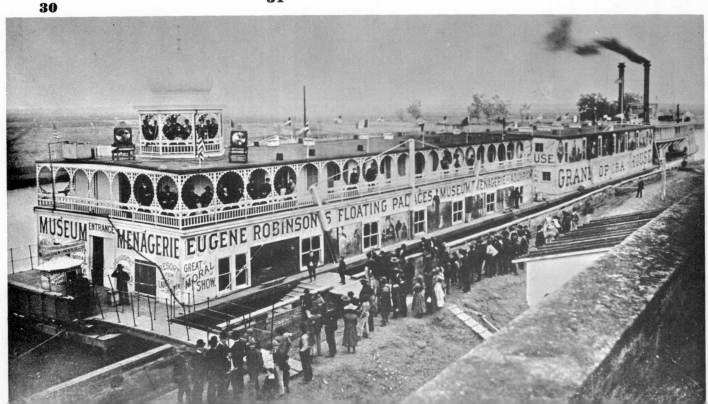

33

32

32 Le Petit Théâtre du Vieux Carré, the oldest of a number of small theatres in New Orleans where plays are produced either by amateurs or professional actors. This one is an outgrowth of the Drawing Room Players, which had its start in 1916. The Little Theatre, as it is better known, had produced plays with amateur actors continuously for fifty-four years. Another well-known theatre is the Gallery Circle, a theatre in the round, which has operated successfully since 1948. The Repertory Theatre, started in 1967 with the aid of a federal grant, is now on its own. It is located in a former synagogue, and professional actors are employed. *Photo by Richard Koch*

French Opera

33 Charles Boudousquié, first impresario of the French Opera House, around 1860. The golden age of opera in New Orleans extended over a period of a little more than a century. Beginning in the 1820s, John Davis yearly brought a group of singers and musicians from France to perform at his Théâtre d'Orléans, and thereafter followed an epoch in which there was scarcely an interruption in regularly scheduled opera performances. Davis would go to Europe each year and recruit his personnel, and soon he was giving operatic performances, including ballet, which were considered to be without equal in the United States. Plagued by constant financial troubles and the fact that he had to reimport a new troupe each year, Davis decided to take his company to eastern seaboard cities in the summer. He did this from 1827 to 1833 (except 1832) and during these summers his New Orleans troupes performed 212 pieces (opera, plays, ballets, concerts, and separate musical numbers) in New York, 203 in Philadelphia, 54 in Baltimore, and 19 in Boston. His companies were acclaimed everywhere, his orchestras being particularly praised. At home, Davis's troupes staged hundreds of performances in the eighteen years that he operated the Théâtre d'Orléans. These were not only operas but plays, ballets and concerts, and during this time the opera became very much a part of New Orleans life. In 1837, Davis, then sixty-four, relinquished control of the opera, and he died two years later.

34 Architects' sketch of the New Orleans Opera House, 1858. Boudousquié found himself at odds with the Théâtre d'Orléans' owner in 1858 and determined to erect another, more modern opera house. Promoting a stock company with a capital of $100,000 in early 1859, he retained the architect-builders Gallier and Esterbrook to design and construct the new building. Work on the Opera House started in May, 1859, and opened with a gala performance of *William Tell* on December 1. Seating about two thousand, the building occupied a site at the uptown woods corner of Bourbon and Toulouse streets, on which the Downtowner Hotel now stands. It was of Greek Revival design, and its pilastered and colonnaded front measured 166 feet on Bourbon by 187 feet on Toulouse, and its 80-foot-high fly loft towered above the surrounding buildings. Like most important New Orleans buildings of the time, it was constructed of brick with

34

plastered walls and embellished with moldings and other plaster ornaments. *Howard-Tilton Memorial Library, Tulane University*

35 A fashionable crowd entering the French Opera to attend a performance, ca. 1860. Watercolor by Boyd Cruise. A contemporary wrote:

> There was not a single building in Louisiana as closely identified with the history of our festivals and revelries of the highest order as the old French Opera House. . . . The lyric temple on Bourbon Street was truly the patrimony of all Louisianians, the scene of wondrous gatherings and sumptuous receptions at which generations of New Orleanians met on pleasure bent, in order to forget the ills and cares of life 'neath the dispelling influence of suave and rapturous music.

36 From 1859 until it burned in 1919, the French Opera House was the scene of many carnival balls. This sketch, by C. E. H. Bonwill, shows a masquerade ball held in the Opera House on Washington's birthday, 1864. This was given by Mrs. Nathaniel Banks, wife of the Federal general occupying New Orleans.

37 Ladies and gentlemen in the corbeille level, 1866. In 1871, the English illustrator Alfred R. Waud was sent to New Orleans with Ralph Keeler, a journalist, by a Boston magazine. Waud, who had visited New Orleans in 1866, has left us some of the best sketches

35

36

37

38

39

of people at the French Opera. "They . . . are fine looking people and some of the women would be considered beauties in any part of the world."

38 A Creole family at the opera, 1871. "We have given you in our picture of the occupants of the proscenium box a representation of one of the old aristocratic families."

39 The Negro Gallery, 1871: "The *dii superi* of the fourth tier, or gallery, are Negroes in all stages of coatlessness and inverse civilization. . . . We find them in a very tropical temperature, against which the cheap lemonade that a boy is selling prevails them not."

40

40 The Loges Grillées, 1871. A quote from a contemporary: "These latticed stalls extend around the whole house. They are for the benefit of those who want to see and not be seen; they are used often by people in mourning. The lattice is drawn down on only a few of them, and the rule is represented in the engraving, that the fair occupants are not only visible, but flirting between the acts."

41 Premiere, or opening night, at the French Opera, ca. 1901. Taken from the stage, this view shows the audience that packed the house from the *parquet* (orchestra) to the *quatrièmes* (fourth gallery). The *Daily Picayune* described the interior of the French Opera House on December 2, 1859, a day after the opening:

41

The house is constructed so as to afford a full view of the audience from almost every point and its gracefully curved tiers of boxes, rising one above the other, each gradually receding from the line of the other and then filled, in a great degree, with ladies in grand toilette, presented a spectacle that was richly worth viewing. The private boxes on each side of the proscenium are elegantly draped with crimson damask and are occupied by families for the season. The whole house is painted white and the decorations of the front of the boxes are in gold; the first circle with rich festoons, and those above it with panel work. A magnificent mirror in a gold frame on the wall on each side of the proscenium adds greatly to the picturesque effect of the auditorium. . . . The entrances to the house are numerous, spacious and commodious, and the concert-room, ladies retiring room, etc., are constructed upon a scale of great elegance and convenience.

42 The French tenor Léonce Escalaïs, who, in 1910, performed the sensational feat of reaching fifteen high C's in the aria "Supplice infâme" in *Le Trouvère* (better known to opera lovers as "Di quella pira," in *Il Trovatore* at the French Opera House (including four encores). René J. Le Gardeur, Jr., a lifelong opera enthusiast, reminisced about this performance and in general about the French opera in the following letter, which is excerpted. (As a high-school boy, Le Gardeur and a chum, the late Albert L. Voss, who later became the leading authority on the New Orleans French Opera, attended performances beginning in the early 1900s.) He writes:

The significant thing about this old opera, which distinguished it from any other opera association in the United States at any time, and certainly from any opera today, is that it was primarily a French institution, bound up very closely with the French (Creole) culture in the city. Except on rare occasions, and in the case of some visiting troupes, the operas were sung in French, and operagoers knew the words by heart, and understood everything that was going on. It was quite common at my house (and in many other Creole families too) to hear young and old sing the arias—quartets and choruses did not deter them either—from memory, and "just for fun," with appropriate gestures and stage business. *Faust* was the favorite opera, and we often sang, at home, the Garden Scene quartet, relishing particularly the ironic humor of Mephistopheles's words.

The Creoles took their opera seriously. They had favorites among the artists, and there would be arguments, sometimes fights and duels, between partisans of rival artists. I know of no such cases at first hand, but often heard them talked about.

Sunday night was devoted to French comic operas. Some of them were rather risqué and the ladies would avoid these. During my opera days I never saw people in evening dress on Sunday nights

42

43

and there were seldom any ladies, except some married and elderly ones perhaps, when "safe" operas were being given. The principal performers on Sunday nights were an entirely different troupe from those who did the regular operas.

Albert L. Voss Collection. Courtesy Mrs. Raymond J. Boudreaux

43 Mlle. Stella Bossi, the premier danseuse of the French Opera Company of the 1901–1902 season. *Albert L. Voss Collection. Courtesy Mrs. Raymond J. Boudreaux*

44 During its most successful years, it was the custom for the impresario of the New Orleans French Opera to go to France and gather a troupe of singers and bring them to the city for the season. This photograph was made in 1910, when impresario Emile Durieu (*ninth from left*) paused to have a picture of his troupe taken en route to New Orleans. On a less happy occasion, in 1866, Charles Alhaiza, impresario, had gathered fifty-seven French artists and sailed with them from New York on the steamer *Evening Star.* On October 3, the vessel went down in a violent storm off Tibee Island, Georgia, and Alhaiza and the entire cast along with most of the other passengers were lost.

44

45

45 On the afternoon after fire destroyed the French Opera House in 1919. For sixty years the French Opera House had had a checkered career. Although it was successful at first, the Civil War intervened, and by 1873 the Opera Association found itself in debt and the building was sold by the sheriff. In 1889, a new French Opera Association was formed, which bought the building from an insurance company that held the mortgage, and reorganized. A most brilliant season was that of 1880–1881, and in the succeeding years until 1887 the opera flourished. From that time on, for no ascertainable reason, interest in opera declined in New Orleans, not to be revived until 1906. A typical troupe that played the 1909–1910 season was composed of 130 members—25 artists, 40 choristers, 22 members of the ballet, 40 musicians, 2 orchestra leaders and a stage manager, besides electricians, carpenters, and stagehands.

The season 1919–1920 began brilliantly on Armistice night, November 11, but fire, starting mysteriously in the small hours of December 4, 1919, gutted the sixty-year-old opera house. Five persons, asleep over the Café de l'Opéra, barely escaped with their lives. All scenery, costumes, and music were completely destroyed.

46 The cover of the last season of the French Opera House. In the half century since the fire there has been much talk of rebuilding, but New Orleans remains without a home for the performances that the New Orleans Opera Association mounts regularly each season in the Municipal Auditorium. In 1972, the new cultural center will provide proper facilities.

Concerts

47 While opera was extremely popular with New Orleanians, there were other musical interludes. In early 1851, Jenny Lind, the "Swedish Nightingale," arrived by steamer in New Orleans. So great was the crowd at the levee to greet her that P. T. Barnum, her impresario, had to employ a ruse (by escorting two veiled ladies down the gangplank with the crowd in pursuit) so that she could go on separately to her quarters in the upper Pontalba Building. Miss Lind sang thirteen concerts to the delight of her admirers who paid $87,600 in admissions.

48 Louis Moreau Gottschalk (1829–1869) in 1853 at the time of his return to New Orleans, the first American artist to win acclaim in Europe. Gottschalk was a child prodigy at the piano, and at thirteen he was sent to Paris to study. At his first public appearance three years later, he won the praise of Berlioz and Chopin, and was launched on a highly successful career both as a pianist and composer. Many of Gottschalk's compositions were based on Louisiana folk tunes. On a visit to his birthplace in 1853, Gottschalk gave several concerts, which were enthusiastically received. At the conclusion of one, Mayor A. D. Crossman presented him with a sixteen-ounce gold medal as a testimonial from his fellow citizens.

46

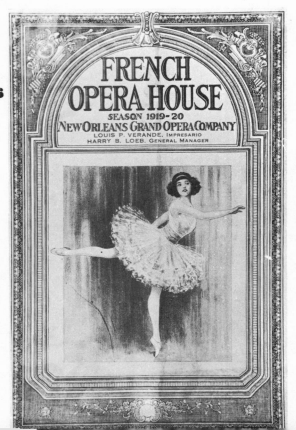

FRENCH OPERA HOUSE
SEASON 1919-20
NEW ORLEANS GRAND OPERA COMPANY
LOUIS P. VERANDE, IMPRESARIO
HARRY B. LOEB, GENERAL MANAGER

47

48

49

49 The New Orleans Zither Club in concert dress. This group gave concerts at the turn of the century at Tulane Hall and at the Athenaeum. Before the advent of professionally managed touring concert artists, serious amateur musicians of New Orleans had organized themselves into clubs, which gave concerts. Most of these were groups of singers, such as the Orphéon Français, the Polyhymnia Circle, the Quartet Club, and the Choral Symphony Society. In the late 1890s when the Tyrolean zither became popular, this New Orleans Zither Club was organized by Victor Huber, a young Viennese composer and teacher who had settled in New Orleans.

50 The Festival Hall of the New Orleans Saengerfest. In 1890 there were no less than five German singing societies. Under the able leadership of Professor John Hanno Deiler, of Tulane University, the North American Saengerbund was invited to New Orleans, and with the help of local German-American businessmen, this large wooden hall seating five thousand spectators, with a stage accommodating fifteen hundred singers, was built at Lee Circle. A series of six concerts was given, all to capacity audiences, and the event was both a cultural and financial success.

50

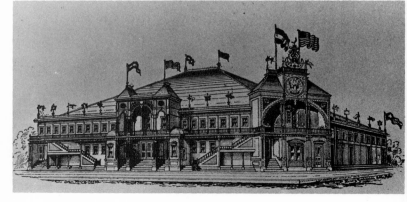

ATHENAEUM

The Philharmonic Society
Of New Orleans

MARGARETE MATZENAUER

Dramatic Soprano Metropolitan Opera

FIRST CONCERT
Wednesday, October 24, 1917
At eight-thirty p. m.

BOARD OF DIRECTORS OF THE PHILHARMONIC SOCIETY

OFFICERS
Miss Corinne Mayer,
President
Mrs. Mark Kaiser,
First Vice-President
Mrs. Jane Austen Tuttle
Second Vice-President
Mrs. Philip Werlein
Secretary-Treasurer

DIRECTORS
Mrs. Frederick W. Bott
Miss Camille Gibert
Miss Violet Hart
Mrs. T. L. Lyons, Jr.
Miss Blanche McCord
Miss M. V. Molony
Miss J. K. Newman
Mrs. J. H. Stauffer

51

Kreisler

Direction C. J. FOLEY
Boston, Massachusetts

Jerusalem Temple   .   .   New Orleans
Friday Evening, February 15, 1924 at 8.15

Tickets, $2.50, $2.00, $1.50, $1.00, on sale Monday, Feb. 11th
at Grunewald Music Co., 735 Canal Street.   Mail orders now
to Philharmonic Scholarship Fund, 1103 Fern Street, will
receive prompt attention.

STEINWAY PIANO

52

53

51 52 The Philharmonic Society of New Orleans was organized in 1906 by a group of music lovers headed by Miss Corinne Mayer, Mr. and Mrs. H. T. Howard, Mr. and Mrs. Mark Kaiser, and others for the purpose of bringing great concert artists to the city. The organization, later run entirely by women, was highly successful, and many of the world's greatest artists came to New Orleans under its auspices. The Philharmonic Society is now part of the New Orleans Philharmonic Symphony Society. Seen here are pages from the programs of Margarete Matzenauer and Fritz Kreisler.

53 The New Orleans Philharmonic Symphony Orchestra in rehearsal. This organization had its beginning in May, 1936, when the Philharmonic Society of New Orleans sponsored the New Orleans Civic Symphony Orchestra. Arthur Zack, formerly of the Cincinnati Symphony Orchestra, was employed to direct the infant organization, and the first concert was given on May 18, 1936. *From* New Orleans Item, *April 14, 1936*

54 Now in its thirty-fifth season, the New Orleans Philharmonic Symphony Orchestra has grown in its

54

number of musicians (approximately 90), in performances (130 in the 1970–1971 season), in length or season (now 36 weeks), and in musical stature. Since 1963, the symphony has been under the direction of the dynamic Werner Torkanowsky.

Jazz

55 How did New Orleans jazz come to be born? There have been almost as many explanations as performers. Certainly New Orleans was always a lively town with a solid background of grand opera and reputation for innumerable balls, dances, and parades, which were necessarily enlivened by music. The eminent authorities Al Rose and Dr. Edmond Souchon wrote of its origins in *New Orleans Jazz Family Album:*

> We feel that Jazz was not invented at all, but that it came into being so gradually that any attempt to pin down a first time would be based on the most specious types of reasoning. Credit for the

creation of Jazz is due no individual, man or race. If anything, it is a product, an inevitable product we think, of the avenues and alleys of an unique city, polyglot, multiracial, seething with love and conflict, a battleground of nations and cultures, a landscape of mire and magnolias.

And recently Richard B. Allen, associate curator of the Tulane University Archive of New Orleans Jazz, defined the music: "Jazz is a Creole Gumbo. There's a little of everything in it. It draws from African work chants, European and American folk music, grand opera, French quadrilles, Spanish dance forms, Negro spirituals—almost any kind of music played or sung in New Orleans during the nineteenth century when the city was one of the nation's chief musical centers." Contrary to the generally accepted belief that New Orleans jazz originated in the red-light district (Storyville, 1897–1917), from taped interviews of old-time jazzmen and from other sources, students of the subject have come to the conclusion that jazz, then known as ragtime, had been played years before this era. A

55

number of bands did play in the cabarets that fringed the district, a circumstance that probably gave rise to the story, but by and large most of the lively music of the time was played at balls, dances, picnic outings, and parades.

Emile ("Stalebread Charley") Lacombe (1885–1946) formed this skiffle band with its boy performers and homemade instruments in 1897. He called his group the Razzy Dazzy Spasm Band, and they performed in the streets of Storyville in the late 1890s. Stalebread, though blind, was an active performer in New Orleans jazz bands in the 1920s and 1930s. He is the second from the left. *Courtesy Dr. Edmond Souchon*

56 This band is about to depart for Felix Park, a picnic ground opposite the Jefferson Park Race Track on the interurban line of the Orleans-Kenner Electric Railway, where they were to make music for an Easter

Sunday dance. They are at the O-K ticket office, 127 S. Rampart Street. *Photo by John J. DePaul*

57 The Streckfus steamboats, for years a part of the New Orleans harbor scene, employed good jazz bands for dancing aboard their *Sydney, J.S., Capitol,* and *President.* This band, led by Fate Marable (at the piano), and including (from extreme left) Baby Dodds, William ("Bébé") Ridgely, Joe Howard, Louis Armstrong, David Jones, Johnny Dodds, Johnny St. Cyr, and Pops Foster, is pictured aboard the Steamer *Sydney* in 1918.

58 Louis ("Satchmo") Armstrong, the most famous of all jazzmen, was born in New Orleans in 1900. Armstrong began to play in the Waifs' Home band and became a protégé of the talented King Oliver. From the mid-1920s he led his own band. Armstrong's ready smile, gravelly voice, and genial personality, coupled with his superb musicianship on the trumpet, had made him one of the most beloved of entertainers.

59 King Oliver (playing the trumpet) played jazz in New Orleans until 1918 when he left for Chicago. There his Creole Jazz Band, one of the greatest jazz organizations in the early and mid-1920s, played at the Lincoln Gardens. In this band, Louis Armstrong made his first appearance in the big time. Armstrong is shown in this 1923 photograph posing with a slide trumpet. This group recorded "Mabel's Dream" for Okeh Records, now a collector's item.

56

57

58

59

60 The Six and Seven-Eighths String Band in 1915 aboard the *Aunt Dinah,* the Jahncke family houseboat. Left to right, kneeling, are Howard McCaleb, Charlie Hardy, Hilton ("Midget") Harrison, Edmond Souchon, and Bill Gibbens. Standing are Bob Reynolds, Commodore Ernest Lee Jahncke (later un-dersecretary of the United States Navy), and Shields O'Reardon. The band was formed in 1911 and got its name because one of its seven members was so much shorter than the others. It was still in existence fifty-seven years later, although time took its toll of some of the original members. *Courtesy Dr. Edmond Souchon*

60

61

61 Johnny DeDroit's Band in the 1920s. Johnny DeDroit was a widely known New Orleans jazzman who started playing trumpet solos at the age of twelve. From left, standing: Rudolph Levy, saxophone; Henry Raymond, saxophone and clarinet; Frank Cuny, piano; Russ Papallia, trombone; Paul DeDroit, drums; John DeDroit, trumpet. In 1917–1918, he had his own band playing in the cave of the Grunewald Hotel, and he and his boys were the first white jazz band to play in tuxedos. DeDroit and his band played for years (during the 1920s) at Kolb's restaurant; he once took his band to New York for an engagement, but soon returned to his hometown where until his retirement in the 1960s the DeDroit band was in great demand for dances, nightclub engagements, theatres, hotels, and carnival balls.

62 Johnny Wiggs (John Wigginton Hyman), a world-renowned New Orleans jazzman, with the WSMB radio band of 1946. Every one of these musicians was a distinguished player. Left to right: Julian ("Digger") Laine, trombone; Arthur ("Monk") Hazel, drums; "Chink Marten" (Martin Abraham, Sr.) bass; Johnny Wiggs, cornet; Armand Hug, piano; Leonard ("Boogie") Centobi, clarinet. Wiggs began playing in the 1920s with the New Orleans Owls. In 1927, he led his own Bayou Stompers, which made recordings for Victor. After jazz had almost died in New Orleans in the 1930s (nearly killed by the hillbilly music craze), it was largely through Wiggs's efforts that jazz was revived in the city of its birth. *Courtesy Johnny Wiggs*

63 The custom of accompanying the corpse to the grave with a band of music playing funeral dirges was practiced in New Orleans, as it was elsewhere in the nineteenth century. The custom was gradually aban-

62

63

doned by whites, but persisted with Negroes. Seen only occasionally today (generally at funerals of older jazzmen), the bands play slow music going to the cemetery and "fast" coming back. This brass band is marching in a funeral procession in the 1940s. *Courtesy Howard-Tilton Memorial Library, Tulane University*

64 From the 1920s to the 1940s, "spasm bands," generally composed of young Negro boys who danced to "music" made by assorted pans, tin cans, and the clapping of hands, were a common sight in New Orleans.

65 Oscar ("Papa") Celestin (trumpet), venerable New Orleans jazzman (1884–1954), wrote "My Josephine," "Marie Laveau," and "Down by the Riverside." He founded the original Tuxedo Brass Band in 1911. *Courtesy New Orleans Public Library*

66 Sweet Emma Barrett, "The Bell Gal," pianist and singer, started in 1923 with Papa Celestin. A popular bandleader, she has played with some of the city's top "reading" bands, although Sweet Emma can't read a note. She earned her sobriquet by her habit of wearing belled garters.

67 Bill Mathews (1889–1964), New Orleans jazz trombonist. He played with Jelly Roll Morton, the Original Tuxedo Orchestra, and with Papa Celestin. *Courtesy New Orleans Public Library*

64

65

66

67

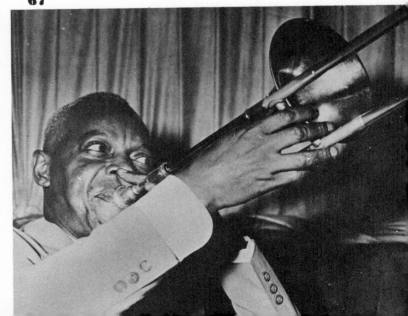

68

68 After suffering an eclipse, New Orleans jazz has been revived and today is more popular than ever. The founding of the Jazz Museum by the New Orleans Jazz Club and the establishment of such places as Preservation Hall for the performance of New Orleans jazz has done much to enhance the city's heritage. Led by its uninhibited grand marshal, Fats Houston, this marching band is eagerly followed by "second line" jazz enthusiasts, who keep in step with the marchers. *Photo by Leon Trice*

69 "Fats," as grand marshal, leading the Olympia Brass Band at the funeral of a New Orleans jazzman. *Photo by Ralph Uribe. Courtesy Times-Picayune*

69

70

70 Alphonse Floristan Picou (1878–1961). This famous New Orleans jazzman's funeral, held during the carnival season in 1961, was one of the biggest in New Orleans history. *Courtesy New Orleans Public Library*

71 The Onward Brass Band, 1964. The occasion was a parade and concert at McAllister Auditorium, Tulane University. *Photo by Bob Martel. Courtesy New Orleans Public Library*

71

72

74

73

72 Pete Fountain, whose unique New Orleans tone on the clarinet has made him a local and national favorite, is a leading exponent of swing and Dixieland jazz. Pete's Half-fast Marching Club with its one-hundred-odd costumed members, marches each Mardi Gras before the Rex parade.

73 Al Hirt, world famous jazz trumpeter, combines a remarkable blend of musicianship and showmanship. His virtuosity, drive, and energy have captured popular fancy. His New Orleans style has made him known to millions everywhere, and like Fountain he is at the forefront of his brand of music.

74 Jazz parades in New Orleans are still a common occurrence. This one is the Onward Brass Band marching up Royal Street with the usual crowd of "second-liners" tagging along. *Photo by Terry Friedman. Courtesy New Orleans Public Library*

Education

75 Samuel Jarvis Peters (1801–1855), best remembered as "the father of the public school system of New Orleans." A Canadian of American descent, he had come to New Orleans at twenty years of age, and without initial capital succeeded by dint of hard work within eight years to acquire a commanding position in the commercial affairs of the city. Elected to the city council, he was instrumental in having many of the streets of the city paved, sidewalks laid, and the levees graded and shelled. He and James Caldwell were the developers of the second municipality, the section above Canal Street, which they turned from a swamp into the most thriving part of New Orleans. With Caldwell and others, he built the magnificent St. Charles Hotel and the Merchants' Exchange, and made many other improvements in the burgeoning

75

American section of New Orleans. Peters was a leader in the movement that resulted in the establishment in 1841 of New Orleans's first tax-supported free public school system. By the time of his death in 1855, there were twenty-six public schoolhouses in the city, a tribute to his perspicacity. Two schools have been named after Peters, and each year on Founders' Day, a delegation from the present Samuel J. Peters Junior High School brings flowers to his grave in Lafayette Cemetery on Washington Avenue. *Courtesy Samuel J. Peters Junior High School*

76 McDonogh No. 1, Laurel Street between Philip and First streets, made possible by $750,000 from a legacy left the city by John McDonogh. It was used to build thirty-five public schools in New Orleans. Although Governor Claiborne had tried to establish a public school as early as 1804, apparently this came to naught, and the youth of the city attended private schools of which there were a number. In a study made in 1931 by Stuart Grayson Noble of Newcomb College he states:

> The educational needs of New Orleans during the first quarter of the nineteenth century were of a practical character. The schools were called upon to assist in overcoming the language difficulty brought about by the merging of the Anglo-American, French and Spanish elements in the community. The French and Anglo-Americans, it is true, often had separate private schools for their children, but, even in these, more than one language was taught. . . .
>
> The cultural demands were largely elementary. Girls were taught a smattering of the fine arts, needlework, and manners. Boys might study Latin, but seldom Greek. Books were scarce and reading was more for information than pleasure.
>
> The first public schools were viewed with some suspicion. In the Second Municipality, out of a

possible attendance of 3,000, only 13 pupils came when the first school opened, but the schools were soon accepted and by 1850, 6,385 children were attending when the total population was only 31,000 in this section of town.

77 In 1857, the St. John Evangelical Lutheran Congregation founded this grade school, which has had an uninterrupted history of more than a century of operations. August C. Reisig, the principal of the St. John School, is seen with some of his pupils in 1903.

78 Madame Picard's School, as it looked in 1860. Madame Picard's School (Markey-Picard Institute) was a typical Creole private school for boys and girls of the 1880s and 1890s. It was located at 2308 Esplanade. It still stands, but has been so badly mutilated that it is scarcely recognizable from the original structure. This large galleried mansion originally was the home of Michel Musson, a successful businessman who had once been postmaster of New Orleans. When Musson's nephew, the famous painter Edgar Degas, came from Paris for a visit in 1872–1873, he lived in this house and did much of his work there. *Courtesy Mrs. Milton L. Reisch*

77

76

78

79   80

79 St. Simeon's Select School, 1906. This large suburban residence, built in 1834, was the property of François Saulet. It was located on Annunciation Street between Melpomene and Thalia streets. After the Civil War, the building was occupied for many years by St. Simeon's Select School, and it later became part of Mercy Hospital before it was demolished in the 1960s to provide a site for a supermarket. *Courtesy Library of Congress*

80 Sophie Bell Wright (1866–1912) operated a girls' school called Home Institute, in its time one of the most prominent private schools in the city. Miss Wright also ran a night school for poor working girls—a pioneer venture in New Orleans.

81 Public libraries followed public schools by some years. In 1894, when this picture was made, the Fisk Free Library occupied quarters in Tulane Hall on University Place near Canal Street. The Fisk brothers, Abijah and Alvarez, through bequest and gift, were the founders of this library in the 1840s. The New Orleans City (Lyceum) Library, which had been housed in Gallier Hall, was consolidated with the Fisk Library in 1896, and the New Orleans Public Library was formed with thirty thousand volumes. Its first home was in St. Patrick's Hall (site of the old Post Office Building on Camp Street).

82 In 1906, Andrew Carnegie gave $250,000 (later increased to $375,000), which, supplemented by appropriations of the city council, was used to build this library at Lee Circle (1908). The building served until 1959 when it was demolished and the library moved to the present structure on Tulane Avenue.

81

82

83

83 The first institution of higher learning in Louisiana was the Collège d'Orléans, seen here in 1812, from the plan of the city of New Orleans and suburbs by J. Tanesse, city surveyor, 1817. Though projected in 1805 by Governor Claiborne, it did not open until 1811, but in 1825 the college closed its doors. The school was located on a site near the present St. Augustine's Catholic Church on St. Claude Avenue. Probably its most famous alumnus was the historian Charles Gayarré.

84 At a point when the first public school system was flourishing, the University of Louisiana had been in its infancy, seen here in the 1850s in this watercolor by Boyd Cruise. The university "campus" was located on Common Street between University Place and Baronne Street. It consisted of three buildings, all done in the Greek Revival style characteristic of New Orleans of the period, the medical department being housed in the largest central structure. The University of Louisiana was founded by constitutional mandate in 1847, and it absorbed the Medical College of Louisiana, which was established in New Orleans in 1834 through the efforts of seven physicians who saw the necessity for training men in that profession locally. Preparatory, law, and academic departments were organized at the new university, but poor student enrollment and meager state appropriations hindered growth. A disastrous yellow-fever epidemic in 1853 was an almost fatal blow, and the university had to close entirely during the Civil War. The university

fared a little better during Reconstruction times through appropriations by the state, although the actual funds were not always available. Despite its financial problems, the university made progress. *Courtesy Joseph Merrick Jones, Jr.*

85 Paul Tulane (1801–1887), founder of Tulane University, successor to the University of Louisiana. In 1881, an aloof, retiring, and austere bachelor, Tulane, then eighty years of age, made a decision in his home in Princeton, New Jersey, which was to change the picture of higher education in New Orleans. Tulane had come to New Orleans in 1822 and started a merchandising business, which, with shrewd investments in real estate, had brought him a fortune. In 1882, at his request, a board of administrators was formed in New Orleans, and Tulane deeded real estate worth half a million dollars to it to found an institution of "a higher grade of learning." The question of founding an entirely new university (which Paul Tulane favored) or amalgamating with the University of Louisiana, which still suffered from chronic financial difficulties, was resolved when a tax decision of the Supreme Court changed Paul Tulane's mind. He and the administrators agreed that they would take over the older institution. Thus, in 1884, a tax-exempt institution was formed, and the name of the university was officially changed to Tulane University of Louisiana in honor of Paul Tulane's beneficent gift.

85

84

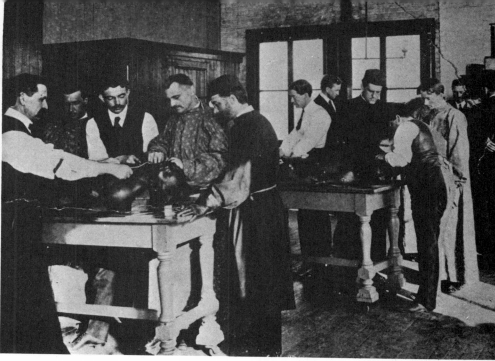

86

88

86 Josephine Le Monnier Newcomb (1816–1901), founder of Newcomb College at Tulane University. At Paul Tulane's death in 1887, the board of administrators had expected to receive the residue of his estate, but no will was found and the estate went to relatives. However, the year before, Josephine Le Monnier Newcomb, an extremely wealthy widow who called New Orleans her home, donated $100,000 to the board of administrators of Tulane University for the founding of a college for women in memory of her only daughter, Harriot Sophie Newcomb, who died at the age of fifteen in 1870. Like Tulane, Mrs. Newcomb was at times difficult to deal with, but unlike Tulane she left a will by which the university received $2,668,307 for Newcomb College endowment. She had previously given about $1 million, about the same amount Tulane had given. Newcomb was the first women's college in the country to be coordinated as part of a university.

87 Tulane University campus, 1895. By 1888, old buildings of the university on Common Street were in such poor shape that the board of administrators had decided to obtain a larger site for the university. In

1891, the Foucher tract opposite present-day Audubon Park was purchased for $37,500. An additional tract adjoining was purchased in 1893, thus increasing the site to fifty-eight acres. In January, 1894, the cornerstone of the first of three buildings on the new campus was laid. The building, now Gibson Hall, was named for United States Senator Randall Lee Gibson, whose diplomatic handling of the early negotiations with Paul Tulane paved the way for the establishment of the university. In the nearly three quarters of a century that have elapsed since Tulane moved "uptown," the university has grown from a "trolley-car," parochial seat of learning to an internationally recognized institution with eight thousand students from the United States and sixty foreign countries, and a faculty of distinguished educators. *Courtesy Dr. John P. Dyer*

88 Intent students learning dissecting techniques during a Tulane Medical School anatomy class in the 1890s at the Richardson Memorial Building on Canal Street. *Courtesy Medical Information Services, Tulane School of Medicine*

87

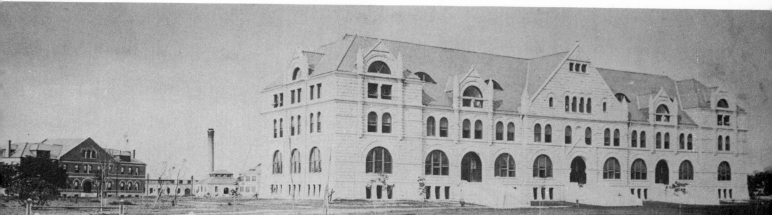

89

91

89 Tulane Medical School, which is not on the campus. The school comprises three buildings, the Hutchinson Memorial Building (1930), the Libby Memorial Building (1954), and the Burthe-Cottam Building (1963). The total area of the complex is in excess of half a million square feet. *Courtesy Medical Information Services, Tulane School of Medicine*

90 Another outstanding New Orleans school is Loyola University of the South, which began in 1904 as Loyola Academy under the leadership of Father Albert Biever, S.J. The academy later developed into a college of arts and sciences, and in 1910, as Loyola College, it merged with the College of the Immaculate Conception on Baronne Street when the latter became the Jesuit High School. On April 15, 1912, Loyola Col-

lege was incorporated as a university and authorized by the Louisiana Legislature to confer degrees. Schools of dentistry, law, music, and business administration were added through the years, and today Loyola is the largest Catholic university south of St. Louis, with an enrollment of 4,300. Marquette Hall, queen of Loyola's buildings and centerpiece of its campus horseshoe, was erected in 1911. *Courtesy Loyola University of the South*

91 Students for a Democratic Society from Tulane and Loyola universities marching on October 15, 1969, to protest the United States involvement in the war in Vietnam. *Courtesy Major Henry M. Morris, Chief of Detectives, New Orleans Police Department*

90

Literature

92 New Orleans has produced few world-famous authors, although many came to the city to observe and write. Among the first to settle in New Orleans was François Xavier Martin (1762–1846), seen here at sixty, a native of France who emigrated first to Martinique and later to New Bern, North Carolina, before coming to New Orleans. Martin had a colorful career as printer, lawyer, writer, and jurist. While most of his writings (thirty-four published volumes) consist of legal reports, he wrote the first comprehensive *History of Louisiana*. It was published in New Orleans in 1827.

93 Charles Gayarré (1805–1895), scholar and pioneer Louisiana historian, was the grandson of New Orleans's first mayor, Jean Étienne Boré, and spent his childhood on Boré's plantation. He entered politics, eventually being elected United States senator in 1835. Failing health induced him to resign and travel to France for treatment. It was during this period that he did extensive research on Louisiana in the French Archives in Paris. His *Histoire de la Louisiane* was published in French in 1846–1847 and his monumental *History of Louisiana* in four volumes from 1854 to 1866. It was largely through his efforts that many original documents relating to Louisiana were purchased from France and Spain and returned to New Orleans.

94 A page from *De Bow's Review*, edited by J. D. B. De Bow in New Orleans and published between 1857 and 1870. The review was almost the sole literary effort in New Orleans in the barren period immediately after the Civil War. De Bow managed to sandwich between its articles on commerce and economics an occasional essay or poem and some well-written information pieces on contemporary life.

95 J. D. B. De Bow.

92

93

94

95

DE BOW'S REVIEW,
INDUSTRIAL RESOURCES,
ETC.

EDITED BY J. D. B. DE BOW,
PROFESSOR OF POLITICAL ECONOMY IN THE UNIVERSITY OF LOUISIANA.

TABLE OF CONTENTS.

ART. I.—THE UNITED STATES MAIL.......... 553
    By D. D. Leach, of Washington, D. C.
ART. II.—STATISTICAL CONGRESS OF NATIONS AT BRUSSELS.......... 570
ART. III.—EDUCATION AND CRIME AT THE NORTH AND THE SOUTH.......... 575
    By J. T. Trezevant, of Tennessee.
ART. IV.—EMANCIPATION IN JAMAICA—ITS WORKINGS.......... 581
ART. V.—SEA-COAST CROPS OF THE SOUTH.... 589
    By R. F. W. Allston, of South Carolina.
ART. VI.—GREAT CITIES OF THE WEST—CINCINNATI. No. III.......... 615

ART. VII.—SUBMARINE TELEGRAPH ACROSS THE ATLANTIC.......... 625
    Letter by Lieut. Maury.
ART. VIII.—SYSTEM OF COTTON MANUFACTURES IN THE U. S.......... 629
ART. IX.—THE GREAT SOUTHERN CONVENTION IN CHARLESTON.......... 633
ART. X.—THE BATTLE OF NEW ORLEANS.......... 641
ART. XI.—INTERESTING RAILROAD STATISTICS. 647
ART. XII.—RAILROADS.......... 649
ART. XIII.—COMMERCE AND NAVIGATION OF THE UNITED STATES.......... 652
ART. XIV.—EDITORIAL, BOOK NOTICES, ETC.... 655

PUBLICATION OFFICE, MERCHANTS' EXCHANGE, (OVER POST OFFICE,) NEW-ORLEANS—WASHINGTON-CITY.

☞ Postage Two Cents a Number, if Prepaid Quarterly.

96   **97**

99

100

96 Lafcadio Hearn (1850–1904) came to New Orleans from Cincinnati in 1877 and spent ten years there, first working for the *Item* and later for the *Times-Democrat*. Hearn's delightful newspaper sketches of Creole life were later collected and published by Albert Mordell in *An American Miscellany* and by Charles W. Hutson in *Editorials and Fantastics and other Fancies*. His *Chita*, the story of the hurricane that destroyed Last Island, earned him the reputation of a "lapidary in words." Hearn and George Cable collaborated with W. H. Coleman in the *Historical Sketch Book and Guide to New Orleans and Environs*, which was published at the time of the Cotton Centennial Exposition in 1884.

97 George Washington Cable (1844–1925) was born in New Orleans, and at only fifteen was thrown upon his own resources. After serving in the Confederate army he returned to New Orleans, worked for a cotton firm, and as a reporter for the *Picayune*, meanwhile absorbing the local scene and making notes for his inimitable stories. *Scribner's Magazine* published his "'Sieur George" in 1873, and Cable, who had opened a heretofore unexplored vein in his stories of New Orleans Creole life, found himself hailed as a genius. So well did Cable use the New Orleans locale in his stories, that three of his fictional houses are still pointed out—'Tite Poulette's Dwelling at 710 Dumaine Street, Madame John's Legacy at 632 Dumaine Street, and 'Sieur George's House at 640 Royal Street, all fortunately preserved. Other well-known works include *The Creoles of Louisiana, Old Creole Days, The Grandissimes, Dr. Sevier,* and *Kincaid's Battery.*

98 Madame John's Legacy, rebuilt after the original was destroyed by fire in 1788.

98

99 Grace King (1851–1932) was the daughter of a distinguished southern family and early came under the influence of a Creole teacher, although no Creole herself. Miss King had a passionate love for her city and region, a feeling that quickened when she met and grew to know well the Creole historian Charles Gayarré. A contemporary of Cable, she felt that his writings distorted the Creole way of life, and when Richard Watson Wilder, editor of *Century Magazine*, challenged her with, "If Cable is so false to you, why do not some of you write better?" she wrote *Monsieur Motte*, which was published in 1886. Encouraged, she wrote *New Orleans, The Place and the People; Creole Families of New Orleans; De Soto in the Land of Florida; Sieur de Bienville;* and a number of other books, which have earned her a high place among New Orleans writers.

100 While recuperating on the Gulf Coast, Dorothy Dix (Mrs. Elizabeth M. Gilmer, 1870–1951), met Mrs. E. J. Nicholson, the owner of the *Picayune*. Dorothy sold her first story to the *Picayune* for $3 and shortly thereafter joined its staff and began her articles for women. In 1901, she went to work initially for the *New York Evening Journal* and remained in the metropolis for twenty years. By the 1920s, she was the highest paid woman writer in the world and her column on advice for the lovelorn was carried by newspapers all over the country.

101   **102**   **103**

101 O. Henry (William Sydney Porter, 1862–1910). He arrived in New Orleans in 1896 after fleeing from Texas where he had been charged with embezzlement. It was here, he told an interviewer, that he adopted his pen name and took up his literary work in earnest. He frequented the restaurant of Madame Begué and later used her in one of his stories. While only in New Orleans a comparatively short time, he stored up enough background for four of his stories of the city: *Cherchez la Femme, Whistling Dick's Christmas Stocking, Blind Man's Holiday,* and *Renaissance at Charleroi.*

102 In 1921, Julius Friend (*left*), Albert Goldstein (*center*), Basil Thompson (*right*), with John McClure (*not shown*) founded *The Double Dealer,* a "little" literary magazine, which, breaking with past traditional southern romanticism, printed the early works of the then unknown William Faulkner, Ernest Hemingway, and Thornton Wilder. During the almost five and a half years of its existence, *The Double Dealer* achieved a national reputation as an excellent literary journal. In the 1920s, before the restoration movement had taken firm hold in the Vieux Carré, the French Quarter was a sort of Left-Bank Paris, which attracted struggling artists and young writers. These types reveled in the picturesque atmosphere of the decaying old buildings and found the low rents helpful to the pocketbook. Attracted to this scene were the artist William Spratling, and the writers Sherwood Anderson, William Faulkner, Oliver La Farge, Lyle Saxon, E. P. O'Donnell, and John McClure. From time to time other literary lights dropped in, among them Gertrude Stein, John Dos Passos, Erskine Caldwell, and John Steinbeck. Anderson came in 1922 and lived in the Vieux Carré until 1925. While here, he was the central figure of the Vieux Carré literary group. He wrote the novel *Many Marriages* in New Orleans and contributed a number of pieces to *The Double Dealer.* Faulkner wrote most of his first novel, *Soldier's Pay,* during his stay in 1924–1925.

103 Frances Parkinson Keyes (1885–1970), world-famous novelist, was a part of the New Orleans scene for thirty years. Coming in 1940 when she wrote *Crescent Carnival,* she soon returned and, fascinated by the wealth of material for her novels in Louisiana, made New Orleans her winter residence and determined to write about this region. Restoring the historic Beauregard mansion and garden, she gave it to a non-profit foundation for the eventual benefit of the citizens of New Orleans. From her studio in Beauregard House have come a score of novels about New Orleans and Louisiana, among them *Steamboat Gothic, The Chess Players, Madame Castel's Lodger,* and *Dinner at Antoine's.* This last reached a sale of 2 million copies. Mrs. Keyes wrote some fifty books, many of which have been published in twelve foreign languages. *Photo by André Snow*

104 Part of the Federal Writers' Project in New Orleans, 1936. These workers were employed to measure and draw the most important of New Orleans's old buildings, compile and publish translations of old city records, steamboat statistics, genealogical records in cemeteries, etc., much of which has been of great value to historians.

104

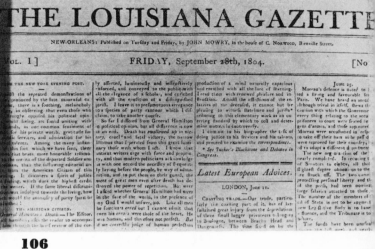

105

105 *Moniteur de la Louisiane,* the first newspaper in New Orleans, published in 1794 by Louis Duclot. It was established under the Spanish regime, a quarter of a century after French rule had ceased. Sanctioned as the official news organ of the government, the *Moniteur* devoted very little space to local news events, as happenings in the city were usually common knowledge long before the paper came from the press. A conglomeration of advertisements, clippings from foreign papers, poems, fiction, and "cards" from readers, the paper somehow survived for twenty years, well into the American era. This edition is dated October 23, 1802. *Courtesy New Orleans Public Library*

106 Masthead of *The Louisiana Gazette,* September 28, 1804, the year of its founding, one of the first English newspapers to be published in New Orleans. During the early nineteenth century, French newspapers were dominant, springing up like weeds—seven before 1810, three between 1810 and 1820, and six between 1820 and 1830. There was an immigration of men both enterprising and competent to edit, and a population eager to read newspapers. Factional jealousies between Creoles and Americans probably also played a part. Most of the newspapers of the period died within a year but *L'Abeille,* founded in 1827, nearly reached the century mark, expiring in 1925. *Courtesy New Orleans Public Library*

107 Masthead of the first issue of *The Picayune,* Jan-

uary 25, 1837. Two printers, Francis Asbury Lumsden and George Wilkins Kendall, published this first edition of what was to be the only paper (with numerous combinations through the years) to survive to the present. Patterning their paper after the northern penny press, they sold it for a picayune (6¼¢) and filled it with brief light articles, even flippant in tone, a new treatment of news in New Orleans journalism. There were five other daily newspapers in 1837—*The Louisiana Courier, Louisiana Advertiser, L'Abeille, True American,* and *The Commercial Bulletin.*

108 Colonel Francis Asbury Lumsden (1800–1860), Kendall's partner in founding *The Picayune.*

109 George Wilkins Kendall (1809–1867), cofounder of *The Picayune.*

108   **109**   **111**

110

THE PICAYUNE.
[NO. 72. CAMP STREET.]
By F. A. LUMSDEN & G. W. KENDALL.
Friday Evening, October 20, 1837.

Our Horse.

Just look at him—see how he bounds o'er hedge and stlie—see how his legs fly and never touch the ground—observe how the Bee and Bulletin are in pursuit of him—see how our printer's devil hails him with the greeting of "go it Pic.!"—look what a good humored rider he has—see how he cracks his whip and leaves his pursuers in the lurch—observe his look of independence—scan his eye glistening with fun and pleasure—now just look at the flush of conscious victory which plays upon his brow as he lets fly the streamer bearing the words "you're all too late—my news is for the Picayune!" And that is the way the Picayune will do business this winter. It will be the first to publish all news, commercial, political, and foreign. Our horse is a capital animal—we are delighted with him. Mr. Gibson's horse used to run last winter an *hour* in thirty minutes; our horse will go it in 2½ minutes precisely. It is thus that we will outrun all our neighbors and instil new life and vigor into the press of New Orleans.

110 Before nine months of publication, the *Picayune's* proprietors inaugurated a pony express to hasten the news from the east. It was before the invention of the telegraph and the expansion of the railroads, and mail was carried by stage. Kendall and Lumsden's system brought their "slips" (clippings from eastern papers) in sooner than did their competitors. This issue is the announcement of the *Picayune's* pony express, October 20, 1837.

111 When E. J. Holbrook, editor of the *Picayune*, died in 1876, his young widow, better known as the poet Pearl Rivers, took over the management and editing of the paper. This remarkable woman, born Eliza Jane Poitevent, was probably the first woman journalist in the South, having worked on the *Picayune* as literary editor prior to her marriage. The *Picayune* was heavily in debt at the time of her husband's death, but she resolutely set about to direct its affairs. In 1878, she married George Nicholson who had been with the paper since 1842 and who was then its business manager. So successful was this pair in the operation of the paper, creating new departments, championing reforms, and increasing the advertising, that by 1891 the *Picayune* had the largest circulation of any New Orleans newspaper. *From* New Orleans Yesterday and Today

112 Mastheads of seven newspapers published in New Orleans between 1838 and 1854. *Courtesy New Orleans Public Library*

112

New-Orleans Price-Current,
AND
COMMERCIAL INTELLIGENCER.
PRINTED AND PUBLISHED WEEKLY BY BENJAMIN LEVY.....EDITED BY GEORGE B. YOUNG.

VOL. IX.—No. 24.   NEW-ORLEANS, SATURDAY, JUNE 9, 1838.   NEW SERIES.

List of Vessels in the Port of New-Orleans.

113 In this 1857 city directory frontispiece, no fewer than seven buildings occupied by newspapers are depicted as an example of the engraver's art. *Courtesy New Orleans Public Library*

114 Political cartoons began to appear in New Orleans newspapers in 1876. This one, from *L'Abeille*, April 23, 1899, was meant to needle the authorities to hurry with the repaving of Chartres Street.

115 Cover of *Comptes Rendus de l'Athénée Louisianais*, March, 1955, a well-written French periodical still published today—the only French publication in Louisiana. Almost imperceptibly since the coming of the Americans in 1803, French culture in New Orleans had begun to decline. The French, who had dominated the Germans (who had come to Louisiana in an earlier day), were themselves gradually dominated by the greater aggressiveness and numerical superiority of their American fellow citizens. The Civil War caused further separation between the Creoles and France; no longer did they travel to France, and the public schools here deprived their children of the study of French. The older Creoles, therefore, founded *l'Athénée Louisianais* in 1876 and in the following year began to publish *Les Comptes Rendus*.

113

La Nouvelle-Orléans, Mars 1955

COMPTES RENDUS
de
L'ATHÉNÉE LOUISIANAIS

Fondé en 1876

SOMMAIRE

Ephémérides—Saison 1953-1954

Concours de 1955

Lionel Charles Durel
Nécrologie par James F. Bezou

Hommage aux Acadiens
Dagmar Renshaw LeBreton

Les Contes Populaires de la Louisiane
Calvin Claudel

En Marge d'une Affiche de Théâtre de 1799
René J. Le Gardeur, Jr.

Le Théâtre d'Orléans en Tournée
dans les Villes du Nord 1827-1833
Sylvie Chevalley

Revue Littéraire:
A Propos de Deux Livres
Simone de la Souchère Deléry

Une Nouvelle Histoire de la Louisiane
George Raffalovich

La livraison: $1.50
Siège Social, 1925 Esplanade Avenue
New Orleans 16, Louisiana

Imprimerie E. P. Rivas, Inc., La Nouvelle-Orléans

115

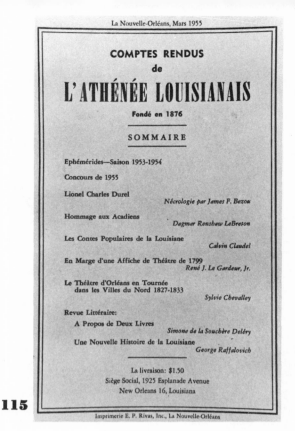

116 Cover of *The Louisiana Historical Quarterly*, October, 1930. A valuable source of Louisiana historical material is contained in the thirty-four-year run. This publication came to full flower under the editorships of Henry P. Dart and Walter Prichard.

116

114

La Rue de Chartres en 1900.

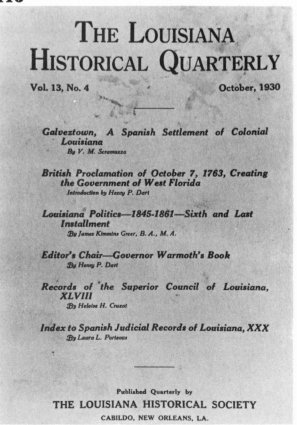

THE LOUISIANA
HISTORICAL QUARTERLY

Vol. 13, No. 4   October, 1930

Galveztown, A Spanish Settlement of Colonial
Louisiana
By V. M. Scramuzza

British Proclamation of October 7, 1763, Creating
the Government of West Florida
Introduction by Henry P. Dart

Louisiana Politics—1845-1861—Sixth and Last
Installment
By James Kimmins Greer, B. A., M. A.

Editor's Chair—Governor Warmoth's Book
By Henry P. Dart

Records of the Superior Council of Louisiana,
XLVIII
By Heloise H. Cruzat

Index to Spanish Judicial Records of Louisiana, XXX
By Laura L. Porteous

Published Quarterly by
THE LOUISIANA HISTORICAL SOCIETY
CABILDO, NEW ORLEANS, LA.

Fine Art

117 The earliest known painter who worked in New Orleans was Jean Pierre Lassus, the surveyor-painter. But he did not remain long in the colony. His *Veue et Perspective de la Nouvelle Orleans,* painted in 1726, hangs on the walls of the French National Archives in Paris. Any portraits or scenes of New Orleans painted in the French regime would have been destroyed in the great fires of 1788 and 1794 because the next earliest painter we know about is Francisco Salazar. Salazar probably painted the portrait of Don Andrés Almonester y Roxas and others, especially that of the Montégut family. In 1803, J. L. Bouqueto de Woiseri painted his *View of New Orleans from the Plantation of Marigny.* French artists Félix Achille Beaupoil de Saint-Aulaire and Charles Alexandre Le Sueur have left us several interesting mementos of their stay here in the 1820s and 1830s.

In the 1830s the growing wealth and culture of New Orleans attracted a number of painters, mostly portraitists. One of the best known was the well-trained Frenchman Jean Joseph Vaudechamp, who painted in the style of Ingres. Vaudechamp painted the leading citizens and their wives, and many of his portraits are in the Louisiana State Museum and in private collections. Two visiting Frenchmen painted memorable New Orleans pictures. One was Hippolyte Sebron, who painted the best-known steamboat picture, *Giant Steamboats at New Orleans* and the famed impressionist Edgar Degas, whose *Cotton Market of*

New Orleans is one of the prized possessions of the Museum of Pau, France.

In the 1880s there was an art revival in New Orleans. The Southern Art Association was formed in 1883 and soon had a membership of five hundred. In 1887, Ellsworth Woodward, himself a painter of no mean ability, founded the art department of Newcomb College. The Newcomb Art School flourished, and in 1897 Ellsworth and his brother William added a pottery department, which in the next two decades won worldwide acclaim for its output. In the 1920s the Arts and Crafts School, 712 Royal Street, was founded, and for a number of years trained many artists. *Courtesy French National Archives*

118 The Isaac Delgado Museum of Art, opened in 1911, became the repository of several New Orleans collections—the Hyams Barbizon and Salon paintings, the Morgan Whitney jades, and the Howard collection of Greek pottery. WPA workers are seen here at the museum during the 1930s. *Courtesy New Orleans Public Library*

119 A handsome Greek Revival building located in City Park, the museum for years was a kind of art mausoleum, and it was not until the arrival of its first professional director, Alonzo Lansford in 1948, that the institution took on new life. He and Arthur Feitel, the president of the Delgado board, secured thirty-

two Italian Renaissance paintings of the Kress collection, and paintings of modern schools began to appear on its walls. Lansford's successor, Sue Thurman (1958–1961), and its present director, James B. Byrnes, who came in 1962 under a completely reorganized Isaac Delgado Museum of Art Association, have done wonders in scheduling shows and in the acquisi-

tion of important works of art through purchase or gifts. In 1970, three large wings were started to more than double the size of the museum and provide a much-needed auditorium. This is how the expanded Isaac Delgado Museum of Art will look. *Courtesy Isaac Delgado Museum of Art*

120

120 One of the most fascinating objects in the collection of the Louisiana State Museum at the Cabildo is the death mask of Emperor Napoleon Bonaparte. It was made by Francisco Antommarchi, who had attended the emperor in St. Helena when he died. *Courtesy Louisiana State Museum*

Cuisine and Restaurants

121 New Orleans has always had a reputation for good food. In 1885, the gastronomic guide in *Coleman's Guide to New Orleans* wrote:

> For an ordinary dinner, a hungry man, dropping casually into a restaurant, should take a soup and some fish; then an *entrée,* say a sweetbread, or a lamb chop; then say a spring chicken, or roast beef, or roast mutton or veal, with one or two dishes of vegetables. For dessert, some fruit or jelly, and cheese, and a cup of coffee. With a half bottle of claret, this would cost from $1.50 to $2.00.

He could have been writing about McDonnell's restaurant, seen here in 1859. The city's restaurants are bracketed with the best of those in New York and San Francisco, and nearly every visitor samples the cuisine of at least one or two restaurants. Such palate-pleasing specialties as oysters Rockefeller, pompano en papillote, shrimp bisque cardinal, filet of beef marchand de vin, creole gumbo, filet of trout meunière or amandine, trout marguery, bouillabaisse à la marseillaise (with a Creole touch), soufflé potatoes, buster crabs, cherries jubilée, café brûlot diabolique, and other dishes equally tempting are readily available in the leading restaurants.

122 A pompano dinner at the lake (1872), sketch by Alfred R. Wand.

New Orleans is not considered really visited without a trip to the lake for a fish or game dinner. There are three places to choose from: Milneburg, West End and Spanish Fort, and several restaurants at each. . . .

McDONNELL'S

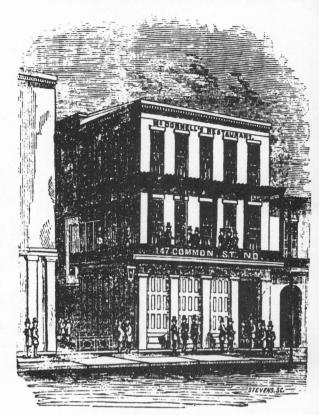

RESTAURANT

121

From Coleman's Guide to New Orleans, *1885*

122

123

124

125

123 At mid-nineteenth century, one of the most delightful places to dine was Boudro's restaurant in Milneburg. Lucien Boudro, noted for his court bouillon and other fish dishes, operated this restaurant for twenty-five years, and his successors continued in business for years after his death in 1867. Boudro was engaged by the Baroness Pontalba as caterer for Jenny Lind when she came to New Orleans in 1850 and was the baroness's guest. But Boudro's name was immortalized by William Makepeace Thackeray when the latter came to New Orleans in 1856 to lecture and was taken to Boudro's for dinner. Thackeray, who had a liking for good food and wine, wrote in *A Mississippi Bubble:* "At that comfortable tavern on Pontchartrain we had a bouillabaisse than which a better was never eaten at Marseilles; and not the least headache in the morning. I give you my word, on the contrary, you only wake with a sweet refreshing thirst for claret and water." Boudro's restaurant adjoined his home and garden, seen in this watercolor. *Courtesy Richard Koch*

124 There were many small restaurants in the Vieux Carré in the late nineteenth century. This one bore the title Au Rendezvous des Compagnons de l'Art Culinaire, and was located on Chartres Street. Sketch by William Woodward, 1904.

125 One of the favorite restaurants of a great many New Orleanians is Galatoire's at 209 Bourbon Street. Galatoire's is a seafood restaurant *par excellence,* although they prepare meat and chicken dishes very well too. Some of their specialties are trout marguery, a heavenly mixture of trout, shrimp, and other seafood served with a rich white sauce; trout meunière amandine, a filet of trout coated in milk and fried in butter and garnished with almonds; oysters en brochette; crabmeat maison, eggs Sardou, broiled pompano or broiled redfish and stuffed eggplant—all delicious dishes. Galatoire's doesn't advertise, accepts no reservations, and there is usually a line in front of the door by 11:45 in the morning, soon after the restaurant opens. Beyond the small marble-fronted building,

Galatoire's interior is lined with mirrors, and coat hangers are attached to the wall every few feet. More than one patron has said that the interior of Galatoire's is reminiscent of a large, old-time barbershop. But it's been that way since 1905 when the brothers Galatoire started in business, and the present members of the family intend to keep it that way; their steady patrons agree with them. *Courtesy The Vieux Carré Survey*

126 Bégué's Restaurant, 1906. Hippolyte Bégué and his German-born wife ran this eating place (right-hand corner) opposite the French Market. Madame Bégué was a good cook, the fame of her dishes spread, and the place became well patronized. After Hippolyte's death, his widow continued to operate the restaurant, which then became known as Madame Bégué's. *Courtesy Library of Congress*

127 There was nothing fancy about Bégué's—Madame cooked on this cast-iron, wood-burning stove.

128 129 Bégué's became well known and loved by gastronomes for Sunday morning breakfasts. These gentlemen, each with his own bottle of wine, were snapped while enjoying one such breakfast.

126

128

129

Madame Begue's Breakfast Menus for a Week.

MONDAY
Toast Bread Omelet
Broiled Ham   Potatoes with White Sauce
Jambalaya of Chicken and Ham
Roast Turkey
Mayonaise of Celery and Shrimps
Fruit   Coffee

TUESDAY
Chicken a la Creole
Kidney with Tomato Sauce   Veal Omelet
Mayonaise of Fish   Stuffed Tomatoes
Pineapple with Port Wine   Coffee

WEDNESDAY
Blanquette of Veal
Spaghetti with Shrimps   Ham Omelet
Liver a la Begue   Roast Duck
Strawberries with Madeira Wine   Coffee

THURSDAY
Broiled Beefsteak   Sweetbread Omelet
Court Bouillon   Fried Eggplant
Broiled Sausage   Anchovy Salad
Fruit   Coffee

FRIDAY
Turtle Soup   Fish with Tomato Sauce
Potato Omelet   Stuffed Eggs
Jambalaya of Rice and Shrimps
Fruit   Coffee

SATURDAY
Mutton Feet with Creole Sauce
Oyster Omelet   Snails
Liver a la Begue   Egg Salad
Fruit   Coffee

SUNDAY
Bouchees a la Reine   Creamed Cauliflower
Veal Omelet   Eggs with Tomato Sauce
Eggplant with Rice and Ham
Roast Turkey stuffed with Truffles

127

130

131

132

130 Fabacher's restaurant. Anthony Fabacher, one of a family of restaurateurs, operated this one in 1906 at Royal and Iberville streets. It succeeded one founded in 1881 by Joseph and Lawrence Fabacher.

131 Brass token issued by Louis Martin, who started his Bohemian Tavern on Iberville and Exchange Alley in 1904 (still in operation by his sons). The token was free with a five-cent glass of beer. It could then be taken to the lunch counter and exchanged for food. *Courtesy Arthur Martin*

132 The most famous restaurant in New Orleans is undoubtedly Antoine's. Founded in 1840, Antoine's, with its old-fashioned building and unpretentious interior (except for the hundreds of framed pictures of the great and near great who have dined there that adorn its walls), is a *must* for tourists who come to the Crescent City. Antoine's is noted for oysters Rockefeller, pompano en papillote, shrimp cardinal, trout amandine, soufflé potatoes, filet of beef marchand de vin, and many other mouth-watering dishes. *Photo by Charles L. Franck*

133 Interior of Antoine's. For many years the restaurant has catered to the inner circle of New Orleans carnival Krewes. Its Rex Room, with pictures of former kings of carnival and mementos of nearly a hundred years of Rex rule, is the scene of many private banquets, this one for the former kings of carnival. *Photo by Teunisson, ca. 1910*

133

134

134 View of the wine cellar at Antoine's, which contains over twenty thousand bottles of imported wines and liqueurs. *Courtesy New Orleans Public Library*

135 View of the kitchen at Antoine's in 1951. Up until about 1965, the cooking was done on French coal ranges, but lack of parts forced the restaurant to change to gas ranges. *Photo by R. E. Covey. Courtesy New Orleans Public Library*

136 Maylie's Restaurant—Maylie and Esparbé's—which catered to the butchers of the Poydras Market. Established in 1876, it has survived the passing of the old market and is well patronized today. A notable feature is the huge wisteria vine that blooms each spring over the upper gallery of this Poydras Street establishment. Its trunk, more than a foot in diameter, was once indoors, but when the street adjoining was widened, it again came into the sunshine. Maylie's Restaurant was long noted for its soup and its excellent soup-meat, which was a traditional dish. *Photo by Charles L. Franck*

135

136

137 The great dish of New Orleans, and which it claims the honor of having invented, is the GOMBO. There is no dish which at the same time so tickles the palate, satisfies the appetite, furnishes the body with nutriment sufficient to carry on the physical requirements, and costs so little as a Creole Gombo. It is a dinner in itself, being soup, *pièce de résistance, entremet* and vegetables in one. Healthy, not heating to the stomach and easy of digestion, it should grace every table.

From Coleman's Guide to New Orleans, *1885*

137

138

139

140

141

138 Brennan's French Restaurant, 417 Royal Street, is physically one of the most attractive. Occupying an ancient bank building, which was also the home of the world's champion chess player, Paul Morphy, Brennan's has been elegantly restored and adapted to its new use. It is noted for its New Orleans–style breakfasts, which can sometimes begin at 9:30 A.M. and end as late as 2:00 in the afternoon! Breakfast, if the weather is good, usually starts with an eye-opener or two (Bloody Mary, Sazerac, Gin Fizz) in the lovely tree-shaded patio at the rear of the restaurant. Once at table, there is a bewildering choice of foods, from creole cream cheese through the marvelous egg dishes, such as eggs hussarde, eggs à la Nouvelle Orléans (poached eggs, lump crabmeat, cream sauce with brandy), eggs Sardou and eggs Portuguese, and sautéed bananas to mention but a few. *Courtesy New Orleans Public Library*

139 Arnaud's is another well-known New Orleans restaurant at 813 Bienville Street. Its shrimp Arnaud and filet of redfish with lump crabmeat hollandaise are famous. The restaurant is especially known for its luncheons.

140 Commander's Palace, 1403 Washington Avenue, in the Garden District, is known for oysters Bienville, crabmeat imperial, stuffed flounder, and soft-shell turtle stew. Commander's Palace serves outdoors in good weather on an attractive patio, and the decor of its indoor dining rooms is Victorian.

141 Kolb's Restaurant, 125 St. Charles Avenue. Kolb's is situated in two old buildings that still retain their cast-iron balconies so characteristic of the New Orleans of a century ago. Creolized versions of German dishes are served in a charming old-world dining room.

These and others, which range from the grand New Orleans French and Creole restaurants to oyster bars, poor-boy sandwich shops, and neighborhood restaurants, are listed and rated for cooking, decor, price, and service in *The New Orleans Underground Gourmet* by Richard H. Collin. *Courtesy Times-Picayune*

4. PERSONALITIES AND CUSTOMS

Famous Visitors

1

2

1 New Orleans has played host to many famous people, always extending warm cordiality for which it bears an enviable reputation. Marie Joseph Paul Yves Roch Gilbert du Motier, Marquis de Lafayette (1757–1834), was among a long line of distinguished visitors.

In 1825, the sixty-eight-year-old Lafayette on a tour of the United States had accepted the invitation of New Orleans to visit the Crescent City. The city government moved out of the Cabildo and the building was redecorated as his residence.

Leaving Mobile on his tour, Lafayette boarded the steamboat *Natchez* on April 8, and after a stormy voyage through Mississippi Sound in which everyone became seasick, the *Natchez* landed at the Chalmette battlefield in a downpour of rain where the general was met by Governor Johnson and the party escorted to New Orleans. Arriving at the Place d'Armes, he was welcomed by Mayor Roffignac under a triumphal arch that had been erected in his honor amid the roar of cannon, the pealing of bells, and the acclaim of hundreds who threw their hats in the air or waved handkerchiefs and shouted "Vive Lafayette!" Festivities went on for six days until April 15 when an immense crowd gathered at the Cabildo, "Lafayette's House," to see him off on his voyage upriver to Baton Rouge,

Natchez, St. Louis, and other cities. Illustration by Julien, lithographed by Bichebois, 1830.

2 The ornate Arc de Triomphe erected in the Place d'Armes for Lafayette's visit. It was designed by the city's engineer, J. Pilié, and made by J. B. Fogliardi, who also made this engraving. It was sixty-eight feet high, fifty-eight feet wide, and twenty-five feet deep. The top was forty feet above the street. It is believed to have been constructed of canvas over a wooden framework; the base was painted to resemble green marble and the top portion yellow marble. Painted on the base were figures representing Justice and Liberty; adorning the arch were two allegorical forms depicting Fame with trumpets and ribands bearing the names of Washington and Lafayette. The roof bore inscriptions in French and English: "A grateful Republic consecrates this monument to Lafayette." The topmost figure was that representing Wisdom crowning a bust of Franklin. *From* Visite de Général La Fayette à la Louisiane, *1825*

3 Brown Pelican—one of the 1,065 birds that John J. Audubon drew for *The Birds of America*, published in England in the famous Elephant Folio between 1826 and 1838. While in New Orleans, Audubon drew at least fifty-six birds of the 489 distinct species in this

3

here has made the town one scene of wild joy and happy commotion."

In September, 1863, General Ulysses S. Grant came fresh from the federal victory at Vicksburg to confer with General Nathaniel P. Banks. Grant was thrown from his horse as he was riding up St. Charles Avenue when the horse shied at a locomotive.

Grant next visited New Orleans in 1880 on a tour that he hoped would generate support for his nomination for a third term as president.

Like Grant, Teddy Roosevelt also visited New Orleans twice. The first time was when he was passing through the city in 1898 with more than nine hundred Roughriders on his way to Cuba. His next time was a whirlwind nine-hour visit on October 18, 1905. So great was the cheering of the huge crowd at City Hall that speeches of welcome by Governor N. C. Blanchard and Mayor Martin Behrman could not be heard, and Roosevelt had to cut his speech to a few words. *Photo by Mathew B. Brady*

5 William McKinley, the first President of the United States to visit New Orleans while in office, May 2, 1901, at the balcony of the Cabildo. *Photo by John N. Teunisson*

6 President William Howard Taft visited New Orleans twice in 1909. In February, he attended a carnival ball and was guest of honor at a banquet attended by four hundred persons. He came again in October 30, 1909, traveling by steamboat, and was accompanied by 117 senators and congressmen, 24 governors, and 3 diplomats to inspect possibilities for waterway improvements. He is seen here playing golf during his second visit. President Warren G. Harding visited New Orleans on Nobember 18, 1920, on his way to Panama.

rare first edition, which numbered only about 190 sets (and sold in those days for $1,000 a set).

4 General Zachary Taylor. Before Taylor's visit in 1840, the city had turned out to welcome General Andrew Jackson, who was invited to attend the twenty-fifth anniversary of the Battle of New Orleans. There were military reviews, a theatre party at the St. Charles Theatre, and Jackson laid the cornerstone for a monument in the Place d'Armes (eventually to be surmounted by his own bronze figure) before he left.

But then in 1847, an even bigger celebration was accorded General Zachary Taylor, "Old Rough-and-Ready," the hero of the war with Mexico, who paid a short visit to New Orleans December 3 to 5. Another triumphal arch was erected in the Place d'Armes, and the general, who had adopted Louisiana as his home and had a plantation near Baton Rouge, was welcomed by forty thousand persons who jammed the square and nearby streets. After much festivity, the legislature presented him with a sword before he left, and the *Daily Picayune* commented, "His presence

4

5

6

7

7 President Franklin D. Roosevelt came to New Orleans on April 29, 1937, to dedicate Roosevelt Mall in City Park. Here he attends a banquet at Antoine's. On October 17, 1953, President Dwight D. Eisenhower reviewed a mock carnival parade of floats from both Comus and Rex organizations on the occasion of the sesquicentennial celebration of the Louisiana Purchase. President John F. Kennedy made a quick and unexpected trip to New Orleans on May 4, 1962, where he addressed a group attending the dedication of the dock board's Nashville Avenue wharf.

Notable Residents

8 New Orleans has always had its share of outstanding citizens, among them Judah Touro, one of the benefactors of New Orleans. Touro was born in Newport, Rhode Island, in 1775. The son of a rabbi, he was left an orphan at twelve and reared by his mother's family in Boston. Entering his uncle's business, he began a mercantile career that was eventually to make him one of the richest men in New Orleans

(he arrived penniless in 1801 at the age of twenty-six). Opening a store, he soon had a profitable business. Always courteous, completely honest in his dealings, and prompt in his payments, Touro soon expanded his activities and became a trusted representative of eastern firms, a shipowner, and a real-estate investor. Touro became a philanthropist who helped both Jew and Gentile alike. In 1822, when the First Presbyterian Church at Gravier and St. Charles was about to be sold by the sheriff, Touro bought it and presented it to the congregation, whose minister, Dr. Clapp, he greatly admired. Later he bought the old Episcopal (Christ) Church on Bourbon and Canal streets, remodeled it, and presented it to the newly organized Jewish congregation. He also contributed funds to this congregation, which built the classical edifice (later the Knights of Columbus Hall) on Carondelet Street. In 1852, he bought two buildings on Gaiennie Street and converted them into a hospital under the direction of Dr. Joseph Bensadon. This, with a bequest after his death, was the beginning of the Touro Infirmary.

Judah Touro died in his Canal Street home on November 18, 1854, at the age of seventy-nine, leaving bequests to more than sixty charities, Jewish and Gentile, and the residue of his estate to his faithful friend Shepherd, who had saved his life nearly forty years before. Among his bequests was $80,000 to establish an almshouse, which after many vicissitudes still functions as the Touro-Shakspeare Home for the elderly in Algiers. Today both Touro Synagogue and Touro Infirmary honor the name of one of New Orleans's most self-effacing and generous men.

9 Judah Touro was a contributor to the building of this synagogue on Carondelet Street. The building, in the best Greek Revival style, later became the Knights of Columbus Hall. It has been demolished. *Photo by Charles L. Franck*

10 John McDonogh, the godfather of public education in New Orleans, painted by Helene Maas, 1890. Born in Baltimore in 1779, he began his career in the employ of a flour merchant, coming to New Orleans at

8   **9**

10　　　　　　　　　**11**

twenty-one years old. He soon went into business for himself, trading in sugar, molasses, hides, indigo, and pig iron, accumulating a sizable fortune, which he cannily invested in real estate.

McDonogh fought in the Battle of New Orleans with Beale's Rifles, and in 1817 he moved to Monplaisir, the old house originally built across the river from New Orleans by the Chevalier Jean de Pradel in 1750. Here he lived until his death on October 26, 1850. McDonogh was regarded as a miser during his lifetime, and great was the surprise when his will was filed, leaving an estate valued at more than $2 million for the education of boys and girls in his native Baltimore and adopted New Orleans. After lengthy litigation, the two cities received money with which New Orleans laid the foundation of its public school system, building thirty-five schools, a number of which are still in existence. McDonogh owned slaves, but initiated a scheme for their emancipation by crediting them with earnings made in their free time until the price of their freedom was saved. Some of his slaves were repatriated to Africa by the American Colonization Society in 1842. In his will, McDonogh asked that

"it may be permitted annually to the children of the free schools to plant and water a few flowers around my grave." McDonogh was temporarily buried in McDonoghville, but in 1864 his remains were removed to Baltimore. However, New Orleans didn't forget—in 1898, a monument in Lafayette Square was dedicated to his memory, paid for by the contributions of school-children, and each year on McDonogh Day (the first Friday in May), delegations of children brought flowers to this monument. They still do each year to a later monument built near the present city hall.

11 On December 29, 1898, McDonogh's birthday, the first monument to the philanthropist was dedicated. The money to pay for it, $7,000, had been raised mostly by the five-cent contributions of school-children. *Photo by O. H. Williams*

12 McDonogh's well-known thrift was cartooned by an artist who showed him being rowed across the river from his home in McDonoghville to New Orleans by one of his slaves to save the ferry fare.

12

Mc Donogh's last trip and last picayune saved for the poor ~~lawyers~~

13

14

15

13 Alexander Milne was another of the fabulous characters of old New Orleans. He was born in Fochabers, Scotland, in 1742, starting life as a footman in the family of the Duke of Richmond and Gordon. When that nobleman decided to put his household in livery, so the story goes, and required Milne to powder his bright red hair (of which he was quite proud), Milne quit and came to America. Coming to New Orleans during the Spanish regime in 1790, he entered business. Prospering in the hardware trade, he ultimately branched into a large brickmaking operation, meanwhile thriftily accumulating capital. Milne became imbued with the idea that the swamplands that adjoined Lake Pontchartrain would become valuable and he purchased large tracts. At the time of his death at the age of ninety-four in 1838, he owned twenty-two miles along the lake extending from the Rigolets all the way into Jefferson Parish.

Milne directed that his estate be used to establish a school in his native Fochabers and allocate funds for the establishment of orphan asylums for boys and girls, the Society for Destitute Orphan Boys, and the Poydras Asylum. Legal complications and long-drawn-out lawsuits resulted in the inevitable shrinkage of the estate. It was not until the twentieth century that, after still more legal legislative actions, the Milne Homes for girls and boys became a reality. A portion of the Louisiana legislative acts 2 and 3 of 1839 establishing the Milne Orphan Asylums is carved in the granite face of his monument, perhaps as a perpetual reminder of his intentions. The town of Milneburg, once a delightful resort at the end of the Pontchartrain Railroad, bore his name until it was absorbed into the encroaching city. The statue representing him ornaments the Gothic structure of Milne's Free School, built in his native Fochabers in Scotland. The school is still in existence. *Courtesy Gordon Baxter, Esq.*

14 Bernard de Marigny (1785–1868), who was called by his biographer, Edward Larocque Tinker, "a fabulous figure; swaggering, gallant, and fantastic, his pride overbearing, his courage unquestioned and his temper like tinder." Born the son of one of the richest men in Louisiana, who had large land holdings below Canal Street, Bernard's way of life, his extramarital affairs, and, particularly, his gaming forced him to sell his lands piecemeal. When the Civil War came, Bernard was in his middle seventies. He was too old to fight, and the war couldn't ruin him as he had already lost practically everything. Bernard lived to be eighty-three and died as a result of a fall on February 4, 1868. Of him, Tinker says:

Thus died the man who had lived the history of his state, who had seen the flags of Spain, France, the United States, and of the Confederacy, float over his city. . . . The last great Creole gentleman, *grand seigneur* of the New World, who had received the Marquis de Lafayette and had *tutoyéed* a king of France, was gone. A fabulous figure, he was a relic of the golden era of his race, epitome of their virtues and their faults. There will be no more like him, for the conditions that produced him have disappeared.

Lithograph by Pierre Villain. *Courtesy Louisiana State Museum*

15 Judah P. Benjamin (1811–1884). Born a British subject on the island of St. Thomas, as a child he moved to Charleston with his parents. Educated in North Carolina and after two years at Yale, he came to New Orleans in 1828. Copying documents in a notary's office while he studied law, he passed the bar examination at the age of twenty-one and embarked on a legal career that earned him large fees, and then on to a political career, which successively took him to the state legislature, the United States Senate, and to a membership in the cabinet of the Confederate States of America. Possessed as he was of a shrewd, inquiring mind, infinite patience, and tireless energy, it was not without reason that he was called "the brains of the Confederacy."

After the close of the Civil War, Benjamin fled, and, eluding pursuers, made his way after many vicissitudes to England, where at the age of fifty-five he started life over again, studying English law and rising to be queen's counsel. His practice increased to such an extent that he was forced to confine it to cases before the House of Lords and the Privy Council.
Courtesy Louisiana State Museum

17

16 Margaret Gaffney Haughery (1813–1882), one of New Orleans's best-loved women, from a painting by Robert Geddes presented to the Female Orphan Asylum. Born in County Cavan, Ireland, in 1813, Margaret came to Baltimore at the age of five with her parents. They died when she was nine, and Margaret was brought up by a Mrs. Richards. At twenty-one she married Charles Haughery, and they left for New Orleans where a daughter was born. Haughery's health failed, and he died after a sea voyage in a vain effort to recuperate. Their only child also died, and Margaret, left a childless widow, thereafter devoted herself to helping orphaned children. By 1840, she was not only making a living for herself, but had succeeded in raising funds to erect St. Theresa's Asylum on Camp Street. Through the years she worked untiringly to help orphans, of which New Orleans had an unusually large share. In 1859, she became the owner of a bakery then nearing bankruptcy. Margaret's shrewdness and keen business sense soon put the bakery on a paying basis. Using much of the profits of

her enterprise, she did an ever-increasing amount of charitable work, and at her death in 1882 three prosperous asylums owed their origin and success to her untiring energy and philanthropy—St. Vincent de Paul, the Female Orphan Asylum, and St. Elizabeth's Asylum. In her will she calculated that her business was worth about $30,000, nearly all of which was bequeathed to New Orleans orphan asylums—Catholic, Protestant, and Jewish. She signed her will with an X; she had never learned to read or write.

17 The Margaret monument sculpted by Alexander Doyle, who did the figure of Robert E. Lee atop the column at Lee Circle. The statue, paid for by public subscription, is in a little triangular park bounded by Camp, Prytania, and Clio streets. It is white marble and simply lettered "Margaret."

18 Margaret's Bakery, 74, 76, 78 New Levee Street, about 1880, from an advertisement in a carnival parade paper.

16

18

19   20

19 Myra Clark Gaines (1805–1885), commonly regarded as the daughter of Daniel Clark, wealthy New Orleans landowner, business and political figure of the early nineteenth century. She was the principal and ultimate victor in a series of sensational lawsuits against the city of New Orleans, which were in the courts for nearly sixty years. Myra endeavored to recover the patrimony which she said was hers under a will that was never produced in court. In the process, she spent a fortune in litigation, and near the end of the dozen times that the case went to the United States Supreme Court more than forty thousand pages of manuscript testimony were part of the record. At her death, she left a relatively small sum to her grandchildren, for in the end she had accomplished nothing whatever by one of the longest, most romantic, and complicated lawsuits in the history of the United States. *From* The Court Circles of the Republic

20 Daniel Clark (1766–1813). Always a restless schemer, he became absorbed in politics and was appointed American consul at New Orleans. After the formation of the Territory of Orleans, Clark became its first delegate to Congress. He and Governor Claiborne were bitter enemies, and Clark wounded Claiborne in the thigh in a duel.

21 Paul Morphy, brilliant chess genius. He is playing "blind" eight games simultaneously, Paris, 1858. He was born in New Orleans in 1837. Of Creole parentage, he was a precocious youngster who took to chess naturally. By the time he was thirteen, he had defeated the Hungarian chess master, A. J. Lowenthal, who was visiting New Orleans. He later defeated the best players in Europe, at twenty-one, and was declared world champion after defeating Adolf Andersen, the then current world champion, in December, 1858, in Paris. Morphy returned to the United States to receive tumultuous welcomes in New York, Boston, and, ultimately, New Orleans. With no more chess fields to conquer, he renounced the game, as far as the public was concerned, and began to practice law.

21

Characters

22

22 A multiracial society made for a rich mixture of occupations and activities. By 1803 New Orleans had a polyglot population of about eight thousand Frenchmen, Spaniards, Americans, Germans, Indians, and Negroes. The blacks, both slave and free, made up about a little more than half the total. Portrait of an unknown woman wearing a tignon (a Madras headkerchief) and clasping her prayer book. This sensitive portrait was painted in 1841 by L. Lotta. *Courtesy Louisiana State Museum*

23 Indians were a common sight in 1803, particularly at the market. Sketched by Benjamin Latrobe. *Courtesy Samuel Wilson, Jr., and Mrs. Ferdinand Claiborne Latrobe*

24 Negro nursemaids in Lafayette Square, 1880. *From* America Revisited *by George Augustus Sala, London, 1886*

24

23

"Blackb

C.M.Luria.
Old Praline Mammy

"Vegetables !"

25   **26   27**   **28**

25 *The Cala Woman,* sketch by E. W. Kemble. A cala (pronounced "cahlah") is a rather coarse rice fritter made of flour, eggs, butter, milk, sugar, boiled head rice, and yeast sponge-mixed into a stiff batter. The calas were formed by dropping spoonfuls of the batter into deep hot fat. Cala women, carrying their wares on their heads in covered wooden bowls, were generally abroad early in the morning to sell their calas for breakfast. The cry of the vendor was "Bels calas, bels calas, tout chauds" (fine fritters, fine fritters, very hot). *From* Century Magazine, 1886

26–28 These three once-familiar figures, sketched by Corinne M. Luria, have completely disappeared from New Orleans. The blackberry woman, whose familiar cry was "Bla-a-ck berries, berries very fine," would journey to the outskirts of the city to pick the glistening berries she peddled, and trudge the city streets calling her wares. The praline mammy would vend her own delicious products—brown pecan and pink or white coconut pralines—from a basket. The vegetable peddler with her basket of fresh vegetables was welcomed by housewives unable to go to the city markets.

29

29 For years, even into the twentieth century, these Choctaw Indian squaws would come from their habitat near Bayou Lacombe in St. Tammany Parish across Lake Pontchartrain to the French and Poydras markets to sell herbs, roots, and "filé" (pounded dried sassafras leaves for making gumbo). These women also made and sold baskets, one of which holds a papoose. *From* New Orleans Characters *by Leon J. Fremaux, 1876*

30 Section of the French Market, sketched in 1866 by Alfred R. Wand. It had its beginnings in 1791 when Spanish authorities erected a building on the site of the present market. The French Creoles promptly christened it La Halle des Boucheries. The building was destroyed in 1812, and an arcaded structure designed by city surveyor Jacques Tanesse was erected the next year. Parts of the vegetable market were added in 1823 and the market extended from Dumaine to St. Philip streets. *From* Harper's Weekly

31 Situated on the levee near the Place d'Armes, the market house held more than one hundred stalls and was about three hundred feet long, extending along the levee. The market was erected at a cost of $30,000.

30

Its low-pitched tile roof and arcaded sides made it an impressive building, particularly thrilling to those who approached it by water. Sketch by Charles Alexandre Le Sueur. *Courtesy Musée d'Histoire Naturelle, Le Havre, France*

32 This famous market is situated near Jackson Square. Its extent and antique appearance, the various languages spoken there—English, French, German, Spanish—which make it a perfect Babel, and the abundance and variety of the articles sold in the stalls, make it an object of curiosity to every stranger visiting New Orleans. As early as three o'clock in the morning the market is crowded with sellers and buyers, and it is almost impossible to move about. By nine o'clock the place is almost deserted. Even by daylight it looks picturesque and attractive.

From Harper's Weekly, *January 21, 1882*

33

The butchers scorn to use all those blandishments that the lower grades of market society make use of to attract purchasers. Like Mohomet, the mountain must come to them. From the ceiling hang endless ropes of spider's webs, numberless flies, and incalculable dirt. The stalls [i.e., wooden chopping blocks] are deeply worn by the scraping process; in some yawn pits, apparently bottomless; and lastly, the floor of the market is not at all clean, but covered with mud and dirt from the feet of its patrons.

Thus the butchers in the French Market are described in the *Guide to New Orleans,* issued at the Cotton Centennial Exposition, 1885. *Photo by George F. Mugnier*

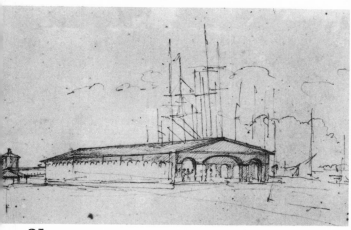

31

32

33

34

35

36

34 "Making Market"—a New Orleans colloquial expression—is what this woman with her basket on her arm is doing: going to the French Market to shop. This photograph was taken about 1906. The buildings were extensively remodeled in the 1930s under the WPA, and a colonnade around the meat market was constructed. *Courtesy Library of Congress*

35 The Poydras Market, built in 1838 by the American element in the first municipal district as a substitute for the French Market in the Creole district. It was erected in the middle of Poydras Street between Baronne and South Rampart streets. Until it was remodeled in 1898, it was almost as picturesque as the old French Market. "On week days," says *The Pica-*

yune's Guide to New Orleans (1903), "there may be seen standing in the middle of the market rows of colored women waiting to be employed to wash or scrub." The market was demolished in 1930. This view is of the Baronne Street entrance, taken by Mugnier, ca. 1895.

36 This clothespole man, whose characteristic street cry was "clo-o-othespoles," was photographed by George F. Mugnier, ca. 1895. Before the day of the mechanical dryer, the family wash was strung out in backyards on slack clotheslines, which were then raised and made taut by the introduction of a clothespole. These poles were saplings, cut and trimmed of branches, except near the top where several, three or four inches long, were left to serve as V's to engage the line.

37 Leon J. Fremaux's satirical drawing *On the flags* (on a flagstone pavement). Two would-be speculators listen to a third tell about the money he could have made if he had sold the imaginary stock he never owned. *From* New Orleans Characters *by Leon J. Fremaux, 1876. Courtesy Howard-Tilton Memorial Library, Tulane University*

38 *Cooling Their Coppers,* sketch by Alfred R. Wand. Made in 1872, this sketch of a Canal Street drugstore shows a group of heavy drinkers trying to

37

38

39

alleviate the pangs of their hangovers from a night-before spree by drinking Vichy and Kissengen waters. In the first days of steam engines, boilers were made of copper, and the expression "cooling their coppers" was slang for getting rid of a hangover. *From* Every Saturday

39 New Orleans drugstore, 1880. George Augustus Sala in *America Revisited* (London, 1886) wrote: "A grave and bald headed gentleman sat in a rocking chair at the door of the *pharmacie* reading *Abeille de la Nouvelle Orleans*. His equally grave spouse was enthroned, spectacled, behind the counter perusing the *Propagateur Catholique*. In the dim recesses of the store you could discern rows of shelves laden with tall white gallipots; and about the whole place there was a gentle soporific odour of aromatic drugs."

40 This scene of a day more leisurely than ours was probably photographed about 1900. The building in the background is the Cosmopolitan Hotel, and the loungers out front on Bourbon Street are no doubt guests.

40

41

41 A sociable gathering with the boys at the Commercial Club, located on Canal Street near Baronne. *From* The City of New Orleans—the Book of the Chamber of Commerce and Industry of Louisiana, *published by George W. Englehart, 1894*

42 Tobacco shops have all but vanished from the American scene, their function taken over largely by drugstores, although a few still exist in the business district. This one (ca. 1898) was located on Baronne Street near Gravier and was operated by Manuel Suarez, who stands behind his counter. From the showcases he dispensed Melachrino, El Cubo, Chancellor, Van Dyck, Ruy Lopez, La Preferencia, El Far, Owl, Fatima, New Bachelor, Havana Ribbon, Satin, Abbey, Webster, and Choctaw cigars and cigarettes, Polar tobacco, and Union Leader Cut Plug. *Courtesy Mrs. Milton L. Reisch*

42

43

43 In former years, New Orleans abounded in itinerant repairmen who mended umbrellas, repaired household utensils, or sharpened scissors and knives. This one, photographed by Francis Benjamin Johnson around 1895, carried a small machine shop. He could grind scissors, file saws, and make keys. Besides his odd toppiece, he called attention to his services by means of a small bell, which he operated with his thumb. *Courtesy Library of Congress*

44 This milkman is making a delivery to the La Louisiane Hotel and Restaurant on Iberville Street in 1903. Most dairymen who supplied New Orleans with milk in this era were French. The milk is dispensed from spigots in the two large galvanized milk cans into the buyers' pitchers. That great New Orleans delicacy, creole cream cheese, was also peddled from these carts. *Courtesy Library of Congress*

45 *The Bottle Man* would exchange used bottles for small sums or candy. Such once-popular itinerants have long since disappeared from the streets of New Orleans. *From* Picayune's Guide to New Orleans, *1903*

44

45

46 "Buglin' Sam" Dekemel (*right*), with his father, who was the chef, made and sold delicious sugar-coated hot waffles in their horse-drawn wagon. "Buglin' Sam," whose real name was Matthew Dekemel, specialized in playing jazz tunes on a regulation army bugle and used his horn to attract trade. The view is the front of the Elks clubhouse, ca. 1920.

47 A quaint New Orleans custom, unhappily passed away, was the giving of cake or candy or some small gratuity (called lagniappe) to children or servants when they made a purchase at a grocery store. The word is pronounced "lan yap" and is derived from the Spanish "la ñapa"—a small present.

46

47

48

50

51

48 Many New Orleans youths learned to swim in the Mississippi, an exhilarating but dangerous sport, which annually took the lives of some hapless beginners. These boys were caught by John J. DePaul's camera on a summer's day about 1912.

49 These men in front of the barber's sign (note the prices in 1910!) are drinking beer poured from "growlers," a pitcher or can that was taken to a bar to be filled with beer for consumption outside. "Rushing the growler" was once a popular custom in New Orleans. *Photo by John J. DePaul*

49

50 Two "white wings," taken ca. 1910. These public street cleaners wore white uniforms in the old days, hence the name. *Photo by John J. DePaul*

51 A hurdy-gurdy and attentive music lovers, ca. 1915. These barrel organs, or street pianos, were once a common sight in New Orleans. Mounted on wheels, they were pulled through the streets by Negro organ grinders, who stopped wherever they could to gather a few coins from listeners. The hurdy-gurdy's tinny music was produced by turning a hand crank. *Photo by John J. DePaul*

52

53

of stripped palmetto fronds attached to a weighted rope. With the advent of gas heating, this Negro tradesman passed from the scene. *Photo by Hermann B. Deutsch*

53 *Gas Lighter,* sketch by G. F. Castledon. The lamplighter with his ladder was a familiar figure when the city was lighted by gas. *From* The Jack Lafaience Book *by James J. McLaughlin, 1922*

52 The chimney sweep's trademarks were his battered silk high hat and his call, "R-r-r-r-ramoner la cheminée" (sweep the chimney). In a day when most New Orleans houses were heated by coal burned in grate fires, chimney sweeps were employed to clean the flues of soot. This they did with the aid of a bunch

54 Fuel distribution in New Orleans in 1920. Before the introduction of natural gas, kerosene was widely used by New Orleanians to heat their homes. These peddlers are ready to start on their routes, their wagons loaded with one-gallon "safety" containers of "Stanocola Burning Oil." *Photo by Charles L. Franck*

54

55

56

55 Scrubbing the front steps of their modest cottages with powdered brick as a detergent was a Saturday morning ritual practiced by many New Orleans housewives for years. The coarse grains of the brick wore away the paint on the steps, and the bleached wood was highly regarded as a symbol of good housekeeping. *Courtesy Times-Picayune*

56 For this densely crowded slum area, just sitting on the front steps and exchanging gossip was a mild pleasure relished by the whole neighborhood. The banquette is paved with brick in a herringbone pattern, once a common type of sidewalk paving. *Courtesy Library of Congress*

57 A crowd in front of the entrance to Simon Gumbel & Company's office at 838 Gravier Street, awaiting their weekly nickel dispensed to them by the firm. For nearly half a century, every Saturday morning one hundred or so old women, Negroes and whites alike, would collect here. This odd custom, which by 1930 had cost the firm $10,400 in nickels, was begun by Simon Gumbel as a hobby. Many of the old women looked forward to this weekly nickel for years, and would walk miles to stand in line to receive it. *Courtesy Howard-Tilton Memorial Library, Tulane University*

58 Banjo Annie, a familiar character in the streets of the Vieux Carré for twenty years, was said by tavern-keepers to have been the most famous drinker in modern Quarter history. She would appear in the doorway of a bar and sing, accompanying herself on guitar. Just as she would hit the high note in "The Old Concert Hall on the Bowery," the bartender would spray her with soda water. Annie died in 1951.

57

58

59

60

Saloons

59 The interior of a New Orleans barroom about 1850, from a French woodcut. New Orleans has been long famed as the home of civilized drinking, and some of its mixed drinks are as famous as its incomparable cuisine. The word "cocktail," so one story goes, was the invention of a Royal Street pharmacist, Antoine Peychaud, who concocted a brandy toddy and added a dash of bitters of his own compounding to give it zest. He served it to his friends in an egg cup (the old fashioned double-end kind), this piece of crockery being known in French as a *coquetier*. From it, we get "cocktail." Peychaud's bitters have had a long and honorable history. Three of the best known, and still available, New Orleans mixed drinks are the Sazerac cocktail, the Ramos gin fizz, and dripped absinthe frappé. A tipple greatly prized by the Creoles of New Orleans of the middle nineteenth century was the Roffignac. Roffignac was a much-respected mayor whose name seems to have been attached to the product of a contemporary, François *Roffiac,* who was by trade a distiller of cordials. The Roffignac was made by pouring a jigger of cognac into a highball

glass, adding a portion of raspberry or grenadine syrup (the sweetings used in New Orleans a century ago) ice, soda, and water. Three of these and anybody was mayor for the day!

60 "WELCOME TO ALL" reads the lettering over the central mirror of this bar. The gent in the center holds an "old-fashioned" in his hand, and the barkeeper stands in front of some seventy assorted bottles used in his trade. A primitive slot machine graces the left side of the bar, ca. 1890.

61 The front of a typical saloon of the 1890s. The sign on the corner of the building informed the thirsty that pure Cincinnati lager beer was served within, and the four empty beer barrels waiting to be picked up told the onlooker that business had been brisk. Saloons of this period generally had swinging doors, and their walls carried frames for posting bills. These posters announced that Madame Modjeska was soon to be heard and that *La Traviata* was to play at the French Opera House. *Courtesy Henry A. Gandolfo*

61

64

62

63

62 In 1898, there were eight hundred saloons in New Orleans. This one was called the Congo Square Saloon and Confectionary and was adjacent to the square of that name (now Beauregard Square in front of the Municipal Auditorium). *Courtesy New York Public Library*

63 The old Absinthe House bar in 1903. The old Absinthe House, on Bourbon Street, was probably built about 1806, but did not become a tavern until 1861. The bar was noted for its excellent absinthe

frappé, which was slowly "dripped" from its fountains. In later years (before Prohibition), it became a custom to tack the cards of patrons on the walls and ceilings, giving the place a very picturesque look. General Jackson, contrary to the legend, did *not* meet with Lafitte, the pirate, in this house (or any other house) to plan the Battle of New Orleans. *Courtesy Library of Congress*

64 The Sazerac Bar in the 1930s. Note the prices. *Photo by Charles L. Franck*

65

66

67

Voodoo

65 Congo Square, gathering place each Sunday of slaves who amused themselves by dancing, sketch by Edward W. Kemble for "Creole Slave Songs" by George W. Cable. The square was the scene of such dances as the calinda, an immodest African dance in which the men formed in one line and the women, facing them, in another, and the Bamboula, seen here performed to the beat of a drum of bamboo. *From* Century Magazine, *April, 1886*

66 These slaves brought with them the practice of voodoo, particularly those who came from Saint-Domingue via Cuba in the early years of the nineteenth century. The devotees of this African religion worshiped a snake in secret rites that concluded with orgiastic dancing. The powers of the Deity were ascribed to the serpent, and the queen of the sect was the "voice" of the god. This voodoo dance sketch was made in 1885 by Edward W. Kemble for "Creole Slave Songs."

67 Marie Laveau (1796?–1881), the best known of the voodoo queens, with her daughter, sketch by Edward W. Kemble for "Creole Slave Songs" by George W. Cable. This onetime hairdresser rose to great power among the superstitious members of her race, and many white people consulted her for advice and for the gris-gris (pronounced gree-gree), charms for good or evil, which she sold. Marie Laveau, ac-

cording to William A. Read in *Louisiana French,* concocted a gris-gris of salt, gunpowder, saffron, and dried dog dung. Gris-gris balls, as large as oranges, were fashioned of gaudy feathers and secreted in a pillow or in a bed. Other gris-gris consisted of placing a cross of wet salt on the doorstep (trouble) or a small coffin on the gallery (death). A favorite good-luck gris-gris was to wear a dime with a hole in it about the ankle. *From* Century Magazine, *April, 1886*

68 A gris-gris of wet salt on the gallery in the shape of a cross meant trouble for the householder (if he were superstitious).

68

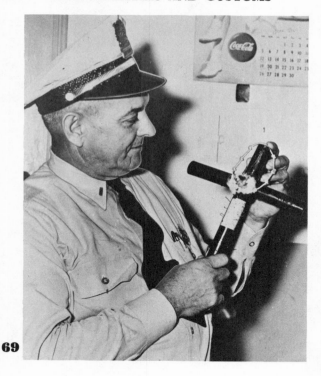

69

70

71

69 Police Lieutenant Chester Keating with a voodoo black cross, June 13, 1949. As late as 1956 one could buy "Money-drawing Incense" and "Love Powders" for 50¢ and "Boss-fixing Powder" for $1 at the Cracker Jack "drugstore," 435 South Rampart Street. This store sold Alka-Seltzer and Gillette blades, but was in reality a voodoo dispensary with all kinds of gris-gris on hand. *Courtesy Times-Picayune*

Storyville and Prostitution

70 In the first part of the nineteenth century, the Swamp, a section of Girod Street near the river, was long regarded as the toughest part of town. A succession of barrel houses, cheap lodgings, and bordellos lined the street. The prostitutes were tough females, many of whom could fight as well as men, as this disgruntled customer found out to his sorrow. Patronized by the rough flatboatmen who moored their boats nearby, the Swamp was for years a local den of iniquity.

71 Gallatin Street, a short alley that once ran from the French Market to the Mint, was New Orleans's second tenderloin district. Here in saloons and dance houses prostitutes plied their trade on unwary seamen.

72 *Working a Sucker in a Concert-Saloon*—a waitress picking the pocket of her drunken customer. The concert saloon was a forerunner of the modern nightclub. It generally had a dance floor and sometimes a stage. Food and drink were served by girl "beer jerkers," who worked on commission and usually augmented their earnings by prostitution in their leisure hours.

72

South Robertson streets, the west side of Robertson Street from Customhouse to St. Louis streets, and the south side of St. Louis Street from South Robertson to Basin. To the intense disgust of Alderman Story, the area soon became known as Storyville.

74 Storyville was dominated by Tom Anderson, political figure, owner of several saloons, head of an oil company, and a member of the state legislature. Anderson's Arlington Annex was figuratively the district's city hall and Anderson its mayor. This advertisement of Anderson's three saloons and his picture appeared in a souvenir program of the National Convention of Chiefs of Police held in New Orleans in 1903!

75 Basin Street with Tom Anderson's saloon at the corner of Iberville, and the "plush" houses of pleasure "down the line." No less than fourteen brothels in this and the next block of Basin Street advertised in one edition of the *Blue Book*. These included such notorious landladies as Josie Arlington, "Countess" Willie Piazza, Emma Johnson, and Lulu White. *Courtesy Dr. Edmond Souchon*

73

73 Street hustling. In 1857, the city passed an ordinance "Concerning Lewd and Abandoned Women," which legalized prostitution. It set up a restricted area of operations and a license system for houses and women engaged in the trade, but this was ineffective and was soon abandoned. After the dislocation caused by the Civil War and Reconstruction, social life in the New Orleans underworld assumed a new status. By the 1880s, a venal police force bossed by even more corrupt politicians who closed their eyes to a growing evil gave New Orleans the reputation of uncontrolled vice. Reform agitation began in the 1890s, and a school of thought developed advocating the establishment of a restricted district for the control of prostitution. This eventually found expression in a plan by Alderman Sidney Story, when an ordinance setting the limits of such a district was enacted during the reform administration of Mayor Flower. Thus came into existence the New Orleans restricted district, easily the most amazing spectacle of legalized vice in America. The limits of the restricted district were the north side of Customhouse (Iberville) Street from Basin to

THE STAG
712-714 Gravier Street

ARLINGTON
110-114 N. Rampart Street

THE ARLINGTON ANNEX
Corner Basin and Customhouse Streets

T. C. ANDERSON, Proprietor.   NEW ORLEANS

74

75

Blue Book

76

77

80

78

79

81

76 Cover of the *Blue Book*. In the Arlington Annex for twenty-five cents one could obtain a copy of the official guide and directory to Storyville, the *Blue Book*. Here were listed in alphabetical order the more than seven hundred white, octoroon, and Negro prostitutes and their addresses in the district. Besides beer, whiskey, and cigar advertisements, it also contained full-page puffs of various landladies and their houses, some of which were illustrated.

77 The advertisement of The Arlington, operated by the notorious Josie Arlington. *From* The Blue Book

78–81 The Basin Street "palaces" were lavishly furnished in what the advertisements called gorgeous style—heavy draperies, tapestries, "real" oil paintings, leopard skins, potted palms, and curios, to set off the heavily-carved plush-covered furniture—a rococo atmosphere that must have thrilled the damsels who worked there and the "sporting" men who were their customers. The American Parlor; The Vienna Parlor; A boudoir; Josie Arlington's bagnio. *From* The Blue Book

82 Just a short distance away were the rows of "cribs" in decaying hovels, whose furnishings consisted of a bed, a table, and a chair, and whose occupants, forbidden by law to leave the premises, were often known to snatch off the hat of any unwary male who stopped to listen to their solicitations.

83 Storyville doings were chronicled in a column called "On the Turf," published in a scurrilous rag called *The Mascot.*

84 A housing project occupies much of what was Storyville, and about the last memento left in the neighborhood was the name "Tom Anderson's" in front of the site once occupied by his Arlington Annex saloon. For twenty years, Storyville had operated full blast. Very few visitors to New Orleans missed at least a quick ride through its dozen city squares to view iniquity firsthand. But time was running out, and during World War I the end of Storyville came when Josephus Daniels, secretary of the navy, requested the city, which with some reluctance passed an ordinance on July 10, 1917, to close the district in an effort to curb vice because of the proximity of armed-services personnel.

85 A fragment of the lurid past—the transom that once identified Lulu White's bagnio, 235 N. Basin Street. *Courtesy New Orleans Jazz Museum*

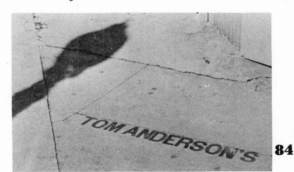

84

82

85

83

86

Victorian Home Life

86 One of these women has closed her eyes in fear of the flashlight, but her companion to the right knits imperturbably. C. Milo Williams, who took this picture, was an architect who lived in Carrollton. His hobby was photography, and his flashlight pictures of his home and family printed from glass negatives made in the 1890s give us glimpses of a time long past.

87 A corner in the home. An artistic family, and their love of art is evidenced by the great number of framed pictures that graced this room and the *objets d'art* in view.

87

88

89

88 A family musicale. Only the little boy to the extreme right seems resigned to the whole affair.

89 A Sunday afternoon on the lawn of a house on Bayou St. John. Two derbied dandies pose in the background, a bearded gentleman and two ladies listen to the music of a guitar player, and the family cat seems otherwise preoccupied. *Courtesy Louisiana Landmarks Society*

90 This group of well-dressed women gathered at McDonogh No. 23 School to celebrate Columbus Day, about 1895. Those in black in the rear of the photograph wear widows' bonnets; those seated in front wear dresses with leg-of-mutton sleeves. *Photo by C. Milo Williams*

90

5. DIVERSIONS

Biggest Free Show on Earth

1 New Orleans has always loved a parade. Mardi Gras aside, the earliest such public procession of which we have records took place in 1734 when the Ursuline nuns moved from their temporary quarters at Chartres and Bienville to the first of their four successive convents. Bienville himself was a spectator, and the marchers consisted of, besides the nuns and children dressed as angels, the clergy, soldiers, and townspeople, all stepping to music.

This is the Gem Café on Royal Street near Canal, which in its day was a gathering place for the elite young men of the city. It was also the birthplace of the New Orleans carnival as we know it today, for it was here that the Mystick Krewe (Comus) was organized, the first New Orleans carnival organization.

The New Orleans carnival season starts just after Christmas and goes on until Lent. During this period, which could vary from four to nine weeks, depending when Ash Wednesday falls, are staged some sixty large-scale balls and more than two dozen colorful street parades, culminating in the elaborate Rex and Comus pageants on Mardi Gras (Fat Tuesday or Shrove Tuesday). About five hundred thousand people, New Orleanians, Louisianians, and visitors from far and near, line the streets along the parade route. Over fifty thousand are costumed, and from sunup to sundown they may wear masks. These and the organized marching clubs, with their colorfully decorated trucks, music bands, and jolly costumed people aboard, participate in the revelry presided over by Rex, king of carnival.

Nearly two decades before New Orleans was founded in 1718, Mardi Gras had become a part of the local geography, for it was on Mardi Gras in 1699 that d'Iberville rediscovered the Mississippi River and camped for the night on the banks of a little bayou, which he appropriately named Bayou du Mardi Gras —the first place-name in Louisiana. Early in New Orleans's history, the French settlers celebrated Mardi Gras in one fashion or another. When Governor Claiborne inaugurated the American regime in New Orleans in 1803, he was impressed by the passionate love of the Creole population for dancing and holding masked balls. The early years of the nineteenth century enhanced New Orleans's reputation as a gay, carefree town. Public ballrooms, such as John Davis's adjoining his Théâtre d'Orléans, were the scene of an almost continual round of subscription and masked balls when these were permitted by the authorities. Masquerade costumes were advertised in *L'Abeille*, February 26, 1828, but apparently the first mention of an organized masquerade parade in carriages was not documented until 1837. In the 1840s, more and more

1

maskers thronged the streets on that day, many armed with small paper bags of flour, which they tossed at spectators.

2 Encouraged by the enthusiastic reception given their first efforts in 1857, Comus and his krewe produced an even better parade in 1858, "The Classic Pantheon," with thirty-one floats, on which rode maskers dressed to represent Jupiter, Minerva, Apollo, Janus, Ceres, Flora, Pan, and Bacchus. This pageant, which reportedly cost the members $20,000, was described as one of "taste, brilliancy and beauty." Even the far-off *Illustrated London News* ran this woodcut and a description of it on May 8, 1858.

In the late 1840s to the mid-1850s, while the balls continued to flourish, rowdyism on the streets had so invaded Mardi Gras that the New Orleans press clamored for the abandonment of this once merry festival that "had become vulgar, tasteless and spiritless."

New Orleans was changing, constantly growing in size and wealth. The newcomers brought with them customs and religions that were alien to the Creoles, yet they were readily adapted to the Gallic spirit permeating the social life of New Orleans. One of the great contradictions, in a city of contradictions, is the fact that six Anglo-Saxons from nearby Mobile, Alabama, saved the great Latin festival of carnival for New Orleans and gave to this world-famous celebration its present form and substance. By bringing imagination and organization into play, the Americans developed the Mardi Gras into an institution of fantasy, which the "Creole soon acknowledged with pride and in which his spirit and genius have remained predominant."

The club Mystick Krewe of Comus sprang almost full-blown from the minds of the six young Mobilians. They had been members of a carnival group in Mobile, the Cowbellion de Rakin Society, formed about 1831. They now had chosen a minor Greek god of festive mirth as their patron, and the young organization soon had eighty-three members, most of whom bore Anglo-Saxon names. All members of the Mystick Krewe were pledged to secrecy. By dint of prodigious labor (and considerable help from the Cowbellions of Mobile), Comus and his cohorts presented on Mardi Gras night, February 24, 1857, a torchlight street parade, which had for its theme "The Demon Actors in Milton's Paradise Lost." All characters were on foot except Comus and Satan, who rode on decorated floats. After the parade, the Mystick Krewe repaired to the Gaiety Theatre for a tableau ball.

2
3

3 Comus parade, March 5, 1867. By 1861, pageants and glittering tableau balls had become part of the local scene, but the Civil War put a temporary end to Mardi Gras festivities. In 1862, New Orleans fell to Farragut, and it was not until 1866 that Comus returned once more with a street parade and ball. The subjects were "The Past, the Present, and the Future," which depicted the "Horrors and Sorrows of War," the "Blessings and Beauties of Peace," and the "Hope of a Smiling Future."

The 1870s saw a further increase in carnival organizations. The Lord of Misrule, king of the Twelfth Night Revelers, made his bow on the streets on January 6, 1870, with a parade and tableau at the Opera House, which featured an immense Twelfth Night cake surrounded by the court of the Roi de la Fève.

In January, 1872, another organization came into being—Rex, which would have the greatest influence on the yearly celebration of Mardi Gras. Rex was hurriedly organized by a group of leading businessmen when they learned that New Orleans would receive on Mardi Gras His Imperial Highness Alexis Romanov Aleksandrovich, brother of the heir apparent to the throne of all the Russias, and that city and state officials had not made preparations to welcome the distinguished visitor.

That same year the Knights of Momus, organized along the same lines as Comus, held their first parade. Five years later, during the dying days of Reconstruction and unchecked political corruption when New

Orleans had two sets of legislatures and two governors simultaneously, Momus and his knights staged a pageant entitled "Hades—A Dream of Momus." Like the parade of Comus two years before, it was a travesty on the political situation, which in Louisiana and in the whole United States had about reached an all-time low. *From* Frank Leslie's Illustrated Newspaper

4

5

6

4 Grand Duke Alexis Romanov Aleksandrovich, whose visit to New Orleans on Mardi Gras, 1872, inspired businessmen to form the Rex organization. Alexis had been in America two and a half months before he was scheduled to arrive in New Orleans.

He had arrived the day before Mardi Gras on board the palatial Mississippi River steamer *James Howard,* and on the great day, after being formally received at City Hall by Governor Henry Clay Warmoth, Mayor B. F. Flanders, and General James Longstreet, His Highness somewhat woodenly reviewed the first Rex parade. This mile-long spectacle was preceded by guns of a local artillery unit, followed by a white-bearded Rex who, clad in purple silk velvet generously loaned the krewe by the actor Lawrence Barret (then playing at the Varieties Theatre), rode a bay charger. Rex was followed by the boeuf gras, alias Old Jeff, the decoy-bull of the local stockyards; the Pack, who were maskers representing the fifty-two playing cards in the deck; and some five thousand maskers on foot and in groups on wagons and carriages. Interspersed were a number of bands that had been commanded to play the official Mardi Gras tune, "If Ever I Cease to Love." The tune, the Rex organization learned, had been sung by the warbler Lydia Thompson in the burlesque *Bluebeard* in the east where Alexis had heard it and liked it, and by a happy coincidence, Lydia Thompson, immensely popular, was playing in New Orleans at the Academy of Music. The tune therefore was transposed into march time and dedicated to the grand duke. The catchy music, with its numerous choruses ("If ever I cease to love, May oysters have legs and cows lay eggs . . . May little dogs wag their tails in front, If ever I cease to love"), has ever since been the national anthem of Rex, king of carnival. *From* His Imperial Highness the Grand Duke Alexis, 1872. *Courtesy Library of Congress*

5 "Hyenas Laugh and Drop the Crunching Bone." This figure was easily recognized as the hated Benjamin F. ("Spoons") Butler. Through most of the bitter Reconstruction period Comus had continued to parade. In 1873, the krewe put on "The Missing Link to Darwin's Origin of Species," a parade satirizing Darwin, the Republican party in Louisiana and in the nation, and the New Orleans Metropolitan Police, who kept the radicals in power. Except for two cars, the entire krewe marched disguised in great papier-mâché masks, representing crustacea, fishes, reptiles, insects, rodents, ruminantia, carnivora, and quadrumana. The parade was described in a clever poem, which was painted on transparencies carried along. Not every mask was a satire, although such appeared frequently. Among those easily recognizable were the tobacco grub, whose face bore a strong resemblance to President Grant; the hated General Benjamin ("Spoons") Butler, whose harsh occupation of New Orleans with federal troops in 1862 was then still fresh in mind and who unmistakably had the body of a hyena; and the chief of the Metropolitan Police, General A. S. Badger, who was caricatured as a hound dog. The parade, led by the despised Metropolitans (and the police still lead parades to this day), was turned back by a group of jeering, defiant men who formed into a solid mass of humanity and refused passage when the pageant reached Canal Street. The Krewe thereupon turned back with their ineffectual escort and entered the Varieties Theatre for their ball, leaving some ten thousand spectators on the downtown side of Canal Street waiting in disappointment. *Courtesy William B. Wisdom Collection, Tulane University Library*

6 "Tobacco Grubs Essay the Loftiest Stalk" bore the unmistakable likeness of General Grant. *Courtesy William B. Wisdom Collection, Tulane University Library*

7 "The Missing Links" was the first parade to be constructed in New Orleans. Previously, the big masks and animal figures had been made in France, but in 1873, local artisans were able to make them stronger and, no doubt, cheaper, and a new industry was born. The illustration shows the interior of a "den" where carnival masks and costumes are being prepared for the 1880 Mardi Gras. *From* America Revisited *by George Augustus Sala, London, 1886*

8–15 Original sketches from the 1873 Comus parade. *Courtesy William B. Wisdom Collection, Tulane University Library*

14   **15**

16

18

16 *New Orleans Carnival Flag*, lithograph by J. Curtis Waldo, ca. 1880. Working feverishly, Rex and his krewe laid plans for a gigantic Mardi Gras celebration. A carnival flag was designed—a diagonal bar of gold from upper left to lower right forming an upper triangle (green) and a lower triangle (purple) with the crown of Rex in the center. A series of royal edicts was proclaimed, ordering a half holiday on Mardi Gras, buildings to be decorated, the royal flag displayed, and setting forth the order of marching in his parade.

17 The parade of Comus passing the City Hall, Mardi Gras, 1872. City Hall was elaborately decorated for the grand duke's visit. A semicircular platform was erected at the front of the building, and its railings trimmed with evergreens and small flags. In the center of the platform was a crimson canopy ornamented with gold fringe and lace. Flags of the United States, Russia, France, Prussia, Britain, and the Confederate stars and bars also flew on either side of the entrance, and an archway of gas jets with crystal shades topped the decorations. From this vantage point Alexis viewed the procession of Rex in the daytime and that of Comus that evening. *From* Frank Leslie's Illustrated Newspaper, *March 9, 1872*

18 19 In 1873, in the second Rex parade, the king rode a horse and the boeuf gras was paraded behind him. For the first time at a New Orleans Mardi Gras, Rex had organized into one parade the unorganized little groups of maskers, and it had been a tremendous

17

19

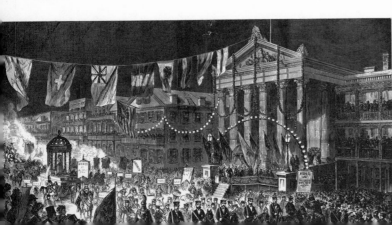

success. Rex had great plans for 1873. He would have a grand ball primarily for the entertainment of visitors. Traditionally, the balls given by the existing carnival krewes were exclusive affairs, and visitors coming to New Orleans at carnival time in ever-increasing numbers were unable to get invitations. In 1873, Rex issued four thousand invitations, and his first grand ball, Pro Bono Publico, was held at Exposition Hall on Mardi Gras night.

The ballroom was crowded at an early hour and Rex, preceded by his court, marched in glittering procession twice around the hall. His Majesty cast his royal eyes over the assemblage to choose a queen. He halted before a lady he found most comely—a Mrs. Walker Fearn. Taken completely by surprise, Mrs. Fearn, the wife of a soldier-diplomat who had come to the ball out of curiosity and who had on her second-best black dress, with a bonnet fastened under her chin, rose to the occasion, tossed her bonnet to her husband, and was thereupon crowned Rex's consort, his first queen of carnival. Sketch by J. Wells Champney. *From* Scribners Magazine, *December, 1873*

20 The Rex ball of 1879. Bearded gentlemen in full dress and ladies in gowns with bustles and long trains stroll about the ballroom (Washington Artillery Hall), which had been decorated with flags and featured a garden centerpiece. The king and queen are on a raised dais in the rear center. In the early 1880s, more organizations were born. The Independent Order of the Moon was founded by a group of funmakers whose purposes were similar to those of the Phunny Phorty Phellows and who cavorted on Mardi Gras day each year from 1878 until 1888 with floats ridiculing practically everything. In 1882, the Krewe of Proteus was organized by a group of young men from the New Orleans Cotton Exchange.

The custom of choosing a queen began with Twelfth Night Revelers as early as 1871, followed by Rex in 1873, Momus in 1881, and Proteus in 1882. In 1884, at the Comus ball at the French Opera House, when the daughters of General Robert E. Lee, Stonewall Jackson, D. H. Hill, and Jefferson Davis were honored guests, Comus "took out" Miss Mildred Lee. From then on Momus annually selected a queen to rule with him over his ball.

In 1889, the Edison Company inspired the Knights of Electra to design a parade to demonstrate the incandescent lamp. A 12,000-pound steam generator mounted on a float and drawn by 16 mules supplied the power, conveyed through wires hidden in ropes, to light globes on the helmets of some 128 participants who marched to "exemplify the practicability of electricity as an illuminator of moving bodies like processions . . ."

21 Starting in 1876, Rex had begun to "arrive" in his carnival capital on the Monday before Mardi Gras, usually by water, after an elaborate buildup in the newspapers describing the trip from his mythical kingdom. In 1879, he arrived at the levee on the steamer *Rob't E. Lee*, was met by a welcoming committee, and escorted through the streets with a military guard of honor. This started a custom much enjoyed by the populace—"Seeing the King Come In." The flag-bedecked boats and ships in the harbor formed a water pageant of welcome, and Rex arrived amid the booming of cannon and the chorus of steam whistles. This custom lasted until 1917, and was revived in 1971 on Rex's Centennial. For many years Rex arrived at the foot of Canal Street on the royal yacht *Stranger. Courtesy Library of Congress*

20

21

22

22 23 After exchanging greetings, he was escorted to his royal chariot at the Canal Street ferry-house. Accompanied by a military guard of honor, His Royal Highness then paid an official call on the mayor at City Hall. *Courtesy Library of Congress*

24 The arrival of Rex on the riverfront in 1906. Ac-

tually, another member of the organization impersonated Rex on the Monday before Mardi Gras. Those accompanying His Majesty are Colonel George Soulé, William Murray, Judge Albert G. Brice, and Morris Newman, all wearing high hats. Members of the krewe, costumed and masked, followed. *Courtesy Dr. Edmond Souchon*

23

24

SOUVENIR CARNIVAL PPP

HONI SOIT QUI MAL Y PENSE

NEW ORLEANS MARDI-GRAS FEBRUARY 22 1898

PRICE, TEN CENTS.

26

25

Papers," lithographed in colors by a local firm and sold folded and ready to mail for a dime on the streets. Elaborate booklets, such as the ninety-four-page souvenir of Momus entitled *The Ramayana, the Iliad of the East*, a flowery book of verse illustrated by sixteen lithographs of the floats of the parade, which appeared in 1882, were published occasionally.

27 Invitation to the ball. This opens from the top and is about a foot high. Invitations were souvenirs, which usually typified the design of the pageant and tableau. In the gilded age, these were often of the most elaborate and fanciful design, lithographed in several colors and in gold and delivered by special messenger. Some of the invitations were made in Paris, but as New Orleans had its share of able lithographers, many were produced in the city. Great care was exercised in

27

25 Judging by the crowd's inattention, this impressive birdlike float seems to have a more compelling competitor, not seen here, but approaching.

26 A group of the members of Mississippi Fire Company No. 2 formed a new carnival club in 1878, Phunny Phorty Phellows. While the older krewes paraded with mythological subjects, the Phellows took more earthy themes, and for years their parades, designed for plain fun, were awaited with great eagerness by thousands who crowded the streets of New Orleans to watch. This cover is of a publication commemorating their 1898 contribution.

The first black-and-white pictures of the individual cars making up a carnival parade appeared in the late 1870s in *The Weekly Budget*. In the 1880s, several New Orleans newspapers issued "Parade

choosing guests, and invitations to the exclusive balls were much sought after. In 1877, two invitations to the Comus ball were stolen. Comus advertised a $2,000 reward for their return. The invitations were not used, nor was the reward claimed.

28 The Knights of Electra parade of 1889 marching to popularize the incandescent lamp. Unfortunately, the parade was rained out; a second postponement because of boiler trouble caused great disappointment to the thousands who had come to view the spectacle; a third attempt suffered from lack of participants who had heard a rumor that they might receive a fatal shock from the wires. Electricity did not again play a part in the street spectacles until the Krewe of Nereus in 1900 mounted their pageant on regulation electric-trolley trucks to portray "The Christian Era." There were delays, and the electric cars became separated; the incongruity of the trolley poles sticking up through the decorations of the "floats" caused widespread disapproval. Nereus retired thereafter from public parades and has since staged only tableau balls.

29 *Promiscuous Maskers on Canal Street*, by B. West Clinedinst. The last years of the nineteenth century had seen the establishment of a number of societies formed to participate in the carnival celebration. Some of these were Atlanteans (1891), Elves of Oberon (1895), Nereus (1896), High Priests of Mithras (1897), Les Mystérieuses (1896), and Consus (1897). Following these were the Falstaffians (1900) and The Mittens (1901). With the beginning of the new century, the pageantry of carnival assumed a fixed pattern, which continued with only minor changes. In the leading carnival organizations, men were the social arbiters. Working in secrecy, they devised the themes of tableau and pageant; passed on the names of those to be invited to the ball; selected

29

one of their members to be king, and generally chose his queen and her attendants. The work fell upon the captain of the krewe and his lieutenants, who assumed full responsibility for the success of the parade and the ball.

In the gilded age, most parades consisted of eighteen to twenty floats, including the title float and the king's throne car. The parades were designed by highly skilled carnival artists and built by trained artisans who created in wood, papier-mâché, cloth, paint, gold, and silver leaf the mythological, legendary, fanciful, satirical, or comical subjects chosen for the spectacle. The floats of the first parades were drawn by horses, but later these were replaced by mules which, after humbly pulling the city's garbage wagons on other days, had three nights and a day of glory at carnival time. The night parades were illuminated by colored flares and by flambeaux (gasoline reflector torches) carried by coonjining Negroes who had as much fun as the krewe on the floats. Carnival for the man in the street was the biggest free show in the world and he loved it.

With minor variations, in each carnival there were

28

the parade and the ball of Momus on the evening of Thursday before Mardi Gras; the arrival amid pomp and ceremony of Rex at the levee on Monday noon; the Proteus parade and ball on Monday evening; the daytime parade of Rex and street-masking of the people on Mardi Gras day; and the evening parade of Comus, climaxed by the balls of Comus and Rex. *From* Frank Leslie's Illustrated Newspaper, *1893*

30 Mardi Gras maskers in homemade costumes. Two monkeys with tails are in the front row and an Uncle Sam and a Happy Hooligan bring up the rear, ca. 1910. *Courtesy New Orleans Public Library*

31 Plutocrats for a day, Mardi Gras, ca. 1915. This group with rented high hats and homemade full dress suits has hired a barouche to see the sights, and the face of the lad clutching the cigar is marked with hauteur in keeping with his role. *Photo by John J. DePaul*

30

31

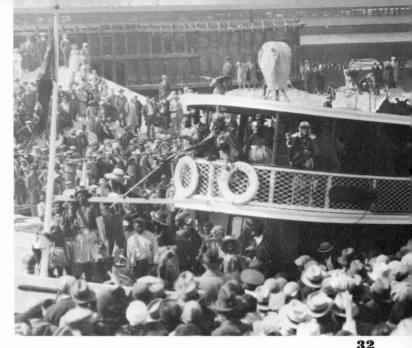

32

32 "The Greatest Free Show on Earth" was enjoyed by the Negroes of New Orleans probably even more than by the whites. They often made very elaborate costumes, the favorite being "Indians." The Zulu Aid and Pleasure Club each year selected a king, and on Mardi Gras morning for many years the monarch and his grass-skirted dukes would arrive at the head of the New Basin Canal aboard a tug, then mount the royal floats and parade—with numerous stops for liquid refreshment—in neighborhoods largely populated by Negroes. The Jahncke tug *Claribel* bore the royal party on Mardi Gras day, 1923, when this picture was made. *Photo by Charles L. Franck*

33 Negro flambeau bearers.

33

35

36

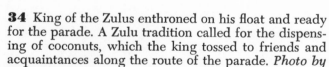

34

34 King of the Zulus enthroned on his float and ready for the parade. A Zulu tradition called for the dispensing of coconuts, which the king tossed to friends and acquaintances along the route of the parade. *Photo by Ray Cresson*

35 A typical carnival ball, ca. 1937. These were held through the years at various halls and theatres, such as the Washington Artillery Hall, the French Opera House (a favorite place for years until it burned in 1919), the Athenaeum, and presently the Municipal Auditorium. The maskers (members of the krewe) are dancing with ladies who have been "called out" by members of the reception committee from the audience. The balls are always opened with a pageant directed by a captain and feature the presentation of the young women of the court and are climaxed by the appearance of the king and queen. *Photo by Charles Genella*

36 The Boston Club at night during the Carnival season. The initials stand for Knights of Proteus, and this krewe was to parade that night. *Courtesy New Orleans Public Library*

37

37 By throwing peanuts and candy to the outstretched hands of parade viewers in 1881, Rex's krewe aboard the carnival floats started a custom that still persists—throwing literally tons of beads, cheap trinkets, and doubloons to the crowds. Mardi Gras, 1963.

38 Bourbon and Bienville streets, Mardi Gras, 1967. Bourbon Street in the French Quarter is a year round play spot for many visitors. On Mardi Gras, it particularly lives up to its reputation for gaiety, with great crowds of merrymakers and some of the most un-

39

inhibited maskers strolling about. *Courtesy Major Henry M. Morris*

39 Rex, 1971, Mardi Gras, pauses at the Louisiana Club. *Photo by Beau Bassich*

38

40

Parades

40 Through the years almost any event of any consequence would bring out the marchers. This parade is on Chartres Street in front of the St. Louis Cathedral to inaugurate the Jackson statue in 1856. *From* Ballou's Pictorial Drawing Room Companion

41 Some of the most colorful parades in New Orleans were those of volunteer firemen. Starting in 1837 or 1838, these pageants were an annual feature for more than fifty years. Held on March 4, the anniversary date of the founding of the Firemen's Charitable Association, they drew thousands of spectators. Each year before parade time the volunteers would repaint their engines and shine the brass and silver ornaments on them. Then the parade would start to the delight of the thousands of spectators who lined the street to watch. This painting by V. Pierson and P. Poincy is of the thirty-fifth annual parade of the volunteer firemen of New Orleans, March 4, 1872. *Courtesy Louisiana State Museum*

42 43 Not all parades were organized for gaiety and fun; some were very solemn affairs indeed. Witness the parade held on December 9, 1852, when a crowd estimated at between forty and fifty thousand watched as a funeral car drawn by six gray horses headed a parade in memory of three great American statesmen who had recently died—John C. Calhoun, Henry Clay, and Daniel Webster. Some five thousand persons marched, and these included the governor, the mayor, clergymen, judges, various federal and state officials, the fire department, the Masons, the Odd Fellows, benevolent societies, military units, and various trade unions. The funeral car carried three urns, each bearing the name of one of the distinguished statesmen, and these were solemnly deposited at the conclusion of the parade in a huge wood-and-canvas cenotaph painted to imitate marble that had been constructed in Lafayette Square, while the crowds dispersed to three halls to hear eulogies. The procession took one hour and a half to pass a given point, and its length was a mile and a half.

41

42

signed by A. Mondelli. It measured eighty-four by sixty feet and was sixty feet high. It consisted of a platform on which a classical dome-surmounted little temple sheltered an altar. From *A History of the proceedings in the City of New Orleans on the occasion of the Funeral Ceremonies in honor of Calhoun, Clay, and Webster, which took place on Thursday, December 9, 1852.*

44 Ralph Keeler, a journalist from Boston, who visited New Orleans in 1871, has left us as vivid a picture of a New Orleans parade as did the English illustrator Alfred Waud, who sketched it. Keeler wrote: "There is

43

44

The Clay, Calhoun, and Webster funeral car was decorated in black velvet and ornamented with silver fringe. The cenotaph in Lafayette Square was de-

never a Sunday and scarcely a week day in New Orleans without a procession of some kind. Canal Street would hardly look natural without its procession and accordingly you have The Seven Wise Men in full force in our engraving. This is one of the largest of the countless associations in which New Orleans delights, and which, whatever their other objects may be, can always be counted upon for a parade." The "Seven Wise Men" are preparing for a parade. The curious iron structure to the right of the illustration is Belknap's fountain, which featured miniature steamboats, swans, ducks, and cupids all set in motion by water power, and was, as Keeler described it, "a queer combination of arabesque and advertisement." *From Every Saturday, July 1, 1871*

45 Lee Circle, at the junction of St. Charles and Howard avenues. On a rainy February 22, 1884, a crowd estimated by the *Daily Picayune* at 15,000 turned out to witness the unveiling of this 16½-foot statue of Robert E. Lee (facing north) atop a 60-foot Doric column at what was then Tivoli Circle. While not actually a parade, the event contained much of the trappings. The schoolchildren in the photograph are appropriately dressed and massed to form the stars and bars of the Confederate flag. The statue was the work of Alexander Doyle, and the column was designed by John Roy, who wrote that he had selected the Doric order because it was "unsurpassed in sublime majesty, righteous in all its proportions, strength and beauty combined in an appropriate memorial to a great and good man." *Courtesy Charles F. Weber*

45

46

46 Celebrating Christmas Eve was more than a parade. The New Orleans custom of celebrating Christmas and New Year's with fireworks apparently had its origin sometime after the Battle of New Orleans. Despite repeated city ordinances penalizing the use of fireworks, the custom has continued to this day. This illustration, made at Christmas, 1884, portrays a crowd of noisy, horn-blowing revelers on Canal and Royal streets. Roman candles arch skyward, and to the left can be seen a hand firing a revolver. *From Frank Leslie's Illustrated Newspaper, January 3, 1885*

47 The Thin Gray Line—Confederate Veterans's parade on St. Charles Avenue in 1904. *Courtesy New Orleans Public Library*

47

Movies

48 When they weren't watching a parade, New Orleanians were at a movie. New Orleans's first movies were projected from the booth shown in the center of this photograph of West End. The pictures were

48

50 Fred Knaps, who has worked for fifty-five years as a projectionist, took this picture of the New Dixie Theatre, Canal and University Place, in 1915. Playing was Mae Marsh in *The Victim*. Admission was five cents.

51 By the time World War I had been declared, there were a number of Canal Street movie houses in operation. The Triangle, 814 Canal, the Dream World, 632 Canal, the No Name, 1025 Canal, and the Alamo, 1027 Canal, were some of the more popular theatres. Later came the Globe, Canal near Camp, seen here in 1922.

50

shown on a large canvas screen, which was unrolled in front of the bandstand. On June 28, 1896, Allen B. Blakemore, an electrical engineer for the New Orleans City & Lake Railroad, set up Edison's "Wonderful Vitascope." He had rigged up this small, square booth six feet above the decking of the resort to house the projector, and an old-time circus man named Billy Reed cranked the first flickering films. Blakemore used the five-hundred-volt current from the trolley line, reducing it by a water rheostat, for his machine. The first films were short subjects, since the first full-length movie, *The Great Train Robbery*, was not made until 1903. A short time after the open-air performance at West End began, Vitascope Hall, at Canal and Exchange Place, opened for business showing short subjects, such as *Shooting the Chutes, The May Irwin and John Rice Kiss, The Corbett-Courtney Fight*, and *Niagara Falls*. Admission was ten cents. *Photo by Detroit Photographic Company. Courtesy Library of Congress*

49 Movie houses proliferated. This one, the Acme Theatre, was located on Baronne Street. The posters advertise a six-reel show for five cents. *Courtesy Fred Knaps*

49

51

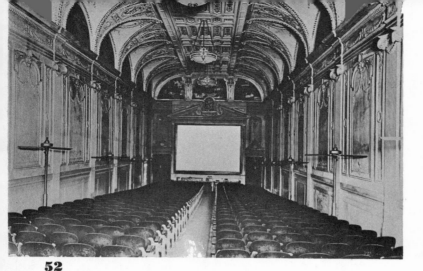

52

52 One of the more fancy movie houses was the Trianon, Canal between Baronne and Carondelet. In 1940, there were nearly fifty neighborhood movie houses. In 1971, more than two-thirds of these are gone, the victims of television and changing times.

Resorts

53 For more active diversion, there were the pleasure resorts—West End, Spanish Fort, Milneburg. This is a view of West End, then celebrating the French national fete day in New Orleans, July 14, 1881. First known as New Lake End, West End had its inception in 1871 when the city took over the partially built embankment thrown up in Lake Pontchartrain some eight hundred feet from shore at the terminus of the New Basin Canal and the Seventeenth Street Canal, raising the one-hundred-foot-wide bank to a height of

eight feet. In that year, the New Orleans City and Lake Railroad started its steam "dummy" and cars, and soon a large wooden platform was constructed over the water, and a hotel, restaurant, and various structures intended to house amusements were built, and a garden was laid out on the embankment. By 1880, New Lake End was rechristened West End, and for the next thirty years this lake resort was very popular with pleasure seekers. *From* Frank Leslie's Illustrated Newspaper, *August 13, 1881*

54 The New Basin Shell Road, a toll road. This 1906 photograph shows the tollgates, the toll-collector's house adjacent to Métairie Cemetery, and the tug *N. S. Hoskins* towing a couple of schooners and barges loaded with sand and bricks. The New Basin Canal (now filled and part of Interstate Highway 1–10), which ran from Lake Pontchartrain to a turning basin near the present Union Terminal, was dug by hand through the swamp in back of the city between 1831 and 1835 at a cost of $1,226,070. The canal was built by the American element above Canal Street to compete with the older Carondelet Canal, which had its terminus in the lower part of the city, at a time of intense rivalry between the Creoles and Americans. For more than a century, until it was filled in in 1950, products such as sand, gravel, shells, lumber, bricks, cordwood, and charcoal were carried on it from "across the lake" to the heart of the city. The New Basin Canal was sixty feet wide and six feet deep and about six miles long. On the canal's west side, the earth from the excavation formed the base of the famous New Basin Shell Road seen here, where antebellum New Orleans put its blooded horses through their paces. The Shell Road became famous throughout the country, and the expression "2:40 on the Shell Road," when that was the limit of speed for trotting horses, had its origin here. In later years, this road was a favorite with early automobilists, who would take their "machines" to West End for a spin on warm summer evenings. It is now part of Pontchartrain Boulevard. *Courtesy Library of Congress*

53

54

55 The bandstand and pavilion at West End in 1901. In 1898, the railway line to West End was electrified, and the exhilarating 6½-mile ride from downtown New Orleans on the West End trains, which in summer consisted of a motorcar pulling several opensided trailers, was enjoyed by thousands of patrons who flocked to the lake. It was here in 1896 that the first movie shown in New Orleans was viewed. *Courtesy Library of Congress*

56 West End boasted a scenic railway built entirely over water, seen here in 1901. At one end of the tracks was a "tunnel of love," which gave a swain a good opportunity to kiss the girl he had taken for the ride. *Courtesy Library of Congress*

57 West End in 1912, before development of West End Park. When the thirty-year lease of the railway company was about to expire, a disagreement between

55

56

57

it and the city over improvements the government wanted to make resulted in the utility company's acquiring and redeveloping Spanish Fort (1909), another pleasure spot for New Orleanians. The city then constructed a sea wall five hundred feet further out in the lake and filled in the space between the old embankment to form the present thirty-acre West End Park, these improvements being completed in 1921. *Courtesy Dr. Edmond Souchon*

58 Plan of Spanish Fort and other areas showing hotel, bathhouse, etc., built April 30, 1828. Fort San Juan (Spanish Fort) was constructed at the mouth of Bayou St. John after the Spanish took over Louisiana in 1769. By 1793, it was in need of repairs, and Governor Carondelet made these and stationed a garrison there. At the time of the Battle of New Orleans, General Jackson sent Major Jean Baptiste Plauché's battalion and a company of artillery under the command of Captain Zacheus Shaw to the fort, more for observation than for defense. The land occupied by the old fort was sold as surplus by the government in 1823 to Harvey Elkins who erected the Pontchartrain Hotel within its walls and laid out a pleasure garden, which became very popular. *Courtesy National Archives, Washington, D.C.*

59 It was at the Pontchartrain Hotel that the Duke of

59

Saxe-Weimar was entertained on his visit to New Orleans in 1825. This structure was rebuilt in 1874 about the time that a railroad was constructed to connect the resort with downtown New Orleans. Moses

58

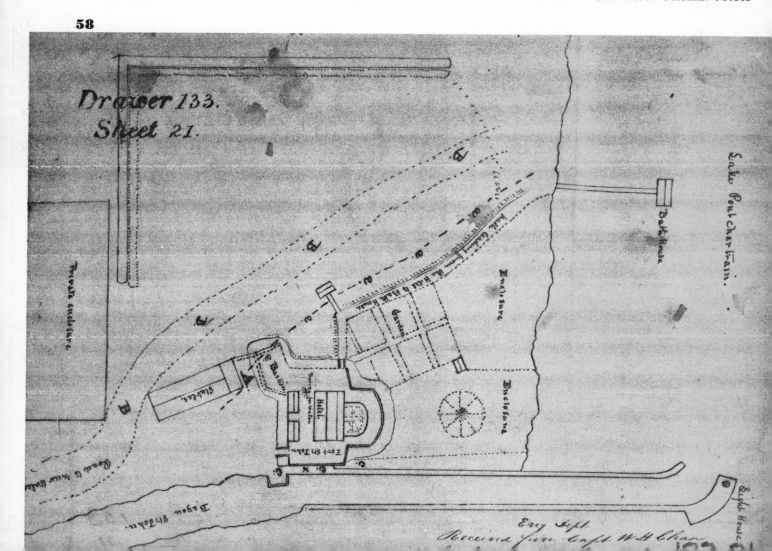

Schwartz bought Spanish Fort in 1878; in 1881, he built a casino, where excellent table d'hôte meals were served for $1, and a theatre that featured light opera and band concerts. By 1883, Spanish Fort had reached its zenith as an amusement resort. It was here that Oscar Wilde lectured on his visit to New Orleans. This view of the Spanish Fort pavilion is from *Peoples Illustrated and Descriptive Family Atlas of the World*, Chicago, 1886.

60 The band concerts at old Spanish Fort in the 1880s drew many pleasure seekers to the resort. One of the bands was Professor G. Sontag's Military Orchestra and a popular number performed was "The Blacksmith in the Woods," by Michaelis. An arrangement for piano of this piece, engraved for T. Fitzwilliam & Co., was published in New Orleans about 1886. Its fancy cover showed the entrance to Spanish Fort, the train which ran there, and a picture of Professor Sontag. This sheet music was a gift to the author from the family of Louis D. Fincke, a member of whose family played in Sontag's orchestra.

61 Ruins of Fort San Juan (Spanish Fort) on Bayou St. John, ca. 1890. *Photo by George F. Mugnier*

62 A view about 1895 of Spanish Fort park with the Over the Rhine restaurant in the background. This

60

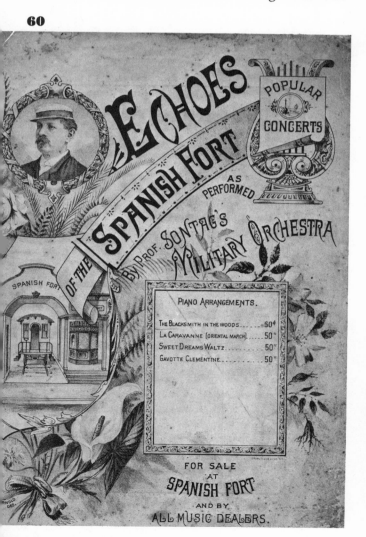

61

62

restaurant was still in operation in 1913. Spanish Fort went into eclipse when steam railroad service was suspended in 1903 and its buildings burned in 1906, three years before the property was acquired by the New Orleans Railway and Light Company, who extended their electric car lines to the resort in 1911 and rebuilt and reopened it as an amusement center in competition to the then popular West End. *Photo by C. Patterson*

63 Bathing from the Spanish Fort bathhouse was a popular sport in 1922 when this photograph was made. The two young women on the pier wear very modest bathing suits, set off by stockings and shoes. *Photo by Charles L. Franck*

63

64 An aerial view of Lakeshore Drive as it crosses Bayou St. John. All the land in this view was reclaimed from the lake bottom in a giant program carried out by the Orleans Levee Board in the 1930s. The plans of the board in 1928 to develop the whole lakefront between West End and the Industrial Canal had written finis to Spanish Fort as a pleasure resort. The remains of the old fort still stand, but the area surrounding it has been built up with fine residences.

65 The lighthouse at the mouth of Bayou St. John on Lake Pontchartrain. Saint-Aulaire made this picturesque view in 1821 on a day the lake was quite rough. *Courtesy Bibliothèque Nationale, Paris*

66 When the Pontchartrain Railroad began operations in 1831, its terminus on Lake Pontchartrain was called Milneburg. It soon became a favorite suburban place of amusement with a hotel, bars, restaurants, bathing facilities, and shooting galleries. The lighthouse seen here was built in 1855 to replace an earlier structure. By 1929, it had outlived its usefulness, and the bureau of lighthouses presented it to the Orleans Parish Levee Board. The board filled in the lakeshore in the 1930s. Practically nothing remains today of Milneburg except the old lighthouse that now stands high and dry at the Pontchartrain Beach amusement park. Milneburg (mispronounced Millenburg) lives on—it is the title of a popular jazz composition, "Millenburg Joys." *Photo by Richard Relf*

65

66

67

69

67 The *New Camelia* with a happy crowd of excursionists aboard, ca. 1910. The sidewheel steamer, beloved by thousands of excursionists who rode her from Milneburg or Spanish Fort to Mandeville, came to New Orleans in 1862. She had been built ten years before and christened *Zephyr.* After the Civil War, she was bought by a New Orleans cotton merchant named August Bone and put into the Gulf Coast trade. In 1879, this durable vessel was rebuilt and rechristened *New Camelia,* and until about 1917 she was the most famous of the Lake Pontchartrain excursion boats. Worn out and laid up, she sank in 1920.

68 Milneburg from the air. In this photograph, made in 1921 by H. J. Harvey, about a hundred "camps" built out over the water may be counted. This little Venice was demolished when the lakeshore development took place in the 1930s. *Courtesy Dr. Edmond Souchon*

68

69 For several miles along the shallow shores of Lake Pontchartrain from West End to a section called Little Woods, there were several hundred such cottages or camps built over the water on pilings. They were the summer homes of many Orleanians of modest means. *Courtesy Howard-Tilton Memorial Library, Tulane University*

70 One of the wonders of the amusement world that fascinated New Orleans in the 1850s was Spalding and Rogers's *Floating Palace.* This two-hundred-foot long vessel, which had been built in Cincinnati in 1851, was a super-showboat. It could accommodate 3,400 spectators, and more than a hundred people worked aboard her—crew, trainers, business staff, and performers, besides the horses and animals of the menagerie. There was even a daily newspaper published aboard, and besides the circus performance there were minstrel and dramatic performances and a museum that the proprietors said contained "100,000 curiosities." This circus wintered in New Orleans for several years, performing in the Academy of Music on St. Charles and Perdido streets. When spring came, the performers and animals were loaded aboard the *Floating Palace* for the trip upriver. The *Floating Palace* was converted into a hospital in 1862 by the Confederates.

70

71 The interior of the *Floating Palace*, lithograph by A. Forbriger. One of the chief attractions of the circus was its performing horses, which are shown in the principal view and in the side vignettes. *Courtesy New-York Historical Society*

72 Advertisement for Spalding and Rogers's Amphitheatre & Museum. *From* Gardner's New Orleans Directory, *1860*

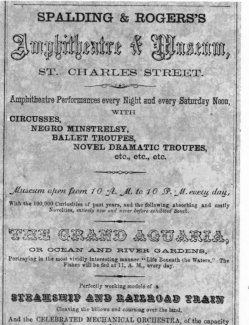

SPALDING & ROGERS'S

Amphitheatre & Museum,

ST. CHARLES STREET.

Amphitheatre Performances every Night and every Saturday Noon, WITH

CIRCUSSES,
NEGRO MINSTRELSY,
BALLET TROUPES,
NOVEL DRAMATIC TROUPES,
etc., etc., etc.

Museum open from 10 A. M. to 10 P. M. every day,

With the 100,000 Curiosities of past years, and the following absorbing and costly Novelties, *entirely new and never before exhibited South.*

THE GRAND AQUARIA,

OR OCEAN AND RIVER GARDENS,

Portraying in the most vividly interesting manner "Life Beneath the Waters," the Fishes will be fed at 11, A. M., every day.

Perfectly working models of a

STEAMSHIP AND RAILROAD TRAIN

Cleaving the billows and coursing over the land,

And the CELEBRATED MECHANICAL ORCHESTRA, of the capacity

72

Parks and Amusements

73 New Orleanians were always nature lovers and took to the parks early. New Orleans's first park was Tivoli Gardens, located on the outskirts of the city on Bayou St. John. This illustration by Paul Cavailler in the early part of the nineteenth century shows a fête champêtre, or rural festival. There are people eating and drinking at tables under the trees, and pavilions are in view. *Courtesy Samuel Wilson, Jr.*

74 Another popular amusement place was the Jardin du Rocher de Ste. Hélène (Garden of the Rock of St. Helena). While no view of this amusement place, which was operating in the 1840s, has come down to us, the plan shows the park to have been quite extensive: bowers for picnic tables, a bowling alley, pavilions of various kinds, and a formal garden. The site was Carondelet Canal between Galvez and Miro streets. *Courtesy Notarial Archives of Orleans Parish*

75 Crowning the May Queen under the oaks in City Park, sketch by R. J. Hamilton. The story of City Park is linked with Louis Allard, who once owned it. Allard was a member of an old Creole family that had sent him to France to be educated. When he returned he was a brilliant, cultured gentleman, but an impractical planter who borrowed on his ancestral holdings and

Paul Cavailler del. et Lithe.   Lithe L. Magny, Passage de la Bourse N° 15.

73

74   **75**

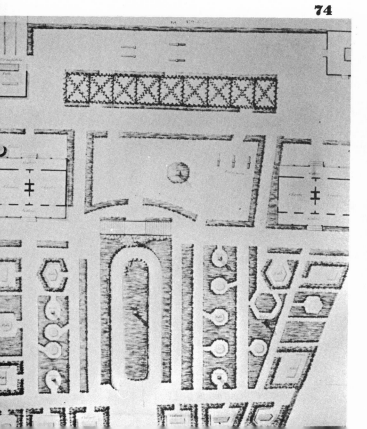

gradually sold his land. Two years before he died in May, 1847, John McDonogh seized the site of the park in a sheriff's sale, paying $4,500 for it. He permitted Allard to live out his life on the place, and in his will McDonogh directed that the site be sold to provide money for New Orleans schools. The city fathers wisely kept the land and in 1891 set up the board of commissioners of the New Orleans City Park Improvement Association to operate it. In 1898, a plan was adopted to landscape eighty-five acres of the park area, and a lagoon was formed by enlarging a portion of Bayou Métairie, which flowed for more than half a mile in the park area. This part of the park is noted for its huge live oak trees, many well over a century old. In 1926, the city paid $1,750,266 for the 1,100 acres, virtually all swamp, between the park and the lakefront, and this was largely developed during the days of the WPA.

An old brick-plastered tomb under one of the oaks near the Isaac Delgado Museum is often pointed out as Allard's tomb. Records in the St. Louis Cathedral archives show, however, that he was buried in a private tomb in St. Louis Cemetery No. 2 on May 18, 1847. *From* Harper's Weekly, *June 6, 1863*

76 The peristyle in City Park, a colonnaded pavilion that not only serves as a shelter but lends grace to the park. The lagoon in the foreground was originally Bayou Métairie. *Courtesy New Orleans Public Library*

77 The entrance to City Park in 1911. The iron arch has long since been removed. *Courtesy Ellis P. Laborde*

78 One of the joys of going to City Park on Sunday was to listen to the band concert and, if one stayed until dark, to view the free moving pictures, which were projected on a screen at the bandstand. This photograph of Joseph Sporrer's Band was made before a Sunday concert in 1899. Professor Sporrer is second from the right, first row. *Courtesy Mrs. Wilbert H. Reisig*

76

77

78

79 WPA workmen in 1937, beginning the construction of a new concrete road in the City Park extension, part of the general improvement plan. *Courtesy New Orleans Public Library*

79

80 Audubon Park. This park comprises a 247-acre site directly across from Tulane and Loyola universities on St. Charles Avenue. The site, originally part of the Foucher and Boré plantations, was purchased by the city in 1871 and first called New City Park, the name being later changed to Audubon Park to honor the famous artist and ornithologist John James Audubon. The park was the site of the World's Fair and Cotton Centennial Exposition in 1884–1885.

Audubon Park contains a memorial flagstaff honoring men who served in World War I, a statue of Audubon erected in 1910, a large swimming pool, the Odenheimer Aquarium and seal pool located in the beautiful Popp Gardens, a golf course, and a zoo. There are also many fine live oaks and a large lagoon, and a pavilion where a good view of the Mississippi River can be had. The park also contains an artificial hill constructed by WPA labor in the 1930s, so that children could have a hill to climb in pancake-flat New Orleans. The lagoon is in the foreground, with the tower of the Holy Name of Jesus Catholic Church in the background. *Courtesy Times-Picayune*

81 On May 4, 1907, a promoter named Charles C. Mathews advertised the opening of White City, an amusement park, located on the site now occupied by the Fontainebleau Motor Hotel on Tulane and Carrollton. On opening night, it featured a performance of *Kismet* by the Olympia Opera Company. The grounds were illuminated by fifteen hundred electric lights, and, beside the main attraction, one could ride on the "Flying Horses" or the "Figure 8," play the "Japanese Ball Game" or view "Katzenjammer Castle." White City was eventually closed and Heinemann Baseball Park (later Pelican Park) was built on the site in 1914. This is White City in 1908.

82 While parks would become an ideal place for bicycles and skates, the bicycle did not appear in New Orleans until 1868, a year before the first roller skates came into use. The first bicycles were curious affairs with a four-foot wheel in front and a smaller one-foot wheel in the rear as in this 1885 version. The rider had to exercise considerable skill to keep from tumbling,

81

82

80

which he often did when the front wheel hit an obstacle in the road. Despite the clumsiness of the first bicycles, riding quickly became a fad, and a number of clubs were organized and spirited races were held. Into the early 1900s cycling was very popular.

83 Penny Wonderland, ca. 1900. Your palm read, or your fortune told for one cent, and nearly a hundred stereoscopic machines with risqué or sentimental scenes to tempt one—all for a penny. *Photo by Teunisson. Courtesy New Orleans Public Library*

84

83

Cotton Centennial Exposition

84 More than a diversion, at what is now Audubon Park, on December 16, 1884, New Orleans proudly unveiled the wonders of its World's Fair and Cotton Centennial Exposition, spread out on a 249-acre tract in uptown New Orleans. Though the city's economy still bore the scars of war and Reconstruction, this did not deter the exposition's promoters, who financed and built a world's fair that equaled and even surpassed the fairs of much larger cities. Set in tastefully embellished grounds, the exposition's largest structure, the Main Building (*right center*), covered thirty acres. Its Horticultural Hall (*below*), a 600- by 194-foot house of glass, was the largest conservatory in the world. There were a number of other buildings (Government and States, Art Gallery, etc.), and for the first time at a world's fair electricity was used to provide light for buildings and grounds. The illustration is a bird's-eye view of the grounds and buildings.

85 The exposition was formally opened when Colonel Gus A. Breaux read the address of President Arthur, who had been invited to attend but was unable to come. Sketch by Charles Graham and T. de Thulstrup.

86 The approach to Horticultural Hall. This sketch, by T. de Thulstrup and Charles Graham, was made shortly after the opening of the exposition. When the fair closed, Horticultural Hall was kept as a conservatory, and it was one of the sights of New Orleans until it was wrecked by the tropical storm of September, 1915. *From* Harper's Weekly, *January 3, 1885*

87 One of the wonders of the Cotton Centennial Exposition was the electrically illuminated fountain in the center of Horticultural Hall. In the hall were displayed more than twenty thousand pieces of fruit in a setting of tropical and semitropical plants, flowers, and shrubbery. Sketch by C. Upham. *From* Frank Leslie's Illustrated Newspaper, *January 17, 1885*

88 One of the sights of the exposition was the Liberty Bell sent down from Philadelphia. Sketch by E. W. Kemble. *From* Century Magazine, *1885*

85

87

86

88

6. SPORTS

Crossed Swords Under the Oaks

1 While not exactly a sport, dueling among gentlemen in nineteenth-century New Orleans was the accepted way of settling disputes, misunderstandings, fancied insults, and quarrels. The city's proud, overly sensitive Creoles and its bragging adventurers contributed to many duels, some bloody and fatal, a few almost comic. Although laws had been passed forbidding the practice and though the church interdicted it on moral grounds, the *Daily Picayune* could remark on July 29, 1837, that duels were "as common these days as watermelons." The fear of loss of honor was greater in this age than the dread of dying. The numerous fencing masters had a large following, and it almost became a necessity for a young gentleman to become proficient in the use of arms. In the more genteel encounters, the rapier and the colichemarde, a sharper-pointed triangular blade, were used in preference to the more brutal broadsword or pistol. In 1866, Don José Quintero, a Cuban who had settled in New Orleans and who was an expert on the subject, wrote a curious little book, *The Code of Honor,* which one could consult to find out how, when, and where to be insulted, and what to do about challenges and seconds, and how to comport oneself in the duel itself. Here the handkerchief is about to be dropped.

2 "The Oaks"—the famous New Orleans dueling ground as it appeared in former days, sketched by Harry Fenn. According to popular legend, most duels in New Orleans took place "under the oaks" in what is now City Park. Actually, many took place in other secluded places near the edge of town or in the streets.

3 Pepe Llulla (Señor Don José Llulla), seen here in old age, is almost synonymous with dueling in New Orleans. Llulla, who was born in 1815 in the Balearic islands, settled as a youth in New Orleans and served his apprenticeship in arms under L'Alouette, a famous fencing master. Mastering the art, he eventually opened a *salle d'armes* of his own. Llulla was not only an expert swordsman but also a crack shot. Though he was known to have engaged in at least twenty duels, he could not remember the number of times he had served as a second. Llulla was also a venturesome businessman, who alternately owned a slaughterhouse and bought and sold flatboats. In 1857, he bought the St. Vincent de Paul Cemetery and ran this until he died in 1888.

1

2

4 In 1866, Alfred Waud attended and sketched a duel between the husband of a singer at the French Opera and another member of the cast who had given him cause for jealousy. The duel was held in the early morning in the rear of the Halfway House, then a tavern in a building still standing at the junction of City Park Avenue and the Pontchartrain Expressway. On the third round, after two rounds without any results, the husband was shot in the leg, and his opponent, apparently horrified because he thought he had killed his enemy, clapped both hands to his head and fainted. The seconds declared that honor had been satisfied, and Waud wrote: "The event proved to be an excellent topic for breakfast and it was revived with fresh interest at intervals throughout the day; the jealous husband meanwhile gnashing his teeth over his wounded leg and disappointed revenge—a beautiful instance of the futility of dueling!" *From* Harper's Weekly, *July 14, 1866*

5 After the Civil War, the glamour of personal encounters seems to have slowly disappeared. Dueling met with public disapproval, and it was very often ridiculed. The last mention of a duel in the press was made in 1889 when two duelists, after blazing away three times at each other and missing, were arrested by a policeman, who, attracted by the shots was probably disgusted at the poor marksmanship. The illustration is of a typical dueling pistol.

Fights Between Animals

6 Fights involving bulls, bears, tigers, and dogs were held in New Orleans as early as 1817. This fight between a large slate-colored bull called Napoleon IV and a four-hundred-pound grizzly bear took place before a frenzied crowd in 1853. The bull threw the bear several times and the bear chewed the bull's head, but after a while the bear retired to his corner and refused to fight. *From* The Illustrated News, *April 23, 1853*

7

8

7 "New Orleans," wrote Carp, a roving sportswriter, in an article printed in the *Daily Picayune* in 1885, "was for years a noted place for cockfighting and lovers of the sport were wont to gather there from all parts of the South." In the 1830s, a popular pit in the rear of the Union Hotel in the Vieux Carré advertised cockfights every evening. In 1866, Alfred Waud described a Sunday afternoon visit to a New Orleans cockpit:

> We were driven along Esplanade Street and not far from Beauregard's mansion, stopped at a place where right upon the street, entrance money was taken at a little ticket-office window before the spectator was admitted to the pit, where a fight between two game chickens was progressing fast and furious, the spectators betting furiously in English and French. Here full-blooded negroes and elegant mulattoes sat side by side with whites, and among the latter were Yankee merchants, Southern planters, professional gamblers, Mexicans, Cubans, Frenchmen and Spaniards.
>
> One of the unfortunate chickens being soon killed, the business of matching and weighing others occupied a little time, which our party expended in visiting the cages where the stock of fighting cocks was kept, a special privilege, the proprietor himself accompanying us in the inspection. These as the reporters used to say in the army, "were all aching for a fight," fine healthy birds with no immediate occupation other than crowing lustily.

Watching two more fights, Waud concluded, "Once in a while the attendants would pick up the bleeding roosters, sprinkle water from their lips upon them, and revive them for another round." Laws prohibiting cruelty to animals were passed in Louisiana in 1880, thus ending legal cockfighting, but these by no means stopped the "sport."

A Gambling Town

8 Gamblers, as depicted in *The Illustrated News,* 1853. From the start, New Orleans was a gambling town. C. C. Robin, a visitor at about the time of the Louisiana Purchase, wrote: "In the evening when the business of the day is over, fortunes are lost over and over again at it. . . . All indulge in it." Robin thought the prevalence of the habit arose from lack of education and stimulating intellectual activity, and that since the men of the city had nothing to talk about except business and politics they turned to gambling as an exciting way to pass their leisure hours.

The first gambling-house operator of note was John Davis, who operated games in conjunction with his Théâtre d'Orléans and opened a suburban branch on Bayou St. John. Davis ran high-class places, but there were many more gambling houses that became focal points for crime and disorder. There have been plush establishments catering to the well-to-do where huge sums were won and lost, and "joints" where those of more modest means could play keno. At times in the city's history (particularly during the carpetbag period), New Orleans was a virtual gambling hell. In 1880, when Mayor Joseph Shakspeare divised a system of unofficial suppression of gamblers, there were eighty-three large gambling houses in existence. From Davis's day to today, authorities have attempted to control gambling by various means.

9 *Louisiana State Lottery.* This illustration, taken from a lottery order blank in the Howard-Tilton Memorial Library, Tulane University, depicts Generals Beauregard and Early with their assistants in the act of drawing for prizes. Shown in vignettes are the rubber tube in which the numbers were encased and

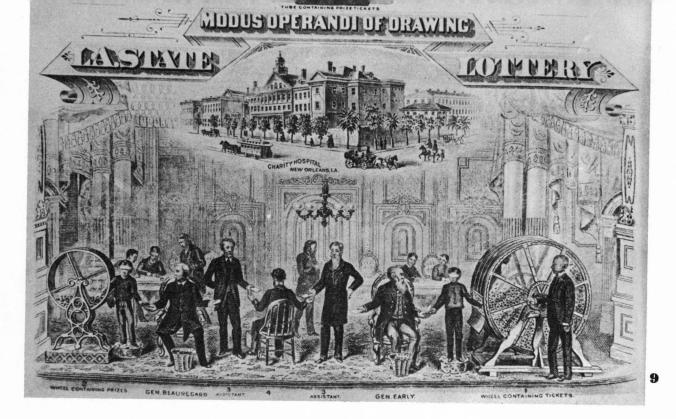

MODUS OPERANDI OF DRAWING

9

WHEEL CONTAINING PRIZES   GEN. BEAUREGARD   ASSISTANT   ASSISTANT   GEN. EARLY   WHEEL CONTAINING TICKETS

the Charity Hospital, which was the yearly beneficiary of $40,000 from the operators of the lottery.

In 1868, John A. Morris, a capitalist with New York connections, and Charles T. Howard formed the Louisiana State Lottery Company, which succeeded in obtaining from the Warmoth Republican administration an exclusive franchise to operate for twenty-five years. For this franchise, Morris and his associates had agreed to pay $40,000 a year for the Charity Hospital fund.

For several years, the Louisiana State Lottery Company made very little money. When they were about to quit, a Dr. Maxmilian A. Dauphin, who had been working for the concern in a very minor capacity, came to the management with a scheme that he felt sure would make the lottery pay. Dauphin had steeped himself in the business of lottery operations. He realized that what was needed to put the lottery over was dramatic publicity of the right kind. Accordingly, in 1877, he drew into the scheme two well-known heroes of the Confederacy, General P. G. T. Beauregard of Louisiana and General Jubal A. Early of Virginia, offering them each a reputed $30,000 a year to act as commissioners and to supervise the drawings. The drawings, well publicized with the names of the commissioners in every advertisement, were conducted with unimpeachable fairness, first in theatres and later in their own building.

10 This was the smaller of the two wheels used in the lottery drawings. It was known as the prize wheel, and General Bureaugard read out the prizes from tubes selected by a blindfolded boy to match the lucky numbers drawn from a much larger wheel containing one hundred thousand numbers.

Limited by franchise to issuing one hundred thousand tickets, the Louisiana State Lottery Company had started operations with twenty-five-cent tickets and a capital prize of $3,750, but as business increased the prices of a ticket rose to $40, with a $600,000 capital prize. People could buy fractions of tickets. In one instance, a New Orleans barber won $300,000 on an investment of $20.

The lottery company had a narrow squeak in 1879 when the legislature repealed its charter, but a federal court annulled the act of the legislature. That same year, a new state constitution was drawn up and the company was rechartered but without a monopoly clause, and with a provision that after 1895 all lotteries in Louisiana were to be prohibited. *Courtesy Louisiana State Museum*

10

11 A newspaper advertisement of the Louisiana State Lottery Company in June, 1880. If it is assumed that all tickets were sold at $10 each, the total intake would be $1 million. Since the prizes were only $522,500, the company would make a gross profit of $477,500 or nearly 48 percent (less their expenses, of course) on this one drawing! (This is really over 91 percent on the total prize money paid out.) The company also ran a "policy" business in New Orleans, which in the 1880s reached such proportions that it was able to pay the entire expenses of the lottery operations with the nickels and dimes bet by the thousands of players who daily thronged the hundred policy shops operated by the company. Business spread rapidly, and soon there were agents in cities all over the United States. In Boston and New York, there were monthly sales of $50,000; in Chicago it reached $85,000. The lottery company once stated that only 7 percent of its revenue came from Louisiana. In 1890, nearly 45 percent of the receipts of the New Orleans post office was lottery business, with $25 million a year coming through the mail.

12 A New Orleans lottery vendor, sketch by W. T. Smedley, 1892. The Louisiana State Lottery Company acquired the fitting nickname of "The Octopus." Strictly for advertising purposes, it contributed lavishly to any charity or cause which would bring its philanthropies to the public eye; at the same time its tentacles went deep into the pockets of the poor and entwined around the necks of legislators or anyone of prominence who could be bought. Growing bolder with each passing year, the lottery company was finally a dominant influence in the state, until leading citizens formed an anti-lottery league and laid plans to rid the state of this "debaucher of politics and debaser of the people." Urged on by the anti-lottery league, Congress passed a law on September 19, 1890, prohibiting the use of the mail for the transmission of all letters, circulars, and newspapers relating to the business of lottery. This and the results of a long, bitter

12

13

struggle in the state election of 1892 were the death blows that finally forced the Louisiana State Lottery to end its existence.

13 Typical Louisiana State Lottery Company tickets —drawings of May 14, 1889, and October 20, 1893.

14 One of the most active anti-lottery fighters was Reverend Dr. Bevery Caradine. The illustration is from his book, *The Louisiana State Lottery Company Examined and Exposed*, 1890.

15 For more sophisticated gambling, there were always the riverboat types. George Devol (1829–1892) was one of the more colorful riverboat gamblers. He had abandoned the steamboats at the outbreak of the Civil War and sought refuge in New Orleans. In his autobiography, Devol tells that he and other stranded riverboat gamblers formed a handsome military company, the Wilson Rangers, which they themselves called the Blackleg Cavalry. Every morning they would mount their horses and gallop back of the city ostensibly to drill. The first orders they would receive from their commanding officer would be:

"Dismount! Hitch horses! Hunt shade! Begin

11

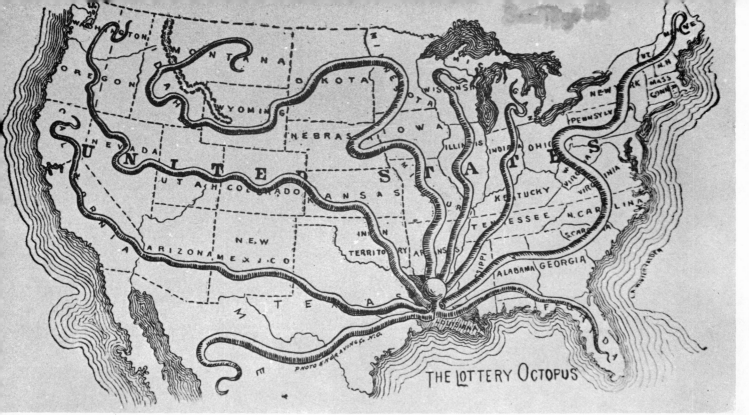

THE LOTTERY OCTOPUS

15

Greetings from
NEW ORLEANS, LA.

16

playing!" . . . in less than ten minutes there would not be a man in the sun. They were all in the shade, seated on the ground in little groups of four, five and six; and in each group could be seen a little book of tactics (or at least it looked like a book at a distance). We would remain in the shade until the cool of the evening, when the order would be given: "Cease playing! Put up books! Prepare to mount! Mount! March!" When we would get back to the city, the people would come out, cheer, wave handkerchiefs and present us with bouquets for we had been out in the hot sun, protecting their homes from the Northern invaders.

When Farragut launched his attack on the Confederate forts below New Orleans, Devol's company was sent downriver with other detachments to engage a federal land force that had been reported to be marching to the city. Wrote Devol: "As we went through the streets, the ladies presented us with bouquets, and cheered us; but there was but little cheer in that fine body of gamblers." About six miles below the city one of the federal ships fired a salvo on canister at them, whereupon the Blacklegs retreated at full speed. When they got back to the city, they hurriedly dismounted, cut the buttons off their coats, buried their sabers and tried to make themselves look as much like peaceful citizens as possible. Devol concluded: "We had enough of military glory and were tired of war."

16 Shooting craps was an ever-popular amusement, particularly among Negroes. This illustration, copied from a postcard postmarked February 7, 1910, shows a game in progress among roustabouts aboard a Mississippi River steamboat.

17 "Beyond the city limits in the adjacent parishes of Jefferson and St. Bernard," states the *New Orleans City Guide*, 1938, "are several large and elaborately appointed gambling houses. . . . Although gambling is, strictly speaking, illegal, these places are usually open for business from dusk to dawn." One of these was the Hi-Li (Jai Alai) Club, 137 Friscoville Avenue, in St. Bernard Parish, in those days a seventy-five-cent taxi drive from downtown New Orleans. This club featured the extremely fast game of jai alai played by imported American or Spanish players who tossed balls with incredible speed against a wall with the aid of a cesta, a curved basketlike device attached to the arm.

17

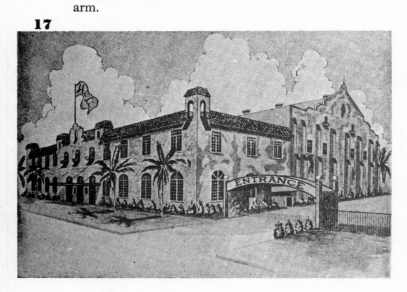

Sport of Kings

18 In 1847, when the Mexican War broke out, New Orleans was the leading horse-racing center of the United States. The city boasted four tracks, three on the east side and another across the river. These were the Métairie, the Eclipse, the Union, and the Binga-man, and the newspapers gave about equal coverage

to the doings at the tracks as to the war with Mexico. The first racetrack was laid out in 1820 by François Livaudais on his Live Oak Plantation, which was near the intersection of St. Charles and Washington avenues. Livaudais invited his friends to view informal matching and racing. Then followed the Jackson Course in 1825, established a few miles below the city, and, in 1837, the Eclipse Track, occupying part of the site of Audubon Park, was laid out. The next year saw the beginning of the Métairie Race Track seen here during spring meeting. *From* Frank Leslie's Illustrated Newspaper, *May 4, 1872*

19 The main entrance to the Métairie Race Course. In 1853, the Métairie Jockey Club was founded. This exclusive organization took over the management of the track, built a massive grandstand, and soon the Métairie course became a shrine for the outstanding thoroughbreds of the day, as well as a mecca for horsemen from all over the United States. The ten years before the Civil War was a decade forming one of the most glorious pages in the annals of American turf, and in

19

18

this period Métairie attained its full glory. Crowds exceeding twenty thousand filled the stands and lined the rails. *From* Frank Leslie's Illustrated Newspaper, *December 18, 1869*

20 The racer Lexington, who provided some of the best-remembered races at the Métairie track in the thrilling Lexington-Lecompte contests in 1854 and 1855. Lecompte, foaled and reared in Louisiana, won the first contest on April 8, 1854. The races were for four miles, and Lecompte, finishing in 7:26, bettered the record time of Fashion at the Long Island track in 1842. On April 2, 1855, Lexington, running against time, ran the four miles in 7:19¾, bettering Lecompte's record by 6¼ seconds. In a race with Lecompte on April 14, Lexington won easily in 7:23¾, and this con-

test probably aroused as much interest at the time as the famous steamboat race between the *Rob't E. Lee* and the *Natchez* in 1870. Lithograph published by N. Currier, 1855. *Courtesy Fair Grounds Corporation*

21 *Life on the Métairie—The Métairie Race Course*, a painting by Victor Pierson and Theodore S. Moise, 1867. Among the sixty personalities in this painting for the Métairie Jockey Club is General P. G. T. Beauregard. The Métairie track had closed for the duration of the Civil War, reopening in 1866. But it was not the same Métairie. The old Métairie Jockey Club had disintegrated, and Reconstruction troubles and quarrels within the ranks of management forced the owners to sell. In 1872, a group of businessmen bought the track and converted the site into the Métairie Cemetery, which would in time become one of the outstanding burial places in the United States. *Courtesy Fair Grounds Corporation*

22 In 1872, the Louisiana Jockey Club, a new group, took over the old Creole Race Course (the present Fair Grounds that got its name from the fairs the Mechanics and Agricultural Association held there

20

22

21

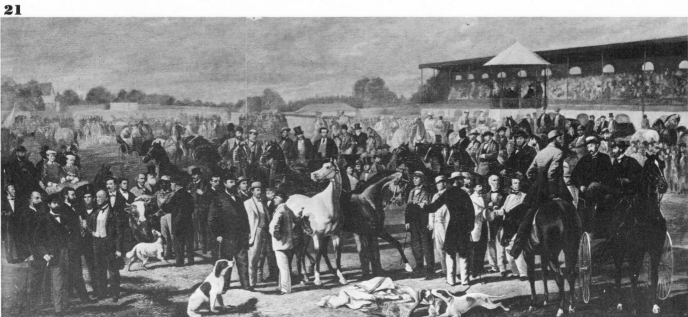

after the war). The Louisiana Jockey Club also bought the adjoining Luling mansion on Esplanade to serve as a clubhouse, shown here, and it is still standing. The estate with 500-foot frontage and a depth of 2,500 feet with its flower gardens and orchards was one of the most impressive in the city. The organization built a new grandstand and started operations with a six-day inaugural race meet in April, 1872. *From* Jewell's Crescent City Illustrated, *1873*

23 Spring meeting of the Louisiana Jockey Club, sketch by Ph. G. Cusachs. Limiting its membership to four hundred, the club included the city's wealthiest and most prominent citizens. The elite gathered at the Fair Grounds for the races and also for concerts, drills, tournaments, and fêtes champêtres. *From* The New York Daily Graphic, *April 24, 1874*

24 Ladies' Day at the races. A special section of the stands was designated the "Beauty Corner" and was reserved exclusively for the fair sex. The Fair Grounds track had a checkered history. A new jockey club was formed in 1880; another, the Crescent City Jockey Club, was founded in 1892, which ran the Fair Grounds until 1908; and somewhere along the line the Luling mansion-clubhouse was lost. In 1905, competition in the form of the City Park racecourse developed with the result that there was literally too much racing. In 1908, the Louisiana Legislature abolished the sport.

24

25 Finish of handicap, Crescent City Jockey Club, 1906. By 1915, racing was again legal, and the Fair Grounds reopened under the auspices of the Business Men's Racing Association. In 1918, the grandstand burned to the ground, and it was rebuilt in the almost miraculous time of about seventy-two hours as to be ready for the season's opening on New Year's Day. Changes in management took place again in 1926, in

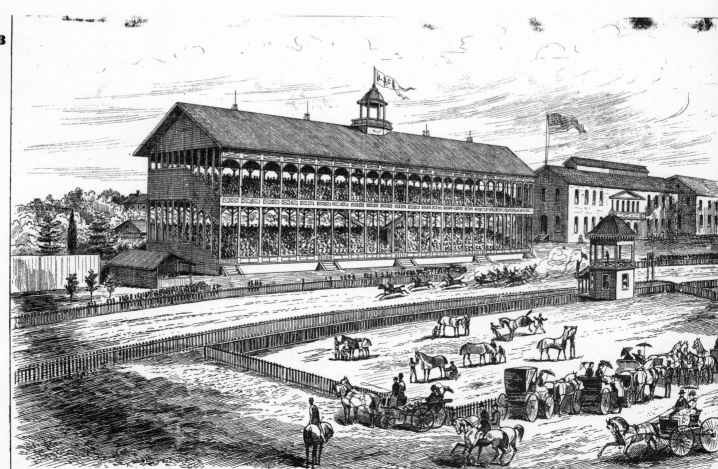

23

25

1934, and in 1940, when the highly successful Fair Grounds Corporation was organized. The Fair Grounds and horse racing are very much part of the New Orleans scene and have been for three quarters of a century. *Courtesy Library of Congress*

Sailing

26 The first Southern Yacht Club, second oldest in the United States, in the 1880s. The club was founded in 1849 at Pass Christian, Mississippi (many New Orleanians spent the summer on the Gulf Coast to avoid the yellow-fever epidemics that plagued the Crescent City in those days). Racing began in 1850 and con-

tinued until the Civil War. By 1878, the club had grown to three hundred members. The clubhouse was built in 1879 at West End and a yacht harbor created. *Courtesy Howard-Tilton Library, Tulane University*

27 Fish Class sloops in a race at the Southern Yacht Club, 1940s. In 1919, Rathbone DeBuys, an architect intensely interested in yachting, feeling the need for a sturdy sailboat of a type that could be used for training or racing, designed a 15'-10" gaff-rigged yacht, and the club built six of them, which were rented to members. Other clubs followed suit, and by 1950 there were eighty-four of these Fish Class sloops in the dozen Gulf Coast yacht clubs of the Gulf Yachting Association. Hundreds of skippers were trained on these boats, and each year the Fish Class boats contend for the handsome challenge trophy Sir Thomas Lipton presented to the club in 1919. A number of internationally famous yachtsmen are members of the Southern Yacht Club. *Courtesy Southern Yacht Club and Erston Reisch*

27

26

28

28 The Southern Yacht Club of today from the air. *Courtesy Southern Yacht Club and Erston Reisch*

29 A rowing race in the New Basin Canal opposite West End, ca. 1895. Rowing clubs were also popular. The first rowing club established in New Orleans was the Wave Boat Club in 1835, with headquarters in the New Basin Canal. Within a few years, six more clubs were formed, and these built their clubhouses on the upper side of Algiers Point on the Mississippi River and did their rowing in that stream. The sport grew quickly, and soon regattas were being held. Unfortunately, in 1844, high water swept away the Algiers clubhouses and the sport languished. Revived again in 1872 by the St. John Rowing Club, which built its clubhouse on Bayou St. John near the Harding Drive Bridge, the club soon had rivals with boathouses on the bayou, river, and lake. The twentieth century saw a gradual diminution in interest in the sport. The September, 1915, hurricane destroyed the St. John Boat Club at the mouth of the New Basin Canal; fire destroyed the Pontchartrain Rowing Club in 1927, and the remaining landmark, the former St. John Rowing Club on Bayou St. John, was demolished in 1928 as part of the City Park beautification program. *Courtesy Dr. Edmond Souchon*

29

Boxing

30 While prizefighting was illegal in Louisiana, New Orleans from the end of the Civil War was a fight-happy town. In the days before gloves came into use, these bareknuckled contests drew great crowds of fans. One such was recorded in January, 1869, when a New Orleans fighter named King fought and beat Farrell, a Philadelphian in an eighty-three-round contest held near the Halfway House. Another fight between Jim Mace and Tom Allen took place in 1870 in Kenner, and seven hundred "sporting men" made the trip to see the match.

New Orleans was the ring capital of the world during the 1880s and 1890s. Every boxer of note appeared in New Orleans during these years and again in a brief rebirth of prestige between 1910 and 1915.

John L. Sullivan, the Boston strong boy, who trained at the Young Men's Gymnastic Club, was matched with Jake Kilrain in a fight that couldn't be held in New Orleans because Governor Nicholls called out the militia to prevent it. Mississippi, too, had laws against prizefighting but the promoters scheduled the fight there on July 8, 1889, in Richburg, a sawmill town of two hundred, near Hattiesburg. New Orleans went fight-mad. Crowds on Canal Street before the fight resembled those at Mardi Gras, and nearly three thousand men in two trainloads bought tickets to an unnamed destination to see the contest. Sullivan beat Kilrain in seventy-five rounds, fighting bareknuckled for two hours, sixteen minutes, and twenty-three sec-

onds for a purse of $10,000. Sullivan and Kilrain were arrested, tried, and convicted "as criminals who outraged decency and defied the laws." Stiff jail sentences and fines were dealt both men, but later the State Supreme Court reduced the fines and remitted the sentences. This scene of the fight is the seventh round as Kilrain locked his arm around Sullivan's neck. *Courtesy New Orleans Athletic Club*

31 Louisiana legalized glove contests in 1890, the first state to do so. The leading athletic club in the 1890s was the Olympic. The club's arena on Royal Street between Montegut and Clouet adjoined clubrooms with such social attractions as a bar, billiard room, library, lounging rooms, and a dining room. In 1891, Bob Fitzsimmons knocked out Jack Dempsey (the "Nonpareil") for a purse of $12,000 with 3,500 fans looking on. In 1892, the Olympic reached the zenith of its career in promoting "The Carnival of Champions." Boxing with gloves was now legal, and on three successive days, September 5, 6, and 7, customers paid a total of $101,557.80 to witness Jack McAuliffe knock out Billy Meyers for the world lightweight championship (purse $9,000); George Dixon knock out Jack Skelly for the world featherweight championship (purse $7,500); and James J. Corbett knock out John L. Sullivan (*below*) for the world heavyweight championship. Gentleman Jim got $25,000, while poor old John L. Sullivan lost his title and got nothing. In 1893, the Olympic matched Andy Bowen, a local boy, against gentleman Jack Burke of Galveston for the lightweight championship of the South. This fight,

30

31

witnessed by an enormous crowd, was the longest battle in ring history—with or without gloves. It lasted 110 rounds, and the men fought for seven hours and nineteen minutes. Both men refused to continue, and the referee called it "no contest."

32 New Orleans has produced, besides several scores of boxers who never quite reached the top, two who made the Boxing Hall of Fame. One of these was Tony Canzoneri, who, although born in Slidell, rose from a shoeshine boy around New Orleans to the pinnacle of boxing. One of the greatest lightweights of all time, the 5-foot-4-inch Canzoneri started as an amateur boxer at only ninety-five pounds. During his career Canzoneri held eight titles, including his amateur championships.

33 The other New Orleans boxer to reach the Hall of Fame was Pete Herman. Born Peter Gulotta of Italian parentage, the diminutive Herman started his boxing career in 1912. He won the world bantamweight title from Kid Williams in a twenty-round bout in New Orleans on January 7, 1917, and lost it to Joe Lynch on December 20, 1920, in Madison Square Garden. On July 25, 1921, Herman did what few fighters can ever do—regain a championship. He did this by beating Lynch in Brooklyn in fifteen rounds, only to lose the crown two months later to Johnny Buff. Pete Herman fought for the last time on April 24, 1922, when he whipped Roy Moore in a ten-rounder in Boston. Increasing difficulty with his sight caused him to retire and he eventually became blind. He has been operating a nightclub in New Orleans.

34 Nat Fleischer, the New York authority on boxing and editor and publisher of *Ring Magazine,* rates three other fighters born in New Orleans as of national importance. One of these is a Negro, Harry Wills, a powerful heavyweight born on May 15, 1889, who fought for over twenty years. Wills and Sam Langford, "the Boston Tar Baby," fought twenty-two matches over the years; Wills won six, Langford two, and there was no decision in fourteen. Wills's last fight was in 1932 when he was knocked out in Brooklyn by Jankassa. He retired from the ring and went into the real-estate business. He died in New York in 1958.

35 Pal Moran is one of the three great New Orleans fighters named by Fleischer. This New Orleans boy who came up from the French Market neighborhood fought seven world champions, including the great Benny Leonard, between 1912 and 1929. He fought Rocky Kansas in 1926, featherweight champion Kid Kaplan the same year, and junior lightweight champion Jack Bernstein in 1923. He received his biggest purse, $22,500, in his fight with Dundee. After retiring from the ring, he worked at local racetracks as a mutuel clerk for more than thirty years.

36 The last Fleischer selection is Joe Mandot, the pride of the French Market area, the fighting baker boy who was a superb boxer in the days before World War I. During his career, Joe Mandot fought eight men who became world champions. He lost decisively only to one. His opponents included such greats as Ad Wolgast, Willie Ritchie, Freddy Welsh, Johnny Kilbane, Johnny Dundee, Rocky Kansas, Ted ("Kid") Lewis, and Benny Leonard. A fighter who depended on speed and cleverness rather than on stamina and punching power, Joe Mandot was one of the most popular boxers to call the Crescent City his hometown. Other New Orleans fighters were Marty Burke, Eddie Coulon, Johnny Fisse, Battling Shaw, and Happy Littleton.

32   **33**   **34**   **35**   **36**

37   **38**   **39**

37 Charles Abner Powell (1860–1952), the "father" of the New Orleans Pelicans, came to New Orleans in 1887 and became a member of the city's first professional team. As manager of the Pelicans, he invented the rain check, conceived the idea of covering the diamond with tarpaulin to prevent flooding of the field during rainstorms, and introduced Ladies Day to fans here.

Baseball had got its start in the East in the 1840s. New Orleans amateur teams started playing in the 1850s. The first local games in which the press showed an interest were played in July, 1859, on a cleared field on the Delachaise estate near today's Louisiana Avenue by teams of a league which called itself the Louisiana Base Ball Club. By 1870, New Orleans had three baseball parks (one with a grandstand that could accommodate 1,200 persons) and half a dozen amateur teams. In April of that year, New Orleans saw its first professional games when the Cincinnati Red Stockings, the first entirely professional ball club, then on a national tour, played a series of five games with local amateurs including the Pelicans. The results were predictable, in favor of Cincinnati. By 1901 Abner Powell was so dissatisfied with the performance of his now professional team that he journeyed to North Carolina, bought a new one for $12,000, brought it back to New Orleans, and fired his old team. The newcomers greatly improved the Pelicans's standing. After Powell, three other remarkable Pelican managers—Charley Frank (three pennants), Johnny Dobbs (two pennants), and Larry Gilbert (five pennants)—bossed the New Orleans teams through 1938 (with the exception of two years). These years were the brightest, the great days of New Orleans baseball—the days of Dixie Walker, Joe Martina, and Cotton Knaupp.

38 Larry Gilbert (1891–1965), named manager in 1922. A New Orleans boy who had grown up in the ball park, Gilbert had a meteoric rise to fame after playing with teams in Victoria, Texas, and Michigan

(Battle Creek) before making the majors where he played with Milwaukee. After that he was with the Braves, a team that won the World Series in 1914. Gilbert was the first New Orleanian to play in the major leagues and the first to play in a world series. Eventually returning to his hometown and the Pelicans, Gilbert managed the team until 1938 (with the exception of 1932). When Gilbert left New Orleans, the glorious days of the Pelicans were ended. From 1939 to 1959, when the team disbanded, there were no fewer than thirteen managers and several affiliations with various major league teams and changes of ownership, but with the exception of two years when they came closer to first place, the Pelicans never won another pennant. The old magic was gone.

39 Before the days of professional baseball the sport was a social highlight. This sketch by Alfred R. Waud, made in 1871, shows players on the fringe of a crowd of dancers at the Fair Grounds. *From* Every Saturday

40 "Shoeless" Joe Jackson, a rough-and-ready player, played in the Carolinas in his bare feet. He com-

40

plained that the rough field made the ball "wingy," but didn't open his mouth to complain about his feet. ("Shoeless" seems to have forgotten what he is famous for in this picture.) Jackson played for the Pelicans and later for the Chicago White Sox. *From* The Chicago White Sox *by Warren Brown*

41 Alexander Julius Heinemann (1876–1930), "Heine" to the fans, was largely responsible for the development of the Pelican franchise into one of the most valuable minor league properties in the country. Heine was not a ballplayer—he started in baseball by vending soft drinks in the stands, but by 1914 he was the Pelicans's general manager, and from that time on his team began to win games and make money. It was he who moved the Pelican stadium from Carrollton and Banks to a site on Tulane and Carrollton where it bore his name until 1938. It was in Heinemann Park at one of the climactic games in the 1927 series that with 15,411 fans in the stands, a crowd of 2,000 broke down the gates and rushed in to see the game. Despite his financial success, Heine was not a favorite with the fans. He roamed the stands during a game, habitually wearing an old straw hat, and this never failed to bring calls of "cheapskate." Plagued by financial reverses in the 1929 crash, Heinemann ended his own life in 1930.

42 The pennant-winning Pelican team, 1923. This photograph was the proud possession of Cotton Knaupp, who played more than fifteen hundred games in the Southern Association and who, on August 8, 1916, made the only unassisted triple play on record in Southern Association history. *Courtesy Mrs. Henry Knaupp*

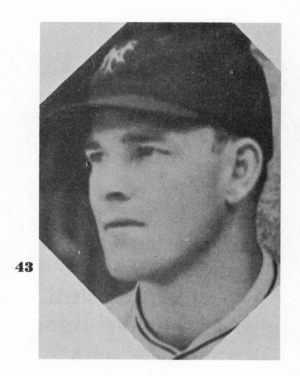

43

43 Melvin Thomas Ott from Gretna (on the west bank of New Orleans) was born in 1909. He was the greatest baseball player to come out of the New Orleans area. He began a twenty-two-year career with the New York Giants in 1926. During that span, he hit 511 home runs to set a National League record. He played in 2,730 major league games, went to bat 9,456 times, scored 1,859 runs, including 488 doubles, 72 triples, and the 511 homers. He batted in 1,860 runs and retired with a lifetime batting average of .304.

42

41

Pelicans
1923

MATTISON, P.   BOGART, O.F.   GILBERT, MANAGER   TUCKER, O.F.
THOMAS, P.   EWOLT, S.S.   WALKER, P.   HENRY, 1ST B   DOWIE, C.   WINN, P.
WHITTAKER, P.   NITZE, C.   MARTINA, P.   SCHICK, O.F.   KNAUPP, 2ND B   FOSS 3RD B

44 Pelican Stadium, at Tulane and Carrollton avenues, as it operated in 1955 a few years before it was demolished to build the Fontainebleau Motor Hotel. Its playing field—458 by 610 feet—was one of the largest in the country. *Courtesy Times-Picayune*

Football

45 Hugh and Thomas L. Bayne, brothers who had played football at Yale, taught the game to students at Tulane and, dividing them into two squads, on New Year's Day, 1890, put on the first football match to be seen in New Orleans. About seven hundred people attended the game, which was held at Sportman's Park in the rear of the Halfway House on City Park Avenue and the New Basin Canal. Enthusiasm for the sport spread, and students at Louisiana State University became interested. In 1893, Tulane played its first game with "The Old War Skule," and the score was Tulane 34, Louisiana State University 0. In the early days, there were no bands or cheerleaders. The players wore nondescript uniforms, and the game was characterized by battering-ram tactics. The rules were different, too. The center rolled the ball back, and it had to be touched by two players before it was in play. Touchdowns counted four points; goal after touchdown, two points. Halves were generally forty-five minutes, and there were no substitutes. If a man was knocked out, the game went on just the same without him, and it was considered something of a disgrace to be knocked out. Footballs cost $5. In the early 1890s, one of the games came to a sudden conclusion when the ball collapsed—it was the only football in town! This photograph is of the Tulane varsity team, 1902.

46

47

46 Tulane vs. Auburn, 1903. Tulane's colors—olive and blue—were selected in 1893, although the team didn't become known as the Green Wave until 1920. During the first two decades of football, Tulane's teams had a checkered career. In 1895, they won four and lost two games; in 1899, they lost all their games, but in 1900 they were undefeated. Although 1908 was a good year, with only one loss, between 1909 and 1914 the record of the teams was dreary.

47 Things began to look up in 1915 when Clark D. Shaughnessy came to Tulane as football coach. He revolutionized football with the development of the modern T formation. Shaughnessy came to Tulane fresh from Big Ten honors at Minnesota, and, with a one-year gap (1921), coached the Green Wave for ten seasons. Under his coaching, by 1919 Tulane emerged as a major competitor in southern collegiate football. His greatest teams were the 1924 Greenies, who upset Vanderbilt, and his unbeaten 1925 team. Shaughnessy later coached at Chicago, Maryland, Pittsburgh, and Stanford before joining the staff of the Chicago Bears. He died in 1970.

48 From 1920 to 1940 was the golden age of Tulane football. This is the Tulane team of 1925, captained by Lester J. Lautenschlaeger. They won all their games except for a tie with Missouri; their greatest game of that season was an upset victory, 18–7, over Northwestern in Chicago. Under four coaches—Clark Shaughnessy, 1915–1920, 1922–1926; Bernie Bierman, 1927–1931; Ted Cox, 1932–1935; Lowell ("Red") Dawson, 1936–1941—the Greenies played in a Rose Bowl

and two Sugar Bowls and were conference champions (or co-champions) six times. In that period, seven Tulane players were named All-American players—Charles ("Peggy") Flournoy, 1925; Willis ("Bill") Banker, 1929; Gerald ("Jerry") Dalrymple, 1930 and 1931; Donald ("Don") Zimmerman, 1932; Claude ("Little Monk") Simons, 1932; Harley Ray McCollum, 1939; and Ralph Wenzel, 1939. *Courtesy Dr. John P. Dyer*

49 Bernie Bierman was brought to Tulane by Shaughnessy to be his assistant in 1923. He left three years later to become head coach of Mississippi A. & M., now Mississippi State. When Shaughnessy, too, left Tulane, for Loyola, across Freret Street, Bierman returned in 1926. His 1929, 1930, and 1931 teams were unbeaten in the South, and he took the latter eleven to the Rose Bowl. Bierman was succeeded by Ted Cox, who had as his backfield coach Lester Lautenschlaeger. In the next four years this happy combination's Green Wave won 71 percent of its games: 6–2–1 in 1932; 6–3–1 in 1933; 9–1–0 in 1934; 6–4–0 in 1935. But that year, the team lost 41–0 to L.S.U., and despite the fact that Cox and Lautenschlaeger had developed a conference championship, won a Sugar Bowl game, and produced an All-American player, the Tulane athletic council pressured the coaches to resign. Their successor was Lowell ("Red") Dawson whose record had much to commend it—62 percent of games won, a Sugar Bowl game, and three All-American players. But the loss of four out of six games with Tulane's traditional enemy, L.S.U., between 1936 and 1941 caused the alumni and Tulane supporters to become

48

so critical that Dawson resigned after the 1941 season.

50 When Dawson departed in 1941, he was succeeded by another former Tulane star, Claude ("Little Monk") Simons—whose father (*below*) pioneered Tulane's athletic programs—who coached the teams through the difficult years of World War II. In 1946, Henry E. Frnka, who had brought two Tulsa University teams to the Sugar Bowl game, assumed the coaching responsibility. Frnka resigned after the 1951 season, having posted a six-year record of thirty-one victories, twenty-three defeats, and four ties.

Tulane's football program underwent moderation under Coach Raymond ("Bear") Wolf (1952–1954), and it continued under Andy Pilney and Tommy O'Boyle in low key. Jim Pittman, who became Tulane

coach in 1966, compiled a record of twenty victories, thirty defeats, and one tie during his five-year tenure. Pittman resigned to go to Texas Christian University after leading Tulane in 1970 to its most successful season in twenty years—seven victories against four defeats—topping it off with a Liberty Bowl victory over Colorado. As Pittman's successor, Tulane engaged Bennie Ellender, a former Tulane quarterback, who had a successful coaching career at Arkansas State.

51 A capacity crowd viewing a Sugar Bowl football game in the 1960s. The Sugar Bowl began after several years of urging by Fred Digby, sports editor of the *New Orleans Item,* and James M. Thomson, publisher, for a midwinter calendar of amateur sports in

49

50

51

New Orleans. Their idea was crystallized by Warren V. Miller and Joseph M. Cousins and their friends whose efforts resulted in the formation in 1934 of the New Orleans Mid-Winter Sports Association. Also, enough guarantors to finance the first Sugar Bowl game were secured. The first contest, between Tulane and Temple, was played on January 1, 1935, in the Tulane stadium, which had been built in 1926 after a whirlwind campaign that raised $300,000 in two weeks; the concrete stands had an original capacity of 30,000. It was a thrilling game and a financial success, and within a year plans were laid to enlarge the stadium. Additions were made to the structure in 1937, 1939, and 1947, bringing the total seating capacity to 80,985. Thirty-six successive New Year's games between some of America's finest collegiate football teams have made the Sugar Bowl a nationally known New Orleans institution. An estimated 40 million Americans view the classic on television. The New Orleans Mid-Winter Sports Association also sponsors tennis and basketball tournaments, a track meet, and a sailing regatta, all highly successful. *Aerial photo courtesy New Orleans Mid-Winter Sports Association*

52 New Orleans also fields a pro team, the Saints, whose Dan Abramowicz is seen here in action. He was named NFL's leading receiver in 1969. The New Orleans Saints obtained a National Football League franchise in 1966. The seventeenth team in that league, the Saints became an immediate favorite with football fans, some seventy-five thousand of whom jam the Tulane Stadium when they play home games. *Courtesy New Orleans Saints*

53 Saints Mam'selles at halftime. The home games have been noted for their between-the-halves spectaculars. So great has the interest in the Saints' Sunday games become that a number of churches have changed their hours of service so that their members could avoid the traffic congestion that ensues. *Courtesy New Orleans Saints*

52

53

7. NATURAL DISASTERS

Epidemics

1 2 From 1796 on, almost annually the city was stricken with sickness mostly transported by commerce with the West Indies, Cuba, and Mexico. In 1832, the city was visited by a frightful cholera epidemic. Its effect can be seen from the contrast between a usual burial—from funeral to interment—seen here, and the account of the epidemic by Dr. Theodore Clapp, a Protestant minister who came to New Orleans in 1822, and described in detail his experiences in this fearful time. In his *Autobiographical Sketches and Recollections during a Thirty-Five Years' Residence in New Orleans,* he wrote:

Many persons, even of fortune and popularity died in their beds without aid, unnoticed and unknown, and lay there for days unburied. In almost every house might be seen the sick, the dying and the dead. All the stores, banks and places of business were closed. There were no means, no instruments for carrying on the ordinary affairs of business; for all the drays, carts, carriages, hand and common wheel barrows, as well as hearses, were employed in the transportation of corpses instead of cotton, sugar and passengers. Words cannot describe my sensations when I first beheld the awful sight of carts driven to the graveyard, and there upturned, and their contents discharged as so many loads of lumber or offal, without a single mark of mourning or respect, because the exigency rendered it impossible.

Often I was kept in the burying ground for hours in succession by the incessant, unintermitting arrival of corpses, over whom I was requested to perform a short service. One day I did not leave the cemetery till nine o'clock at night; the last interments were made by candlelight. Reaching my house faint, I found my family all sobbing and weeping for they had concluded from my long absence, that I was certainly dead.

3 Theodore Clapp (1792–1866), who courageously buried the dead in the great cholera epidemic of 1832.

4 The potter's field where hundreds of victims of the 1853 epidemic were buried in hastily dug graves. This cemetery was on the edge of a swamp, and the "wet grave" became a byword. Between 1817 and 1860, and twenty-three yellow-fever epidemics, 28,192 deaths from yellow jack were recorded. The worst of these took place in 1853 when recorded deaths from yellow fever were 7,849, although many authorities estimate that 12,000 lost their lives. William L. Robinson, of the Howard Association, a group of thirty men who ministered to the indigent sick during several of the epidemics, has left a vivid pen-picture of the yellow fever of 1853. In his *Diary of a Samaritan,* he wrote:

By the 10th of August the mortality had reached an appalling height. The whole city was a hospital. . . . The streets were deserted save for

1

2

4

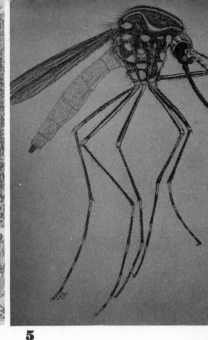

5

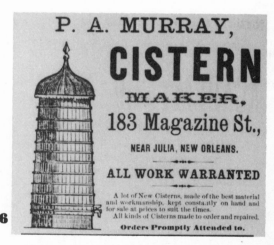

6

7

the hasty pedestrian on an errand of mercy. The rattling of an omnibus and the swing of the doctor's gig, as either rapidly passed, were the only disturbing sounds. The vociferations of the coalman, the knife-grinder, and other callings that enliven the thoroughfares were silenced by fear of the disease. . . .

The morning train of funerals . . . crowded the road to the cemeteries. It was an unbroken line of carriages and omnibuses for two miles and a half. The city commissary's wagon and carts of the different hospitals with their loads of eight or ten coffins each, fell in with the cortege of citizens. . . .

From The History of the Yellow Fever in New Orleans, *Summer, 1853. Courtesy Howard-Tilton Memorial Library, Tulane University*

5 Yellow fever, which in a century had caused more than 150,000 deaths and sickened more than half a million people in the South, was transmitted by the *Aëdes aegypti* (stegomyia) mosquito. The mosquitoes, hidden in imported cargoes from the tropics, found New Orleans, with its semitropical climate, its watery surroundings, its unscreened houses, and its thousands of rainwater cisterns, an ideal place to multiply. Drawing by George E. Beyer. *Courtesy Museum of Tropical and Parasitic Diseases, Tulane University School of Medicine*

6 New Orleans used rainwater cisterns to catch the water from the roofs of houses for drinking. The still, clean water in these receptacles was a perfect breeding place for the yellow-fever mosquito.

7 *Burning Sulphur and Tar Barrels to Disinfect the Streets.* William L. Robinson in his *Diary of a Samaritan,* 1860, said:

All manner of experiments were used to try to alleviate the spread of the disease. Tar was set on fire around and in the cemeteries and lime profusely thrown on the cracked and baked earth covering the coffins in the trenches. The Board of Health, in an

unthoughtful moment, adopted a suggestion of firing cannon throughout the city to disturb the atmosphere. This was not continued beyond the first day, as it was attended with melancholy results upon the nervous systems of the sick and convalescent. The gas-works threw open to the use of the citizens their stores of tar. Besides those used in the yards of private houses, drays were engaged to drop half a barrel of tar at distances of 150 feet in the middle of Canal, Rampart and Esplanade Streets. At sunset, when all were simultaneously fired, a pandemonium glare lighted up the city. Not a breath of air disturbed the dense smoke, which slowly ascended in curling columns until it had reached a height of about 500 feet. Here it seemed equipoised, festooning over our doomed city like a funeral pall, and remaining until the shades of night disputed with it the return and reign of darkness.

These experiments did not visibly diminish the ravages of the pestilence . . . 1186 died in the first week of August, 1526 the second, 1534 the third and 1628 the fourth.

From Frank Leslie's Illustrated Newspaper

8 *The Household Hospital—The Last of the Family.* There was a period after the Civil War when there were just a few cases, but a virulent yellow-fever epidemic broke out again in 1867 when more than 3,300 died of the disease. In 1870, there was a lesser epidemic and again in 1873. Just as the people of the city were beginning to feel optimistic about the elimination of the disease, since there had been only one death from the scourge the year before, the third worst epidemic struck the city in 1878. There were twenty-seven thousand cases with more than four thousand deaths. Then followed a few years of comparative healthfulness until 1897 when the disease again reached epidemic proportions and about three hundred people died.

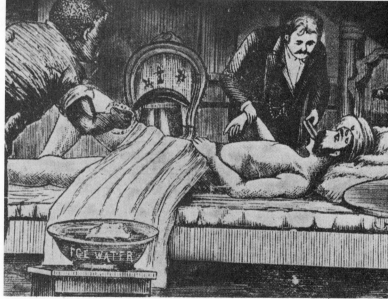

9 A member of the Howard Association aiding a stricken victim. *From* Doctor Dispachemquic: The Story of the Great Southern Plague of 1878

10 One of New Orleans's favorite shrines is the chapel dedicated to Saint Roch in the cemetery of that name. Built by Father Peter Thevis in 1868 to fulfill a vow he made when his congregation was spared from a yellow-fever epidemic, it resembles the chancel of a small Gothic church. Its altar is ornamented by a carved wooden statue of Saint Roch with his faithful dog. At one time the shrine's walls were hung with countless replicas of limbs, discarded crutches, and little marble "thanks" blocks, which were brought there by the faithful to testify to the cures that were wrought through the intercession of the saint. *Photo by Charles Genella*

11 This broadside, printed by *The Picayune*, probably in 1905, as a public service, was written by Dr. Quit-

11

man Kohnke, the city's health officer. It gave instructions for treating the sick room, preventing the spread of disease, and treating the sick. In the first years of the twentieth century, major strides had been made toward the elimination of the disease. The work of the Walter Reed Associates on the Havana Yellow Fever Commission had proved conclusively that the *Aëdes aegypti* mosquito was the carrier of the disease, and a small group of physicians together with Dr. Kohnke who had studied the experiments of Dr. Reed in Cuba had urged the city's inhabitants to adopt these protective measures. The response to these suggestions was not too encouraging, and in 1905 what was to be the last of the epidemics broke out. By July 12, there were more than a hundred cases and twenty deaths, which proclaimed to the world that Bronze John was again visiting New Orleans. But in that year New Orleans won the battle against yellow fever.

After shotgun quarantines were erected around the city, the local authorities asked the federal government to take charge of the campaign to rid the city of the epidemic. The United States Public Health Service and Marine Hospital Service under the leadership of Dr. Joseph H. White outlined the strategy along lines that had been laid down by Walter Reed. Under the direction of Dr. Kohnke, a vigorous campaign was started to eliminate the mosquitoes. Volunteer organizations systematically checked every house and all possible breeding grounds; gutters were salted and some sixty-eight thousand cisterns were screened or oiled. For years the citizens of New Orleans had fought a hopeless fight against their ancient enemy; now they knew the cause of their trouble and set out with a vim to conquer. This they did and, although 423 people died of the disease in 1905, New Orleans has never had an outbreak of yellow jack since.

Floods and Hurricanes

12 Disaster was not confined to death by disease. The site that Bienville had selected for New Orleans in 1718 created problems almost from the beginning, when a year after the little town was laid out, the Mississippi overflowed and a low levee had to be constructed to keep out the water. From that day to this, drainage has been a continual, expensive problem, which has only begun to be solved in the first years of this century.

First attempts at drainage consisted of open ditches emptying principally into Bayou St. John, which flowed into Lake Pontchartrain. In 1835, a drainage company was organized, and primitive drainage machines (huge paddle wheels) were installed. More of these machines were installed between 1846 and 1871, but they were so inefficient that after a heavy semitropical rain, the low areas sometimes remained flooded for days afterward. Between 1735 and 1927, there were thirty-eight major floods in the lower section of the river. Nine times the river water flooded New Orleans, not because the city's levees failed, but because backwaters had flowed into the city from breaks elsewhere. A crevasse in Kenner in 1816 brought water as far as Chartres Street, and the Sauvé crevasse in May, 1849, flooded 220 squares

12

in New Orleans and drove 12,000 people from their homes. This street was flooded by the Sauvé crevasse.

13 14 In 1871, there was a great crevasse at Bonnet Carré, the site of the present spillway above New Orleans. The overflow of the Mississippi River reached Lake Pontchartrain, raising the level of the lake, and north winds blew the water cityward. When a protection levee at Hagan Avenue proved inadequate, the city was flooded. These two views, Canal Street, near Claiborne Avenue, and an interior on Bienville Street, are by the ubiquitous Alfred R. Waud who was in New Orleans at the time of this flood. *From* Every Saturday, *July 8, 1871*

15 In 1903, when this photograph was made, the Mississippi had risen to the top of the levee, and it was necessary to pile on sandbags to keep the water from coming into the streets. *Courtesy Library of Congress*

15

13

14

16 April 29, 1927, immediately following the blast that saved the city. Unusually heavy rains upriver had caused the Mississippi to rise dangerously. Greenville, Mississippi, was almost wiped out; Little Rock, Arkansas, was under water; and breaks were sweeping the flood to New Iberia, Louisiana, a hundred and fifty miles from the river. New Orleans became panicky, and although every measure was taken to strengthen the levees, the cry "Cut the levee below the city" was on everyone's lips. Permission was granted, and the levee was dynamited at Caernarvon, Louisiana, after the people of St. Bernard Parish had been evacuated and guaranteed reimbursement for losses. The engineers in charge eventually opened a breach a thousand feet wide, the yellow water poured into the land, and the river above the city began to drop. *Courtesy Department of the Army, New Orleans, Corps of Engineers*

17 The Bonnet Carré spillway. After the flood of 1927, the United States government recognized its responsibility for flood control. In 1931, the Bonnet Carré

spillway was built. This controlled outlet can divert 250 million cubic feet of water a second—nearly twice the flow of Niagara Falls—into Lake Pontchartrain and eventually into the Gulf of Mexico. The river was shortened by cutoffs, the great Atchafalaya floodway built, and levees strengthened, thus removing the fear of floods from New Orleans for good. The Bonnet Carré spillway has only been used twice—in 1937 and 1945—and each time it has performed the work it was designed to do.

18 September, 1929, when parts of the uptown section of the city were under water. The photograph, by Dr. Willard R. Wirth, shows the high water on Jena and Tonti streets. An earlier flood had occurred on Good Friday, April 15, 1927, when fourteen inches of rain fell in twenty-four hours and lightning struck the main power cable of several of the drainage plants.

19 Drainage Pumping Station No. 6 on the Métairie Relief Outfall Canal, the largest of fourteen stations that keep New Orleans relatively dry. These stations

16

18

17

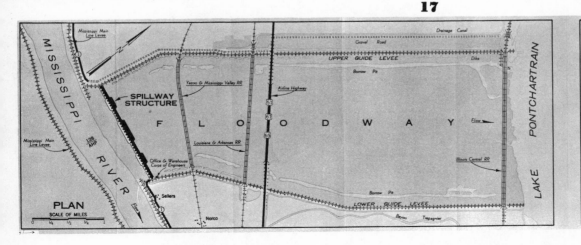

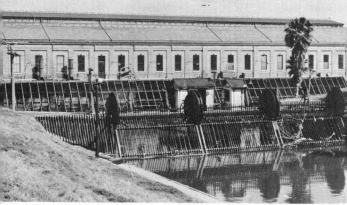

19

are supplied by power generated by the sewerage and water board's own generating station and underground power cable system. Since New Orleans is virtually surrounded by levees, the rainwater that falls into the city must be pumped out into Lakes Borgne and Pontchartrain. As the annual precipitation is almost sixty inches, this creates a most unhappy predicament. To overcome this disadvantage, a primary drainage system of 167 miles of open or covered canals and 45 miles of pipeline, which are served by fourteen pumping stations having a capacity of 28,000 cubic feet per second, had to be created. To date, more than $60 million has been spent on the drainage system and another $28 million program was started in 1967. To the New Orleans Sewerage and Water Board is due the credit for creating a soundly engineered and well-administered system. *Courtesy New Orleans Sewerage and Water Board*

20 New Orleans has also had its share of hurricanes. On September 29, 1915, a hurricane struck the Mississippi Gulf Coast, and New Orleans was battered by winds that reached a velocity of 120 miles an hour. There was $13 million in property damage, and several persons lost their lives. In the next two weeks more than twenty-two inches of rain fell, and this added greatly to the damage done by the hurricane, since the roofs of most buildings previously damaged could not be repaired in time. The entire side of this building (part of "bedbug row," as the Crescent block on Canal Street between Prieur and Roman was known) was peeled off by the storm.

21 These curious citizens are traveling the flooded streets to "see the sights."

20

21

22 Among the church steeples destroyed on September 29, 1915, were those of the First Presbyterian, St. Paul's Lutheran, and, shown here, Felicity Methodist Church. *Photo by John J. DePaul*

23 Fifty years later, almost to the day, on September 9, 1965, Hurricane Betsy roared out of the Gulf of Mexico into Louisiana. The center of this most destructive storm passed thirty-five miles southwest of New Orleans, and by 10:20 P.M., winds of over one hundred fifty miles per hour struck the city. The hurricane brought tidal surges, which overtopped the protection levees in the lower sections of the city and caused a devastating flood. The tremendous force of the wind, which accounted for about half the damage to homes and businesses, caused the Mississippi to rise nine feet in a few hours. For days after, more than thirteen thousand homes and places of business were flooded, some to a depth of seven feet or more, and the owners lost most of their personal possessions. Ships in the river were blown to the riverbanks, and several sank; there was great damage to the port facilities. Strangely, only about four inches of rain fell, and the death toll in the city was comparatively light, although property damage exceeded $121 million. The one hundred thousand trees, long the city's pride, after suffering great damage from the prolonged freezing weather in February, 1962, were battered still further. Hundreds of trucks were employed for weeks afterward clearing the debris from the city's streets. *Photo by G. R. Arnold. Courtesy Times-Picayune*

22

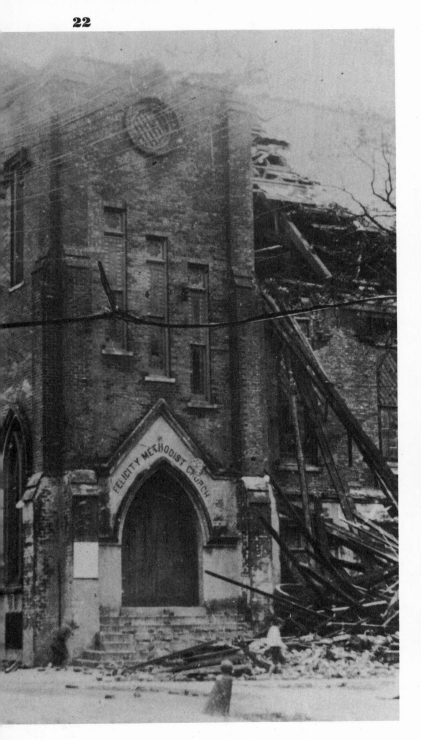

23

8. MUNICIPAL SERVICES

Early Mail

1

1 When Louisiana was purchased, all that was necessary to complete mail service to the capital of the new territory was to contract for a route between Natchez and New Orleans. Natchez was the principal town of the Territory of Mississippi, and to reach it a road straggled from Washington through Knoxville and Nashville. Mail was transported by horseback over this wilderness trail, known as the Natchez Trace, as far as Fort Adams, an American outpost on the Mississippi River just below Woodville, Mississippi. The new schedules called for twenty-four-day delivery between Washington and New Orleans, which in winter and spring was not always possible because of high water and muddy roads. The diorama shows a post-rider on the Natchez Trace in 1809. *Courtesy Public Roads Administration*

2 Blaise Cenas, a Philadelphian, first postmaster of New Orleans, who came to the city in 1804 to open the first post office. Cenas was a very able man and did much to establish the first postal routes. President Jefferson sought a shorter route than the Knoxville-

2

Nashville-Natchez Trace forest trail and sent a surveyor to lay out a more direct way between Washington and New Orleans. Isaac Briggs made the hazardous five-month trip, and in 1805 Congress sent the first mail to New Orleans, also by horseback, over what came to be known as the Southern Route. The mail was carried over this route, which ran to New Orleans through Virginia, the Carolinas, Georgia, Alabama, and Mississippi, with indifferent results, which generally aroused the ire of New Orleans merchants who loudly protested its inadequacy. *Courtesy Louisiana State Museum*

3 In 1823, Congress authorized the surveying of a direct route between Washington and New Orleans that would have cut the distance to about 1,150 miles. This illustration shows the Army Engineers' *Map of Reconnaissance,* on which they projected two routes, neither of which was ever built.

4 Postriders who rode the mail over the Washington–New Orleans route via Georgia and Alabama faced incredible hardships. The routes were sometimes little more than blazed trails, and often these postmen had to swim their horses over flooded creeks. This illustration shows a postrider on a corduroy road, which consisted of logs laid across soft or swampy places to permit passage.

5 Meanwhile other factors were coming into being. Steamboats operating out of New Orleans beginning in 1812 soon carried mail to upriver points, and the coming of the railroads started what was to become the most dependable means of transporting mail. This poster, dating from about 1840, advertising the "Old Southern Route," illustrates the progress—a combination of steamboat travel from New Orleans to Montgomery via Mobile and from Montgomery to Columbus, Georgia, by rail. As added attraction to passen-

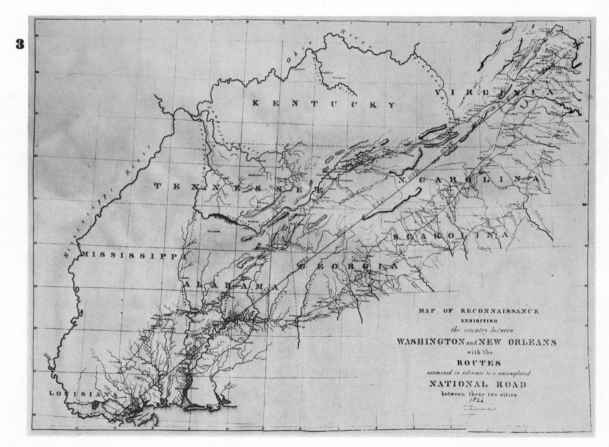

3

MAP OF RECONNAISSANCE
EXHIBITING
the country between
WASHINGTON and NEW ORLEANS
with the
ROUTES
examined in reference to a contemplated
NATIONAL ROAD
between these two cities
1826

4

5

6

7

gers, the poster advised that since the route avoided Florida, "No Danger is to be apprehended of any Attack by Indians." *Courtesy Louisiana State Museum*

6 The New Orleans Post Office in 1842 was unique. It was housed in the lower story of the Merchants' Exchange—a marble-fronted building, which stood until a few years ago on Royal Street near Canal—and post-office boxes of subscribers were located in the main reception hall. There was also a fifty-foot bar in the building, and merchants who came for their mail could get a drink while waiting for their letters. The quarters later became Gluck's restaurant. *From Norman's New Orleans and Environs, 1845*

Waterworks

7 New Orleans's first waterworks, the pumphouse of Latrobe's waterworks, postdating the colonial system where river water was peddled by the hogshead to householders who poured it in large stone vessels to let the sediment settle. This building, which was completed in 1813 on a site near the French Market on Ursuline and Levee streets, was made to house a steam pump to pump river water into a system of wooden pipes throughout the city. Its designer, architect-inventor Benjamin H. B. Latrobe, unfortunately died of yellow fever before he could install the ma-

chinery. The plant was completed, however, and operated from 1823 to 1836, when a larger system was inaugurated. Lithograph by Saint-Aulaire. *Courtesy Bibliothèque Nationale, Paris*

8 Plan of New Orleans's first water system. This drawing, which is in the New Orleans city engineer's office, shows the scheme to distribute Mississippi water through cypress log pipes, which had been drilled especially for the purpose. The cross section of the pump house shows the reservoirs for the water.

8

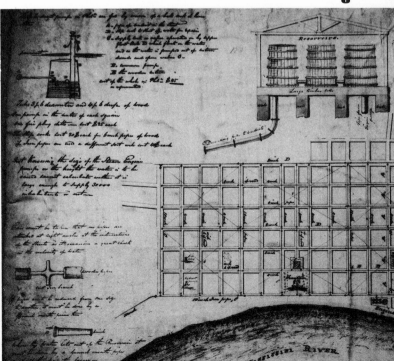

9

10

12

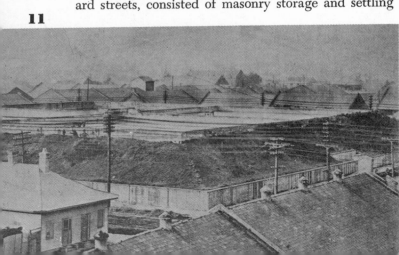

11

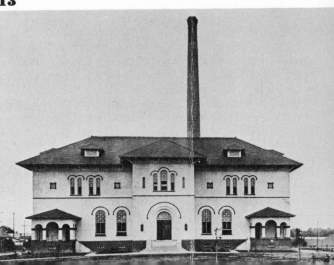

13

9 The bored cypress logs are remnants of the first water-supply system in New Orleans. *Courtesy Louisiana State Museum*

10 Just before the Civil War, a new waterworks neared completion. This massive cast-iron building, ca. 1870, was located at the head of Canal Street and had a reservoir capacity of 175,000 gallons. Construction stopped, and the building was used as the Free Market, a food distribution center for the poor in the early days of the war.

11 The reservoir of the New Orleans Water Works Company, ca. 1908. By the early 1830s, the city had outgrown the original system, and in 1836 a new system of pumps and reservoirs was put into operation. This waterworks, which was located on a site bounded by St. Thomas, Market, Religious, and Richard streets, consisted of masonry storage and settling tanks, 250 feet square, built on a mud mound 21 feet above street level, with the necessary steam engine to pump the water from the river. Cast-iron pipes were used for mains, and the plant had a maximum capacity of 3 million gallons of unfiltered water a day. *Courtesy Reservoir of the New Orleans Water Works Company*

12 When the present filtration plant was put into use in 1909, the tanks of the old reservoir were drained, and in August, 1911, leased to the Sugar Planter's Storage and Distribution Company of Louisiana for the storage of blackstrap molasses. Some days after, when the tanks had been filled, the walls of the reservoir burst, and with a roar six hundred thousand gallons of blackstrap cascaded into the nearby streets. Molasses was seven feet deep opposite the tanks, and the gutters for blocks around were filled with it. The nearby residents rushed to the scene with pots and pans to scoop up some of the sweet, sticky flood, and barefoot boys waded in molasses-filled gutters until the sewerage and water board, formed in 1889, flushed the gooey mess away from the area. Meanwhile, flies and ants had a holiday, and the company estimated that $40,000 had gone down the drain. *Photo by John DePaul*

13 The water purification pumping station, 1909. Before 1909, New Orleans depended largely on wooden cisterns for drinking water. Rainwater caught by gutters from the roofs of houses was stored in these wooden tanks. By modern standards, the water thus

supplied was not completely sanitary, and in a drought the cisterns would often run dry. Piped river water was available, but the customers had to filter it themselves. Improvements had begun in 1900 when the sewerage and water board appropriated $20,000 to construct an experimental water purification plant. Attempts by the predecessor company at filtering the muddy Mississippi water had failed, but the board engaged the services of a firm of New York consulting engineers, who sent Robert S. Weston to New Orleans to operate the pilot plant that was built in Audubon Park. Within two years, after much experimentation, a great deal had been learned about the most economical way to supply the city with clean, cheap water, and construction began on the present filtration plant.

As for a sewerage system, until the twentieth century New Orleans used primitive backyard cesspools. The first sewerage pipes were laid in 1903, but the system was not fully completed until 1908. *Courtesy Herbert C. Swan*

Fire Department

14 Efforts were made to protect the city from fire as early as 1807 when an ordinance was passed prescribing that householders maintain two water-filled buckets on hand at all times, and requiring theatres to dig wells. But it was not until 1829 that the first volunteer fire company was formed, which was followed by others. By 1834, there were six companies in existence, and the Firemen's Charitable Association was founded. By 1855, there were twenty-four companies, and the Firemen's Charitable Association was a potent force in city affairs. This engraving, showing volunteer firemen of New Orleans, July, 1844, was presented to John Adams, an active fireman for six years.

14

15 The men who made up these early volunteer companies were leaders from various walks of life. As time went on and as the city grew, membership was recruited from the best class of mechanics and laboring men. Volunteer firemen were a dedicated lot—proud of their engines, and ready to respond to an alarm day or night. They fought fires with primitive hand-pumping equipment and a water supply that often failed

15

when it was most needed. Many lost their lives. The Firemen's Charitable Association furnished doctors and medicine for the men, aided widows and orphans, and helped with funeral expenses when a member died. The engine of Mississippi No. 2, seen here, was made in New York and shipped to New Orleans in 1830. *Courtesy Louisiana State Museum*

16 There was great rivalry between various companies. John Malloy, of Columbia Company No. 5, is sitting on a barrel covering the nearest hydrant until his company arrives. (One wonders what happened to the property on fire meanwhile!) *From* A History of the Fire Department of New Orleans *by Thomas O'Connor*

17 Members of Columbia Steam Fire Engine Company No. 5, ca. 1885. *Courtesy Mrs. Charles Eichling*

18 Fire of the Orleans Cotton Compress, February 11, 1844. New Orleans customarily received, stored, and compressed large quantities of cotton for shipment abroad, and when a cotton compress caught fire, as a number did, the conflagration was spectacular. This building was two blocks long, cost $753,558 to build in 1833–1835, and had a storage capacity of twenty-five thousand bales. *From an insurance policy courtesy Samuel Wilson, Jr.*

19 The volunteer firemen were so attached to their hand pumpers that when the first clumsy steam fire engine, *Young America*, which weighed nine tons, was brought to New Orleans from Cincinnati in 1855 by the city council and a group of fire underwriters, the volunteers resisted the change. *Young America* was soon superseded by an engine that weighed half as much, which was constructed locally, but an attempt to organize a paid fire department was challenged by the men. After a peppery exchange between the Firemen's Charitable Association and the city council, which got nowhere, the firemen revolted, and on November 20, 1855, brought twenty-eight fire engines solemnly up Camp Street to Lafayette Square where they surrendered them to the mayor.

16

18

17

20 Steam engine of Eagle Company No. 7, 1868. After 1855, the city council advertised for bids for a department. The Firemen's Charitable Association underbid the rival underwriters' group and secured the contract at $70,000 annually. For the next thirty-six years, until 1891, when the present paid fire department was organized, the Firemen's Charitable Association and its volunteer firemen controlled the New Orleans fire department. In 1891, a board of fire commissioners was established and seven fire districts set up under the direction of Thomas O'Connor as chief, and an appropriation of $302,278 made to run the department for the next year. The volunteers soon realized that steam pumpers were far more efficient than the hand-operated apparatus they had been using, and by 1861 six companies had converted to steam. *From* A History of the Fire Department of New Orleans *by Thomas O'Connor*

19

20

21

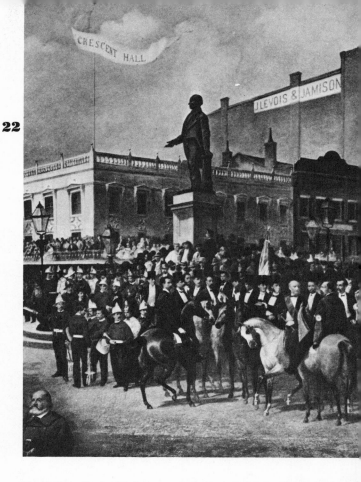

22

21 The fire mark of the People's Insurance Company of New Orleans, which operated between 1870 and 1887. Fire marks came into use in England after the great London fire of 1666 when the first fire-insurance companies devised a lead plate in the form of a phoenix rising from the flames. This they nailed to a prominent spot on all houses insured by the company to enable firemen readily to identify insured from uninsured properties. The idea spread to America, and in 1752 when the first fire-insurance company was founded in Philadelphia, one hundred fire marks were cast and placed in use. The use of fire marks eventually reached other cities, among them New Orleans. Fire marks stood as a guarantee to all volunteer fire departments that the insurance company would handsomely reward the brigade that extinguished a blaze on premises identified by a shield. With the inauguration later of a paid fire department, there was no longer a necessity for fire marks. Thus passed from use an interesting bit of Americana. *Courtesy Insurance Company of North America and Thomas A. Greene*

22 The thirty-fifth annual parade of the volunteer firemen of New Orleans, March 4, 1872, painting by V. Pierson and P. Poincy. *Courtesy Louisiana State Museum*

23 Steamer No. 13 in the heyday of the dashing horse-drawn steam pumper, ca. 1907. The firehouse, at Perdido between St. Charles and Carondelet streets, is in the left background. *Courtesy Chief Edward J. O'Brien*

23

24

26

24 The fire-engine house of the Louisiana Hose Company, draped in black in 1885 to mourn the passing of Charles T. Howard, a member of the company and "one of the best friends of the Volunteer Fire Department." The engine is an earlier model. *From* A History of the Fire Department of New Orleans *by Thomas O'Connor*

25 Fighting a big fire, January 7, 1908, at the furniture store of William G. Tebault at 217 Royal Street. This three-alarmer brought out no fewer than seven steam pumpers, which are drawing water from a fire cistern, one of eighty-three in the city at the time. Fire cisterns were connected to huge mains that could be turned on with a large key. Even with seven engines drawing water from this cistern, the well is overflowing. *Courtesy Chief Edward J. O'Brien*

26 A vault slab in Cypress Grove Cemetery. The Firemen's Charitable Association founded the Cypress Grove Cemetery, using the proceeds of a bequest left them in 1838 by Stephen Henderson, a wealthy citizen who admired their aims. The cemetery was dedicated on April 25, 1841, with more than a thousand persons present. Its imposing entrance, in the Egyptian architectural style, is still a New Orleans landmark. William Kelly had been a member of Phoenix Fire Company No. 8. When he died in 1862 at the age of twenty-one, his brother had this tombstone carved of William gazing at the company engine. *Photo by Guy F. Bernard*

27 Many fire companies had their own tombs. This one, with its interesting carved pumper, was erected by Jefferson Fire Company No. 22 in 1852 and still stands in Lafayette Cemetery No. 1 on Washington Avenue. *Photo by Guy F. Bernard*

25

27

28

28 Monument to Irad Ferry in Cypress Grove Cemetery, erected by the first and second municipalities of the city. On January 1, 1837, Irad Ferry, a fireman and a leading businessman, was killed in a fire and his death so touched the hearts of all citizens that he was given an elaborate funeral. The governor, mayor, judges of the Supreme Court, members of the legislature, fellow volunteer firemen, and hundreds of mourners marched.

29 New Orleans firefighters in action today. *Courtesy Leon Trice*

29

30

Police Department

30 The New Orleans police force had its origins just before the city was relinquished to the United States in 1803 when the French commissioner, Pierre Clément Laussat, organized the Gens d'armes, composed of former Spanish soldiers and free mulattoes. These were frequently beaten up by the tough flatboatmen who often caroused in the taverns near the riverfront after their long trips down the Mississippi. In the first years of the American era, several attempts were made to form a stable police force, but these seem to have met with little success. The Gendarmerie was succeeded by the Garde de ville, or city watch, but they proved as ineffectual as the Gens d'armes. Instead, a force of eight men, or constables, was organized, and their efforts were supplemented by militia patrols who marched with armed citizens in small groups. As the city grew, the nightly patrols gradually were abolished, while the number of paid constables increased.

31 A New Orleans constable of the 1840s. To the populace, he was known as "Charley." In 1840, after several years of debate, the council of the first municipality had adopted an ordinance to reorganize the poorly run police department. The force, fifty-eight officers and men, was divided into a day and a night watch. The men were stationed at three posts: City Hall, the Faubourg Tremé, and Bayou St. John. The ground floor of the Cabildo, then City Hall, was used as the central police station, and the cells at its rear served as a jail. Thirty-four constables, two corporals, a sergeant, a lieutenant, and a captain had their headquarters there. The constables carried no firearms, their only weapon being a spontoon, or short pike, which during the night they were to strike on the pavement when they came to a street corner on their beats. In case of trouble, they were provided with rattles and would "spring their rattles" to call for assistance. The ordinance did not specify the style of uniforms, but each man on duty was ordered to wear "a painted leather cap, numbered to correspond with the roll of the district in which he may serve." For his

31

32

33

services, he was paid $35 a month; corporals received $50; sergeants, $60; lieutenants, $100; and the captain, $150. Two of the men were to attend the fire bell, and there was to be a sentinel at City Hall and one at the meat market.

The ordinance contained a joker that was to bedevil the police department for nearly half a century. It gave the mayor and the recorder the right to appoint all policemen, except the captain and lieutenants. It was a day of "to the victor belongs the spoils," and one's appointment as constable depended almost entirely on political friends.

32 33 With the increased enforcement of discipline, the morals and efficiency of the department improved greatly. The politicians, particularly Mayors Shakspeare and Fitzpatrick, had quarrels with the police commissioners: the old powers of patronage were hard to give up. These resulted in two court battles that found the police commissioners victorious. From 1894 on, after the last of these contests, there was relative harmony, and in 1912 other improvements were made in the system of police administration. Mayor Joseph A. Shakspeare served from 1880 to 1882 and from 1888 to 1892. The tenure of office had increased between his two terms. Mayor John Fitzpatrick served from 1892 to 1896, and was the second president of the police board.

34 Mayor Gerard Stith (1858–1860), who was somewhat of a dandy, helped to reform the police department. Stith was born in Virginia, but raised in New Orleans. He was a printer, and became foreman of the composing room of the *Picayune* and head of the Printers' Association, thus being accounted leader of organized labor in the city. He became mayor after successfully holding several political offices. Stith consistently advocated public improvements, and during his administration much of the large square granite pavements were laid, which were characteristic of this city's streets for more than half a century. By 1872, the still cumbersome police organization was headed by New Orleans's first chief of police, John Youenes, who had been appointed by Mayor A. D. Crossman. From that time on (except for the period of military rule and during Reconstruction), the heads of the department as well as a large percentage of the body of the police rarely outlived an administration that had ap-

34

pointed them. In these years, the police department, inefficiently organized, underpaid, woefully inadequate in equipment and numbers, and subject to little or no discipline, was the focal point of graft and corruption. By 1886, a citizens' committee, calling itself "The Committee of One Hundred," denounced the police force to the legislature as "partisan and corrupt, inefficient and wanting in every characteristic, physical, moral and intellectual." It was not until 1888 when Act 63 was passed by the state legislature that the modern police force had its beginnings. This act placed the administrative power in the hands of a board of unsalaried commissioners and the mayor. A thorough reorganization of the police force then took place, with David C. Hennessy as superintendent. Although most old members of the force were retained, rules were tightened and new applicants had to undergo rigid examinations. Engraving by A. H. Ritchie.

35 In June, 1858, just before Stith's election, in which he ran against Major P. G. T. Beauregard, a large group of citizens, aroused over the familiar disorders accompanying a New Orleans election, secretly organized and without fanfare took possession of Jackson Square. They occupied the courtrooms of the Cabildo, and seizing the arsenal in its rear, armed themselves. This group, under Captain Johnson K. Duncan, then publicly announced its intention to take over the civil government of the city to ensure a fair election without "disorder, outrage and unchecked assassination." This was during the time when the Know-Nothing party was active, and included other political overtones. For five days, a vigilance committee, Mayor Waterman, candidate Stith, the city council, and an opposition group of sixteen hundred, who were hastily sworn in as police deputies, conferred, pleaded, threatened, and did everything but fight. Then came election day, "one of the most orderly in the history of the city," in which the American party of Stith won, and the vigilance committee, whose headquarters are seen here, evacuated its position and faded away. *From* Ballou's Pictorial Drawing Room Companion, *July 10, 1858*

36 David C. Hennessy, first superintendent of the New Orleans police department. He was assassinated on October 15, 1890, by members of the Sicilian Mafia who had settled in New Orleans and whose nefarious activities he had vigorously investigated. The subsequent arrest, trial, and acquittal of nineteen Italians implicated in the assassination plot precipitated the lynching of eleven of them.

37 Outraged citizens on March 14, 1891, following the acquittal of the Italians, collecting before the door of Parish Prison. The Parish Prison served New Orleans for sixty years between 1834 and 1894. It was a grim, forbidding-looking structure located in the square bounded by Orleans, Tremé, St. Ann, and Marais streets, a site in the rear of the Municipal Auditorium. More than two dozen hangings, several of them public, took place here, and there were suicides and murders committed within its gloomy walls. The Parish Prison accumulated its own unique traditions and legendary lore.

38 Citizens using a huge wooden beam broke into the Parish Prison. About sixty armed men were admitted by the vigilance committee, and they hunted the Italians who had been set free by their jailers to escape if they could by hiding. Nine of the Mafia were shot, and two were hanged outside the prison. Two, luckier than the others, hid in a doghouse and were

HEAD-QUARTERS OF THE NEW ORLEANS VIGILANCE COMMITTEE.

35

36

37

38

40

saved. Sketch by W. R. Leigh. *From* Scribner's Magazine, *February, 1896*

39 Lynching the Italians in the yard of the Parish Prison. Sketch by Charles Graham. *From* Harper's Weekly, *March 28, 1891*

40 The courtyard at the time of the lynching.

41 "I'm lost, mister policeman," 1903.

39

41

42 A bit of the Nile in the Irish Channel. This is the former sixth precinct station on Rousseau Street near Jackson Avenue. The building was at one time a Jefferson Parish courthouse and jail and was later remodeled in the Egyptian style. It is still standing and serves as a city sign shop.

43 The tenth precinct police station, about 1900. This station, located on the New Basin Canal and City Park Avenue, then had a complement of ten patrolmen, who had an enormous though thinly settled district in the rear of the city to patrol.

44 These were the officers of the fourth precinct police station in 1903. They were commanded by Captain Thomas Capo, and the squad contained one patrolman who did his work on a bicycle on which he is shown leaning. By 1900, the department had a force of 325 men, and there were 12 precinct stations. Patrolmen wore heavy coats, buttoned to the neck with twin rows of brass buttons, and their headgear resembled a cross between a football helmet and a construction laborer's hard hat (light color for summer and dark for winter wear).

45 The paddy wagon answering a call, 1903.

46 During Chief Inspector James W. Reynolds's term (1911–1917), the force was increased to 250 and the first motorcycles were employed; by 1922, twenty-one policemen on motorcycles chased speeders. The police force is seen here in 1911 when nearly two hundred officers gathered for a group portrait in Elks Place before the Criminal Courts Building for annual inspection. Chief Inspector Reynolds is on the extreme left, front row. In 1917, "the most exciting half-hour in history" resulted in the murder at headquarters of Chief Inspector Reynolds by a disgruntled and crazed

44

43

policeman named Mullen and the mistaken killing of Capt. Gary Mullen when in the excitement someone yelled, "Mullen killed Reynolds." *Courtesy Major Henry M. Morris, Chief of Detectives, New Orleans Police Department*

47 A helmeted policeman (John H. Behrman) posed for this picture in 1912. *From* The Behrman Administration *by Thomas J. Nolan*

48 The grim House of Detention, Tulane Avenue at Broad Street. Originally built as a hospital, it was later converted to a jail and demolished in the late 1920s when the present Criminal Courts Building was erected on the site.

49 The old Criminal Courts Building, Elks Place, ca. 1912. This rusty brick and sandstone Criminal Courts Building with its clock, towers, and turrets was long a

45

46 **47**

48

49

New Orleans landmark. Located at Tulane Avenue and Saratoga Street, it was built in 1893–1895 amid charges of improper construction and misuse of funds by city officials. Besides the criminal courts, the building also housed the first precinct police station, and the Parish Prison adjoined it at the rear. Poorly constructed, by the 1920s the structure was practically worn out by constant severe use. In 1931, the criminal courts and Parish Prison, along with police headquarters, were moved to the new buildings at Tulane and Broad streets, and thereafter a modern police radio communications system was inaugurated. In the 1930s, the old Criminal Courts Building retained several minor courts and the precinct police station. Enterprising newspaper reporters at the time discovered that tramps had set up housekeeping under its ground floor. These vagrants had even tapped the

electric current for lighting and were snugly ensconced in what the reporters nicknamed the "Hotel de Bastille," just a few feet from their traditional enemies, the police.

50 When this picture was taken, sometime before World War I, Michael Walsh, who had been appointed in 1856, was the oldest policeman on the force. *Courtesy Major Henry M. Morris, Chief of Detectives, New Orleans Police Department*

51 The traffic squad in 1912. The motorcycles ridden by these policemen resembled today's motorbikes. The men are Harry Duval, later captain of the motorcycle squad, Walter Jacobs, Edward A. Theard, and Frederick Krummel, who lost his life in a cycle accident in 1942. In 1947, the first emergency unit was set up, using a panel-body truck. By 1950, the police force numbered 950, and there were 80 squad cars, 7 patrol wagons, and 66 motorcycles besides other mobile equipment; a police training school (including courses at Loyola University) was constructed and a central complaint bureau was in operation. In writing the new city charter of May 1, 1954, the board of police commissioners was abolished and the operation of the department placed under the mayor with a police advisory board to counsel him. *Courtesy Major Henry M. Morris, Chief of Detectives, New Orleans Police Department*

52 Annual inspection of the police and fire departments, Jackson Square, April 30, 1961. Mayor deLesseps Morrison (in uniform, back to camera) salutes, while the police band plays. The inspection was followed by a mass in St. Louis Cathedral.

Today, there are some fifteen hundred commissioned personnel (police officers and detectives) and a staff of over three hundred civilians to aid them. Some five hundred automobiles and trucks are in service and well over one hundred motorcycles and three-wheeled cycles. The $4 million police headquarters and central lockup, dedicated in June, 1968, marked the beginning of another era in the history of

50

there, and the hospital was regarded as one of the best run in America. Since most of the patients were foreigners or out-of-state Americans, a tax paid by ship captains on each immigrant they brought to New Orleans provided a substantial part of the hospital's revenue. *From* Ballou's Pictorial Drawing Room Companion, *1858*

54 Charity Hospital's amphitheatre and ward, from *Harper's Weekly*, September 3, 1859. The ward was described as follows:

54

52

this colorful department, whose motto is "to protect and to serve." *Courtesy Major Henry M. Morris, Chief of Detectives, New Orleans Police Department*

Hospitals

53 The Charity Hospital outgrew its old quarters on Canal Street, and this new building was erected in 1832 at a cost of $150,000. During the early 1850s about eighteen thousand patients a year were treated

53

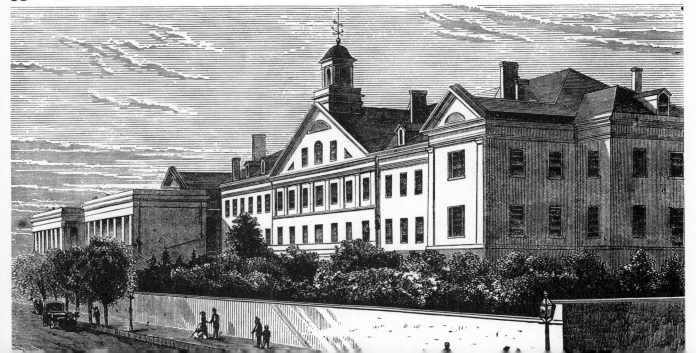

Here are the sick wards, constantly crowded with patients of every age and sex, of every color, from blue-eyed, fair-browed Anglo-American to the tawny, sun-browned child of the Tropics, speaking every language from the liquid lapse of the vowely Italian tongue to the guttural harshness of the Celestial empire. Here you will find every type of disease and every gradation of bodily injury from a simple cold to the malignant vomito, and from the spraining of a finger to compound comminuted fracture of the thigh bone.

55 In 1885, Charity Hospital inaugurated its first ambulance service. A story current at the time had it that it took so long to receive and answer the first call that the patient had recovered and left the scene before the ambulance arrived. The driver and intern, not wishing to return empty-handed, picked up a Negro boy who was perfectly well, and returned in triumph to the hospital with their "patient." *Photo by Louis Cormier*

56 A horse ambulance of the Louisiana State Society for the Prevention of Cruelty to Animals, an organization that dates from 1888.

57 Maison de Santé, also known as Dr. Stone's Infirmary, was one of a number of private hospitals that operated prior to the Civil War. It was built in 1839 at the corner of Canal and Claiborne. It closed its doors in 1867 and Dr. Stone died shortly thereafter. *From New Orleans Directory, 1852*

57

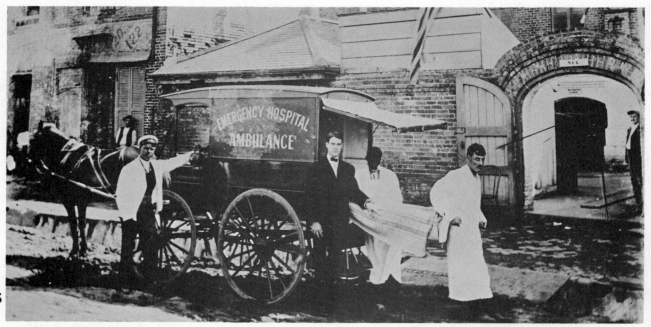

55

56

58 Hotel Dieu, the oldest private hospital in New Orleans in point of continuous operation—113 years. It was built about 1858 for the Sisters of Charity (Daughters of Charity of St. Vincent de Paul), who had previously been connected with Dr. Stone's Maison de Santé. *From* Jewell's Crescent City Illustrated, *1873*

59 Touro Infirmary, founded in 1852 by Judah Touro. Its first director was Dr. Joseph Bensadon. When Touro died in 1854, he directed that the hospital be continued as a charitable institution, and the Corporation of Touro Infirmary was organized. The hospital remained open until 1861 when the outbreak of the Civil War forced its closing. During the war years it was used as an almshouse for members of the Jewish faith. The infirmary reopened in 1869. *Courtesy Touro Infirmary Public Relations Department*

60 Touro Infirmary, about 1890. In 1881, this site on Prytania between Delachaise and Aline streets was bought and these buildings were erected. In 1906, a new plant was needed, and a $300,000 hospital building was constructed. Since that time, several additions have been built to make Touro Infirmary one of the leading private hospitals in this area.

61 Ochsner Foundation Hospital and Clinic (1970), Jefferson Highway, a short distance above New Orleans. Founded by the world-renowned surgeon Alton Ochsner and his associates, this hospital enjoys a very high reputation not only in New Orleans but in Latin America, where many of its patients come from for treatment. *Courtesy Times-Picayune*

59

60

61

58

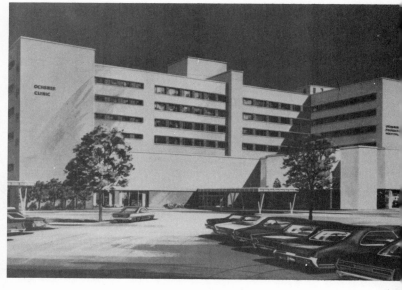

9. TRANSPORTATION

Street Transportation

1 The first means of public rapid transit in New Orleans was an omnibus line started in 1832 when the need developed for transportation from downtown New Orleans to the Pontchartrain Railroad Station and the Levee Steam Cotton Press. This line was located in the third district of the city. Omnibus lines expanded, and by 1858 there were a dozen operating on various streets, uptown and downtown. The vehicles generally seated fourteen persons and were drawn by two horses. The bus shown operated from the St. Charles Hotel (in the background) to the New Orleans, Jackson & Great Northern Railroad Station on S. Robertson and Clio streets in the 1850s.

2 The tremendous rise in New Orleans population during the 1850s and the realization that iron wheels on iron rails enabled a horse or mule to pull a heavier load faster brought the street railway into existence for better mass transportation. As in other large cities, New Orleans discarded the omnibuses for the mule car, and the change took place shortly before and soon after the Civil War.

To the four pioneer street railways operated by the New Orleans and Carrollton Railroad Company since the mid-1830s were soon added eight more lines. By 1873, more than 15 million passengers were being carried annually by the mule cars, 1,641 horses and mules, and 671 employees. In that year, more than 23 million people were carried, and the fare was a nickel. This bobtailed-horsecar of the Girod & Poydras line was owned by the Canal & Claiborne Streets Railroad Company. Often this line, because of poor service, was called G & P—get out and push.

3 The most famous mule-car driver on the New Orleans and Carrollton Railroad (now the St. Charles Avenue streetcar line) was none other than Sir Thomas Lipton, the famous tea merchant, who arrived in the city in 1872 when he was a young man. He is seen here at age twenty-seven.

4 In the 1880s, the New Orleans and Carrollton Railroad Company employed mule cars on its route up St. Charles as far as Napoleon Avenue. From that point to Carrollton during the cotton Centennial Exposition little steam engines for motive power were used. One of these was sketched in 1884 by John Durkin. *From Harper's Weekly, December 20, 1884*

5 A steam dummy of the New Orleans City and Lake Railroad, with its string of open-sided trailer cars just before starting a trip to West End, viewed on Canal Street about 1895. A dummy engine was a small street

railway steam locomotive that had its boiler and running gear completely enclosed. Steam dummies were discarded in 1898 when the line was electrified. *Courtesy Edwin H. Gebhardt*

6 The first electric streetcars were brought to New Orleans and run as exhibitions at the New Orleans Cotton Centennial Exposition in 1884–1885. Yet, by 1890 the mule cars were still running and even a new line was started. The city at that time had a population of 242,039, and the mule cars, which had a top speed of eight miles per hour, seemed quite satisfac-

4

5

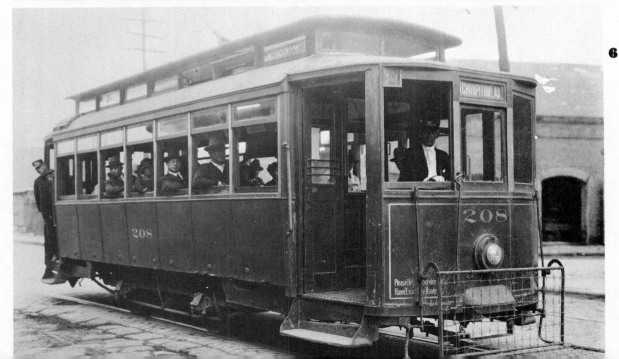

6

tory. At long last the New Orleans city council gave permission to electrify a line, and the first electric streetcars were placed in service on the St. Charles line on February 1, 1893. One line after another was electrified during the next few years, and by 1900 there were four companies operating 28 lines over 173 miles of track. The illustration shows an early type (1899) New Orleans electric streetcar. These four-wheel cars bobbed up and down as they moved. This one was still in service on the Tchoupitoulas line in 1925. *Photo by Charles L. Franck*

7 The electric car lines in operation between 1900 and 1925 are shown on this map compiled by E. Harper Charlton for his *Street Railways of New Orleans*. As can be readily seen, there were extensive track duplications. The peak year of trolley operation in New Orleans was in 1926 when 148 million passengers rode New Orleans Public Service, Inc.'s, twenty-eight railway lines and five motor bus lines.

8 Rush hour on Canal Street, 1904. More than twenty streetcars are visible in this photograph, which was made near Chartres Street. No fewer than twenty-five companies operated streetcar lines in New Orleans through the years. The first amalgamation came in 1903, but it was not until 1922, when the New Orleans Public Service, Inc. was chartered by law, that final unification came. *Photo by John N. Teunisson*

9 Spanish Fort "trains" carried thousands of pleasure seekers to the lake resort. These generally consisted of a powered car, which pulled three trailers. At one time

7
8

a pier, serviced by a shuttle car, extended three quarters of a mile from the shore at Spanish Fort for the convenience of passengers of the lake steamers. The Spanish Fort line was in operation from 1911 until 1932 when buses were substituted. *Photo by H. J. Harvey. Courtesy Dr. Edmond Souchon*

10 Composite-combination car of the OK line, 1928. Between 1915 and 1930, New Orleans had its only interurban line—the Orleans-Kenner Traction Company, which ran its cars from South Rampart near Canal to the town of Kenner. Successful at first, the line succumbed to hard-surfaced roads and the increased use of automobiles. *Photo by Charles L. Franck*

11 The most famous of all streetcars. Tennessee Williams's hit play, *A Street Car Named Desire,* made this New Orleans streetcar line known throughout the world. The Desire line served the antique shop district along Royal, the nightclub section along Bourbon, and a densely populated residential section along the lower part of its route. The line was discontinued in 1948. *Photo by Charles F. Weber*

12 The end of the line. Two "Cemeteries" streetcars are shown at the terminus of that line at Canal Street and City Park Avenue at the rush hour in April, 1964. On May 30, 1964, 101 years after the first cars had started operation on the Canal Street line, the last (excepting the St. Charles Avenue line) cars ceased running, to be superseded by buses. *Courtesy New Orleans Public Service, Inc.*

11

12

9

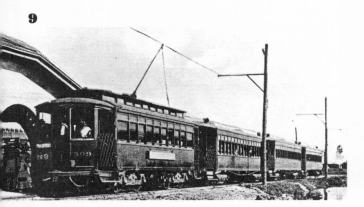

10

13 The last of a vanishing breed—a streetcar motorman at his post today on a St. Charles Avenue trolley as it passes Audubon Park. *Photo by Barney Fortier*

13

291

15 The Canal Street ferries advertised that one could ride all day for a nickel, a bargain even in the days when five cents could buy something. This is the ferry-house with its clock tower. The wing to the left was the harbor precinct police station.

16 An interesting fact about twentieth-century New Orleans ferryboats was that they were twin-hulled catamaran-type vessels. This is the *A. M. Halliday* about to land, probably taken at Mardi Gras time, since many sailors from a visiting warship are about to land at the same time and many flags are flying. The

16

14

14 Ferries on the Mississippi at New Orleans were very much a part of the local scene, almost since the first steamboat came to the city. This is the earliest photograph (1878) of a New Orleans ferry—the Canal Street ferry *Louise*. This boat, which did not have the conventional pilot house perched on its topmost deck, ran between 1867 and 1879. *Courtesy Captain Fred Way, Jr.*

15

twin hulls of the *Halliday* are visible. Such boats were driven by a recessed paddle wheel. The *Halliday* was built in 1903 and was for many years a familiar sight on the river. *Courtesy Captain Fred Way, Jr.*

17 The New Orleans ferry with the most interesting background was the Texas and Pacific Railroad transfer boat, the *Gouldsboro,* seen here in dry dock. She was originally built in 1863 as a federal monitor during the Civil War and named *Chickasaw.* She saw action in Farragut's fleet in Mobile Bay when she overcame the Confederate ram *Tennessee.* After the war, she was sold at auction and stripped to the hull, serving for a time as a barge. In 1881, she was converted into a transfer boat and as such saw service until the advent of the Huey P. Long Bridge when she was retired.

18 In the 1930s, New Orleanians could cross the Mississippi on six ferries. Bridges will ultimately spell the doom of all ferries at the Crescent City. This picture, made in 1958, shows one of the last of the steam ferries, the *Algiers,* silhouetted against the Mississippi River Bridge. *Photo by W. L. D'Aquin*

18

17

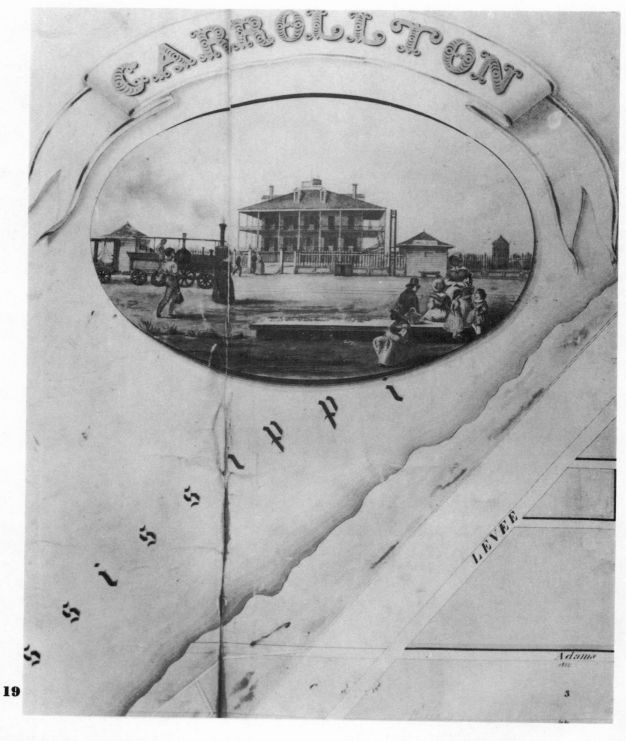

19

19 The only illustration of one of the primitive loco-motives that pulled the first coaches on New Orleans's early railroads is a cartouche on a map in the city's Notarial Archives. This illustration also shows the ticket office and the Carrollton Hotel, the suburban resort so popular in the 1830s and 1840s.

In the 1830s, New Orleans had three short-line railroads—the Pontchartrain, which ran 5.18 miles from the river to the lake; the New Orleans and Carrollton, which ran 6½ miles to the suburb of Carrollton; and the Mexican Gulf Railway, which ran to Bayou Terre-aux-Boeufs 19 miles away in a bid for shorter connections by ship to the east. But the most ambitious railroad scheme of the early days of railroad construction—the New Orleans & Nashville Railroad —came to naught. This was planned to link these two cities 564 miles apart. A set of unfortunate circumstances—the panic of 1837, the parsimony of the state legislature, and prejudice in Mississippi—resulted in the failure of the line after only twenty miles had been constructed. By 1850, the whole state of Louisiana had only eighty-one miles of railroad within its boundaries. The Mississippi River, which had brought New Orleans wealth and power, had so lulled the city's leaders into complacency that it was only when they began to realize that eastern railroads were siphoning off its trade, that New Orleans awoke to its predicament. Thus belatedly came into existence the road to the north, the N.O. & Jackson Railroad (1854–1858), which eventually became part of the Illinois Central system; the road to the west, the N.O. Opelousas & Great Western (1853–1857), now part of the Southern Pacific; the road to the east, the N.O. Mobile & Chattanooga (opened 1870), now part of the Louisville & Nashville Railroad; the line to the southwest, the N.O. Pacific (late 1870s), now part of the Texas-Pacific, Missouri Pacific system; and the road to the southeast, the N.O. & Northeastern (early 1880s), now part of the Southern Railway system. Despite their relatively late start and despite the havoc caused by the Civil War on the Jackson and Opelousas lines, the railroads soon became "The Iron Feeders of Crescent City Commerce," hauling in and out of the city 1,400,-000 tons of freight annually by 1884. By the end of the century, they had all but driven steamboat traffic to the banks forever.

20 Building the roadbed of the New Orleans Opelousas & Great Western through the swamps west of New Orleans was a tremendous task. In 1855, nearly seven hundred men were employed in laying the tracks between Shriever and Gibson. Heat, foul swamp water, mosquitoes, and snakes added to the discomfort of the men, many of whom fell sick of fever. *Courtesy Southern Pacific Company*

21 This little locomotive, the Sabine, was built in 1854 for the New Orleans Opelousas & Great Western Railroad. Captured by General Banks's forces during the Civil War, the Sabine was sold to a plantation after forty-two years of service on the railroad. The engine was discovered on a scrap heap in 1923, repurchased by the Southern Pacific Lines, and restored. The locomotive graced a small park near the station at Lafayette, Louisiana, until 1942 when in a misguided patriotic moment it was donated to the scrap-metal drive during World War II. *Courtesy Southern Pacific Company*

22 Enginemen took great pride in the appearance of their locomotives. This Texas & Pacific engine was in tip-top shape, in addition to being very much deco-

20

21

22

rated with the insignia of the Knights Templars. The occasion was a trip of this masonic organization to Alexandria, Louisiana, on April 27, 1924. *Photo by Charles L. Franck*

23 24 The locomotives (there was more than one) that hauled pleasure seekers from the little station of the Pontchartrain Railway on Elysian Fields Avenue near the river to Milneburg on Lake Pontchartrain were affectionately known to thousands of New Orleanians as "Smoky Mary." The line ceased running in 1932 after an existence of 101 years, the last 52 years of its operation being under the management of the Louisville & Nashville Railroad. No. 2139 faces the river in the 700 block of Elysian Fields before one of its backward runs to the lake, and Smoky Mary, No. 2119, after switching at Milneburg, stands ready for the forward trip to town.

25 Plan of New Orleans, about 1828, showing a canal its promoters hoped to build to connect the river with Lake Pontchartrain. Instead, the pioneer railroad, the New Orleans Pontchartrain and Lake Railroad, was built over the same stretch of land—Elysian Fields Avenue. Only 5.18 miles long, this tiny road was probably the third to have been built (1831) in the United States. The plan shows the growth of the faubourgs, or suburbs, which was taking over plantations both up and downriver. Coming down from the lake, on the top left, is the Bayou St. John, connecting with the Carondelet Canal. *Courtesy Bibliothèque Nationale, Paris*

26 Connecting the Carondelet Canal with Bayou St. John was this Old Basin Canal, which had its origin in a fifteen-foot-wide ditch dug by order of Governor Carondelet in 1796 to connect the outskirts of the infant New Orleans with Bayou St. John in order to supply a navigable water route from the city to Lake

23

24

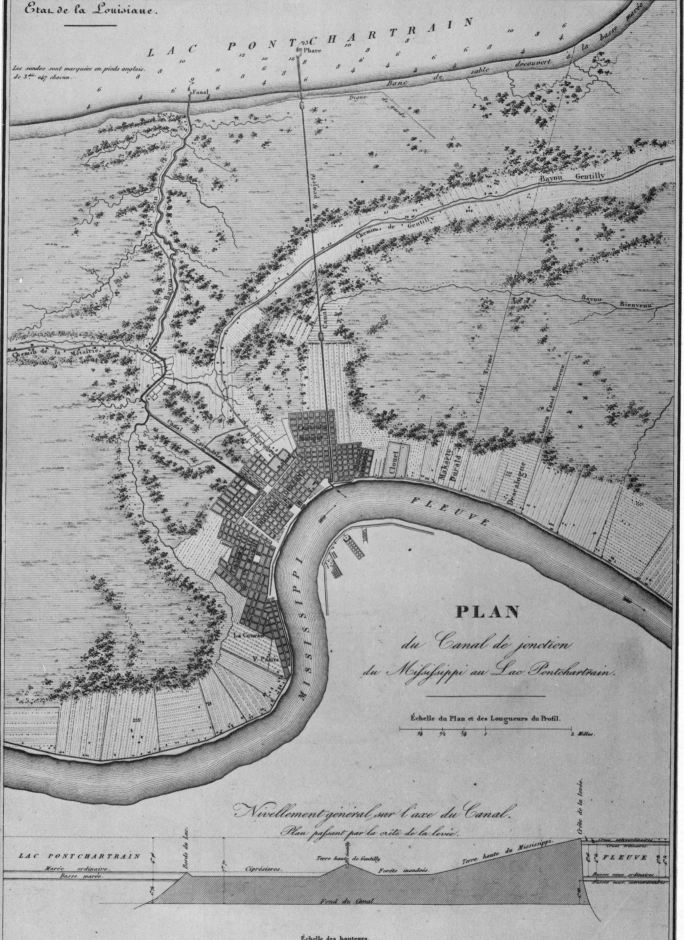

Etat de la Louisiane.

LAC PONTCHARTRAIN

Les sondes sont marquées en pieds anglais.
de 3ᵖᵉ 047 chacun.

Phare

Banc de sable découvert

Fanal

St Jean

Bayou Gentilly

Chemin de Gentilly

Canal

Bayou Bienvenu

Chemin de la Métairie

Canal

Clouet

Macarté Dupald

Decalongue

Canal Terre

Carré

Ancien Canal Ravenaire

FLEUVE

La Course

V. Paures

MISSISSIPPI

PLAN
du Canal de jonction
du Mississippi au Lac Pontchartrain.

Échelle du Plan et des Longueurs du Profil.

2 Milles.

Nivellement général sur l'axe du Canal.
Plan passant par la crête de la levée.

LAC PONTCHARTRAIN
Marée ordinaire.
Basse marée.

Borde du Lac

Cyprésières.

Terre haute de Gentilly

Forêts inondées.

Terre haute du Mississippi

Crête de la levée

FLEUVE

Fond du Canal

Échelle des hauteurs.

Mètres.

25

26

28

Pontchartrain and the Gulf Coast. As time went on, this canal, which also served as a drainage canal, was allowed to fill up, and it did not become serviceable again until 1805, when the territorial council chartered the New Orleans Navigation Company to enlarge it and collect tolls for their trouble. This concern ultimately spent $375,000 in buying land and in enlarging and deepening the canal and its turning basin. In 1852, the company became insolvent, and in 1858 a new group, the New Orleans Canal and Navigation Company, was organized, which ran the canal for more than half a century. Until the digging of the New Basin Canal, the Carondelet Canal was practically the only means of transportation for the commodities originating in the parishes across Lake Pontchartrain. After the rival canal was completed, the Old Basin still continued to function, and through the years countless schooners laden with lumber, firewood, charcoal, and other commodities found their way to the city on its waters. The Carondelet Canal was called "The Old Basin" in local parlance, since it antedated the "New" Basin Canal. The "Basin" was the turning basin at the canal's terminus, located near the St. Louis Cemetery No. 1. The Carondelet Canal was filled in between 1927 and 1938. The boats in this view are charcoal boats, 1906. *Courtesy Library of Congress*

27 The seven-mile-long bridge of the New Orleans & Northeastern Railroad across Lake Pontchartrain was a great engineering feat of the 1880s.

27

28 The first train over the new Huey P. Long Bridge. On December 6, 1935, New Orleans dedicated the $13 million railway-highway bridge across the Mississippi. A great engineering feat, it is 4½ miles long and rises from the base of its foundations to the top of the span as high as a 36-story building. *Photo by Charles L. Franck*

29 A railroad roundhouse—with its turntable and stalls for the engines—was a familiar sight. With the passing of the steam locomotive, the roundhouse fell victim to progress. This one is the New Orleans Public Belt roundhouse, with a typical 1910-vintage switch engine on the turntable. *Courtesy Edwin Gebhardt*

30 The last days of the age of steam. A Southern Pacific train (with oil-burning locomotive) is about to depart, and another train (*right*) is just arriving at Union Station, ca. 1940. *Courtesy Howard Tilton Memorial Library, Tulane University*

31 Side by side are an old and new Public Belt Railroad locomotive, ca. 1950. In 1904, necessary ordinances had been passed to create the Public Belt Railroad, and in 1908 this terminal-switching railroad, which supplies nondiscriminatory service to all who

29

require it in transferring cars from railroad to railroad, from railroads to wharves, and from railroads to industries and public delivery tracks, etc., at nominal charges, began operations. Today the Public Belt is "one of the busiest short-line railroads in the world," servicing 163 miles of track with 13 locomotives, a very important adjunct to maintaining New Orleans's position as second port of the United States. *Courtesy Edwin Gebhardt*

32 New Orleans's first railroad station, viewed from the river by G. W. Sully in 1836. To the left is the terminal of the Pontchartrain Railroad. In the center is the Marigny mansion. *Courtesy Howard-Tilton Memorial Library, Tulane University*

32

33–35 With the opening of the Union Passenger Terminal in April, 1954, five old railroad stations were replaced. Of these, the new terminal occupied the site of a station built for the Illinois Central Railroad in 1892. The four others that vanished were the Louisville & Nashville Station on Canal Street, dating from 1901; the Southern Railway Terminal Station on Canal Street at Basin, opened in 1908; the Texas Pacific Missouri Pacific Terminal at 1225 Annunciation Street, dating from 1916, and the Louisiana & Arkansas, Kansas City Southern Station, on Rampart Street, dating from 1923. Pictured here are the Illinois Central Station, the Louisville & Nashville Station, ca. 1950, and the Southern Railway Terminal Station.

36 37 New Orleans's Union Station and Trans-Mississippi Station, both demolished.

36

33

34

35

37

Beginnings of Aviation

38 In December, 1910, a group of New Orleans businessmen brought eight airmen, headed by John B. Moisant, seen here in his new metal monoplane, with twelve planes to stage what they called the "first real international aviation tournament ever held south of New York City." Moisant was the daredevil who had won the $10,000 first prize in a race across Brooklyn and around the Statue of Liberty, and who had first flown a passenger (his mechanic) across Paris. Just before that, New Orleans got its first close-up of an airplane when Louis Paulhan came to the Crescent City prior to the Mardi Gras in 1910. A debonair Frenchman and an unusually skilled pilot at a time when the profession was something of a fantasy, Paulhan made a hit with New Orleanians—twenty-five thousand of them paid fifty cents to see him perform at the City Park racetrack. Paulhan flew a flimsy-looking Farman biplane powered by a fifty-horsepower seven-cylinder motor, which turned his eight-foot prop fifteen hundred revolutions a minute. He took off at thirty-five miles per hour, and his top speed was sixty.

38

40

39

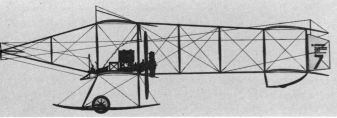

39 This was the type of airplane that Louis Paulhan brought to New Orleans in 1910 for his exhibition flights. It had a wing span of 34 feet 10 inches, and was 38 feet long. With Paulhan aboard, it weighed about 830 pounds.

40 John B. Moisant in his Bleriot monoplane, 1910. The twenty-seven-year-old Moisant, a native of Kankakee, Illinois, had worked in California and the tropics before he took up aviation in France. He had quickly learned his profession and became distinguished for his "firsts" in France before returning to America. At City Park, Moisant and his confreres put on a show that included an attempt to break the altitude record (he failed), a race against an automobile (Moisant lost by a whisker), and other stunts. Things were going so swimmingly that Moisant thought he would attempt to win the $4,000 prize that went with the Michelin Cup for sustained flight. The record was 362.66 miles, and Moisant planned to make his attempt from a field near Harahan. On December 31,

1910, he flew his plane from City Park to the field from which he was to begin his flight. In trying to land, his plane struck an air pocket a few feet from the ground and Moisant was catapulted from it, incurring fatal injuries—the thirtieth fatality among pioneer airmen. New Orleans honored his memory by giving his name to the international airport, near Kenner.

41 A little over a year later on April 10, 1912, George Mestach carried thirty-two pounds of mail from New Orleans to Baton Rouge in one hour and thirty-one minutes. He badly damaged his plane in landing and did not try to carry the mail again. Daily mail service between New Orleans and Pilot Town at the mouth of the river began on April 9, 1923. The flight carried thirty pounds of mail and shortened the mail delivery time between New Orleans and foreign ports by nearly half a day. This is one of the flying boats of the New Orleans Air Line, which flew the mail from New Orleans to Pilot Town in the 1920s. The line, started by Arthur Cambas, was awarded New Orleans's first air-mail franchise by the post office department. The first commercial air transportation service was St. Tammany-Gulf Coast Airways, Inc. They bought a Fokker plane powered by a two-hundred-horsepower engine, put in a bid for carrying the mail from New Orleans to Atlanta, and won the contract. Operations began from Callender Field on May 1, 1928. This concern was later absorbed by American Airlines, Inc., after the former had won a contract to carry the mail to Laredo, Texas.

41

42

43

44

42 James R. Wedell, aviation genius and pilot extraordinary, put Louisiana on the map in the 1930s with his fleet, self-designed planes. In association with New Orleans millionaire Harry P. Williams, he formed the Wedell-Williams Air Service, Inc., and built and raced four revolutionary planes, which set world speed records. Death in plane accidents within two years (1934–1936) snuffed out his life and the lives of his brother Walter and backer Williams. Wedell-Williams had received a contract to build fifty of their fast pursuit planes for the United States Army, which was never fulfilled. *Courtesy Hermann B. Deutsch*

43 Harry P. Williams, the wealthy New Orleans backer of the Wedell brothers, in the cockpit of his plane. *Courtesy Hermann B. Deutsch*

44 The Wedell-Williams "44," so named because, as the revolver and bullets painted on its cockpit proclaimed, it was "hot as a '44' and twice as fast." *Courtesy Hermann B. Deutsch*

45 During the early days of aviation, planes took off and landed in cow pastures around the city and in City and Audubon parks. A favorite field was in the Jefferson Avenue–Claiborne section, which was then open country. Later there was an airfield on the St. Bernard Highway, called Menefee Field; and in 1926 Alvin Callender Field, at Belle Chasse, six miles from New Orleans, was constructed. It was named for Captain Alvin Callender who had been killed in World War I after downing fourteen German planes. Shushan Airport (now New Orleans Airport) was constructed on a pumped-in fill on the shores of Lake Pontchartrain and opened on February 9, 1934. At that time, it was considered one of the finest in the country, but increasing traffic and larger planes made another move inevitable. In 1945, Moisant (now New Orleans) International Airport covering thirteen hundred acres was constructed.

New Orleans International Airport (*below*) opened in 1959. In February, 1960, the first jet passenger planes began to use the facility. The huge, air-conditioned arrival building was built at a cost of $7,500,000. John B. Moisant had been killed not far from the site. *Photo by Leon Trice. Courtesy Times-Picayune*

45

10. BUSINESS

When Cotton Was King

1 Cotton was first planted in Louisiana in 1718, but it was not until Eli Whitney's cotton gin came into use toward the end of the eighteenth century that the crop assumed some importance. By 1809, cotton was a principal crop in the northern part of Louisiana, and the staple was being grown in greater and greater quantities in the upriver southern states. With the coming of the steamboats, New Orleans fast became one of the world's largest cotton markets. Water transportation from tributary streams of the Mississippi, which fanned out into the plantation country, and the city's proximity to the sea, made this inevitable. By the mid-1830s, the Mississippi-Louisiana plantations were producing more than five hundred thousand bales annually, and New Orleans had half a dozen cotton compresses and storage warehouses. Depicted here is the New Orleans levee with its cargoes going and coming from the moored steamboats, 1880. *From* America Revisited *by George Augustus Sala, London, 1886*

2 Weighing cotton bales, 1880. *From* America Revisited *by George Augustus Sala, London, 1886*

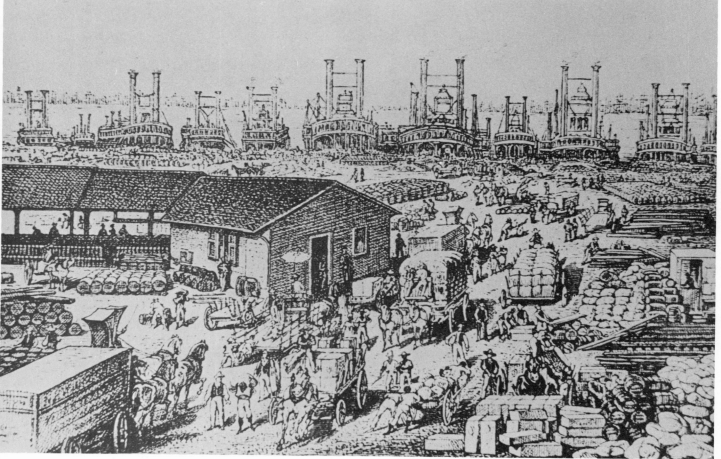

3

3 The largest cotton press in the late 1830s—the Orleans Cotton Press, lithograph by Fishbourne, 1842. It occupied a two-block-long site facing the river. Here baled cotton was recompressed by steam-operated machines, which could handle 150,000 bales a year; twenty-five thousand bales could be stored in its warehouse.

4 *Le Classeur de Coton*—The Cotton Classer, engraving from a sketch by Leon J. Fremaux. Cotton classers were employed by cotton commission merchants to test samples taken from each bale consigned to the merchants. Classified according to grade, condition, and length of staple, the samples, wrapped in paper, were taken to the merchant's sample rooms where they were displayed for examination by cotton buyers. A gentleman always, the classer of the 1880s affected a white linen shirt, wing collar, and bow tie. He protected his tailored clothes from cotton lint by an apron of Manila paper.

5 Compressing cotton, sketch by J. O. Davidson. Huge steam presses recompress the springy fibers into more compact bales so that they will take up less cargo space in ships. *From* Harper's Weekly, *July 7, 1883*

6 *On the Cotton Levee*, 1883. At the time this sketch was made by J. O. Davidson, New Orleans's receipts were already almost 2 million bales of cotton, and the steamboats were still carrying the crop. *From* Harper's Weekly, *July 7, 1883*

7 In 1871, the New Orleans Cotton Exchange was formed by eighteen cotton merchants to facilitate and regulate trading. The first exchange was located in an upper room at Carondelet and Gravier streets. At the time, "Cotton was King," and cotton futures generated intense excitement in the local business community. A writer in *Scribner's* in 1873 gave a vivid description of this atmosphere:

4

5

6

During certain hours of the day, in the American quarter of New Orleans, cotton is the only subject spoken of; the pavements of all the principal avenues in the vicinity of the Exchange are crowded with smartly-dressed, well-to-do looking gentlemen who eagerly discuss crops and values, and who have a perfect mania for preparing and comparing the estimates which are the basis of all speculations in the favorite staple; with young Englishmen with silky beards and miraculously thin toilets, showing that they fancied the climate seven times more heated than the fiery furnace, and with their mouths filled with slang of the Liverpool market; with skippers of steamers from all parts of the west, from alligator-haunted bayous and creeks, and great commercial capitals bordering on the Mississippi; all worshipping at the god cotton. The planter, the factor, the speculator, flit feverishly to and from the portals of the Exchange from high noon until dark, and nothing can be heard above the excited hum of their conversations inside the sacred walk except the penetrating voice of the clerk who reads aloud the latest telegrams.

By 1881, the Cotton Exchange had outgrown its quarters and a new building, pictured here, was built at the corner of Carondelet and Gravier streets. An overornamented structure in the current florid style, this "palace of commerce" was erected at a cost of $400,000 and opened May 12, 1883. When it was demolished in the 1920s for the erection of the present Cotton Exchange, two of the caryatids were preserved and incorporated into a building at 116 City Park Avenue, where they may still be seen. This sketch of the second exchange is by C. Upham. *From* Frank Leslie's Illustrated Newspaper, *March 24, 1883*

7

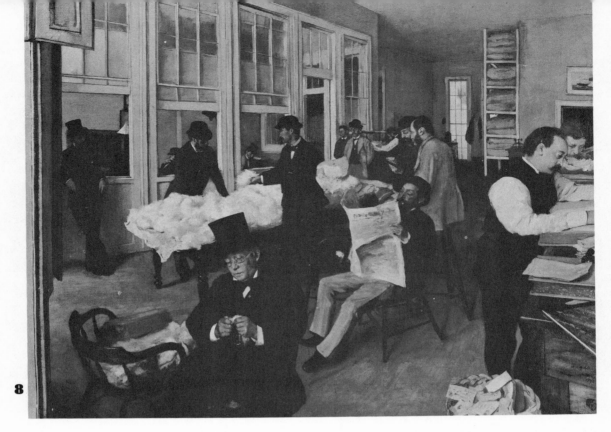

8 The Cotton Market in New Orleans, by Edgar Degas (1834–1917). This masterpiece by Degas was painted in 1873 after the artist visited his brothers Achille and René, successful cotton merchants in New Orleans. René is shown seated reading the *Daily Picayune*, while Achille appears in the left background leaning against a partition. The figure of the elderly man in the foreground examining a sample of cotton is Michel Musson, uncle of the artist and a distinguished New Orleans citizen who was once postmaster. *Courtesy Museum of Pau, France*

9 The interior of the Cotton Exchange was decorated with frescoes depicting Louisiana scenes, and there was a small gallery for visitors. Futures were sold around a small fountain, which can be seen in the illustration, and information concerning the marketing of the staple was posted on blackboards. In 1903, there were about five hundred members of the New Orleans Cotton Exchange. Sketch by C. Upham. *From Frank Leslie's Illustrated Newspaper, March 24, 1883*

10 Absent from New Orleans today are the Louisiana Sugar Exchange and the Cotton Exchange. Federal regulations and changing times have all but eliminated these once potent institutions. But still in existence, and very much alive, is the New Orleans Board of Trade. This organization, housed in a handsome building of 1883 vintage, erected on the site of Banks' Arcade, restored in 1951–1952, and also in 1968, is a meeting place where members are provided market information on quotation boards in the trades of coffee, sugar, cotton, cocoa, grain, and stocks. The board of trade serves as the official grain-inspector agency of the port, and its rooms are a gathering place for the men who direct the green coffee industry in New Orleans. Through the years, the board of trade has played an important part in advocating projects to improve the port and the business climate of New Orleans and Louisiana. *Photo by Leon Trice*

Sugar

11 *The Sugar Industry of Louisiana.* After Jean Étienne Boré had demonstrated in 1796 that Louisiana cane could be made into sugar commercially, within seven years there were seventy-five sugar mills

on the Mississippi River, producing five million pounds of sugar a year. Expert sugar makers were imported from Saint-Domingue to "take off the crop." They commanded high wages, and the sugar planter was always at the mercy of an early freeze or a crevasse that might wipe him out. Nevertheless, production expanded, and the use of steam power for grinding, the invention of the centrifugal machine in 1844, and the filter press in 1855 increased the yield. In the season 1859–1860, the state produced 221,840

hogsheads of sugar, and the crop the year before the outbreak of the Civil War was worth $25 million.

Three times the industry has been threatened with extinction—the first time in 1835 when the tariff was reduced and production dropped 70 percent; again during the Civil War when the plantations and mills were almost paralyzed; and the third time in the 1920s when the mosaic disease cut the yield to $5 million. The introduction of the disease-resistant P.O.J. cane, by the operators of Southdown plantation, near Houma, and their careful replanting of the yield from the first twenty-one eyes (seed) of the new cane until there was enough both for their seven thousand acres and the rest of the cane belt, revived the industry. New and better varieties of cane have since been introduced; these and efficient mechanization have steadily increased the yield and total production. The sketches by J. O. Davidson are: 1. View of sugar district; 2. Stripping and cutting; 3. Bringing in the cane; 4. Plantation quarters; 5. Planting; 6. Planter's residence; and 7. Young sugarcane. *From* Harper's Weekly, *July 21, 1883*

12 The Louisiana Sugar Refinery, built in 1832 two miles below Esplanade Avenue, turned out thirty-five thousand pounds of refined sugar and two thousand gallons of rum daily

13 When a steamboat carrying sugar arrived at the New Orleans levee, the sugar broker would clamber aboard to learn from the clerk if any part of the cargo was consigned to him. If the manifests revealed a lot for the broker, he called for his public weigher and forthwith began boring holes in the casks to extract samples, which he minutely examined and sent to the nearby Sugar Exchange. His weigher meanwhile summoned Negroes to roll the barrels under the arms of the scales and made notations in his notebook as the barrels were weighed. Each barrel was thereupon marked with its weight and the notations eventually transferred to certificates for shipper, broker, and buyer. Like the cotton classer, sugar brokers and weighers were gentlemen who looked and acted the

13

part, whether on the levee, at the exchange, or at the opera. Sketch by Leon J. Fremaux.

14 *Scene at Levee, Handling Sugar*, 1895.

15 The Sugar Exchange building (1895), now demolished, was located at the corner of Front and Bienville streets. A two-storied building, its lower floor contained salesrooms and telegraph offices, while the upper floor housed a library, reading and committee rooms, and a museum.

16 Interior of the New Orleans Sugar Exchange— brisk trading, ca. 1900, drawn by W. A. Rogers. The Exchange boasted portraits of Antonio Méndez, on whose plantation in St. Bernard Parish sugar had been granulated in 1794; of Jean Étienne Boré, who in 1796 first successfully granulated a commercial crop,

12

14

16

and of John J. Coiron, who was the first to use steam power for grinding cane and who introduced a red-ribbon cane from Georgia that was superior to the variety then planted. At the time of this illustration, the Sugar Exchange had 211 members and wielded a powerful influence on the commerce of the state.

17 One cannot pass this section of the Levee without realizing the greatness and importance of the sugar industry in Louisiana. Block after block along about midwinter is packed and crowded with barrels and hogsheads of sugar and molasses. Large as the area is, it scarce affords room for the product that seeks this greatest sugar market in all the United States. The barrels of sweets overflow the sheds, crowd the warehouses in the vicinity, block the sidewalks and overrun the Levee. There is sugar everywhere.

This view of the sugar sheds, 1872, is on a less bustling day. *From* The Picayune Guide to New Orleans, *1903*

15

17

LEEDS & CO.

COR. DELORD AND FOUCHER STREETS,

Manufacturers of

VERTICAL AND HORIZONTAL

STEAM ENGINES,

LEEDS' FOUNDRY,
Cor. Delord & Foucher-Sts.
NEW-ORLEANS, LA.

BOILERS, SUGAR MILLS,

APPARATUS AND FURNACES FOR

BURNING BAGASSE;

Vacuum Pans, Sugar Kettles, Clarifiers and Filters.

STEAM AND HORSE-POWER

DRAINING MACHINES,

SAW MILLS, GIN GEARING,

Furnace Mouths, Grate Bars, &c., &c.

And all Machinery required for the South.

They respectfully call the particular attention of the Planters of Louisiana and the adjoining States to their styles of

STEAM ENGINES, SUGAR MILLS, VACUUM PANS AND DRAINING WHEELS,

Which for strength and durability have not been excelled.

18

19

20

18 The manufacture of the machinery for Louisiana's sugar mills was one of the few industries about which New Orleans could boast in the mid-nineteenth century. One of these was the Leeds Foundry, operated by Charles J. Leeds, which turned out steam engines and boilers for the planters. This plant was the second largest ironworks in the South, and during the early days of the Civil War manufactured cannon and shell for the Confederates. *From* Gardner's New Orleans Directory, *1867*

19 Charles J. Leeds as a young man. He was a civic leader of high caliber and served as mayor of New Orleans from 1874 to 1876, during the Reconstruction period.

Coffee and Bananas

20 New Orleans is famous for its coffee, and is one of the largest coffee importers in the United States. Here we see a shipment of green coffee from Brazil being unloaded from the hold of a steamer at the New Orleans docks. *Photo by Charles Genella*

21 After being unloaded, the sacks await shipment on the wharves, 1930.

22 The smell of roasting coffee pervades several sections of the city, giving them an odor so characteristic that writers who have lived here regard it as part of the New Orleans scene. Here beans are given the "dark roast," which, sometimes with the addition of chicory, produces the characteristic New Orleanian brew. *Photo by Charles Genella*

21

22

23

23 The coffee taster is a highly skilled professional. Later, others may enjoy it as *café au lait* at one of the French Market coffee stands, while munching a delectable sugarcoated doughnut, one of the things that makes New Orleans different from other cities. *Photo by Charles Genella*

24 The interior of the board of trade building, about 1895. When in 1968 the old St. James Hotel, which hid the building from view, was demolished, the delightful loggia and plaza, with fountain, was constructed in front of it.

25 In addition to its coffee imports, New Orleans has an enormous banana trade, which began shortly after the Civil War when the brothers Salvador and Joseph Oteri imported the first shiploads of this prized Central American product. The Oteris and the Macheca brothers continued in business until they were bought out in 1899 by the Boston-based United Fruit Company. United's Great White Fleet (which at one time numbered 102 ships) carried great quantities of bananas to New Orleans and engaged in the passenger business as well. The United Fruit Company's *Talamanca,* seen here about 1950, was typical of the passenger-cargo ships of the Great White Fleet. *Courtesy Robert M. Calder*

24

25

26 Arrival of the *Jamaica*, a United Fruit Company vessel with a cargo of bananas for New Orleans. The gantry-conveyor to the left was lowered into the ship's hold when it docked. *Courtesy Robert M. Calder*

27 28 At dockside, the banana bunches were placed on conveyor belts and then lifted onto the shoulders of laborers who moved in a seemingly endless stream to deposit their loads into waiting refrigerator cars or trucks. *Courtesy Board of Commissioners, Port of New Orleans*

Early Merchants and Merchandising

29 While in the nineteenth century very little manufacturing was done in New Orleans (the city was essentially a trading and shipping center), there was considerable mercantile life. Mallard, the famous New Orleans furniture maker, took a two-page spread in the New Orleans city directory of 1857 to advertise his wares. On one of the pages were pictured rooms furnished with chairs, sofas, tables, a bed, an armoire, and one of his duchesse dressing tables. *Courtesy New Orleans Public Library*

30 Dr. J. A. Sherman operated this odd truss and brace store in 1859. In his advertisement, his showcase displays a dozen different types of braces and trusses, and Dr. Sherman concludes his advertisement with the names of nearly a dozen prominent physicians who recommend his products.

31 In a day when bathing was a rite rather than an everyday necessity and when most homes did not even possess a zinc tub, the public bath flourished. This one, Rollin's Oriental Public Baths, offered great variety. *From Gardner's New Orleans Directory, 1857*

32 Here we have Joseph Etter standing in the middle of his wallpaper and carpeting emporium, 1859.

33 *The Bulletin* was one of New Orleans's news-

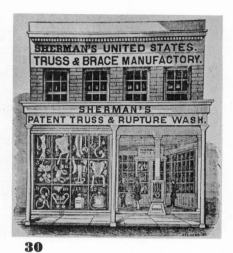

30

29

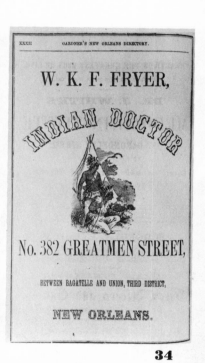

32

34

33

papers, but like most papers of the time, it supplemented its income by doing book and job printing "Neatly, Cheaply, and Expeditiously." *From* Gardner's New Orleans Directory, *1859*

34 New Orleans had its share of quack doctors. As early as 1826, one of them advertised that "by long intercourse with many different tribes of savages, and much practice, he gives relief in desperate cases." Among the ailments he said he could cure were scurvy, bilious complaints, fits, fevers, ague, diabetes, ulcers, cancers, and bed sores. Making no claims, but announcing that he practices as an "Indian Doctor," W. K. F. Fryer placed this advertisement in the 1867 city directory.

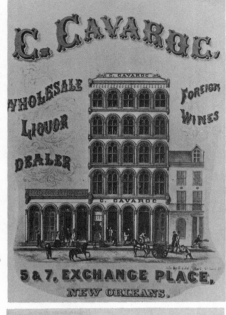

35 C. CAVAROC, WHOLESALE LIQUOR DEALER, FOREIGN WINES, 5 & 7, EXCHANGE PLACE, NEW ORLEANS.

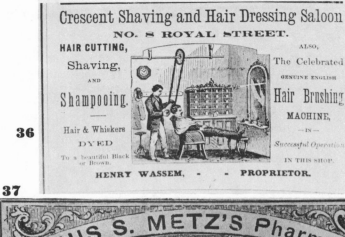

36 Crescent Shaving and Hair Dressing Saloon, NO. 8 ROYAL STREET. HAIR CUTTING, Shaving, AND Shampooing. Hair & Whiskers DYED To a beautiful Black or Brown. ALSO, The Celebrated GENUINE ENGLISH Hair Brushing MACHINE, IN Successful Operation IN THIS SHOP. HENRY WASSEM, PROPRIETOR.

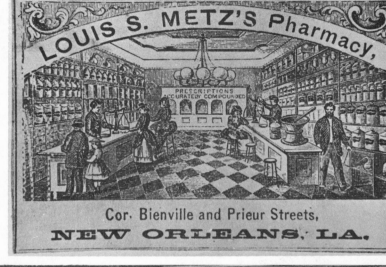

37 LOUIS S. METZ'S Pharmacy, PRESCRIPTIONS ACCURATELY COMPOUNDED, Cor. Bienville and Prieur Streets, NEW ORLEANS, LA.

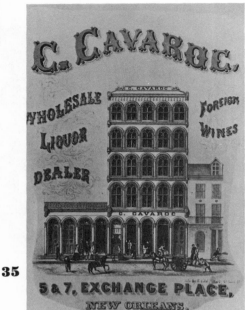

38

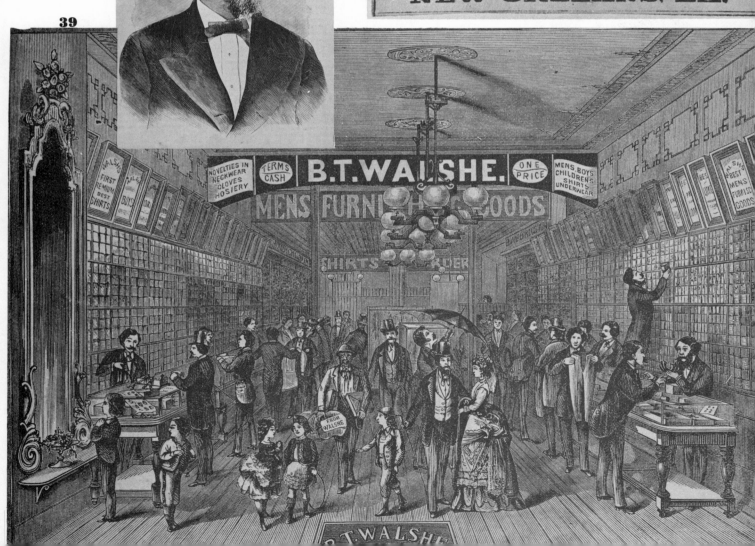

39 B.T. WALSHE. NOVELTIES IN NECKWEAR GLOVES HOSIERY. TERMS CASH. ONE PRICE. MENS, BOYS, CHILDRENS SHIRTS UNDERWEAR. MENS FURNISHING GOODS.

35 In 1867, the wine-importing firm of C. Cavaroc moved into its new five-story building at No. 5 Exchange Place. This structure, which still stands, has a cast-iron facade and is regarded by architectural historians as an important landmark.

36 Henry Wassem was an enterprising barber who not only cut hair, shaved, and shampooed, but also dyed hair and whiskers to a "beautiful Black or Brown," and advertised that he had an English hair-brushing machine.

37 A druggist's label. Louis S. Metz operated a pharmacy at the corner of Bienville and Prieur streets from the 1870s through the 1880s, and this picturesque woodcut was pasted on the bottles of his "prescriptions accurately compounded."

38 39 Blayney T. Walshe came to New Orleans with his parents from Ireland in 1853 when he was thirteen years old. When the Civil War broke out, he volunteered and fought with the Washington Artillery. After the war he opened a men's furnishing store on Canal Street near St. Charles, and realizing the value of advertising, he contracted to take four pages in

Jewell's Crescent City Illustrated, a combination "commercial, social, political and general history of New Orleans," published in 1873.

40 The oldest department store in the city was established in 1842 by Daniel Henry Holmes on Chartres Street. Holmes later erected this four-story store, which is in the Gothic Revival style, on Canal Street. Through the years, the building has been enlarged and remodeled, the present facade being erected in 1964. *From* Jewell's Crescent City Illustrated, *1873*

41 Grunewald Hall, owned by Louis Grunewald, a pioneer music merchant. It was billed as "the finest, most elegantly outfitted and centrally located Hall in the South, suitable for Concerts, Balls, Lectures, Fairs, etc." *From* Jewell's Crescent City Illustrated, *1873*

40

41

42

43

44

42 Long before the day of chain grocery stores, the wholesale grocers of New Orleans did a thriving trade as food distributors. One of these was the longtime partnership of William B. Schmidt and Francis M. Ziegler, whose establishment on Peters Street near Poydras was typical of many in this section of the city. *From* Jewell's Crescent City Illustrated, *1873*

43 Charles Wirth, Jr.'s grocery store, 1904, at 3300 Magazine Street. In the good old days, the Wirth grocery advertised creole eggs at fifteen cents a dozen and butter at twenty-five cents a pound, and the delivery boy brought your box of groceries in his wagon to your back door. *Courtesy Dr. Willard R. Wirth*

44 The store had a lacy cast-iron counter and stools for its customers. *Courtesy Dr. Willard R. Wirth*

45 J. H. Keller's residence adjoins his soap factory. He was listed in the *Picayune* in 1881 as one of the city's wealthiest men with a net worth of $300,000.

46 Trade cards (chromolithographs), bearing the name of the advertiser, were much prized by children. Here we see Santa Claus with Christmas tree in hand

45

46

and a sack full of toys resting under an upturned cart. This was put out by H. Kern, a dry-goods dealer with headquarters in the Moresque Building, Camp and Poydras streets, ca. 1888.

47 Before the days of ethical dentistry, dentists felt free to advertise "painless extraction of teeth."

48 Such quacks as Dr. M. T. McLaughlin advertised electric belts to cure "all weakness in man or woman." *From* Times-Democrat, *February 16, 1904*

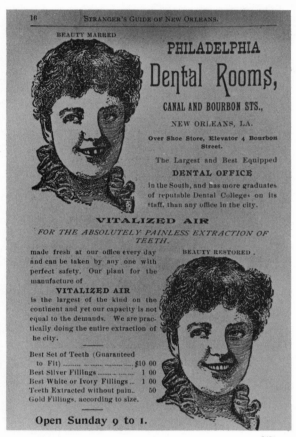

47

48

49 Joseph Schwartz Company, long a distributor for buggies, took on the Buick agency in the early days of the automobile. The mile-a-minute Buick had clincher tires, brass head lamps, and a horn that made a sound like "honk," ca. 1912.

50 There were quite a few tobacco factories in 1880, and this view shows the interior of one.

50

51

51 The A. Delpit Factory, established in 1808, was a tobacco manufactory. Its advertisement, by T. Fitzwilliams Co., which dates from 1884 or 1885, is a superb example of lithography, for which the city had long been noted.

52 Also manufactured in New Orleans was this Windhausen refrigeration machine, 1879, or "air-conditioner." Until 1819 the city had relied on the arrival of sailing vessels for natural ice from the eastern seaboard. In that year, Richard Salmon opened the first "icehouse," an insulated building for storing ice. Ice was sold for eight cents a pound. An experimental ice manufacturing plant opened in 1864, and in 1868 the first plant to manufacture ice on a regular basis was built on Delachaise Street and the river by the Louisiana Ice Manufacturing Company. Within two years, the New Orleans Ice Company, a competitor, appeared. These plants supplied ice at $16 a ton, while natural ice, which was imported as late as 1881, sold

52

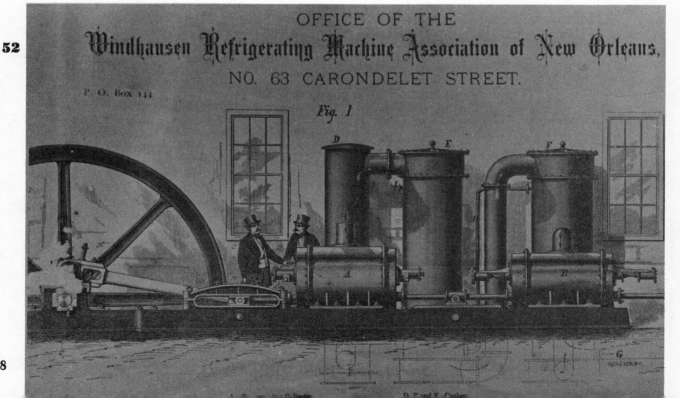

for $20. In 1878, during one of the last great yellow-fever epidemics, the demand for ice exceeded the supply, and ice rose to $60 a ton, wholesale.

In 1879, the Windhausen refrigeration machine, installed in Merz's Brewery, 110 Robertson Street, cooled a large room from normal temperature to 26° at 53 feet, its farthest end, in about three hours. This was perhaps the first attempt at air-conditioning in New Orleans, although the experiment was made to see if the cold would kill certain bacteria and yeast cells. The business end, or the mouth of the machine, delivered a temperature of 26° below zero.

53 The American Express was a frequent visitor here. Its heavily laden two-horse dray is about to pull away from the curb, ca. 1908.

Telephones for the Businessman

54 New Orleans telephone service, which seems to have been designed to serve the businessman, as indicated from this directory, started in 1879 when W. H. Bofinger, president of the American District Telegraph Company, obtained a license from the American Bell Telephone Company and started the New Orleans Telephonic Exchange. This first directory listed ninety-nine subscribers, including a number of firms that are still in business. *Courtesy Southern Bell Telephone and Telegraph Company*

54

LIST OF TELEPHONE SUBSCRIBERS
NEW ORLEANS TELEPHONIC EXCHANGE

OFFICE: 47 CAMP STREET   DECEMBER, 1879   NEW ORLEANS, LA.

INSTRUCTIONS: To call the Exchange give a long ring with the bell crank and when the operator signals back remove the telephone from the hook and give the name of the subscriber wanted. When called by the Exchange give a ring back, then remove the telephone from the hook and say Hello! Hello!

A
Avery, J. E., Fulton and St. Joseph Sts.

B
Ber, H. & B., 76 Baronne St.
Boston Club, 148 Canal St.
Bradstreet Agency, 31 Camp St.
Brown & Jones, 166 Common St.
Buckley, James & Company, 51 Carondelet St

C
Canal Bank, Camp and Gravier Sts.
Canal Street Press, Canal and Claiborne Sts.
Carre, W. W., Euphrosine and Liberty Sts.
Chief of Police, 124 Carondelet St.
City Council Chamber, City Hall.
Clarke & Meader, Napoleon and St. Charles Aves.
Clarke & Meader, 16 Carondelet St.
Coleman, H. Dudley, 9 Perdido St.
Conery E. & Son, Common and Delta Sts.
Coyle, W. G. & Company, 47 Carondelet St.
Coyle, W. G. & Company, Race St.
Crescent Insurance Company, 67 Camp St.
Cromwell Line Steamship Co., Foot of Toulouse St.

D
Del Hondio, K. F., S. Peters and Poydras Sts.
DeWolf & Hammond, 36 Carondelet St.
Dunn, M. F. & Bro., 72 Camp St.

F
Firemen's Insurance Company, 33 Camp St.
Fire Insurance Patrol, 162 Julia St.
Fitzwilliam, T. & Company, 76 Camp St.
Fletcher, I. D., Magnolia and Gravier Sts.

H
Harris, Parker & Company, 48 Perdido St.
Harrison Steamship Line, Foot of St. Peter St.
Horner, Jos. P., 16 Carondelet St.
Huck, W. W., Res., Camp and Third Sts.

I
I. C. Railroad, Tchoupitoulas and Canal Sts.
I. C. Railroad, Carondelet and Gravier Sts.
I. C. Railroad, Calliope and Waters Sts.
International Press, S. Peter and Gaienne Sts.

J
Jewish Widows and Orphans Home, Jackson and Chippewa Sts.

K
Keller, J. H., 110 Gravier St.
Keller, J. H., St. Andrew and Magnolia Sts.

L
Langles, J. J. & Company, Common and Tchoupitoulas Sts.
Langles, J. J. & Company, 5 Triangle Building.
Larue, Edward & Company, 46 Carondelet St.
Lawrence, C. H., 72 Tchoupitoulas St.
Lehman, Stern & Company, 199 Gravier St.
Lhote & Company, 43 Carondelet St.
Lhote & Company, Toulouse & Franklin Sts.
Liverpool & London & Globe Insurance Company, 37 Carondelet St.
Locher, F. Dr. 161 Baronne St.
Louisiana Cotton Press, St. Thomas and Robin Sts.
Louisville & Nashville R. R. Co., St. Charles and Common Sts.

M
Maginnis, A. A. Sons, 111 Magazine St.
Mechanics Insurance Company, 14 Carondelet St.
Meyer, V. & A. & Company, Union and Baronne Sts.
Miller, A. K. & Company, 37 Carondelet St.
Miller, A. K. & Company, St. Mary St.
Miller, D. T. & Company, Union and Baronne Sts.
Milliken, R., 135 Gravier St.
Miltenberger, C. A. & Company, 69 Camp St.
Miltenberger, C. A. & Company, Foot Race St.
Moffett, A. W., Crossman and Levee.
Moore, Lucas E. & Company, 66 Baronne St.
Moulton, Alfred & Company, 41 Carondelet St.
Muir, Duckworth & Company, 54 Union St.

N
Newman, H. & C., 220 Gravier St.
New Orleans Seed Company, Canal Street Ferry Landing.
New Orleans Insurance Association, 3½ Carondelet
New Orleans National Bank, Camp and Common Sts.
New Orleans Picayune, 66 Camp St.
New Orleans Water Works Co., St. Charles and Perdido Sts.
New Orleans Water Works Company, Tchoupitoulas and Richard St.

P
Peet, J. D. & Company, Cotton Exchange Bldg.
Planters Press, Annunciation and Richard Sts.
Planters Crescent Oil Company, Cotton Exchange Bldg.
Planters Crescent Oil Company, Gretna.
Pullman Palace Car Company, St. Charles and Commercial Alley.

R
Ranlett, D. L., 30 South Peter St.
Rice, Born & Company, 91 Camp St.
Roberts & Company, 52 Carondelet St.
Roberts & Company, 307 Gravier St.

S
Schmidt & Ziegler, 51 South Peter St.
Siegfried & Company, 214 Gravier St.
Shardon & Wilson, Jackson and Rousseau Sts.
Shardon & Wilson, Prytania and Felicity Sts.
Smith Bros. & Company, 106 Poydras St.
Stauffer, Eshleman & Company, 71 Canal St.
Stewart Bros. & Company, 46 Union St.
St. Louis & Miss. Valley Trans. Co., 15 Commercial Place.
St. Louis & Miss. Valley Trans. Company, Foot of Julia St.

T
Thomas, S. O. & Company, 39 Perdido St.

U
Union National Bank, Carondelet and Gravier Sts.
Union Oil Company, Cotton Exchange Bldg.
Union Oil Company, Gretna.

W
Walmsley, R. M. & Company, 36 Perdido St.
Wayne, J. A., 52 Carondelet St.
Weeks Silas & Company, 48 Carondelet St.
Weis, Julius & Company, 188 Common St.
Western Union Telegraph Co., 52 St. Charles St.
Wood, B. D. & Bro., 47 Camp St.
Wood, B. D. & Bro., Race St.
Wood, B. D. & Bro., Julia and Levee.
Woodward, Wight & Company, 40 Canal St.

Telephone communications established between stores, offices, cotton presses, factories, residences, etc.

W. H. Bofinger, General Agent   47 Camp Street   P. O. Box 29

55 The first telephone operators were boys who were quickly dubbed "hello boys." However, they were "temperamentally unsuited" for the work (particularly when all deserted their posts during a heavy snowstorm to make and throw snowballs), and women operators replaced them. *Courtesy Southern Bell Telephone and Telegraph Company*

56 Before the days of telephone cables, a multitude of wires were strung on high poles to reach the subscribers. This early photograph shows a pole with ten crossarms. *Courtesy Southern Bell Telephone and Telegraph Company*

57 By 1897, there were 1,641 telephone subscribers. Between 1899 and 1900, New Orleans had two telephone systems, the People's and the Cumberland, but People's sold out to Cumberland. Cumberland's advertised rates did not mention pay station calls, which were fifteen cents. *From* History of the New Orleans Police Department, *1900*

58 In 1919, these Model T Ford roadsters were used by telephone repairmen to do their work. *Courtesy Southern Bell Telephone and Telegraph Company*

TELEPHONES

THE BEST
IS THE CHEAPEST

We not only give you the BEST
but actually the CHEAPEST

Long Distance Equipment

WITHIN THE REACH OF
EVERYONE

Business—as low as **$2** per Month

Residences—as low as **$1** per Month

Our lines not only reach every nook and corner of New Orleans, Algiers and Gretna, but throughout the entire SUGAR DISTRICT of Louisiana, and into the heart of the COTTON COUNTRY, and to all the important cities of the United States and Canada.

**Cumberland
Telephone & Telegraph Co.**

Telephone Building   Carondelet and Poydras Streets

320

59

61

59 New Orleans's banks have had a checkered history. Excessive capitalization, poor banking laws, the panic of 1837, the capture of the city and its long occupation during Reconstruction, the panics of 1873 and 1879, and the bank holiday of 1933 form vivid chapters in the century and a half of New Orleans banking. One of the most interesting old buildings still standing in the Vieux Carré is the Louisiana State Bank, seen here in 1821 at the corner of Royal and Conti streets (now Manheim Galleries). Built from the design of the eminent architect Benjamin H. B. Latrobe, it was chartered in 1818 with a capital of $2 million. Very successfully operated, it withstood the panic of 1837 and went through the Civil War. It was converted into the State National Bank in 1870. *From* City Directory, *1821*

60 Its checks bore vignettes of the steamer *John Randolph* and the pelican and her brood, the state emblem.

61 During earlier days, around 1780, there was a shortage of specie, which was being quickly gobbled up by traders and speculators. Paper currency of various kinds was used in its place, but since this often became worn and illegible through frequent handling, use was sometimes made of cards—even playing cards, which, as the backs were usually plain, could quickly be converted into legal tender by writing in the amounts over an official signature. The illustration depicts a curious example of the use of playing cards as merchandise "scrip," rather than ordinary currency. The cards are numbered, and bear on their backs an inscription entitling the bearer to receive

60

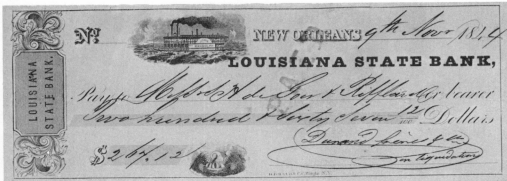

(presumably from a bakery or storehouse) a stated quantity of bread of a given value. Most of them were signed "Bichot" and were good for two loaves of bread each worth one *escalin* (i.e., one "bit" or 12½ sous). *Courtesy Louisiana State Museum*

62 The Bank of Louisiana, chartered in 1824, issued an elaborate bank note, which featured a view of the bank building. Generously capitalized by the state and its stockholders, this bank, too, was successfully operated. In 1830, it had a paid-in capitalization of $4 million and $867,000 in specie on hand. Its handsome colonnaded office, still standing on Royal and Conti streets opposite the Louisiana State Bank building, was erected in 1826. The building is being converted for the Greater New Orleans Tourist and Convention Center.

63 Ruins of the Citizens' Bank of Louisiana. The bank was organized in 1833 and located on Toulouse Street between Royal and Chartres in a stately columned Greek Revival building that ran through the block to the St. Louis Hotel. The building, built in 1836–1838 with J. N. B. de Pouilly as architect, had an interior noted for its vaulted ceiling, "neatly painted in compartments." It was later abandoned, and by 1884 was a crumbling ruin.

64 Like most banks of the period, the Citizens' Bank issued its own bank notes. Printed in both French and English, its ten-dollar bills—the most popular notes issued—bore the word "Dix," the French equivalent of ten—the origination of "Dixie," so the story goes. It seems that when an upriver trader was asked where he was going, if he was headed for New Orleans, as most were, he would answer that he was going after some "Dixies," and in consequence the South was eventually referred to as "Dixie," the land where the ten-dollar bills abounded.

65 Union Bank, chartered in 1832 with a capital of $7 million. It was also generously backed by the state, which issued bonds secured by mortgages on revenue-producing property. The bank's methods of lending were widely copied, and the same principles of operation were used by the Federal Land Bank of another day. This watercolor view by Boyd Cruise is of the Union Bank in 1842, at the corner of Royal and Iberville streets (the site now occupied by Walgreen's drugstore), a substantial Greek Revival structure adjacent to the Merchants' Exchange. *Courtesy Joseph Merrick Jones, Jr.*

66 An advertisement of the New Orleans Canal and Banking Company, corner of Camp and Gravier streets, from the 1884 city directory. This bank was organized in 1831, with a capital of $4 million, to construct a navigable canal (the New Basin Canal) from Rampart Street to Lake Pontchartrain at a cost of about $1 million. Other banks too were organized for particular improvements. The Improvement Bank, organized in 1834, was to build the St. Louis Hotel; the Exchange Bank, chartered in 1835, was to build the St. Charles Hotel.

INCORPORATED MARCH 5, 1831.

New Orleans Canal and Banking Company.

COR. CAMP AND GRAVIER.

J. C. MORRIS, President.

EDW. TOBY, Cashier.   J. B. MONTREUIL, Assistant Cashier.

BOARD OF DIRECTORS.

I. H. STAUFFER, Of Stauffer, Macready & Co.	W. B. SCHMIDT, Of Schmidt & Ziegler.
E. J. HART, Of E. J. Hart & Co.	A. H. MAY, Of Richardson & May.
J. B. LALLANDE, Commission Merchant	J. J. GIDIERE, Of Gidiere, Day & Co.
	J. C. MORRIS.

CAPITAL,	**$1,000,000.**
SURPLUS,	**$200,000.**
UNDIVIDED PROFITS,	**100,000.**

CORRESPONDENTS.

Nat. City Bank, Nat. Bank of Commerce, M. Morgan's Sons, } New York.   Boatmen's Saving Bank, Bank of Commerce, } St. Louis. Britton & Koontz, - Natchez.

66

65

67

68

67 68 There are now eight banks in New Orleans; the oldest in terms of continued operation is the Whitney National Bank, founded in 1883. Four of the banks occupy skyscraper buildings especially constructed for them, and there are some fifty branches of these and other banking houses throughout the city. Seen here are the Whitney National Bank Building erected in 1911, and the Hibernia National Bank, erected in 1925.

11. RIVER AND PORT
Golden Age of Steamboating

1

3

2

2 *Mississippi Raft,* sketch by T. B. Thorpe, 1855.

3 Of necessity, the men who manned the keelboats and flatboats were a hardy lot. When boatmen arrived at New Orleans and sold their cargoes or were paid off, many of them went on hell-roaring sprees. With the coming of steam, those who could afford it rode back home on steamboats. This sketch made aboard an early steamboat by the French artist Le Sueur in June, 1829, shows such a group, probably playing cards.

1 As Americans settled in the Ohio Valley and along the Mississippi, they soon began to depend on the rivers to get their produce to eastern or European markets, loading their grain, cattle, whiskey, lead, salt, and furs on flatboats, keelboats, and rafts, which they floated down to New Orleans. The journey downriver was dangerous enough, but the return trip, a nightmarish battle against the tremendous river, was hazarded by only the heartiest souls. Most crews, before the coming of the steamboat, either walked or rode horseback to their homes via the Natchez Trace.

4 Flatboats stranded at the riverbank, along one of the lively parts of old New Orleans, Levee Street, sketch by J. Dallas. The levee, a low embankment of earth thrown up to prevent the encroachment of the river during high water, was the landing place and market for the great variety of products brought into the city and shipped abroad; it also afforded "an elegant walk," which, a contemporary writer observed, "should be paved with flat stone." Barges, flatboats, and keelboats in great numbers discharged their car-

4

goes of upriver products. When the Mississippi fell and these boats were stranded on dry land, they were generally broken up for lumber to be used for building or firewood. Often the flatboats were later converted into stores, taverns, and boardinghouses, and even places of amusement. *From* Emerson's Magazine and Putnam's Monthly, *October, 1857*

5 Model of the *New Orleans,* the first Mississippi steamboat, in the Campus Martius Steamboat Museum, Marietta, Ohio. It was constructed from plans by Robert G. C. Fee, naval architect. There had been great excitement at the New Orleans riverfront on January 10, 1812. The long awaited steamboat was coming! The waterfront was crowded with the curious; even the territorial legislature had been recessed so that its members could see for themselves this new wonder that Governor Claiborne claimed would soon make New Orleans one of the great cities of the world. At last, with a cloud of smoke pouring from her chimney and with her paddle wheels kicking up a spray of water, the *New Orleans,* named for her home port, rounded to and headed for the landing. The crowd gaped as the strange vessel was being moored. The *New Orleans* was beautifully designed and finished, a striking contrast to the rough flatboats lining the low levee. Painted sky blue, she appeared to an eyewitness "as long as a frigate." Indeed, her 148-foot length and 20-foot beam, her bowsprit and her two masts with their sails furled, and her long sleek cabins outlined by portholes were in the best maritime tradition; only the stack, paddle wheels, and the visible parts of the engine marked this boat as something out of the ordinary.

The *New Orleans* had cost her owners—the Mississippi Steamboat Navigation Company, a group that included Robert Fulton, Robert Livingston, and Nicholas Roosevelt—$38,000 to build. Fulton had induced Roosevelt, an inventor and skilled mechanical engineer, to superintend her construction in Pittsburgh, and Roosevelt commanded the vessel on her first,

thrilling voyage. Actually, the *New Orleans* had started on her epochal trip on September 27, 1811, 3½ months before, but there had been numerous delays because of low water, and, of all things, the repeated shocks of the New Madrid earthquake, which had caused floods, changed the course of the Mississippi, and made navigation extremely difficult. The running time for the 2,000-mile trip from Pittsburgh to New Orleans was 259 hours, or about 8 miles per hour, which confirmed the hopes of her owners that the new steamboat would do well in her trade between New Orleans and Natchez.

Unfortunately, no picture of the first *New Orleans* has come down to us but from descriptions and pictures of other boats that Fulton built on the Hudson, it has been possible to reconstruct this fairly accurate model. *Photo by S. Durwood Hoag*

6 Steamboating didn't exactly mushroom overnight after the first boat had come to New Orleans. The strangling Fulton-Livingston monopoly and many problems in boat design and building had to be overcome. But by 1820 the monopoly was dead, and soon American know-how provided faster and more practical boats adapted to the streams they would navigate. Hulls were made shallower, with boilers and engines on the main deck, and a second deck was added for passengers. Engines used stationary horizontal cylinders with oscillating pitmans, a revolutionary design that became characteristic of Mississippi steamboats. Such a boat was the *Washington,* built in 1825 at Cincinnati. She ran until 1831 when she was destroyed by fire in New Orleans. *Courtesy Captain Frederick Way, Jr.*

7 The first steamship in the coast trade between New York and New Orleans was the *Robert Fulton,* sketched here by Eric Heyl. A wood-hulled vessel 158 feet long and of 702 tons displacement, she had copper boilers and 24-foot paddles (also sails to help out when the wind was right). The *Robert Fulton* was

5

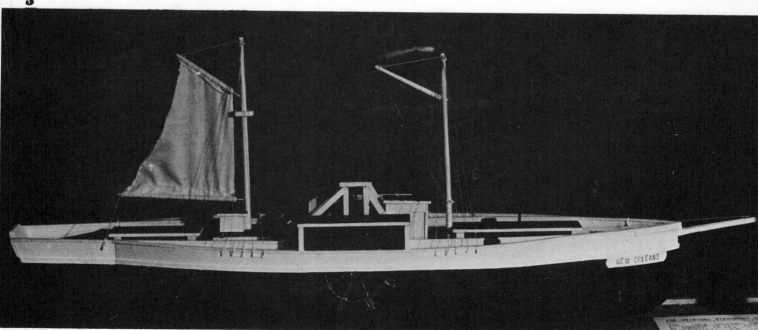

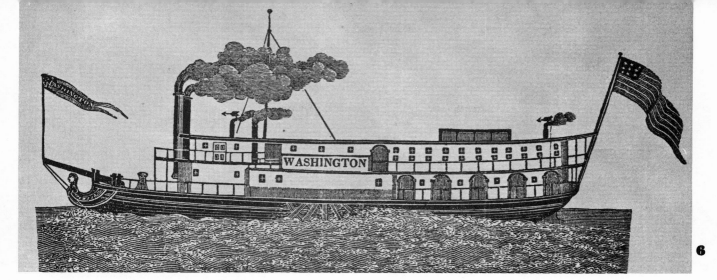

6

7

8

9

the first steamer to be constructed in the United States especially for the high seas. She arrived in New Orleans in May, 1820, and continued in the trade for several years thereafter. *From* Early American Steamers

8 A steamboat of the 1830s, engraving by James Andrews, from a sketch by David Stevenson, 1838. Steamboat builders, mostly on the Ohio River from Louisville to Pittsburgh, could scarcely keep up with the ever-increasing demands for boats. In the decade between 1830 and 1840, 729 steamboats were built. These craft, bringing their cargoes to New Orleans, were responsible for the emergence of New Orleans as one of the great ports of the world.

9 The *New York*, 1837, sketch by Eric Heyl. Charles Morgan, long identified with the coastwise steamship trade, put the *New York* in service between New Orleans and Galveston in 1839. The *New York* was a 365-ton vessel 160′6″ long, 22′6″ wide, and 10′6″ deep, and she was propelled by both steam and sail power. She ran out of New Orleans for several years. In September, 1846, in a hurricane out of Galveston, she foundered with a loss of seventeen lives. *From* Early American Steamers

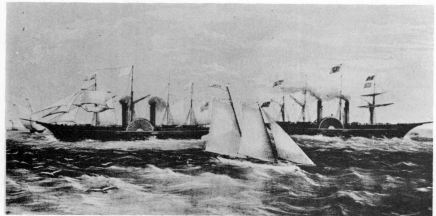

10

10 11 The steamship *Ohio*, with her sister ship *Georgia*. The *Ohio*, of the U.S. Mail Steamship Company, started operations between New York and New Orleans in 1849. At that time she was the largest steamship afloat (2,434 tons, 267′ long, 46′ beam, 29′ depth, 2,700 horsepower engines). The *Ohio* had cost nearly $450,000 to build, and on her maiden voyage the *Daily Picayune* commented: "The departure of the Steamship 'Ohio' last evening was viewed by great numbers of our citizens who had congregated on the levee to witness the event. As she moved majestically down the river, she presented a beautiful appearance, her deck being crowded with people and flags floating from each of her masts." These two boats are advertised at the right. *Courtesy Library of Congress*

12 *The Levee—Third Municipality, New Orleans,* 1854. J. Dallas, whose sketch this is, wrote in that year:

> The levee of the third municipality . . . is remarkable at certain seasons of the year for the receipt of immense quantities of agricultural produce from all parts of the Mississippi valley. From morn-

11

ing until night there is heard the busy hum of labor, voices of every tongue, people of every nation, boxes and bundles, pork and bananas, hams and pineapples, mules and beautiful women, children and old men, Yankees and border-ruffians, Indians and Dutchmen, negroes and molasses, all huddled together in Babel-like confusion, presenting a picture of life and of abundance no where else to be seen in the world.

12

13

13 Steamboats were constructed of wood and carried highly flammable cargoes, thus fire was a constant hazard. During the steam age, there were a number of steamboat fires at the levee. Since the boats were generally moored close to each other, a fire on one would ignite those around her, generally with dire results. This sketch shows the burning of the steamer John Swasey. *From* The Illustrated News, *March 19, 1853*

14 The most frightful steamboat explosion ever to take place at the levee was that of the *Louisiana*, on November 15, 1849. Eighty-six people lost their lives with scores more injured; two boats moored beside the *Louisiana* were also destroyed. A piece of heavy iron was propelled five blocks away; another piece of metal cut a mule in two. The *Louisiana* sank in ten minutes, carrying some trapped passengers to the bottom of the river. *From* Lloyd's Steamboat Directory, *1856*

14

15

15 Steamboat designer-builders at this point had begun to concentrate their efforts above the waterline. With great resourcefulness, they evolved a new architectural form, combining the great, ugly, bulky paddle boxes, towering chimneys, and sprawling superstructure into a graceful vessel that seemed to rest securely on the water rather than tower awkwardly above it. By 1850, the Mississippi River steamboat had reached the apex of design, and no important changes took place after that, except that builders in the 1870s and 1880s made some of their boats bigger and generally yielded to the popular taste that marked the era,

16

17

an exuberance of gingerbread decoration. Between 1840 and 1880, more than 4,800 boats were turned out, and by the end of the steam age more than 6,000 steamboats had plied the rivers. Seen here is a typical pre-Civil War Mississippi steamboat, the *Peytona*, on the Louisville and New Orleans trade, 1859–1863. *From* Harper's Weekly, *March 10, 1860*

16 A busy port with a great future—*New Orleans from the Lower Cotton Press*, lithograph by D. W. Moody from sketches by J. W. Hill & Smith, 1852.

17 One of the greatest boons conferred upon the ocean trade of the city was the steam towboat, one of which, the *Star*, is shown towing a sailing vessel. Since New Orleans is situated more than a hundred miles by river from the Gulf of Mexico, sailing ships—which carried most of the city's foreign trade until the advent of steam-driven ocean vessels—had to make their way slowly upstream by wind power, with a great loss of time. These powerful steam towboats could pull several sailing vessels upriver in a few hours. The tall ladder between the stacks of the *Star* was used by a lookout to spot the masts of approaching vessels at the mouth of the river when the weather was foggy. From a print dated 1856. *Courtesy Smithsonian Institution, Washington, D.C.*

18 By the time war clouds were settling over the Crescent City, New Orleans was the greatest city in the South and West—unique, individual, wealthy. In 1859–1860 alone, there were four thousand steamboat arrivals in New Orleans. Her wharves swarmed with sailing vessels and oceangoing ships from all parts of the globe. Just her river trade for the period was a phenomenal $289 million; her ocean commerce was more than $183 million. The view is of steamboats at the New Orleans levee, ca. 1859. *Courtesy Captain Fred Way, Jr.*

18

19 Perhaps the best of all the pictures of steamboats at the New Orleans levee was painted in 1853 by Hyppolyte Sebron, a French artist, who, better than any artist before or after him, captured the atmosphere of the New Orleans riverfront in the heyday of the floating palaces. The time is about 5 o'clock on a winter evening when many of the boats have pulled away from the docks, bound upstream. Here we see the *Grand Turk*, black smoke pouring from her stacks, already in midstream. The *Gipsy*, her boilers cold, is being unloaded, and three steamers in the background and the loaded docks bear witness to the large trade. *Courtesy Tulane University*

19

20   **21**

A. CARD.

Reports having been circulated that steamer R. E. LEE, leaving for Louisville on the 30th June, is going out for a race, such reports are not true, and the traveling community are assured that every attention will be given to the safety and comfort of passengers.

The running and management of the Lee will in no manner be affected by the departure o other boats.

Je19—otf2dp   JOHN W. CANNON, Master

22

A CARD TO THE PUBLIC.

Being satisfied that the steamer NATCHEZ has a reputation of being fast, I take this method of informing the public that the reports of the Natchez leaving here next Thursday, the 30th inst:, intending racing, are not true.

All passengers and shippers can rest assured that the Natchez will not race with any boat that may leave here on the same day with her. All business entrusted to my care, either in freight or passengers, will have the best attention.   T. P. LEATHERS,

Je25— 5t2dp   Master Steamer Natchez.

21 *The Great Mississippi Steamboat Race*, lithograph by Currier & Ives. "De *Lee* and de *Natchez* had a race. De *Lee* t'rowed water in de *Natchez* face." One of the Leathers's boats provided one of the most exciting chapters in New Orleans river history in July, 1870. This was the famous race between the *Rob't E. Lee* and the *Natchez*, a duel between two river personalities who had been onetime partners, but who now hated each other. Captain John W. Cannon had had the *Lee* built in 1866 and set about making records in his New Orleans trade. In 1869, Leathers had the sixth *Natchez* built, no doubt with an eye on beating the *Lee*. In June, 1870, he took the *Natchez* on a fast trip to St. Louis, beating the record of the *J. M. White*, which had stood for twenty-five years, by an hour and twelve minutes. This precipitated the race from New Orleans to St. Louis, although both Cannon and Leathers disclaimed that their boats were racing and published "cards" in the daily papers to that effect. Cannon set out in earnest to beat the *Natchez*. He stripped his *Lee* down, took no passengers, and arranged for refueling in midstream. Leathers, supremely confident that his boat could beat the *Lee*, took on freight and passengers and made no particular preparations. The results were disastrous for the *Natchez*—the *Lee* broke the New Orleans–St. Louis record, and her speed of three days, eighteen hours, and thirteen minutes was never bettered by a steamboat.

22 Captain Cannon's and Captain Leathers's cards, published in the *Daily Picayune* on the day of the race.

23 Leathers's seventh and last *Natchez*, probably his finest steamer, was built in 1879 at Cincinnati. She was 307 feet long with a 44-foot beam, and her waterwheels were 44 feet in diameter. Her stacks towered 119 feet 6 inches above the waterline, and she was propelled by engines with 34-inch cylinders powered by eight boilers. Her gorgeously equipped cabin was lighted by some hundred painted transom lights depicting Indian chiefs. She ran between New Orleans and Natchez in the early 1880s, but the old captain had to lay her up because of slack times, and she sank in 1887. She is seen here at the wharf in New Orleans, ca. 1883.

20 The Mississippi spawned some heroic figures. One of these was Captain Thomas Paul Leathers, whose career on the river spanned half a century. Starting in the late 1830s, Leathers began to build and operate steamboats. By 1845, he built the *Natchez*, the first of seven fine boats by that name, each one a little bigger and faster than its predecessor. Leathers's boats ran on fixed schedules, a fact that earned him and his partner, Captain Truman Holmes, a profitable mail contract. Leathers was a familiar figure in New Orleans. He lived in a house still standing on Carondelet and Josephine streets. He died after being run down by a "scorcher," a reckless bicycle rider in 1896. *From a portrait in the possession of his family*

23

Captain Eads's Jetties Save
the Port

24 At the mouth of the Mississippi River. The illustration is from a lithograph made by Duke Paul von Würtemburg who visited America from 1822 to 1824. A steam towboat tows a sailing vessel to New Orleans; another sailboat is on its way to the Gulf. The tower, which was a lighthouse and pilot lookout, was built above a blockhouse, and the scattered houses of a village, a wretched village known as the Balize, are in the background. A place with an evil reputation, it was the headquarters of the pilots who boarded incoming ships for the journey upriver. The Balize has long since disappeared. *Howard-Tilton Memorial Library, Tulane University*

24

25 The bars at the mouth of the Mississippi had caused trouble to shipping from the earliest days. Accumulations of silt at the river's mouth had rendered the situation critical by reason of neglect during the Civil War. By the 1870s when ships were being built larger, some vessels would be held up for days and even weeks, caught on a bar, thus holding up other ships. Clearly something had to be done—New

Orleans had dropped from second port to eleventh in the nation. Army engineers proposed to build a canal from a point in the river near Fort St. Philip to Breton Sound to eliminate the trouble. Captain James Buchanan Eads, a self-taught engineer who had constructed river ironclads for the Union during the Civil War in record time, and then built the giant steel arch bridge across the Mississippi at St. Louis, visited the mouth of the river with a congressional delegation, and after studying the situation proclaimed that the proper way to open the river for commerce was by building parallel dikes, or jetties, at the mouths of the passes. This evoked a storm of controversy, and when Eads took a proposal to Congress offering to produce and maintain a twenty-eight-foot channel at the mouth of the Mississippi for $10 million if he succeeded (for nothing if he failed), he was opposed by the army engineers and by New Orleans people, who, fearing that the jetties would cause floods, sent ex-Governor Paul O. Hebert and Professor C. G. Forshey, both West Pointers, to fight Eads's proposal. Eads felt that he was on solid ground: by constructing parallel jetties to be built southward from the mouth of the pass, thus constricting the channel and causing the stream to flow faster, the silt carried by the river would not settle but would be carried out into the Gulf, and the faster the current, the deeper the stream would scour its own channel. After much opposition and long debate, Eads was given a contract to build a jetty at South Pass for $5,250,000 and a $100,000 maintenance fee for twenty years. Work started in June, 1875, and four years later, after Herculean labor

by Eads's men, the middle of the channel measured thirty feet—and the bar had been swept into the Gulf. New Orleans regained its proper place as a world port, and within twenty years the army engineers were constructing another jetty themselves at Southwest Pass. The sketches seen here, by J. O. Davidson, are: 1. Port Eads lighthouse; 2. Bird's-eye view of the jetties. 3. Dredging steamer *G. W. R. Bayley;* 4. Dredging apparatus of *G. W. R. Bayley;* 5. Showing former and present Channel; 6. Seaward end of jetties; 7. Mattress-making; 8. Section of jetty 11,800 feet at sea; 9. Section of jetty; 10. Channel made by current; 11. Concrete works; 12. Inside willow sand barriers; and 13. View within the jetties. *From* Harper's Weekly, *December 8, 1883*

26 Eads's plan to constrict the channel of the river at South Pass called for making two artificial banks seven hundred feet apart and two miles long. Weaving mattresses consisting of stout timbers for supports and willow saplings for bulk, Eads's men towed these into position and sank them with stones, after anchoring them to piles that had been previously driven. These mattresses were laid layer on layer, each layer five feet narrower than the one below it, and very soon the swirling sand carried by the river embedded itself in the willows making a solid bank. After the last mattresses were placed, the top was capped with great stones and eventually with a firm stone paving, to protect the surface from storms. Sketches by Frank H. Taylor. *From* Harper's Weekly, *March 2, 1878*

27

28

27 James Buchanan Eads (1820–1887), who opened the Mississippi's mouth and brought shipping back to New Orleans. To him the city owes an incalculable debt for his perseverance in the face of local opposition, and for his great genius as a civil engineer in building the first workable ship pass, the foundation of New Orleans's greatness as a modern world port.

28 Success at last! *Entrance to Eads Jetties, Mouth of the Mississippi River*, sketch by C. Upham. In the first year after the completion of South Pass jetties, 840 ships had used the facility. *From* Frank Leslie's Illustrated Newspaper, *December 20, 1884*

A Second and Last Breath for Steamboats

29 The Civil War caused an almost complete disruption of commercial steamboat traffic on the Mississippi. When it was over, the finest of the New Orleans packets—which had holed up in tributary streams like the Yazoo—were gone forever, destroyed by the Confederates themselves to avoid capture, or sunk in conflict. But this was not the death knell of steamboating.

In a few years bigger and better boats like the *Ruth, Richmond, Rob't E. Lee, Natchez,* and *Great Republic* made their appearance, and for a long time the steamboats seemed to have caught their second breath. In this watercolor by Boyd Cruise, the *Richmond* is seen passing New Orleans, 1867.

29

30 Many post–Civil War steamers were very large. This one, the *Henry Frank,* is shown about to unload her prodigious cargo of 9,226 bales of cotton at the New Orleans levee on April 2, 1881, a record never exceeded. Woodcut by E. M. Bidwell. *From* Frank Leslie's Illustrated Newspaper, *April 30, 1881*

31 Hundreds of licensed draymen whipped up their teams to carry the flood of merchandise brought down by the steamboats. Their "floats," or springless drays, were once a common sight on the downtown streets of the city. This picture of a cotton float was made about 1890.

32

33

32 The levee was a lively place almost any time of day. This sketch made at the landing place of the steamboat *Bart Able* shows, besides the usual loafers, women food sellers, a banana peddler, a blind beggar and his little girl, and a medicine pitchman hawking his wares, ca. 1875.

33 The open wharves on the levee were a constant temptation to thieves who would paddle under them in skiffs and bore holes into the bottom of barrels stored there, or pilfer from cargo like the cotton thieves shown in this sketch by J. Wells Champney. *From* Scribner's Monthly, *December, 1873*

34 Joseph Horton sketched this scene for *Frank Leslie's Illustrated Newspaper* in 1883. More than thirty steamboats were at the New Orleans levee, literally "a

34

forest of sooty cylinders." Hogsheads of sugar, hundreds of bales of cotton, and large quantities of assorted merchandise were being unloaded on the uncovered wharfs by an army of laborers.

35 New Orleans in 1885, from a sketch by Charles Graham. Every type of contemporary vessel imaginable can be seen.

36 A busy day on the New Orleans docks in 1895. The steamboats were then still carrying an immense amount of freight to New Orleans, and this photograph shows the *Natchez,* the *Garland,* and the *Ouachita,* which is discharging her cargo of cotton. *Courtesy Ray Samuel*

37

37 One of the most picturesque sections of the New Orleans levee was the landing place of the luggers, which brought oysters from the lower coast of Louisiana to the city. *Courtesy Library of Congress*

38 A section of steamboat advertisements from the *Daily Picayune* of March 18, 1881. Twenty-seven boats are advertised, and one could travel on them to Cincinnati, Louisville, Memphis, Vicksburg, Natchez, Helena, and up the Tensas, Ouachita, and the Red and Bayou Lafourche. This reflected only a temporary postwar spurt; the railroads were slowly strangling the steamboats. In the 1890s, more and more boats went to the bank, never to return; in 1909, there no longer existed any St. Louis–Memphis–New Orleans packet lines, and steamboating was dying fast.

38

39

41

39 One of the best known steamboat agents was the firm of Lord & McPeake, 122 Gravier Street, which was in business from about 1869 to 1908. The white-bearded man to the right was an old-time steamboat pilot, Captain Charles H. Fearing, who had been aboard more than 125 Red and Mississippi River steamboats and who once piloted the *Little Fleta* in the perilous journey in the open Gulf between New Orleans and the Rio Grande, a trip which took twenty-seven days. *Courtesy Mrs. Florence Burns*

40 On the New Orleans waterfront, ca. 1890. A steamboat clerk reads a message handed him; the wagon of Bernard Klotz & Co. is delivering supplies; and laborers sit about waiting for a job, while some examine the wares of a "pie wagon." The building in the background is the sugar refinery adjoining the L & N railroad station. *Courtesy Mrs. Samuel Wilson, Jr.*

40

41 Many of the larger steamboats were fitted out with remarkable luxury. These "floating palaces" had elaborate chandeliers, handsomely carved furniture, paintings, Brussels carpets, and often that ultimate of Victorian elegance, a grand piano. This is a glimpse of the cabin of the *Grand Republic*, done in the Gothic style. The photograph shows a social gathering.

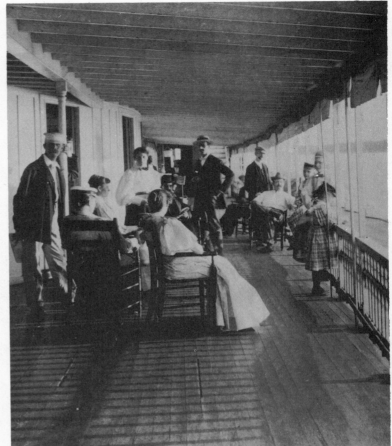

44

44 A group of passengers on the deck of a steamboat, about 1890. The boats seldom traveled more than fifteen miles an hour, and the passengers whiled away the time by reading or simply sitting on the deck and watching the scenery. *Courtesy Library of Congress*

43

42 Steamboat dining tables on the larger boats were beautifully set with massive silverware and the finest of china, often specially designed for the boat. Elaborately folded napkins and knives and forks set in intricate balanced patterns were the pride of the steward of the *City of Monroe*, whose dinner tables are shown here. The *City of Monroe* ran from 1887 to 1896.

43 This was the grand "saloon" of the Anchor Line-steamboat *City of Baton Rouge*, which ran between New Orleans and St. Louis from 1881 to 1890. Commanded by Captain Horace Bixby, who had instructed Mark Twain in piloting many years before, this boat carried the famous author on a voyage to New Orleans in 1882. This photograph was taken from the "gentlemen's cabin." A bar and a clerk's office flank this huge cast-iron stove and spittoons, a necessary adjunct of the times. The carpeted "ladies' cabin" with its dining-room tables is aft.

45 Captain LeVerrier Cooley, one of the last of the old-time New Orleans steamboatmen. Born in 1855, he "learned" the river in the 1870s and trod the decks of steamboats until he died on December 19, 1931. He ran the *Tensas* (which carried a big circular saw swung between her chimneys with a "10" painted on it) in the 1880s; the *Ouachita* in the 1890s; the sturdy *America* in the first two decades of the 1900s; and his last, the "little" *Ouachita*, in the 1920s. Captain Cooley ran his boats up the Ouachita and Black rivers and carried tremendous quantities of cotton to market almost until the end. He once estimated that he had handled eight hundred thousand bales of cotton on the *America* alone, besides large quantities of other cargo.

46 Captain Cooley's *America*, which he loved best of all, loading cotton seed. Pilots on the lower river never tried to bring the steamboats alongside the bank. They took advantage of the sloping, sandy shore and just slid the saucer-shallow hull aground. The boat's tremendous power would get her off as the great paddle threw water under her bottom and washed her loose.

47 When Captain Cooley died, the *America*'s huge bell, which had tapped departure time for so many years, was used as a monument over his grave in Métairie Cemetery in New Orleans—a fitting marker for a steamboatman and for the end of an era.

48

48 The riverfront has always fascinated New Orleanians and visitors to the Crescent City. This photograph, made in 1906, was titled "Sunday on the Levee." The *America,* one of the last of the big packets, is moored before the smaller *Red River,* as a crowd of shirt-waisted ladies and derby-topped men walk past cotton bales on a Sunday afternoon stroll. *Courtesy Library of Congress*

49 The old and new, ca. 1903. This photograph shows the old open wooden wharves and the new steel-cov-

ered docks that were beginning to be constructed on the New Orleans levee in the early 1900s. The board of commissioners of the port of New Orleans, organized in 1896, had taken over the operation of the city's docks in 1901 at the expiration of a contract with private operators and began building the first of the commodious publicly owned dock facilities, which, with the addition of cotton and grain warehouses, have helped make New Orleans the second port of the nation. *Photo by C. Milo Williams*

49

50

50 In October, 1862, after the fall of New Orleans, the Cromwell, New York and New Orleans Steamship Line began operations. They ran their *George Washington, George Cromwell, New Orleans, Knickerbocker,* and *Hudson,* among other vessels. In 1880, the line added the *Louisiana,* seen here, an iron-hulled vessel with a pair of compound beam engines. The *Louisiana* was the fastest vessel in the trade and for many years held the New York–New Orleans speed record.

51

51 New Orleans's steamship lines direct to Europe were run by English, French, and German shipping interests who vied for the cotton trade. Among them was the Harrison Line of Liverpool. This line, which has linked New Orleans with English ports for more than a century, started when the *Fire Queen,* an ex–Civil War blockade runner, arrived at the Crescent City on August 25, 1866. From that time on, the same family, the LeBlancs, have represented the Harrison Line in New Orleans. Seen here is a Harrison Line ship, the *Governor,* at the New Orleans wharf about 1883. Note the mast and sails.

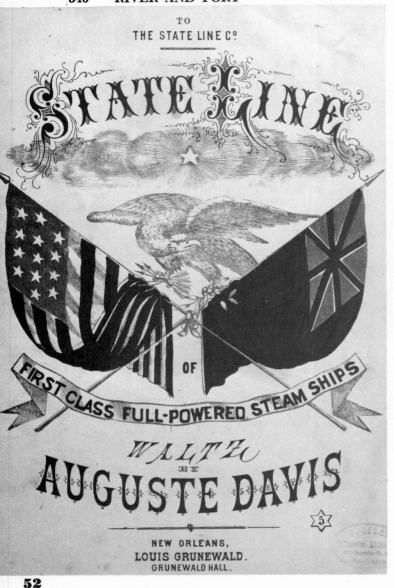

52

53

53 The twentieth century saw the emergence of new lines and the combinations of existing ones. In 1902, the Cromwell Line was purchased by the Morgan Line (Southern Pacific Company), which continued operations between New York and New Orleans until World War II when their ships were sold to the navy. Familiar to many New Orleanians were the *Momus*, the *Creole*, and in later years, the crack *Dixie*. Toward the end of their operations, the company also ran the freight vessels *El Almirante*, *El Capitan*, *El Isleo*, *El Estero*, and *El Lago*. The steamer *Creole* (1907–1934) in the photograph is docking at the New Orleans wharf.

52 Another pioneer steamship line, which ran the *State of Louisiana*, the *State of Minnesota*, and the *State of Alabama* between English ports and New Orleans from 1873 to 1891, had a waltz written for it. This piece, published by Louis Grunewald about 1877, was composed by Auguste Davis, who called it, appropriately, "State Line Waltz."

54 The 8,188-ton *Dixie* was put into passenger-freight service between New York and New Orleans in 1928 by Southern Pacific. The line advertised "One Hundred Golden Hours at Sea," and the *Dixie* (at a cost of $2,400,000) became a favorite with New Orleans travelers. The *Dixie* was the last of the New York–New Orleans passenger liners. She was sold to the United States Navy and renamed *Alcor* in the 1940s. *Photo William B. Taylor Collection. Courtesy Mariners Museum, Newport News, Virginia*

54

55

57

55 Passengers aboard the S.S. *Momus*, built in 1906 for the New York–New Orleans service, were photographed as the ship was about to leave New Orleans, probably about 1907. Most of the men wore derbies, and only two women passengers are in view, one of whom turned away from the camera. *Courtesy New Orleans Public Library*

56 From 1947 until 1969, when they were laid up because they were no longer economical to operate, the three sleek combination passenger-cargo ships of the Delta Line—*Del Norte, Del Mar,* and *Del Sud*—made trips from New Orleans every two weeks for the east coast of South America, with calls at the Caribbean Islands. The *Del Sud,* seen here, could carry 119 passengers. The Delta Steamship Lines of New Orleans was founded by local capitalists in 1919 as the Mississippi Shipping Company. Its ships regularly call at South American and West African ports. *Photo by Eric W. Johnson, Jr.*

57 Today the Delta Line operates fourteen American-flag cargo liners. Shown here is the *Delta Brasil,* built in 1968, an ultramodern automated vessel, one of the five put in recent service. *Photo by C. F. Weber Photography, Inc.*

The Port Today

58 Import and export. The powerful towboat to the right has thirty barges in tow. These vessels have supplanted the steamboats of yesterday and carry tremendous cargoes up and down the Mississippi, Ohio, and Missouri rivers. The sleek cargo ship beside it is typical of the ships of more than forty nations that visit the port each year. *Photo by Angelo J. Mariano. Courtesy Board of Commissioners, Port of New Orleans*

58

56

59

60

59 The port of New Orleans, second in the United States after New York, handled imports and exports valued at nearly $2,630,000,000 during 1969 (United States Department of Commerce figures). Despite a crippling two-month waterfront strike, 4,227 ships arrived and were serviced along the nine miles of wharves operated by the board of port commissioners. The principal commodity handled by the port was grain, representing about 10 percent of the quantity exported by the nation. Shown in this aerial photograph (viewed from the south) are the cotton warehouse (foreground), the public grain elevators, and the new Nashville Avenue wharves. The Huey P. Long Bridge is in the distance; Audubon Park is at the sharp turn to the left; the Garden District is to the right, out of the picture. *Photo by S. R. Sutton. Courtesy Board of Commissioners, Port of New Orleans*

60 The Industrial Canal. This recent air view shows the development of industries along the canal and the junction with the Mississippi River–Gulf outlet (*right center*). The Industrial Canal locks, after nearly half a century of use, are becoming obsolete, and a new and larger lock is now in the planning stage. Southwest, toward the Garden District, is the Mississippi River Bridge, not seen here. The Vieux Carré is about halfway between the mouth of the Canal and the bridge. The triangular shape jutting into Lake Pontchartrain at the top of the picture is the New Orleans Airport. Left of that is Louisiana State University. *Photo by S. R. Sutton. Courtesy Board of Commissioners, Port of New Orleans*

61 The old dream of connecting the river with the lake came to fruition when the Inner Harbor and Industrial Canal was completed in April, 1921. Built at a cost of $19 million, the canal provided industrial sites on deep water, and its great value to the city, for years unappreciated, did not become apparent, for many years after its completion. The scene is dedication day, May 5, 1921.

62

62 This view of the three government warehouses erected in 1917 at the head of the Industrial Canal brings to mind the heroic efforts of Sigmund Odenheimer in establishing an international trade exhibition in New Orleans. One of the warehouses was turned over to a group of New Orleanians to start a New World counterpart of the Leipzig fair. With great energy and much of his own money, Mr. Odenheimer produced an exhibition that covered 16,700 square feet of floor space on which 200 exhibitors displayed the principal economic resources of many states and several foreign countries. For some years, this trade mart was highly successful, but unfortunately, the Great Depression put an end to the venture and it was forced to close in 1931.

61

LOCKS at INDUSTRIAL CANAL, NEW ORLEANS, LA.
LINKING THE MISSISSIPPI RIVER WITH LAKE PONCHATRAIN
May 5th 1923

63

63 The opening of the Mississippi River Bridge to traffic in April, 1958, was the fulfillment of an age-long dream. It put the largely underdeveloped west bank within minutes of the section of downtown New Orleans that lay over the river (and eventually created some monumental traffic jams after the toll was re-moved). Built at a cost of $65 million, this bridge is the nation's longest cantilever bridge. The Mississippi River Bridge is seen here from the eastern side. *Photo by W. L. D'Aquin. Courtesy Times-Picayune*

64 65 One of the marvels of modern industrial New

64

65

Orleans is the Avondale Shipyards located 1½ miles upriver from the port. This concern, under the dynamic leadership of Henry Zac Carter, is the largest industrial manufacturing employer in Louisiana with approximately ten thousand employees. A radically new method of ship construction, virtually a "ship-building machine," is used for the mass construction of destroyer escorts, twenty-seven of which are now under contract. This starts with the hull being assembled in an inverted position, placed in a series of massive turning rings where it is rotated into an upright position, bow, stern, and superstructure added, and the completed vessel launched sideways into the Mississippi. In 1971, the Avondale yards are constructing, besides other work, eleven LASH cargo liners.

66 Another large industry is the Chalmette Works of Kaiser Aluminum & Chemical Corporation, the third largest aluminum reduction plant in the United States,

66

located adjacent to the Mississippi River about seven miles southeast of New Orleans. The plant is a vital part of the economy of the greater New Orleans area, employing about twenty-six hundred with an annual payroll of about $27 million. *Courtesy Kaiser Aluminum & Chemical Corporation*

67 An entirely new concept of cargo handling at New Orleans is CENTROPORT. This $395 million project will provide a spacious industrial complex for port, manufacturing, and distribution facilities in lower New Orleans on the Mississippi River–Gulf outlet and free the banks of the Mississippi of the unsightly steel sheds presently in use for development of choice high-rise riverfront apartments, hotels, tourist terminals, riverfront parks, etc. In 1970, work on CENTRO-PORT had commenced. In the foreground of this artist's conception, drawn from plans of the project, is the Mississippi River–Gulf outlet, to the left the Inner

Harbor Canal, connecting with the Misssissippi (not seen here), and in the background is Lake Pontchartrain with the buildings and wharves of CENTROPORT in the foreground. *Courtesy Board of Commissioners, Port of New Orleans*

68 Just off the Mississippi is the Rivergate, New Orleans's international exhibition facility, which cost more than $13 million. It has an auditorium with a seating capacity of 17,666 persons and a large underground garage. *Courtesy City of New Orleans*

69 The handsome thirty-three-story International Trade Mart Building, designed by Edward Durrell Stone, is a New Orleans riverfront landmark. This photograph was made from the deck of the sightseeing steamer *President*. *Courtesy Chamber of Commerce of the New Orleans Area*

67

68

69

70

70 With the International Trade Mart Building in the background to line it up, the Louisiana Superdome, popularly known as the Domed Stadium, will rise on a fifty-five-acre site in the heart of downtown New Orleans. Test piles were driven in mid-1970 and demolition work was begun toward the end of that year. The Superdome will have a capacity for 84,777 spectators and can be used for football, baseball, ice hockey, arena events, conventions, and exhibitions. The building will have a clear span of 680 feet and a ceiling height of 280 feet. It will be cooled by ten thousand tons of air-conditioning equipment. Comple-

tion is scheduled for 1973. *Photo by Frank Lotz Miller. Courtesy Louisiana Stadium and Exposition District*

71 An aerial view of New Orleans made over the Mississippi River. In the foreground is the International Trade Mart Building; Canal Street stretches to its right; and most of the city's largest buildings are in the triangle between Poydras Street (the wide street to the left) and Canal Street. *Courtesy Chamber of Commerce of the New Orleans Area*

71

1 The space age came to New Orleans in the fall of 1961 when the long-idle nine-hundred-acre Michoud plant fifteen miles east of downtown New Orleans became the National Aeronautics and Space Administration's Michoud assembly facility. Soon thousands of employees began the fabrication of Saturn 1 booster rockets and the gigantic Saturn V boosters—at plants operated by the Chrysler Corporation Space Division, the Boeing Company Launch System Branch, Service Technology Corporation, and Mason-Rust—as part of a tremendous effort by the United States to build rockets powerful enough to put men on the moon. Seen here is the interior of the NASA plant, showing an SA–8 booster under construction in 1963. *Courtesy City of New Orleans*

2 A Saturn V booster made by Boeing at Michoud leaving the plant. As tall as a 12-story building, this first-stage rocket's tanks held 534,000 gallons of propellant, which were used up in 2½ minutes of flight. The booster developed 7½ million pounds of thrust (160 million horsepower), and its job was to lift the Apollo/Saturn V rocket 38 miles above the earth. It then moved at 6,000 miles per hour when it separated and the second stage fired to continue to drive the payload into orbit. *Courtesy Boeing Company*

3 This photograph, made December 21, 1968, at Cape Kennedy, shows the Apollo 8 carrying Astronauts Frank Borman, James Lovell, and William Anders at lift-off. This was the first successful orbiting of the moon, at Christmastime, 1968. The same type of New Orleans–made NASA-Boeing booster carried Apollo 11 and its astronauts Neil Armstrong, Edwin E. Aldrin, Jr., and Michael Collins to the moon on July 20, 1969, when Armstrong and Aldrin became the first humans to trod the dusty soil of earth's satellite. *Courtesy National Aeronautics and Space Administration*

4

4 The Crescent City today. Bienville's little Nouvelle-Orléans occupies a tiny portion of this vast mosaic of avenues, streets, and buildings of modern New Orleans. And Ole Man River, snaking his majestic way past the city, just keeps "rollin' along." *Photo by S. R. Sutton. Courtesy Board of Commissioners, Port of New Orleans*

5 Past and present. Former Mayor Schiro gazes at the bronze and granite monument to Bienville, founder of New Orleans. The memorial, with its bronze figures of Bienville, a priest, and an Indian, is the work of New Orleans sculptor Angela Gregory. It was dedicated April 24, 1955. *Photo by Frank H. Methe*

5

BIBLIOGRAPHY

Alwes, Berchtold C. "The History of the Louisiana State Lottery." *Louisiana Historical Quarterly*, vol. 27, no. 4 (October 1944).

Asbury, Herbert. *The French Quarter: An Informal History of the New Orleans Underworld*. New York, 1936.

Baldwin, Leland D. *The Keelboat Age on Western Waters*. Pittsburgh, 1941.

Baudier, Roger. *The Catholic Church in Louisiana*. New Orleans, 1939.

Biever, Reverend Albert Hubert, S. J. *The Jesuits in New Orleans and the Mississippi Valley*. New Orleans, 1924.

Blain, Hugh Mercer. *A Near Century of Public Service in New Orleans: The Story of the Origins and Progress of the Gas, Street Railways and Electric Service in New Orleans*. New Orleans, 1927.

Blair, Walter, and Meine, Franklin J. *Mike Fink King of Mississippi Keelboatmen*. New York, 1933.

———, eds. *Half Horse Half Alligator: The Growth of the Mike Fink Legend*. Chicago, 1956.

Blue Book, The. *A List of Madams, Houses of Prostitution and Names of Prostitutes*. New Orleans, n.d.

Brooks, Charles B. *The Siege of New Orleans*. Seattle, 1961.

Butler, Benjamin F. *The Autobiography and Personal Reminiscences of Major-General Benjamin F. Butler*. Boston, 1892.

Cable, George W. *Old Creole Days*. New York, 1897.

Caldwell, Stephen A. *A Banking History of Louisiana*. Baton Rouge, 1935.

Capers, Gerald M. *Occupied City: New Orleans under the Federals 1862–1865*. Lexington, Kentucky, 1965.

Carter, Clarence E., ed. *The Territorial Papers of the United States. The Territory of Orleans, 1803–1812.* Vol. IX. Washington, D.C., 1940.

Carter, Hodding, and Carter, Betty Werlein. *So Great a Good—A History of the Episcopal Church in Louisiana and of Christ Church Cathedral, 1805–1955*. Sewanee, Tennessee, 1955.

Carter, Hodding, ed. *The Past as Prelude: New Orleans 1718–1968*. New Orleans, 1968.

Casey, Powell A. *Louisiana at the Battle of New Orleans*. New Orleans, 1965.

———. *Louisiana in the War of 1812*. Baton Rouge, 1963.

Castellanos, Henry C. *New Orleans as It Was*. New Orleans, 1895.

Caughey, John W. *Bernardo de Gálvez in Louisiana, 1776–1783*. Berkeley, California, 1934.

Chase, John C. *Frenchmen Desire Goodchildren and Other Streets of New Orleans*. New Orleans, 1949.

———. *Louisiana Purchase: An American Story Told in That Most American Form of Expression . . . The Comic Strip*. New Orleans, 1954.

Chase, John C.; Deutsch, Herman B.; Dufour, Charles L.; and Huber, Leonard V. *Citoyens, Progrés et Politique de la Nouvelle Orleans 1889–1964*. New Orleans, 1964.

Christian, Marcus. *Negro Soldiers in the Battle of New Orleans*. New Orleans, 1965.

Clapp, Theodore. *Autobiographical Sketches and Recollections During a Thirty-five Years' Residence in New Orleans*. Boston, 1857.

Clemens, Samuel Langhorne (Mark Twain). *Life on the Mississippi*. Boston, 1883.

Clement, William E. *Over a Half Century of Electric and Gas Industry Development in New Orleans*. New Orleans, 1947.

Code of Honor, Its Rationale and Uses by the Tests of Common Sense and Good Morals with the Effects of Its Preventive Remedies, The. New Orleans, 1883.

Corliss, Carlton J. *Main Line of Mid-America: The Story of the Illinois Central*. New York, 1950.

Crouse, Nellis M. *Lemoyne d'Iberville: Soldier of New France*. Ithaca, New York, 1954.

Cruise, Boyd. *Index to the Louisiana Historical Quarterly*. Compiled and decorated by the author. New Orleans, 1956.

Curtis, Nathaniel Cortland. *New Orleans: Its Old Houses, Shops and Public Buildings*. Philadelphia, 1933.

Dabney, Thomas Ewing. *One Hundred Years: The Story of the Times Picayune from Its Founding to 1940*. Baton Rouge, 1944.

Davis, Edwin Adams. *Louisiana: A Narrative History*. Baton Rouge, 1965.

Deiler J. Hanno. *Die Deutschen Kirchengemeinden im Staate Louisiana*. New Orleans, 1894.

———. *The Settlement of the German Coast of Louisiana and the Creoles of German Descent*. Philadelphia, 1909.

Devol, George H. *Forty Years a Gambler on the Mississippi*. 2d ed. New York, 1926.

Dixon, Richard R. *The Battle on the West Bank*. New Orleans, 1965.

Dorsey, Florence L. *Master of the Mississippi: Henry Shreve and the Conquest of the Mississippi*. Boston, 1941.

Dowler, Dr. Bennet. *Researches upon the Necropolis of New Orleans, with Brief Allusions to Its Vital Arithmetic*. New Orleans, 1850.

Du Pratz, Antoine Simon Le Page. *The History of Louisiana*. 3 vols. Paris, 1758.

Duffy, John. *The Rudolph Matas History of Medicine in Louisiana*. 2 vols. Baton Rouge, 1958 and 1962.

————. *Sword of Pestilence: The New Orleans Yellow Fever Epidemic of 1853.* Baton Rouge, 1966.

Dufour, Charles L. *The Night the War Was Lost.* New York, 1960.

————. *Ten Flags in the Wind: The Story of Louisiana.* New York, 1967.

————, ed. *St. Patrick's of New Orleans 1833–1958: Commemorative Essays for the 125th Anniversary.* New Orleans, 1958.

Dufour, Charles L., and Huber, Leonard V. *If Ever I Cease to Love. One Hundred Years of Rex, 1872–1971.* New Orleans, 1970.

————, eds. *Battle of New Orleans Sesquicentennial Historical Booklets.* (Nine brochures on different phases of the British campaign of 1814–1815.) Published by The Battle of New Orleans 150th Anniversary Committee of Louisiana. New Orleans, 1965.

Dyer, John P. *Tulane: The Biography of a University, 1834–1965.* New York, 1966.

Eads, James Buchanan. *Mouth of the Mississippi Jetty System Explained.* Saint Louis, 1874.

Eller, Admiral E. M.; Morgan, Dr. W. J.; and Basoco, Lieut. R. R. *Sea Power and the Battle of New Orleans.* New Orleans, 1965.

Eskew, Garnett Laidlaw. *The Pageant of the Packets. A Book of American Steamboating.* New York, 1929.

Ficklen, John R. *History of Reconstruction in Louisiana (through 1868).* Baltimore, 1910.

Fortier, Alcée. *A History of Louisiana.* 4 vols. New York, 1904.

Fossier, Albert E. *New Orleans: The Glamour Period 1800–1840.* New Orleans, 1957.

Fremaux, Leon J. *New Orleans Characters.* New Orleans, 1876.

Gayarré, Charles. *History of Louisiana.* 4 vols. 5th ed. New Orleans, 1965.

Gibson, John. "Historical Epitome." *Gibson's Guide and Directory of the State of Louisiana and the Cities of New Orleans and Lafayette.* New Orleans, 1838.

Giraud, Marcel. *Histoire de la Louisiane Française.* 3 vols. Paris, 1953, 1958, 1965.

Gleig, George Robert. *The Campaign of the British Army at Washington and New Orleans in the Years 1814–1815.* London, 1836.

Gottschalk, Louis Moreau. *Notes of a Pianist.* Edited by Jeanne Behrend. New York, 1964.

Gould, Captain E. W. *Fifty Years on the Mississippi or Gould's History of River Navigation.* Saint Louis, 1889.

Green, Laurence. *The Filibuster: The Career of William Walker.* Indianapolis and New York, 1937.

Green, Thomas Marshall. *The Spanish Conspiracy. A Review of Early Spanish Movements in the South-West.* 2d ed. Gloucester, Massachusetts, 1967.

Griffin, Thomas Kurtz. *New Orleans: A Guide to America's Most Interesting City.* New York, 1961.

Hennick, Louis C., and Charlton, E. Harper. *The Streetcars of New Orleans 1831–1965.* New Orleans, 1965.

Heyl, Erik. *Early American Steamers.* 2 vols. Buffalo,
New York, 1953 and 1956.

Higginbotham, Jay. *Fort Maurepas: The Birth of Louisiana.* Mobile, 1968.

History of the New Orleans Police Department: Benefit of the Police Mutual Benevolent Association of New Orleans. New Orleans, 1900.

History of the Proceedings in the City of New Orleans on the Funeral Ceremonies in Honor of Calhoun, Clay and Webster, Which Took Place on Thursday, December 9, 1852. New Orleans, 1853.

Holmes, Jack D. L. *Gayoso: The Life of a Spanish Governor in the Mississippi Valley. 1789–1799.* Baton Rouge, 1965.

Huber, Leonard V. *Advertisements of Lower Mississippi River Steamboats 1812–1920.* West Barrington, Rhode Island, 1959.

————. "The Battle of the Handkerchiefs." *Civil War History,* vol. 8, no. 1 (March 1962).

————. *Beginnings of Steamboat Mail on Lower Mississippi.* State College, Pennsylvania, 1960.

————. *Blockade-run Mail from New Orleans and the Louisiana Relief Committee at Mobile.* State College, Pennsylvania, 1953.

————. "Confederate Mail Packets on the Lower Mississippi." *The American Philatelist,* vol. 69, no. 12 (September 1956).

————. "The Golden Age of Opera, Theatre and the Performing Arts." *New Orleans Magazine,* vol. 3, no. 12 (September, 1969).

————. "Heyday of the Floating Palace." *American Heritage,* vol. 8, no. 6 (October 1957).

————. *Impressions of Girod Street Cemetery and a Plan to Rescue Some of Its Moments.* New Orleans, 1951.

————. "Mardi Gras: The Golden Age." *American Heritage,* vol. 16, no. 2 (February 1965).

————. *New Orleans as It Was in 1814–1815.* New Orleans, 1965.

Huber, Leonard V., and Bernard, Guy F. *To Glorious Immortality: The Rise and Fall of the Girod Street Cemetery.* New Orleans, 1961.

Huber, Leonard V., and Huber, Albert R. *The New Orleans Tomb.* New Orleans, 1956.

Huber, Leonard V. and Wagner, Clarence A. *The Great Mail: A Postal History of New Orleans.* State College, Pennsylvania, 1949.

Huber, Leonard V., and Wilson, Samuel Jr. *Baroness Pontalba's Buildings.* New Orleans, 1964.

Huber, Leonard V.; Wilson, Samuel Jr.; and Taylor, Garland F. *Louisiana Purchase.* New Orleans, 1953.

Hunter, Louis C. *Steamboats on the Western Rivers: An Economic and Technological History.* Cambridge, 1939.

Ingraham, Joseph Holt. *The South-West by a Yankee.* New York, 1835.

Jackson, Joy J. *New Orleans in the Gilded Age: Politics and Urban Progress 1880–1896.* Baton Rouge, 1969.

Jacobs, James Ripley. *Tarnished Warrior: Major-General James Wilkinson.* New York, 1938.

Jewell, Edwin L., ed. *Jewell's Crescent City Illustrated.*

The Commercial, Social, Political and General History of New Orleans, Including Biographical Sketches of Its Distinguished Citizens. New Orleans, 1874.

Kendall, John Smith. *Golden Age of the New Orleans Theatre.* Baton Rouge, 1952.

————. *History of New Orleans,* 3 vols. Chicago, 1922.

King, Grace. *New Orleans: The Place and the People.* New York, 1904.

Kmen, Henry A. *Music in New Orleans: The Formative Years 1791–1841.* Baton Rouge, 1966.

Korn, Bertram Wallace. *Benjamin Levy: New Orleans Printer and Publisher.* Portland, Maine, 1961.

————. *The Early Jews of New Orleans.* Waltham, Massachusetts, 1969.

La Cour, Arthur Burton, and Landry, Stuart Omer. *New Orleans Masquerade.* New Orleans, 1952.

Landry, Stuart O. *The Battle of Liberty Place: The Overthrow of Carpet-Bag Rule in New Orleans— September 14, 1874.* New Orleans, 1955.

Latour, A. LaCarrière. *Historical Memoir of the War in West Florida and Louisiana in 1814–1815.* Philadelphia, 1816, and Gainesville, Florida, 1964.

Latrobe, J. H. B. *The First Steamboat Voyage on the Western Waters.* Baltimore, 1871.

Laughlin, Clarence, and Cohn, David L. *New Orleans and Its Living Past.* Boston, 1941.

Laussat, Pierre-Clément de. *Mémoires sur ma vie à mon fils pendant les années 1803 et suivantes . . .* Pau, France, 1831.

Le Conte, René. "The Germans in Louisiana in the Eighteenth Century." Translated and edited by Glenn R. Conrad, *Louisiana History,* vol. 8, no. 1 (Winter 1967).

Le Gardeur, René J., Jr. *The First New Orleans Theatre: 1792–1803.* New Orleans, 1963.

Levasseur, A. *Lafayette in America in 1824 and 1825 or Journal of Travels in the United States.* New York, 1829.

Lloyd, James T. *Lloyd's Steamboat Directory and Disasters on the Western Waters.* Cincinnati, Ohio, 1856.

Long, Edith Elliot. *Madame Olivier's Mansion: 828 Toulouse.* New Orleans, 1965.

Lonn, Ella. *Reconstruction in Louisiana after 1868.* 2d ed. Gloucester, Massachusetts, 1967.

Lytle, William M. *Merchant Steam Vessels of the United States 1807–1868.* Edited by Forrest R. Holdcamper. Mystic, Connecticut, 1952.

Martin, François-Xavier. *The History of Louisiana.* New Orleans, 1827–1829.

Mayo, H. M. *Mme. Bégué and Her Recipes.* Chicago, 1900.

McLaughlin, James J. *The Jack Lafaience Book.* New Orleans, 1922.

McMurtrie, Douglas C. *Early Printing in New Orleans 1764–1810 with a Bibliography of the Issues of the Press.* New Orleans, 1929.

McWilliams, Richebourg Gaillard. *Fleur de Lys and Calumet.* Baton Rouge, 1953.

Meuse, William E. *The Weapons of the Battle of New Orleans.* New Orleans, 1965.

Moehlenbrok, Arthur Henry. "The German Drama on the New Orleans Stage." *Louisiana Historical Quarterly,* XXVI (April 1943).

Morrison, John H. *History of American Steam Navigation.* New York, 1903.

Nau, John F. *The German People of New Orleans, 1850–1900.* Leiden, 1958.

New Orleans City Guide. Federal Writers' Project of the Works Progress Administration for the City of New Orleans. Boston, 1938.

Niehaus, Earl F. *The Irish in New Orleans 1800–1860.* Baton Rouge, 1965.

Nolte, Vincent. *Fifty Years in Both Hemispheres.* New York, 1854.

O'Connor, Thomas. *History of the Fire Department of New Orleans . . . Down to 1895.* New Orleans, 1895.

Owen, William Miller. *In Camp and Battle with the Washington Artillery of New Orleans.* Boston, 1885.

Parkman, Francis. *La Salle and the Discovery of the Great West.* Edited by John A. Hawgood. New York, 1962.

Parton, James. *General Butler in New Orleans.* New York, 1864.

Picayune's *Guide to New Orleans.* 6th ed. New Orleans, 1904.

Pitot, Henry Clement. *James Pitot (1761–1831), A Documentary Study.* New Orleans, 1968.

Quaglia. *Le Père Lachaise ou Recueil de Dessins aux Traits et Dans Leurs Justes Proportions, des Principaux Monumens de ce Cimètiere . . .* Paris, 1828.

Quick, Herbert and Edward. *Mississippi Steamboatin': A History of Steamboating on the Mississippi and Its Tributaries . . .* New York, 1926.

Reed, Merl E. *New Orleans and the Railroads: The Struggle for Commercial Empire 1830–1860.* Baton Rouge, 1966.

Reed, William A. *Louisiana–French,* rev. ed. Baton Rouge, 1963.

Reinders, Robert C. *End of an Era: New Orleans, 1850–1860.* New Orleans, 1964.

Ricciuti, Italo William. *New Orleans and Its Environs: The Domestic Architecture.* New York, 1938.

Richey, Emma C., and Kean, Evelina O. *The New Orleans Book.* New Orleans, 1915.

Ripley, Eliza. *Social Life in Old New Orleans, Being Recollections of My Girlhood.* New York, 1912.

Robin, Claude C. *Voyage to the Interior of Louisiana, 1802–1806.* Translated by Stuart O. Landry, Jr. New Orleans, 1966.

Robinson, William L. *Diary of a Samaritan.* New York, 1860.

Rose, Al, and Souchon, Edmond. *New Orleans Jazz: A Family Album.* Baton Rouge, 1967.

Sala, George Augustus. *America Revisited.* London, 1886.

Samuel, Ray. *The Great Days of the Garden District and the Old City of Lafayette.* New Orleans, 1961.

————. *. . . to a Point called Chef Menteur.* New Orleans, 1959.

Samuel, Ray, and Martha Ann. *The Uptown River Corner: The Story of Royal and Bienville.* New Orleans, 1964.

Samuel, Ray; Huber, Leonard V.; and Ogden, Warren C. *Tales of the Mississippi.* New York, 1955.

Saxon, Lyle. *Fabulous New Orleans.* New York, 1928.

———. *Old Louisiana.* New York, 1929.

Saxon, Lyle; Dreyer, Edward; and Tallant, Robert. *Gumbo YaYa.* Boston, 1945.

Schott, Arthur; Weaver, Charles; Johnson, Phil; and Digby, Fred. *70 Years with the Pelicans. 1887–1957.* New Orleans, 1957.

Scott, Val McNair (Lady Pakenham). *Major-General Sir Edward Pakenham.* New Orleans, 1965.

Ship Registers and Enrollments of New Orleans, Louisiana. 1804–1870. 6 vols. Prepared by The Survey of Federal Archives in Louisiana by the Division of Community Service Programs, Works Projects Administration. Baton Rouge, 1942.

Sinclair, Harold. *The Port of New Orleans.* Garden City, 1942.

Smith, Sol. *Theatrical Management in the West and South for Thirty Years Interspersed with Anecdotical Sketches.* New York, 1868.

Soulé, Leon Cyprian. *The Know Nothing Party in New Orleans: A Reappraisal.* Baton Rouge, 1961.

Stoddard, T. Lothrop. *The French Revolution in San Domingo.* Boston and New York, 1914.

Szarkowski, John, ed. *E. J. Bellocq: Storyville Portraits, Photographs from the New Orleans Red-Light District, Circa 1912.* With a preface and prints made by Lee Friedlander. New York, 1970.

Tallant, Robert. *Voodoo in New Orleans.* New York, 1946.

Thompson, Maurice. *The Story of Louisiana.* Boston, 1888.

Tinker, Edward Larocque. *Creole City: Its Past and Its People.* New York, 1953.

———. *Lafcadio Hearn's American Days.* New York, 1924.

Trollope, Frances. *Domestic Manners of the Americans: With a History of Mrs. Trollope's Adventures in America.* Edited by Donald Smalley. New York, 1949.

Villiers Du Terrage, Baron Marc de. *Les Dernières Années de la Louisiane.* Paris, 1904.

Voss, Reverend Louis. *Presbyterianism in New Orleans and Adjacent Points.* New Orleans, 1931.

Waldo, J. Curtis. *History of the Carnival in New Orleans from 1857 to 1882.* New Orleans, 1882.

Warmoth, Henry Clay. *War, Politics and Reconstruction: Stormy Days in Louisiana.* New York, 1930.

Watson, Elbert L. *Tennessee at the Battle of New Orleans.* New Orleans, 1965.

Way, Captain Frederick, Jr. *Way's Directory of Western Rivers Packets.* Sewickley, Pennsylvania, 1950.

Whitaker, Arthur Preston. *The Mississippi Question: 1795–1803, A Study in Trade, Politics and Diplomacy.* New York, 1934.

———. *The Spanish-American Frontier: 1783–1795, The Westward Movement and the Spanish Retreat in the Mississippi Valley.* 2d ed. Gloucester, Massachusetts, 1962.

Williams, T. Harry. *P. G. T. Beauregard: Napoleon in Gray.* Baton Rouge, 1954.

Wilson, Neill C., and Taylor, Frank J. *Southern Pacific: The Roaring Story of a Fighting Railroad.* New York, 1952.

Wilson, Samuel Jr. "An Architectural History of the Royal Hospital and the Ursuline Convent of New Orleans." *The Louisiana Historical Quarterly*, vol. 29, no. 3 (July 1948).

———. *The Capuchin School in New Orleans, 1725.* New Orleans, 1961.

———. "Colonial Fortifications and Military Architecture in the Mississippi Valley." *The French in the Mississippi Valley.* Edited by John Francis McDermott. Urbana, Illinois, 1965.

———. *A Guide to Architecture of New Orleans 1699–1959.* New York, 1959.

———. "Ignace François Broutin." *Frenchmen and French Ways in the Mississippi Valley.* Edited by John Francis McDermott. Chicago, 1969.

———. "Louisiana Drawings of Alexander DeBatz." *Journal of The Society of Architectural Historians*, vol. 22, no. 2 (May 1963).

———. *Old New Orleans Houses.* (A series of 30 monographs published in *The New Orleans States*, February 7 to November 14, 1953.)

———. *Plantation Houses on the Battlefield of New Orleans.* New Orleans, 1965.

———. *The Vieux Carré New Orleans: Its Plan, Its Growth, Its Architecture.* Washington, D.C., 1968.

———. ed. *Impressions Respecting New Orleans by Benjamin Henry Boneval Latrobe, Diary & Sketches 1818–20.* New York, 1951.

Wilson, Samuel Jr., and Huber, Leonard V. *The Basilica on Jackson Square and Its Predecessors 1727–1965.* New Orleans, 1965.

———. *The Cabildo on Jackson Square.* New Orleans, 1970.

Wilson, Samuel Jr.; Huber, Leonard V.; and Gorin, Abbye A. *The St. Louis Cemeteries of New Orleans.* New Orleans, 1963.

Winters, John D. *The Civil War in Louisiana.* Baton Rouge, 1963.

Young, Perry. *The Mistick Krewe: Chronicles of Comus and His Kin.* New Orleans, 1931.

NEWSPAPERS OF NEW ORLEANS

L'Abeille	The Daily Times
The Bulletin	The Delta
Clarion Herald	The Louisiana Gazette
The Courier	The Mascot
The Daily Democrat	The Orleanian
The Daily Item	The States-Item
The Daily Picayune	The Times-Democrat
The Daily States	The Times-Picayune

The True American
The True Delta

PERIODICALS

Ballou's Pictorial Drawing Room Companion
The Century Magazine
The Daily Graphic (New York)
Emerson's Magazine and Putnam's Monthly
Every Saturday (Boston)
Frank Leslie's Illustrated Newspaper
Gleason's Pictorial Drawing Room Companion
Harper's Weekly
Illustrated London News
Le Monde Illustré (Paris)
New Orleans City Directories, 1823–1969
New York Illustrated News
Scientific American
Scribner's Magazine
Waterways Journal

MISCELLANEOUS SOURCES

Archives Nationales, Paris.
Archivo General de Indias, Seville.
Spanish Judicial Records in the Louisiana State Museum.
Miscellaneous Documents, Manuscripts Division, Library of Congress, Washington.
Reports of the Board of Police Commissioners, New Orleans.
Records of the Deliberations of the Cabildo (1769–1803).
Mayors' Messages to Municipality No. 1 (1804–1853).
New Orleans City Council Minutes and Resolutions.

Abraham, Martin, Sr. ("Chink Marten"), *164*
Abraham Building, *136*
Abramowicz, Dan, 260
Absinthe House, *125*
bar of, *206*
Acadians, 3, 4, *18*, *33*
Adams, Maude, 149
Alaux, Alexandre, 22, *23*
Alexis Romanov Aleksandrovich, Grand Duke, 215, 216, *216*, 218
Alhaiza, Charles, 157
Allard, Louis, 236, 238
Allen, Richard B., 161
Allen, Tom, 253
Almonester y Roxas, Don Andrés, *35*, *48*, 105, 110, 180
American Colonization Society, 191
Andersen, Adolf, 194
Anderson, Tom, 209, *209*, 211
Andrew, John, *46*
Anglin, Margaret, 149
Animal fights, 243–44
Antoine, C. C., 9
Antoine's Restaurant, 185, *185*, 186, *186*
Architecture, 78–141. *See also* Canal Street; Cemeteries; Churches; Hotels; Monuments; Office buildings; Suburban architecture; Vieux Carré
cast-iron fence in cornstalk design, 138, *139*
cottages, 130, *130*, *131*
"double," *131*, *132*
"shotgun," 130, *130*
gallery brackets, *132*
iron lace railing, *126*, *128*
jigsaw ornament, *131*, *132*
servants', or "slave," quarters, *130*
Arlington, Josie, 209, 210, 211
Arlington Annex, 209, *209*, *210*, 211
Arliss, George, 149
Armstrong, Louis ("Satchmo"), *162*, *163*
Arnaud's Restaurant, 187, *187*
Arsenal, the, *103*
Athenaeum, 159, *160*, 224
Aubry, Charles Philippe, 3
Audubon, John J., 188, *188*, 239
Audubon Park, 37, 171, 239, *239*, 240, 248, 273, *348*, 349
Austin, Stephen F., 7
Authors in New Orleans, *173–75*
Aviation, 300–302
Alvin Callender Field, 302
Moisant (now New Orleans) International Airport, 302, *302*
New Orleans Air Line, 301, *301*
New Orleans Airport, 302, *348*, 349
St. Tammany—Gulf Coast Airways, Inc., 301
Wedell-Williams Air Service, Inc., 302, *302*
Avondale Shipyards, *350*, *351*

Badger, A. S., 216
Bailey, Theodorus, 62, *63*

Bananas, *311–12*
Banjo Annie, *204*
Banking, 321–24
American Bank Building, 13, *136*
Bank of Louisiana, 322, *322*
Bank of New Orleans Building, 15
Citizens' Bank of Louisiana, 322, *322*
early paper currency, *321*
Exchange Bank, 323
Hibernia National Bank Building, 13, *324*
Improvement Bank, 323
Louisiana State Bank, 321, *321*
New Orleans Canal and Banking Company, *323*
State National Bank, 321
Union Bank, 100, 323, *323*
Whitney National Bank Building, 13, *324*
Banks, Nathaniel P., 9, 65, 189
Banks, Mrs. Nathaniel P., 154, *155*
Banks, Thomas, 89
Banks' Arcade, 7, 89, *89*, 306
Baptist Bible Institute, 137
Barbé-Marbois, François de, *38*, 39
Barbezan, Paillou de, 1, 22
Baron, Pierre, *28*, *30*
Barrett, Sweet Emma, *165*
Barry, Bernard, 73
Barrymore, Ethel, *149*
Baseball, 255–57
Louisiana Base Ball Club, 255
New Orleans Pelicans, 255–56, *256*
Pelican Stadium, 256, *257*
Baton Rouge, 7
Battle of New Orleans, 6, 30, 44–45, *45–50*, 141, 232
Bayne, Hugh, 257
Bayne, Thomas L., 257
Bayou Bienvenu, 44
Bayou du Mardi Gras, 214
Bayou Métairie, 238
Bayou St. John, 100, *140*, 141, 236, 264, 278, 296, *297*
Bayou Terre-aux-Boeufs, 294
Bayougoula Indians, 21
Beaujolais, Comte de, 4, 35
Beauregard, Pierre Gustave Toutant, 8, 59, 87, 103, *127*, 244, 245, *245*, 249, 280
Beauregard Square, 206
Bégué's Restaurant, 175, 184, *184*
Behan, William J., 11
Behrman, Martin, 11–12, 13, 73, *73*, 87, 189
Bell, Henry, 63
Benevolent Associations, *122*
Benjamin, Judah P., 192, *192*, 193
Bensadon, Dr. Joseph, 287
Bidwell, David, 147, *148*
Bienville, Jean Baptiste le Moyne, sieur de, 1, 2, *17*, 21, 22, *23*, 25, *26*, 28, *109*, 110
monument, *356*
Bienville Plaza, 60

Bierman, Bernie, 258, *259*
Birch, G., *41*
Bixby, Horace, 342
Black Code (*Code Noir*), 21
Blakemore, Allen B., 229
Blanchard, N. C., 189
Blue Book of Storyville, 208, *209*
Board of Trade. *See* New Orleans Board of Trade
Bofinger, W. H., 319
Bohemian Tavern, 185, *185*
Bonnet Carré
crevasse at, 265, *265*
spillway of, 266, *266*
Booth, Edwin, 146
Booth, Junius Brutus, 146
Boré, Jean Étienne, 5, 37, 173, 306, 308
Bossi, Stella, *157*
Boston Club, 224
Boudousquié, Charles, 153, *153*
Boudro's Restaurant, 183, *183*
Bouligny, Francisco, 5
Bourbon Orleans Hotel, 15, 151
Bowen, Andy, 253
Boxing, 253–54
matches in Olympic Athletic Club, 253–54
Sullivan-Kilrain fight, 253, *253*
top New Orleans fighters, 254, *254*
Bradish-Johnson House, 138, *139*
stairway of, *139*
Breaux, Gus A., 240, *241*
Brennan's French Restaurant, 187, *187*
Briggs, Isaac, 270
Broutin, Ignace, *28*, *29*, *30*
"Bucket Ordinance," 6, 273
Building boom in New Orleans, 15, 349–53
Burke, Billie, *149*
Burke, Glendy, 9
Burke, Jack, 253
Burtheville, 10
Butler, Andrew Jackson, 64
Butler, Benjamin Franklin, 9, 63–64, *64*, 65, 105, 216, *216*
hostility by women of New Orleans toward Federal Officers and, 64–65, *65*
infamous "General Order No. 28" of, *65*
Buttre, J. C., *51*
Byrnes, James B., 181

Cabildo (City Hall), 3, 5, 6, 7, 10, 35, *40*, 52, 53, 70, *102*, 103, 104, *104*, 105, *110*, 188, *189*, 278, 280
Louisiana State Museum at, *182*
Cable, George Washington, 9, 174, *174*
Caldwell, Erskine, 175
Caldwell, James H., 143, *143*, 144, *144*, 167
Calhoun, John C., 226, *227*
Cambas, Arthur, 301
Cambioso, Father John, 114
Canal & Claiborne Street Railroad Co., 288
Girod & Poydras line of, 288, *288*
Canal Street, 7, 11, 51, 53, 67, 68, 72, 73,

75, 78, 90, 91, *91*, *107*, *114*, 122,
132, 151, *219*, *220*, 229, 253, 314,
353
architecture along, *92–101, 132*
"bedbug row" on, 267, *267*
floods on, *265*
history of, 90–91
movie houses on, 101, *229*, *229*, *230*
partially completed waterworks on, *272*
steam dummy engine on, 288, *289*
streetcar terminus at, *291*
streetcars on, 290, *290*
Canal Street ferries, 292, *292*
Cannon, John W., 332
Canzoneri, Tony, 254, *254*
Cap Français (Saint-Domingue), *42*
Capdevielle, Paul, 11
Capo, Thomas, 282
Capuchins, 2, 3, *18*
Caradine, Reverend Dr. Bevery, 246
Carnegie, Andrew, 12, 169
Carondelet, Francisco Luis Héctor de, 4,
57, 232, 296
Carondelet Canal, 236, 297, 298. *See also*
Old Basin Canal
Carroll, William, 141
Carrollton, 7, 10, 141
Carrollton Hotel, *141*, 294
Carter, Henry Zac, 351
Casa-Calvo, Marqués de, 5
Casa Capitular of the Cabildo, 5, *36*
"Casket Girls," 30
Cast-iron fence in cornstalk design, 138,
139
Castaigne, André, *38, 39*
Cavailler, P., *52, 53*
Celestin, Oscar ("Papa"), *165*
Cemeteries, 118–25
   Carrollton Cemetery, 119
   Cypress Grove Cemetery, 122, *123*, 277,
      277
      Leeds family tomb in, *123*
      monuments in, *277, 278*
   decorating tombs on All Saints' Day,
      121
   Dispersed of Judah, 122
   Girod Street, or Protestant, Cemetery,
      121, 122
   Lafayette Cemeteries, Nos. 1 and 2,
      119, *277*
   Métairie Cemetery, 123, *123*
      grave of Captain Cooley in, *343*
      Langlés cenotaph in, 124, *124*
   Odd Fellows' Rest, 122
   Potter's Field, 122
   St. John Cemetery, 122
   St. Joseph's Cemetery, 119
   St. Louis Cemetery No. 1, *118, 119*,
      120, 122
   St. Louis Cemetery No. 2, 119, *120*,
      121, 238
      Avet and Lazzize tomb in, *120*
      Pilié tomb in, *120*
      Plauché tomb in, 120
   St. Louis Cemetery No. 3, 119
   St. Patrick Cemeteries, 122
   St. Roch Cemetery, 119
      chapel in, 262, *263*
   St. Vincent's Cemetery, 119, 242
   tombs of benevolent associations, *122*
   wall vaults in, *118, 119*
Cenas, Blaise, 269, *269*
Centobi, Leonard ("Boogie"), *164*
CENTROPORT, 15, 352, *352*

Chaffraix, Madame Désirée, home of, *138*
Chalmette, 6, 9, 45, 50
Chalmette Monument, *50*
Chalmette Plantation, 44
Chalmette Works of Kaiser Aluminum and
   Chemical Corporation, 14, *351, 352*
Charbonnet House, *140*
Charity Hospital, the, 245, *285, 286*
Charles III, king of Spain, 2, 3
Charlevoix, Pierre François Xavier de, 1
Choiseul, Duc de, 2
Christ Church, 92, *92, 93, 114*, 122
Christ Church Cathedral, 114, *115*
Christian Woman's Exchange, *127*
Churches
   Christ Church, 92, *92, 93, 114*, 122
   Christ Church Cathedral, 114, *115*
   Church of the Immaculate Conception,
      114
   Church of Notre Dame de Bon Secours,
      116
   denominations of, 111
   Felicity Methodist Church, *268*
   First Baptist Church, *117*
   First Presbyterian Church, 78, 88, 111,
      114–15, 190, 268
   Holy Name of Jesus Church, *118, 239*
   Jackson Avenue Evangelical Church,
      114, *115*
   Jesuit Church, 92, *93*
   Our Lady of Guadeloupe (formerly
      Mortuary Chapel of St. Anthony),
      112
   Parish Church of St. Louis, 28, 34
   St. Alphonsus Church, 116, *117*
   St. Augustine's Church, 170
   St. Louis Cathedral, 4, 5, 34, 35, *52*, 78,
      102, 103, 110, *110, 111*, 112, 284
   St. Mary's Assumption Church, 116, *116*
   St. Mary's Roman Catholic Church, *116*
   St. Patrick's Church, 53, 78, 88, *112*,
      113
   St. Paul's Lutheran Church, 268
   Strangers' Church (Parson Clapp's
      church), 83, *111*
Cirillo, Padre, 3
City Hall, new, 76
City Hall, old, 278, *279*. *See also* Cabildo
City of Lafayette. *See* Lafayette, city of
City Park, 236, *237*, 238, *238*, 301
   dueling "under the oaks" in, *242*
   Roosevelt Mall in, 190
Civic Center complex, 75, *76*
Civil Courts Building, new, 76
Civil Courts Building, old, 12, 80, *81*
Civil War, 8–9, 58–65
Claiborne, William C. C., 5, 6, *41*, 43, 170,
   194, 214
Clapp, Dr. Theodore, 83, 111, 190, 261,
   261
Clark, Daniel, 194, *194*
Clark, George, 9
Clay, Henry, 94, 226, *227*
   monument, 11, 88, *94, 95, 96*
Cochrane, Alexander, 44, 49
Cockfights, 244, *244*
Coffee industry, *310–11*
Coiron, Joseph, 309
Coleman, W. H., 174
Collapissas Indians, *22*
Collège d'Orléans, 6, *170*
Colson, Jean-François-Gille, *37*
Commander's Palace, 187, *187*
Commercial Club, *200*

Commercial Hotel, 100
"Committee of One Hundred, The," 279
Company of the Indies, 2, 20
Company of the West (later, Company
   of the Indies), 1, 20, 21
Comptes Rendus de L'Athénée Louisianais,
   178, *179*
Concerts, 158–61
   at Athenaeum, 159, *160*
   at Tulane Hall, 159
   Festival Hall of New Orleans Saenger-
      fest, *159*
   New Orleans Philharmonic Symphony
      Orchestra, *160, 161*
   of New Orleans Zither Club, *159*
   Philharmonic Society of New Orleans,
      160
Congo Square, *207*
Continental Guards, 10
Conway, John R., 10
Cooley, LeVerrier, 343, *343*
Corbett, James J., 253
Cotton Centennial Exposition, 11, 239,
   240–41, 288, *289*
Cotton industry, *303–6*
   cotton compressing, *304*
   Levee Steam Cotton Press, 288
   New Orleans Cotton Exchange, 13, 304–
      5, *305*, 306, *306*
   Orleans Cotton Press, 304, *304*
Cotton Market in New Orleans, Degas,
   306
Couret, Gus, 73
Cousins, Joseph M., 260
Cox, Tex, 258
Crabtree, Lotta, 146
Creole Jazz Band, 162, *163*
Creoles, the, 3, 4, 5, 37, 41, 51–52, *52*,
   100, *124*, 142, 156, 178, 205
Crescent City White League, 9. *See also*
   White League
Criminal Courts Building, new, 283
Criminal Courts Building, old, 282, *283*,
   284, *284*
Crossman, A. D., 7, 158, 279
Crozat, Antoine, 19
Culture, 142–87. *See also* Concerts; Edu-
   cation; Fine Art; French Opera
   House; Jazz; Literature; Newspa-
   pers; Restaurants; Theatre
Cushman, Charlotte, 146
Custom House
   of United States, *67, 68*, 72, 73, *107–9*
   original New Orleans Custom House,
      107, 109

Dabbadie, Jean Jacques-Blaise, 2
Dagobert, Père, 3
Daniels, Josephus, 211
Dantoni brothers, 56
Dart, Henry P., 179
D'Aunoy, Pierre, *35*
Dauphin, Maxmilian A., 245
David House, *128*
Davis, Jefferson, 12, 69, 87, *219*
Davis, John, 153, 214, 244
Davis, Molly Moore, 81
   home of, *80*
Davis, Thomas E., 81
Dawson, Lowel, 258
DeBatz, Alexandre, 22, *30*
De Bow, J. D. B., 173
De Bow's Review, 173
DeBuys, Rathbone, 251

DeDroit, Johnny, jazz band of, 164
DeDroit, Paul, 164
Degas, Achille, 306, 306
Degas, Edgar, 168, 180, 306, 306
Degas, René, 306, 306
Deiler, John Hanno, 159
Dekemel, "Buglin' Sam," 201
Delord-Sarpy plantation house, 41
Delta Shipyards, 13
Deming, Henry C., 9
Dempsey, Jack, 253
De Pouilly, J. N. B., 79, 82, 110, 111, 120, 322
Desegregation, 14
De Verges, Bernard, 29
Devol, George, 246–47, 247
Digby, Fred, 259
Directors' House, 27, 30
Disasters, 261–68. See also Epidemics; Fires; Floods and Hurricanes
Dix, Dorothy, 174, 174
Dixon, George, 253
Dobbs, Johnny, 255
Dodds, Baby, 162
Dodds, Johnny, 162
Donaldsonville, 7
Dos Passos, John, 175
Double Dealer, 175
Doullut, Milton, 133
Doullut House ("Steamboat House"), 133
Downtowner Hotel, 15, 153
Drew, John, 149
Duclot, Louis, 176
Dueling, 242–43
   "under the oaks," 242
Duff, William, 143
Dumont, Jean-François, 25
Duncan, Johnson K., 280
Duncan Plaza, 76
Dunn, Oscar J., 9
Duplantier, Armand, 41
Durieu, Emile, 157
Durrell, E. H., 9
Duval, Harry, 284

Eads, James Buchanan, 10, 336
   jetties of, to open river for commerce, 334, 335, 335
Early, Jubal A., 244, 245, 245
Edeson, Robert, 149
Education, 167–72
   Collège d'Orléans, 6, 170
   early public schools, 168, 168, 191
   Home Institute, 169
   Louisiana State University, 348, 349
   Loyola University of the South, 172
   Madame Picard's School (Markey-Picard Institute), 168
   Medical College of Louisiana, 170
   public libraries, 169
   St. Simeon's Select School, 169
   School of St. John Evangelical Lutheran congregation, 168
   Tulane University. See Tulane University
   University of Louisiana, 170. See also Tulane University
Eisenhower, Dwight D., 190
Elizabeth's Asylum, 193
Elkins, Harvey, 232
Ellender, Bennie, 259
Elliott, Maxine, 148
Elssler, Fanny, 146
Epidemics
   cholera, 7, 261, 261, 262

influenza, 13
   yellow fever, 7, 12, 262, 263, 263, 264, 264
Escalaïs, Léonce, 156, 157
Exchange Alley, 80, 185

Fabacher's restaurant, 100, 185, 185
Fair Grounds, 249, 250, 251. See also Horse racing
Farragut, David Glasgow, 8–9, 61, 61, 62, 63
Faubourg Marigny, 5, 140
Faubourg Ste. Marie, 5, 7, 122, 140, 144
Faubourg Tremé, 5, 278
Faulkner, William, 175
Faversham, William, 149
Fearing, Charles H., 341
Federal Building, 114
Federal Confiscation Act, 64
Fee, Robert G. C., 326
Feitel, Arthur, 180
Felix Park, 162
Female Orphan Asylum, 193
Fernandez, J. O., 14
Ferries, 292–93
Ferry, Irad, 278
Festival Hall of New Orleans Saengerfest, 159
Fine arts, 180–82
   Isaac Delgado Museum of Art, 180, 180, 181, 181
   Louisiana State Museum, 182
Fire Department, 273–78. See also Fires of New Orleans
   firefighters in action today, 278
   first steam pumper, 274, 275
   Louisiana Hose Company, 276, 277
   rivalry between companies, 274, 274
Fire mark of People's Insurance Company of New Orleans, 276, 276
Firemen's Charitable Association, 226, 226, 273–74, 275
   Cypress Grove Cemetery founded by, 122, 277, 277, 278
Fires of New Orleans, 4, 12, 33, 34, 110, 274, 277. See also Fire Department
First Presbyterian Church, 78, 88, 111, 114–15, 190
Fisk, Abijah, 169
Fisk, Alvarez, 169
Fisk Free Library, 169
Fitch, Clyde, 148
Fitzpatrick, John, 11, 279, 279
Fitzsimmons, Bob, 253
Flanders, Benjamin Franklin, 10, 216
Floods and hurricanes, 264–68
Flower, C., 11
Fogliardi, J. B., 188
Football, 257–60
   at Tulane University, 257, 257, 258, 258, 259, 260
   New Orleans Saints, 260, 260
   Sugar Bowl game, 259, 260
   Tulane Stadium, 260
Forshey, C. G., 335
Fort Jackson, 8, 61, 61
Fort Maurepas, 19
Fort St. Charles, 46, 47, 90
Fort St. Philip, 8, 44, 45, 48, 61, 61
Foster, Pops, 162
Foucault, Nicolas Denis, 2, 18
Fountain, Pete, 167
Frank, Charley, 255

Franklin, Benjamin, monument of, 88, 88, 89
French, J., 9
French Market, 28, 52, 56, 56, 184, 196, 197, 198, 271
French Opera House, 13, 98, 153, 154–58, 219, 224
French Quarter. See Vieux Carré
French Revolution, 42
Freret, William, 7
Friend, Julius, 175
Frnka, Henry E., 259
Fuller, Charles F., 51
Fulton, Robert, 326

Gaines, Myra Clark, 194, 194
Galatoire's, 183, 183, 184
Gallier, James, Sr., 80, 86, 87, 87, 112
Gallier Hall (Old City Hall), 7, 53, 78, 86, 86, 87, 87, 169
Gálvez, Bernardo de, 3–4, 32, 33, 110
Gambling, 10–11, 244–48
   Hi-Li Club, 248
   Louisiana State Lottery ("Octopus"), 11, 244–45, 245, 246, 246, 247
   riverboat gamblers, 246–47, 247
Garden District, 1, 15, 349
   homes in, 137–39
Garden District Property Owners' Association, 133
Gauche, John, 135
Gayarré, Charles, 170, 173, 173, 174
Gayoso de Lemos, Manuel Luis, 4, 35
Gem Café, 214, 214
Genois, Charles, 7
Gerard, François-Pascal-Simon, 37
German immigrants, 55, 55, 116
   Volksfest of, 55, 55
Gibbs, Samuel, 44, 45
Gibson, Randall Lee, 171
Gilbert, Larry, 255, 255
Gill, Charles, 17
Girod, Nicholas, 6, 81
Girod House (known as Napoleon House), 81
Gluck's Restaurant, 271, 271
Godchaux's, 75
Goldstein, Albert, 175
Gottschalk, Louis Moreau, 158, 159
Government House, 30, 31, 34
Governor's House, 28
Grant, Ulysses S., 9, 10, 189, 216, 216
Great Mississippi Steamboat Race, The, Currier & Ives, 332
Greenville, 10
Greenwall, Henry, 150, 150
Grey, Dr. J. D., 117
Grima House, 127
Grunewald, Louis, 315, 315, 346
Grunewald Hall, 315, 315
Guillemard, Gilberto, 36, 110
Guillotte, J. Valsin, 11
Gulf Yachting Association, 251
Gumbel, Simon, 204

Hackett, James K., 149
Hahn, Michael, 65
Hall, Dominick A., 126
Halle des Boucheries, 196. See also French Market
Harding, Warren G., 189
Hardy, Charlie, 163
Harrison, Hilton, 163

Harvey Canal, 12
Haughery, Margaret Gaffney, 193, *193*
  bakery of, *193*
  monument, *193*
"Haunted House." *See* Lalaurie House
Hayes, Rutherford B., 10, 70
Hazel, Arthur ("Monk"), *164*
Health Education Authority of Louisiana (HEAL), 15
Hearn, Lafcadio, 174, *174*
Heath, Edward, 10
Hebert, Paul O., 335
Heinemann, Alexander Julius, 256, *256*
Heinemann Baseball Park, 239, 256
Held, Anna, 149
Hemingway, Ernest, 175
Hennessy, David C., 11, 87, 96, *96*, 280, *280*
  assassination of, by members of Mafia, 96, 280
Henry, Jean Marie, 142
Henry, Louis Alexandre, 142
Herman, Pete, 254, *254*
Hernandez, Marcellino, 105
Hernsheim, Simon, residence of, 128, *129*
Hewlett, John, 89
Hibernia Bank Building, 13, *324*
Higgins, Andrew Jackson, 14
Hill, D. H., 219
Hill, J. W., 78, 79
Hintermeister, Henry, *40*
Hirt, Al, *167*
History of New Orleans (Kendall), 6
Holbrook, E. J., 177
Holmes, Daniel Henry, 315, *315*
Holmes, Truman, 332
Hombrook, T. L., 46, *47*
Hopper, DeWolf, 149
Horse racing, 248–51
  Fair Grounds, 249, *250*, 251
    Business Men's Racing Association, 250
    Crescent City Jockey Club, 250, *250*
    Fair Grounds Corporation, 251
    Louisiana Jockey Club, 249, *249*, 250, *250*
  Métairie race track, 58, *58*, 248, *248*, *249*
    Métairie Jockey Club, 248, 249
Horticultural Hall of Cotton Centennial Exposition, 240, *241*
Hospitals, 285–87
  Charity Hospital, 245, 285, *286*
  Hotel Dieu, 287, *287*
  Maison de Santé, *286*, 287
  Ochsner Foundation Hospital and Clinic, 287
  Touro Infirmary, 56, 287, *287*
Hotel Dieu, 287, *287*
Hotels
  Bourbon Orleans, 15, 151
  Carrollton, *141*, *294*
  Commercial, 100
  Cosmopolitan, *199*
  Downtowner, 15, 153
  Fontainebleau Motor Hotel, 239, 257
  La Louisiane, 200, *201*
  Monteleone, 100
  Orleans, *70*
  Planters, 92, *93*
  Pontchartrain, 232, *232*
  Roosevelt Annex, 13
  Royal Orleans, 15
  Royal Sonesta, 15

St. Charles, 7, *53*, 63, *66*, 78, 79–80, *83*, *84*, *85*, 111, 144, 167, *288*, 323
St. James, 311
St. Louis, 13, *52*, 78, 79, *79*, *80*, *81*, *82*, 323
Sheraton-Charles, 84
Union, 244
Verandah, *83*, 144
Houston, "Fats," *166*
Howard, Charles T., 245, 277
Howard, H. T., 160
Howard, Joe, *162*
Hoyt, Stephen, 9
Huber, Victor, 159
Huey P. Long Bridge, *298*, 348, *349*
Hug, Armand, *164*
Hurricanes. *See* Floods and hurricanes
Hurstville, 10

Iberville, Pierre le Moyne, sieur d', 1, *16–17*, *18*, *19*, 21, 214
Immigration, 54–57
  from Germany, 55, *55*
  from Ireland, 54, *54*
  from Italy, 56, *56*
Indian temple, 22
Indians, 2, *21*, 22
Industrial Canal, *348*, 349, *349*
Ingraham, Joseph Holt, 92
Inland Waterways Corporation, 12
International Trade Mart Building, 15, 352, *353*
Intracoastal Canal, 12
"Irish Channel," 54
Irish immigrants, 54, 112
Iron lace railing, *126*, 128
Isaac Delgado Museum of Art, 180, *180*, 181, *181*, 238

Jackson, Andrew, 6, 31, 44, *46*, *48*, 49, 50, 105, *109*, 126, 189, 232
  monument, *105*, 226
Jackson, ("Shoeless") Joe, *255*
Jackson, Thomas ("Stonewall"), 219
Jackson Square. *See* Place d'Armes
Jahncke, Ernest Lee, 163
Jardin du Rocher de Ste. Hélène, 236, 237
Jazz, 161–67
  Bayou Stompers, 164
  brass bands at funerals, *164*
  Creole Jazz Band, 162, *163*
  Johnny DeDroit's Band, *164*
  New Orleans Jazz Club, 166
  New Orleans Owls, 164
  Olympia Brass Band, *166*
  on Streckfus steamboats, *162*
  Onward Brass Band, *166*, 167
  origins of, 161–62
  Pete's Half-fast Marching Club, 167
  Preservation Hall, 166
  Razzy Dazzy Spasm Band, 161, *162*
  revival of, 166, *166*
  Six and Seven-Eighths String Band, *163*
  "spasm bands," *165*
  Tuxedo Brass Band, 165
  WSMB radio band, *164*
Jazz Museum, 166
Jefferson, Joseph, 146, 149
Jefferson, Thomas, *38*, 41
Jefferson City, 10
Jesuits, 2, *18*
Johnson, Isaac, 87
Jones, David, *162*
Jones, Thomas Catesby, 47

Kaiser, Mr. and Mrs. Mark, 160
Kaiser Aluminum and Chemical Corporation, Chalmette Works of, 14, *351*, 352
Keene, John, 44, 45
Keller, J. H., 316
Kellogg, William Pitt, 9, 67, *67*, 68, 81, 96
  Metropolitan Police of. *See* Metropolitan Police
Kendall, George Wilkins, 176, *177*
Kennedy, Hugh, 9
Kennedy, John F., 190
Kennedy, Joseph, 90
Kerlérec, Louis Billouart de, 2, *18*, 22, 23, 110
Kerlérec, Madame de, *18*
Keyes, Frances Parkinson, 127, 175, *175*
Kilrain, Jake, 253, *253*
King, Grace, 174, *174*
Knaps, Fred, 50
Knaupp, Cotton, 255, 256
Knights of Columbus Hall (formerly, synagogue), *190*
Kohnke, Dr. Quitman, 263, *264*
Kreisler, Fritz, *160*

Labatut family, 128, *129*
Labranche, Jean Baptiste, 128
Labranche buildings, *128*
Laclotte, Hyacinthe, 44, *45*
Lacombe, Emile ("Stalebread Charley"), *161*, *162*
La Farge, Oliver, 175
Lafayette, city of, 10, *136–41*. *See also* Garden District
  plan of, *136*
Lafayette, Marquis de, 7, 41, 104, 188, *188*, 192
Lafayette Square, 88, *88*, 89, *89*, 95, 114, 191, *195*, 226, 227
Lafitte, Jean, 49
Lafitte's Blacksmith Shop, *125*
Lafrénière, Nicolas-Chauvin de, 3
Laine, Julian ("Digger"), *164*
Lake Borgne, 44, 46, *47*, 53, 267
Lake Pontchartrain, 230–35, 265, 267, 297, 298
  cottages on, *235*
  excursion boats, 235, *236*
  resorts, 230–35
Lakeshore Drive, *234*
Lalaurie House ("Haunted House"), *127*
L'Alouette, 242
Lambert, John, 45
Landrieu, Moon, 15, 77
Lane Cotton Mills, 41
Langlés cenotaph, 124, *124*
Lansford, Alonzo, 180
Largillière, Nicolas de, *16*
La Salle, Robert Cavelier, sieur de, 1, *16*, *18*, 21
Lassus, Jean Pierre, *26*, *180–81*
La Tour, Le Blond de, 1, *24*, 25
Latrobe, Benjamin H. B., 6, 50, 107, *195*, 271, *271*, 321
Launitz, Robert A., 86
Laussat, Pierre Clement, 5, *37*, 41, 278
Lautenschlaeger, Lester J., 258
Laveau, Marie, 207, *207*
Law, John, 1, *19–20*, 21
Leathers, Thomas Paul, 332
Le Carpentier-Beauregard House, *127*
Lee, Mildred, 219

Lee, Robert E., 193, 219
  monument, 228
Lee Circle, 193, 228
Leeds, Charles L., 10, 310, 310
Leeds's Foundry, 310
Le Gardeur, René J., Jr., 156
Le Moyne (sieur) de Bienville, Jean Baptiste. See Bienville
Le Sueur, Charles Alexandre, 180, 197
Levee, The, 328, 328
  steamboat activity on, 309, 337–40
Levees
  construction of, 264
  drainage pumping stations, 266, 267
  dynamiting of, 266, 266
  strengthening of, 266
Levy, Rudolph, 164
Lewis, John L., 8
Libraries, 169
Lincoln, Abraham, 8, 9, 58
Lind, Jenny, 146, 158, 159, 183
Lipton, Sir Thomas, 251, 288, 288
Literature of New Orleans, 173–75. See also Newspapers
  De Bow's Review, 173
  Double Dealer, 175
  Federal Writers' Project, 175, 175
Little Theatre, the, 34
Livaudais, François, 248
Liverpool and London and Globe Insurance Company Building, 136
Livingston, Robert R., 38, 39, 326
Llulla, Don José, 242, 243
Long, Huey P., 13, 74
Longacre, J. B., 41
Longstreet, James, 216
Louaillier, Louis, 126
Louis XIV, king of France, 16, 19
  with his family, 16
Louis XV, king of France, 2, 31
Louis Philippe, 4, 35
Louisiana, admission of, to the Union, 6
Louisiana (American sloop), 44
  commander of, 49
Louisiana Club, the, 225
Louisiana Historical Quarterly, 179, 179
Louisiana Landmarks Society, 134
Louisiana Purchase, 4, 5–6, 40
Louisiana Purchase Treaty, 39
Louisiana State Lottery ("Octopus"), 11, 244–45, 245, 246, 246, 247
Louisiana State Museum, 182
Louisiana State Society for the Prevention of Cruelty to Animals, 286
Louisiana State University, 348, 349
Louisiana Superdome, 353
Lovell, Mansfield, 8, 61, 62
Lowenthal, A. J., 194
Loyola University of the South, 172
Ludlow, Noah, 143, 145
Lumsden, Francis Asbury, 176, 177

Macarty, August, 6
Macarty Plantation, 44, 45
McAuliffe, Jack, 253
McCaleb, Howard, 163
McClure, John, 175
McDermott family, 118
McDonnell's Restaurant, 182, 182
McDonogh, John, 30, 168, 190–91, 191, 238
  monument, 89, 191
Mace, Jim, 253
McEnery, John, 9

Macheca brothers, 311
McKinley, William, 189
McShane, Andrew J., 13
Madame John's Legacy, 174
Maestri, Robert S., 13, 14, 74, 74, 75
Maine, sinking of, 11, 71
Maison Blanche department store, 92, 97, 114, 146
Mandot, Joe, 254, 254
Mansfield, Richard, 149
Mantell, Robert, 149
Marable, Fate, 162
Mardi Gras, 1, 15, 214–25. See also Parades
  arrival of Rex, 219, 219–20
  carnival flag, 218
  masked balls, 214, 215, 219, 221, 221, 223, 224
  organizations of, 222
    Independent Order of the Moon, 219
    Knights of Electra, 219, 222, 222
    Knights of Momus, 215, 219
    Krewe of Nereus, 222
    Krewe of Proteus, 219, 224
    Mystick Krewe of Comus, 214–15, 215, 216, 217–18
    Phunny Phorty Phellows, 219, 221, 221
    Rex, 214, 215, 216, 218, 219, 219–20, 225
    Twelfth Night Revelers, 215, 219
    Zulu Aid and Pleasure Club, 223, 223, 224
  origin of, 214
  parades, 214–15, 215, 216, 217–18, 219, 221, 222, 222, 223
  preparation of masks and costumes, 217
  Rex ball, 219, 219
Marigny, Bernard de, 192, 192
  mansion of, 140, 299
Marigny, Pierre de, 4
Markey-Picard Institute, 168
Marlowe, Julia, 149
Martin, François-Xavier, 173, 173
Martina, Joe, 255
Masonic Temple Building, 13
Mather, James, 5–6
Mathews, Bill, 165
Mathews, Charles C., 239
Matzenauer, Margarete, 160
Mayer, Corinne, 160
Maylie's Restaurant, 186, 186
Mecom, John, Jr., 260
Medical College of Louisiana, 170
Méndez, Antonio, 308
Menken, Adah Isaacs, 146
Merchants and merchandising, early, 312–19
  advertisements, 312, 313, 314, 316, 317, 318
  trade cards, 316
Merchants' Exchange, 79, 100, 167, 271, 271
Merieult House, 34, 125
Mestach, George, 301
Métairie Cemetery, 123, 123
  grave of Captain Cooley, 343
  Langlés cenotaph in, 124, 124
Métairie Race Track (later, Métairie Cemetery), 58, 58, 248, 248, 249
  Métairie Jockey Club, 248, 249
Métairie Relief Outfall Canal, 266, 267
Metropolitan Police of William Kellogg, 216

battle between White Leaguers and, 9, 67, 67, 68, 81, 96, 96
Meyers, Billy, 253
Milhet, Jean, 3
Miller, James F., 9
Miller, Warren V., 260
Milne, Alexander, 192, 192
Milneburg, 234, 235, 296
Miró, Esteban, 4, 33, 110
Mississippi River
  flatboats on, 325, 325
  mouth of, 333
    bars at, 334–35
    jetties of James B. Eads at, 334, 335, 335
Mississippi River Bridge, 350
Mississippi Steamboat Navigation Company, 326
Mississippi-Warrior services, 12
Moisant, John B., 300, 301, 301, 302
Mongoulacha Indians, 21
Moniteur de la Louisiane, 4
Monroe, James, 38, 39
Montpensier, Duc de, 4, 35
Monplaisir House, 30, 191
Monroe, John T., 9, 10, 63, 63, 64
Montégut, Joseph Edgard, 7
  and family, 36, 180
Monteleone Hotel, 100
Montez, Lola, 146
Monuments
  Andrew Jackson, 105, 226
  Benjamin Franklin, 88, 88, 89
  Bienville, 356
  Chalmette, 50
  Henry Clay, 11, 88, 89, 94, 95, 96
  in honor of men who fought in Spanish-American War, 71
  Jefferson Davis, 12
  John McDonogh, 89, 191
  Margaret, 193
  Robert E. Lee, 193, 228
Morales, Juan Ventura, 4, 34
Moran, Pal, 254, 254
Moreno y Arze, Francisco Antonio, 35
Moresque Building, 134, 135
Morphy, Paul, 187, 194, 194
Morris, John A., 245
Morrison, de Lesseps S., 14, 74, 75, 75, 76, 87, 284, 285
Morton, Jelly Roll, 165
Movie houses, 228–30
  Acme Theatre, 229
  Globe Theatre, 229
  Loew's, 101, 101
  New Dixie Theatre, 229
  on Canal Street, 101, 229, 229, 230
  Saenger Theatre, 100, 101
  Trianon Theatre, 230
  Vitascope Hall, 229
Mullen, Gary, 283
Mullen, James Ignatius, 112
Mumford, William B., 64, 90
Municipal Auditorium, 158, 224, 280
Municipal services, 269–87. See also Fire Department; Hospitals; Police Department; Postal service; Waterworks
Museums, 180–82
Musson, Michel, 306, 306
  home of, 168
Musson, Germain, 95
Musson Building, 95

Napoleon I, 5, *37, 38, 42, 43, 44*
  death mask of, *182*
Napoleon House. *See* Girod House
NASA assembly facility at Michoud Plant, *354, 354, 355*
Natchez Trace, *269, 269*, 270, 325
Nethersole, Olga, 149
New Basin Canal, 144, 230, 252, 298, 323. *See also* Old Basin Canal
New Basin Shell Road, 230, *230*
New Lusitano Benevolent Association, tomb of, *122*
New Orleans
  absorption of nearby suburbs by, 10
  architecture of, 78–141. *See also* Architecture
  as busy port city, *330, 331, 331, 349–56. See also* River commerce; Steamboats
  business in, 303–24. *See also* Bananas; Banking; Coffee industry; Cotton industry; Merchants and merchandising, early; Sugar industry; Telephone service
  "characters" of, *195–204*
  culture in, 142–87. *See also* Culture
  disasters of, 261–68. *See also* Epidemics; Fires; Floods and Hurricanes
  diversions in, 214–41. *See also* Cotton Centennial Exposition; Mardi Gras; Movie houses; Parades; Parks; Resorts
  division of, into three municipalities, 51, 52, 53
    map of, *52*
  during Civil War, 8–9, 58–65
  during Reconstruction period, 9–10, *66–70*
  during Spanish-American War, 11, *71*
  during World War I, 12, *72–74*
  during World War II, 13–14, *75–76*
  early street plans of, *24, 26, 27, 41, 46, 52*
    with designation for cemetery, *118*
  events during early growth of, 6–8
  expansion of (1852–1900), 10–11
  expansion of (1900–1971), 11–15
  gambling in, 244–48. *See also* Gambling
  municipal services of, 269–87. *See also* Fire Department; Hospitals; Police Department; Postal service; Waterworks
  notable residents of, 190–94
  official flag for, *73*
  official seal of, *54*
  plan of city commons, 90, *91*
  views of:
    early, *25, 26, 31, 40*
    in 1852, *78, 79*
    in 1863, *78, 79*
    today, *348, 349, 350, 351, 352, 353, 356*
New Orleans (steamboat), 6, *326, 326*
New Orleans Airport, 302, *348*, 349
New Orleans and Carrollton Railroad Company, 7, 141, *141*, 288, *288, 289*, 294
New Orleans & Nashville Railroad, 7, 144, 295
New Orleans Board of Trade, 306
  building of, *307*, 311
New Orleans Canal and Navigation Company, 298

New Orleans City and Lake Railroad, 288, 289
New Orleans Cotton Exchange, 304–5, *305*, 306, *306*
New Orleans Gas Company building, *135*
New Orleans Institute of Mental Hygiene, 56
New Orleans International Airport, 302, *302*
New Orleans Mid-Winter Sports Association, 260
New Orleans Navigation Company, 6, 43, 91, 298
New Orleans Opera Association, 158
New Orleans Pelicans, 255–56, *256*
New Orleans Philharmonic Symphony Orchestra, *160, 161*
New Orleans Public Library, 169
New Orleans Public Service, Inc., 290
New Orleans Railway and Light Company, 233
New Orleans Saints, *260*
New Orleans Sewerage and Water Board, 267
New Orleans Water Works, 144, 272, *272*
New Orleans Zither Club, *159*
New Royal Café, 100
Newcomb, Josephine Le Monnier, *171*
Newcomb Art School, 180
Newcomb College. *See* Tulane University
Newspapers, 176–79
  Commercial Bulletin, 176
  Daily Crescent, 178
  Daily Delta, 177
  L'Abeille, 176, *178*
  L'Orleanais, 178
  Louisiana Advertiser, 176
  Louisiana Courier, 176
  Louisiana Gazette, 176, *176*
  Montieur de la Louisiane, 176, *176*
  New Orleans Item, 174, 259
  New Orleans Price-Current and Commercial Intelligencer, 178
  Picayune, 174, 176, *176*, 177, *177*, 263, *263*, 279
  political cartoons in, *179*
  Times Democrat, 174
  True American, 176, *178*
  True Delta, 178
Nicholls, Francis Tillou, 10, 68–69, *69*, 253
Nicholson, George, 177
Nicholson, Mrs. George (Pearl Rivers), 174, 177, *177*

O. Henry (William Sydney Porter), 175, *175*
O'Boyle, Tommy, 259
Observatory, the, *28*
Ocean Springs, *19*
Ochsner, Alton, 287
Ochsner Foundation Hospital and Clinic, 287, *287*
O'Connor, Thomas, 275
"Octopus." *See* Louisiana State Lottery
Odd Fellows' Hall, *78, 79*
Odenheimer, Sigmund, 349
Odenheimer Aquarium, 239
O'Donnell, E. P., 175
Office buildings, *134–36, 305, 309, 324, 353*
Ogden, Frederick N., 9, 10, 69, 70
O'Keefe, Arthur J., Sr., 13, *73*
Old Basin Canal, *296*, 298. *See also* Carondelet Canal

Oliver, King, 162, *163*
Olympia Opera Company, 239
Olympic Athletic Club, 253–54
Opera. *See* French Opera House
Ordinance of Secession, 8
O'Reardon, Shields, *163*
O'Reilly, Alexander, 3, 32, 35
Orleans, Charles A., home of, *132*
Orléans, Louis Philippe Joseph, duc d' (Philippe Égalité), 4
Orléans, Philippe d', 1, 4, 22, *23*
Orleans Hotel, *70*
Orleans-Kenner Traction Company, 291, *291*
Orleans Parish Levee Board, 234
Oteri brothers, 311
Ott, Mel, 256, *256*
Oursel, Pretextat, 20, *21*
Owen, William Miller, *131*

Packard, Stephen B., 9, 10, 68, 69, *70*
Pakenham, Edward M., 44, 45, *49*
Palmer, Benjamin Morgan, 58, *58*, 114
Parades, 226–28. *See also* Mardi Gras
  in memory of Calhoun, Clay, and Webster, 226, *227*
  of Confederate Veterans, *228*
  of the Seven Wise Men, 227, *228*
  of volunteer firemen, 226, *226*
Parish Church of St. Louis (later, St. Louis Cathedral), 28, *34*
Parish Prison, 11, 96
  lynching of Italians in courtyard of, 280, *280, 281*
Parish Prison (new), 284
Parks, 236–40
  Audubon Park, 37, 171, 239, *239, 240, 248, 273, 348, 349*
  City Park, 190, 236, *237, 238, 238, 242*, 301. *See also* City Park
  Jardin du Rocher de Ste. Hélène, 236, *237*
  Tivoli Gardens, 236, *237*
Patterson, Daniel T., *49*
Patton, Isaac W., 10
Pauger, Adrien, 1, *24, 26*, 102, 110, *118*
Paulhan, Louis, 300, *301*
Payne-Strachan House, *137*
Peace of Ghent 1814 and Triumph of America, The, Plantau, *50*
Peale, Rembrandt, *38*
Pelican Stadium, 256, *257*
Peñalver y Cárdenas, Bishop Luis, 4, 34, *35*
Perchet, Juan M., *34*
Père Marquette Building, 13
Périer, Étienne de, 2, 28, 110
Perkins, George H., 62, *63*
Peters, Samuel Jarvic, 86, 143, 167, *167*, 168
Petit Salon, Le, *128*
Peychaud, Antoine, 205
Philharmonic Society of New Orleans, *160*
Philippe Égalité. *See* Orleans, Louis Philippe Joseph, duc d'
Picou, Alphonse Floristan, *166*
Pilié, J., 188
Pillsbury, Edward, 10
Pilney, Andy, 259
Pinchback, P. B. S., 67
Pitot, James, 5, 43
Pitot House, *43*
Pittman, Jim, 259
Place d'Armes (later, Jackson Square), 3,

5, 10, *28*, *40*, *52*, 53, 60, 77, 78, *102–6*, 188, *280*, *284*, *285*
Arc de Triomphe erected in, for Lafayette's visit, 188, *188*
buildings on, *102–6*
name of, changed to Jackson Square, 105
Plantau, Madame, 50
Plauché, Jean Baptiste, 232
Plaza Towers, 15
Police Department, 278–85. *See also* Metropolitan Police
denouncement of, by "The Committee of One Hundred," 279
House of Detention, *283*
lynching of Italians in Parish Prison courtyard, 280, *281*
origins of, 278–79
Garde de ville, 278
Gens d'armes, 278
precinct stations, *282*
traffic squad (1912), 284, *284*
Pollock, Oliver, 3
Pomarède, Leon, 113
Pontalba, Joseph-Xavier-Celestin Delfau de, 35
Pontalba, Micaela, Baroness de, 105, *106*, *183*
Pontalba Buildings, 79, 102, 105, *105*, *106*
Pontchartrain Expressway, 75
Pontchartrain Hotel, 232, *232*
Pontchartrain Railroad, 7, 234, 294, *296*, 299
Popp Gardens, 239
Porter, William Sydney. *See* O. Henry
Postal service, early, 269–71
Army Engineers' *Map of Reconnaissance*, *270*
New Orleans's Post Office, 89, *271*
Powder magazine, 28
Powell, Charles Abner, 255, *255*
Power, Tyrone, 146
Powers, Hiram, 89
Powers, Leona, 152, *152*
Poydras Market, 198, *198*
Pradel, Chevalier Jean de, *30*, 191
Presbytère, 5, *52*, 53, *102*, *104*, 110
Preservation Hall, 166
Prichard, Walter, 179
Prieur, Denis, 7
Printers' Association, 279
Prostitution, 11, *208–11*
Blue Book of Storyville, 208, *209*
Public Belt Railroad, 12, 298, *298*, 299
Puig family, 128, *129*

Quincy, Samuel Miller, 9
Quintero, Don José, 242

Railroads, 7, 10, 12, 14, 294–300
Mexican Gulf Railway, 294
New Orleans and Carrollton Railroad, 7, 141, *141*, 288, *288*, 289, 294
New Orleans & Jackson Railroad, 7, 295
New Orleans & Nashville Railroad, 7, 144, 295
New Orleans & Northeastern Railroad, 295, *298*
New Orleans, Mobile & Chattanooga Railroad, 295
New Orleans Opelousas & Great Western Railroad, 295, *295*
New Orleans Pacific Railroad, 295
New Orleans Pontchartrain and Lake Railroad, 296

Pontchartrain Railroad, 7, 234, 294, *296*, 299
Public Belt Railroad, 12, 298, *298*, 299
stations:
first, in New Orleans, *299*
Illinois Central, *300*
Louisiana & Arkansas, Kansas City Southern, *300*
Louisville & National, *300*
New Orleans, Jackson & Great Northern, 288
Southern Railway, *300*
Texas Pacific Missouri Pacific, 300
Trans-Mississippi, *300*
Union Station, 298, 299, 300, *300*
Texas & Pacific Railroad, 295, *296*
Reconstruction period, 9–10, *66–70*
Act, 9
Rennie, Robert, 45
Resorts, *230–36*. *See also* Lake Pontchartrain; Spanish Fort; West End
Restaurants, 182–87
Antoine's, 185, *185*, 186, *186*
Arnaud's, 187, *187*
Bohemian Tavern, 185, *185*
Boudro's, 183, *183*
Brennan's, 187, *187*
Coleman's Guide to New Orleans on, 182, *182*
Commander's Palace, 187, *187*
Fabacher's, 100, 185, *185*
Galatoire's, 183, *183*, 184
Gluck's, 271, *271*
Kolb's, 164, 187, *187*
Madame Bégué's, 175, 184, *184*
Maylie's, 186, *186*
McDonnell's, 182, *182*
Reynolds, Bob, *163*
Reynolds, Hampton, *74*
Reynolds, James W., 282, *283*
Rice, Dan, 147
Richards Centers complex, 136
Richardson, Walter P., 152
Riddell, John Leonard, 59
Ridgely, William ("Bébé"), *162*
River commerce, 6, 8, 10, 12, 303, *303*, 325–32. *See also* Mississippi River; Steamboats; Steamers and steamship lines
Riverboat gamblers, 246–47, *247*
Rivergate Exhibition Hall, 15, 352, *352*
Rivers, Pearl (Mrs. Nicholson), 174, 177, *177*
Robb, James, 137
Robb mansion, 137
Robin, C. C., 6, 244
Robinson, Eugene, *151*, 152
Robinson, William L., 261–62
Robinson-Jordan House, *138*
Rochemore, Vincent-Pierre-Gaspard de, 2, *18*
Rodriguez Canal, 44, 50
Roffignac, Louis Philippe de, 6, 188, 205
Romanov. *See* Alexis Alexandrovich, Grand Duke
Roosevelt, Franklin D., 190, *190*
Roosevelt, Nicholas, 326
Roosevelt, Theodore, 189
Roosevelt Mall in City Park, 190
Ross, Alexander, 49
Russell, Lillian, 149

Sailing, *251–52*

Saint-Aulaire, Félix-Achille Beaupoil de, 180
St. Charles Avenue streetcar line, 288, 290, *291*
St. Charles Hotel, 7, *53*, 63, *66*, 78, 79–80, 83, *84*, *85*, 111, 144, 167
St. Cyr, Johnny, *162*
Saint-Domingue, immigration from, 42–43
St. Louis Cathedral (formerly, Parish Church of St. Louis), 4, 5, 34, 35, *52*, 78, *102*, *103*, 110, *110*, 111, *111*, 112, 284
St. Louis Hotel, 13, *52*, 78, 79, *79*, 80, *81*, *82*
slave block in, 81, *82*
St. Patrick's Church, *53*, 78, 88, 112, *113*
St. Patrick's Hall, 89, 169
St. Roch, shrine of, 263, *263*
St. Theresa's Asylum, 193
St. Vincent de Paul (orphanage), 193
Salazar, Francisco, 35, *36*, 180
Salcedo, Juan Manuel de, 5, 35
Saloons, *205–6*
San Antonio (Texas Republic war schooner), *51*
Santerre, Jean-Baptiste, 22, *23*
Saulet, François, 169
Saxe-Weimar, Duke of, 232
Saxon, Lyle, 175
Scheff, Fritzi, 149
Schools. *See* Education
Schwartz, Moses, 232–33
Sebron, Hippolyte, 180
Secession, Ordinance of, 8
Sedella, Father Antonio de (Père Antoine), 35
Seven Years' War, 2
Shakspeare, Joseph, 10–11, 244, 279, *279*
"Shakspeare Plan," 10–11
Shaughnessy, Clark D., 258, *258*
Shenk, Leon, 19
Shepley, George, 9
Sheridan, Philip, 9, 65
Shipyards
Avondale, 350–51
Delta, 13
Higgins, 14
Short-Moran House, 138, *139*
Shot tower, 113, *113*, 114
Shreve, H. M., 48
Shrine of St. Roche, 263, *263*
Simons, Claude ("Little Monk"), 259, *259*
Six and Seven-Eighths String Band, *163*
Skelly, Jack, 253
Skinner, Otis, 149
Slave block in St. Louis Hotel, 81, *82*
Slave traffic, 20, 21, 58, *58*
Smith, B. F., Jr., 78, *79*
Smith, Kirby, 9
Smith, Sol, 145
Solari's (grocery store), *135*
Sontag, G., 233, *233*
Sothern, E. H., 149
Souchon, Edmond, *163*
Soulé, Pierre, 64
Southern Pacific Company building, *134*
Southern Route, the, 270, *271*
Southern Yacht Club, 251, *251*, 252
Spanish-American War, 11, 71
Spanish Custom House, 167
Spanish Fort, 10, *230–33*
Over the Rhine Restaurant, 233, *233*
plan of, *232*
Pontchartrain Hotel, 232, *232*

"trains" to, 290, *291*
Sporrer, Joseph, 238, *238*
Sports, 242–60. *See also* Animal fights;
    Baseball; Boxing; Dueling; Foot-
    ball; Gambling; Horse racing; Sail-
    ing
Spratling, William, 175
Standard Fruit and Steamship Company,
    56
Stanley, Henry M. (formerly, John Row-
    lands), 56, *57*
State House, 96, *96*
State Office Building, 76
State Supreme Court Building, 76
Steamboats, 235, *236*, 303, *303, 305*, 325–
    33, 336–44
  advertisements of, *340*
  America, 343, 344
  City of Baton Rouge, interior of, *342*
  City of Monroe, interior of, *342*
  Enterprise, 47, 48
  fires and explosions on, 329, *329*
  Grand Republic, interior of, *341*
  Great Mississippi Steamboat Race, The,
    Currier and Ives, *332*
  jazz bands on, *162*
  Lord & McPeake (agents), *341*
  Louisiana, explosion of, *329*
  luxurious interiors of, *341, 342*
  merchandise on, 337–39
  Natchez, 332, 332, 333, 333
  New Orleans (first Mississippi steam-
    boat), 6, 326, *326*
  New York, 327, 327
  of Mississippi Steamboat Navigation
    Company, 326
  of U.S. Mail Steamship Company, 328,
    328
  Ohio, 328, 328
  Robert E. Lee, 332, 332
  Robert Fulton, 326–27, *327*
  shooting craps on, 247, *247*
  Spalding and Roger's *Floating Palace,*
    235, *235, 236*
  towboat, 330, *331*
  Washington, 326, 327
Steamers and steamship lines, 345–47
  Creole, 346
  Cromwell, New York, and New Orleans
    Steamship Line, 345, *345, 346*
  Delta Steamship Lines, 347
  Dixie, 346
  Governor, 345
  Harrison Line, 345, *345*
  Louisiana, 345
  Mississippi Shipping Company, 347
  Momus, 347
  Morgan Line, 346, *346*
  Southern Pacific, 346, *346*
  State Line, 346, *346*
Stein, Gertrude, 175
Steinbeck, John, 175
Stempel, Frederick (later known as Fa-
    ranta), 151, *151*
Sterrett, Lee, 152, *152*
Stith, Gerard, 8, 279, *279*, 280
Stolé, Okana, 22, *23*
Stone, Edward Durrell, 352
Story, Sidney, 11, 209
Story Building (Wells Fargo Express
    Building), *135*
Storyville, 11
  and prostitution, *208–11*
  Blue Book of, 208, *209*

Street plans of New Orleans, 24, *26, 27,
    41, 46, 52, 118*
Street transportation, 288–91
  Canal & Claiborne Streets Railroad Com-
    pany, 288
    Girod & Poydras line of, 288, *288*
  Desire Line, 291, *291*
  electric streetcars, 289, *289*
    map of lines, *290*
  New Orleans and Carrollton Railroad
    Company. *See* New Orleans and
    Carrollton Railroad Company
  New Orleans City and Lake Railroad,
    288, *289*
  omnibus lines, 288, *288*
    on Canal Street, 290, *290*
  Orleans-Kenner Traction Company, 291,
    291
  St. Charles Avenue streetcar line, 288,
    290, *291*
  steam dummy engine, 288, *289*
Streets
  Aline, 287
  Annunciation, 41, *169*
  Baronne, 92, *114, 135*, 146, *170, 198,
    229*
  Basin, 209, *209*
  Bayou, 74
  Bienville, *29*, 225, 265, 309,, 315
  Bourbon, 1, 2, 7, 14, 92, *98*, 125, 151,
    153, *183, 199*, 225, 291
  Broad, *283*, 284
  Burgundy, 96
  Camp, 12, 88, *89, 112, 134, 135, 137,
    144*, 151, 193, *193*, 323
  Canal. *See* Canal Street
  Carondelet, 60, *101, 136*, 146, *190, 276,
    304, 305*, 332
  Chartres, 2, 7, *28, 29, 34*, 68, 80, 92,
    127, 183, 226, 264, 322
  Chestnut, 137, *137*
  Chippewa, 114, *115*
  Claiborne Avenue, *114*, 120
  Cleveland Avenue, *131*
  Clio, *193*, 288
  Common, *135, 136, 170*
  Constance, 113
  Conti, 2, 321, 322
  Dauphine, 27, 96, *97*, 114
  Decatur, 27, *28*, 30, 68, *107*
  Delachaise, 287, *318*
  Dumaine, *28*, 174, *174*, 196
  Elysian Fields Avenue, 296, *296*
  Esplanade Avenue, 5, 46, 53, *90, 100,*
    119, *127*
  Exchange Alley, *80*, 185
  Felicity, 10, 53
  First, *137*
  Fourth, 138, *139*
  Front, *309*
  Gallatin, 208
  Galvez, 236
  Girod, *208*
  Gravier, 89, *136*, 146, *147*, 304, *305,
    323, 341*
  Iberville, *28*, 100, *135*, 185, 200, *201,*
    209, 323
  Jackson Avenue, 114, *115*, 282
  Jena, *266*
  Josephine, 332
  Lafayette, *89*
  Laurel, *168*
  Levee, 271, *271*, 325
  Magazine, 89, *316*

  Marais, 280
  Market, 272
  Miro, 236
  Moss, *140*, 141
  Napoleon Avenue, 288
  Natchez, 89
  New Levee, *193*
  North, 88, *134*
  Orleans, *118*, 119, *131*, 151, 280
  Perdido, 276
  Peters, *316*
  Pine, 128, *129*
  Poeyfarre, 41
  Poydras, *134, 186, 198*, 353
  Prieur, 315
  Prytania, 137, *139, 193, 287*
  Rampart, 100, *101*
  Religious, 272
  Richard, 272
  Rousseau, 54, *282*
  Royal, 2, 7, 10–11, *12*, 34, *43*, 67, 80,
    92, 94, *100, 125, 126, 127, 128,
    130, 135*, 167, 174, *187, 214*, 253,
    271, 277, 291, 321, 322, 323
  Rue d'Amour, *127*
  St. Ann, 2, *28*, 280
  St. Charles Avenue, 12, 53, *60, 63*, 78,
    88, 89, 94, *95*, 111, 115, 128, *129,
    137, 138, 144, 147*, 151, 239, 248,
    276, 288, 315
  St. Claude Avenue, 170
  St. Joseph, 113
  St. Louis, 2, *127*, 209
  St. Peter, 2, *34, 128*, 142
  St. Philip, 2, *142*, 196
  St. Thomas, 272
  Saratoga, 284
  South, 88
  South Robertson, 209, 288
  Third, *138*
  Toledano, 10
  Tonti, *266*
  Toulouse, 27, *30*, 153, 322
  Tremé, 280
  Tulane Avenue, 169, *283, 284, 284*
  University Place, 92, *169, 170,, 229*
  Ursuline, 271, *271*
  Washington Avenue, 119, *137, 187*, 248
Stuart, Gilbert, 38
Suburban Architecture, *136–41*
Sugar industry, 306–10
  establishment of, 4
  Louisiana Sugar Refinery, *308*
  machinery for, 310
  New Orleans Sugar Exchange, 308, *309*
  on the Levee, 309, *309*
Sugar Planter's Storage and Distribution
    Company of Louisiana, 272, *272*
Sullivan, John L., 253, *253*
Superdome, 353
Superior Council of the French, 3, 32
Swamp, the, 208, *208*
Synagogues, 190, *190*
  Touro Synagogue, 190

Taft, William Howard, 189, *189*
Talleyrand, Charles Maurice de, 38
Tanesse, Jacques, *46*, 196
Taylor, Zachary, 189, *189*
Telephone service, 319–20
  Cumberland Telephone & Telegraph Co.,
    320
  early operators, 320, *320*
  New Orleans Telephonic Exchange, 319

repairmen, *320*
Tellegan, Lou, 149
Thackeray, William Makepeace, 183
Theatres, 142–53. *See also* Concerts;
    French Opera House; Movie Houses
    Academy of Music (formerly, Dan
        Rice's Amphitheatre), *147*, 216
    American Theatre, *144*
    Audubon Theatre (formerly, Academy
        of Music), 147
    Baldwin Theatre (later, Dauphine), *150*
    Dauphine (formerly, Baldwin), *150, 151*
    Dime Museum and Theatre, 151, *151,
        152*
    Gaiety, 215
    Gallery Circle, 153
    Grand Opera House (formerly, Varieties
        Theatre), 146, 150
    Greenwall Theatre (later, Palace The-
        atre), *150*
    inauguration of matinee in, 147, 148
    Iron Theatre, 151
    Little Theatre of Vieux Carré, *153*
    Repertory Theatre, 153
    Robinson's Floating Palaces Museum,
        152, *152*
    St. Charles Theatre, 152, 189, *215*
        first, *144, 145,* 146
        second, *145,* 146
        stock company in, *152*
        third (later, Orpheum), 145, 146, *146*
    St. Peter Street Theatre, 142
    St. Philip Street Theatre, *142,* 143
    Théâtre d'Orléans, 142, *143,* 153, 214,
        244
    twin theatres, *148–49*
        Crescent, 148, *148, 149*
        Tulane, 148, *148, 149*
    Varieties Theatre, 146, *147*
        "Dixie's Land" first heard in, 146, *147*
Thevis, Peter, 263, *263*
Thompson, Basil, *175*
Thompson, Lydia, 216
Thomson, James M., 259
Thurman, Sue, 181
Tidewater Ship Channel, 15
Tivoli Gardens, 236, *237*
Tonty, Henry de ("Iron Hand"), *16,* 21
Torkanowsky, Werner, 161
Touro, Judah, 98, 114, 190, *190,* 287
Touro block, 98, *98*
Touro Infirmary, 56, 287, *287*
Touro Synagogue, 190
Toussaint L'Ouverture, François Domi-
    nique, *43*
Transportation, 288–302. *See also* Avia-
    tion; Ferries; Railroads; Steamboats;
    Steamers; Street transportation
Treaty of Amiens, 42
Treaty of Fontainebleau, 2
Treaty of Ghent, 45
Treaty of San Ildefonso, 5, 37

Trudeau, Charles, 6
Tulane, Paul, 170, 171, *171*
Tulane Hall, 159
Tulane Stadium, 260
Tulane University (formerly, University of
    Louisiana), 56, 170–72
    campus (1895), *171*
    football teams of, 257, *257,* 258, *258,*
        259
    Medical School of, *171, 172*
    Newcomb College of, 137, 171
        art department of, 180
Turgis, Father Francis, 112
Tuxedo Brass Band, 165
Twain, Mark, 124, 342

Ulloa, Antonio de, 3, *32*
Union Race Course, 55
Union Terrace, *96*
United Fruit Company, 311, *311, 312*
United States Branch Mint, 90, *90*
University of Louisiana, 170. *See also*
    Tulane University
University Place, 92, *169,* 170, 229
Unzaga, Luis de, 3, 32, 110
Ursuline chapel, 48
Ursuline Convent, 5, *29, 30, 48*
Ursuline nuns, 6, *29*

Vaccaro, Joseph, 56, 57
Vaccaro brothers, 56
Vandechamp, Jean Joseph, 180
Vanderlyn, John, *48*
Van Loo, Louis Michel, *31*
Vaudreuil, Marquise, de, *18*
Vaudreuil-Cavagnal, Pierre de Rigaud
    ("The Grand Marquis"), 2, *18,* 110
Verandah Hotel, 83, *144*
*Veue et Perspective de la Nouvelle Or-
    leans,* Lassus, *26,* 180–81
Vidal, Nicolás María, 5
Vieux Carré (French Quarter), 1, 15, *34,*
    52, 56, 77, 79, *100,* 204, *321,* 348,
    349
    architecture of, *125–30*
        double parlor in, 128, *129*
        iron lace railing in, *126, 128*
        servants', or "slave," quarters in, *130*
    authors and artists attracted to, 175
    homes on Esplanade Avenue, *100, 127*
    Little Theatre of, *153*
    restoration of, 13
    small restaurant in, *183*
Vieux Carré Commission, 133
Voodoo, 207–8
Voss, Albert L., 156

Walker, Dixie, 255
Walker, William, *51*
Walmsley, T. Semmes, 13, *74*
Walsh, Michael, *284*

Walshe, Blayney T., *314,* 315
Walton, James E., 60
War of 1812, 6, 44
Warfield, David, 149
Warmoth, Henry Clay, 9, 66, *66,* 67, 216
Washington Artillery battalion (now
    known as First Howitzer Battalion
    of the 141st Artillery of the Loui-
    siana National Guard), 59, *59,* 60,
    60
Washington Artillery Hall, *219,* 224
Waterman, Charles M., 8, 280
Waterworks, 271–73
    plan of New Orleans's first water sys-
        tem, *271*
    reservoir of New Orleans Water Works
        Co., *272*
    water purification pumping station, *272*
Watkins, John, 5
Waud, Alfred R., *54,* 154, *155–56, 182,
    196, 197, 199, 227, 243, 244, 244,
    255, 265*
Webster, Daniel, 226, *227*
Wedell, James, 302, *302*
Weiss, Carl A., Jr., 13
Weitzel, Godfrey, 9
Wells, J. Madison, *65*
Wells Fargo Express Building, *135*
West End, 10, 229, *229,* 230, *230, 231,*
    288
White, Dr. Joseph H., 264
White, Lulu, 209, *211*
White City, *239*
White League, 9, 10, 81
    Sept. 14, 1874 battle of, with Metro-
        politan Police, 9, 67, *67,* 81, 96, *96*
Whiteside, Walker, 149
Whitney Bank Building Annex, 13
Wiggs, Johnny, *164*
Wilde, Oscar, 233
Wilde, Richard Henry, 89
Wilder, Richard Watson, *174*
Wilder, Thornton, 175
Wilkinson, James, 5, *41*
Williams, Harry P., 302, *302*
Williams, Kid, 254
Williams, Tennessee, 291
Wills, Harry, 254, *254*
Wiltz, Louis A., 10, 68
Woiseri, J. L. Bouqueto de, *40, 41,* 180
Wolfe, Raymond ("Bear"), 259
Woodward, Ellsworth, 180
Woodward, William, 180
World War I, 12, 72–74
World War II, 13–14, 75–76
Wright, Sophie Bell, *169*

You, Dominique, 49
Youenes, John, 279

Zack, Arthur, 160
Zemurray, Samuel, 56, 57